Sharon Blackie is a writer, mythologist and psychologist. Her work is focused on exploring and deepening our relationship with the land and with place through the transforming power of myth and story. Originally trained as a psychologist and neuroscientist, Sharon has also practiced as a therapist specialising in narrative, storytelling, creative imagination and clinical hypnotherapeutic techniques. She is the author of *The Long Delirious Burning Blue*, a novel which the *Independent on Sunday* called 'hugely potent. A tribute to the art of storytelling that is itself an affecting and inspiring story'. She is the founder and editor of *EarthLines* magazine, and runs creative courses and retreats for women. For many years Sharon was a crofter, both in the far north-west Highlands of Scotland and in the Outer Hebrides, sandwiched between mountains and sea in one of the wildest and most remote places in the country. She now lives in the hills of Donegal, in a small stone riverside cottage by a waterfall in a wood. www.sharonblackie.net

SHARON BLACKIE

IF
WOMEN
ROSE
ROOTED

The Journey to
Authenticity and Belonging

7 9 10 8

First published in 2016 by September Publishing
This new edition published 2016

Copyright © Sharon Blackie 2016

The right of Sharon Blackie to be identified as the
author of this work has been asserted by her in accordance
with the Copyright Designs and Patents Act 1988.

The title of the book comes from a poem by Rainer Maria Rilke:
'If we surrendered/to earth's intelligence/we could rise up rooted, like trees.',
from *Rilke's Book of Hours: Love Poems to God*, trans. Anita Barrows and Joanna Macy

Typeset in Bembo by Palimpsest Book Production Ltd, Falkirk, Stirlingshire

Printed in Denmark on paper from responsibly managed, sustainable sources
by Nørhaven

ISBN 978-1-910463-66-6

September Publishing
www.septemberpublishing.org

For my mother.
For all the mothers.

Contents

And the Russian women in blue towns
are speaking.
The flower-dressed women of India,
women in orange tents,
dark women
of the Americas
who sit beside fires,
have studied the palms of their hands
and walk toward one another.

It's time
to bless this ground.
Their hair is on fire
from the sun
and they walk narrow roads
toward one another.
Their pulses beat
against the neck's thin skin.
They grow closer.
. . .

Daughters, the women are speaking.
They arrive
Over the wise distances
On perfect feet.
Daughters, I love you.

from 'The Women Speaking' by Linda Hogan[1]

1

Reclaiming Our Stories

The ford, Meenderry, Donegal, Ireland

'Oh what a catastrophe, what a maiming of love when it was made a personal, merely personal feeling, taken away from the rising and setting of the sun, and cut off from the magic connection of the solstice and equinox. This is what is the matter with us. We are bleeding at the roots, because we are cut off from the earth and sun and stars, and love is a grinning mockery, because, poor blossom, we plucked it from its stem on the tree of Life, and expected it to keep on blooming in our civilised vase on the table.'

D.H. Lawrence[1]

It's not quite dawn in this green, fertile valley; there's just the faintest glimmer of pink in the sky to the east. The moon is waxing, gibbous, its light silvering the river which winds through the land, soft like the curves of a woman's body as she stretches out to dip her toes in the sea. A grey heron breaks the silence, shrieking from the banks as I make my way across the narrow bridge, walk slowly up the rising lane. At the crossroads, three hares are sitting quite still in the middle of the road; they scatter when they become aware of me, tails flashing white in the moonlight then vanishing into the dark.

Up I go along the stony, uneven track to the high bog, face to the Seven Sister mountains, silhouetted now against a gradually lightening sky. I wind back along a tiny path to cut home across the fields, but first I have to navigate the ford: a shallow pool in a sheltered hollow through which a deep and fast-flowing stream can be crossed. The ford froths blood-red at the edges with iron precipitates, and I creep down to it carefully, half expecting to catch a glimpse of the *bean nighe*, the Washer at the Ford – the old woman of legend who scrubs clean the bloody clothes of slain warriors. After all, this morning is Samhain,[2] the old seasonal Gaelic festival which marks the beginning of winter. And on this night, my ancestors believed, the passage between this world and the Otherworld is open.

Behind the ford is a single, clearly defined hill, a green breast rising from the soft contours of the land. It is crowned with heather, wiry and dormant now, spreading across its crest like a wide brown nipple. We call it a fairy hill, for these are the places which lead to the Otherworld – the beautiful, perilous dwelling-place of the fairy folk: the Aos Sí,[3] the people of the mounds. Once upon a time, inside a hill like this, Celtic women were transformed into the wisest creatures in the land.

In the Otherworld, wisdom is largely possessed by women, since they are the ones who hold the Cup. The Queen of the Aos Sí decided one day to bestow that gift on human women too, and so she sent out an invitation to all the women of the land, asking them to come to her great hall beneath the hill on a certain date, and at a certain time. The news was carried on the winds and the waves, by the birds and the fish; even the leaves of the trees whispered of it. Soon, women from all over the country began to set out on their journey. Some travelled alone, some came together; and when the appointed day dawned, the doors to the Otherworld opened.

The women streamed inside the hill – and gasped to find themselves in a beautiful hall which was draped with bright cloths woven from nettles and dyed with the blood of shellfish and the sap of plants. Soft animal skins covered the floors and seats, and a feast was laid out on tables of wood and stone, set on plates of pearly shell. A soft green light pervaded the vast hall. When everyone was inside and the watchers saw no more coracles on the water, no more women climbing up the slope of the hill, the doors to the outside world were closed.

Into the hall then came the Queen, bearing herself with kindly dignity, her face shining with a strange but lovely light. She carried a large golden Cup in her hand, bright with unusual marks and carvings; eight fairy women followed behind, each carrying a golden flagon of sparkling liquid which they used to continually fill the Cup. The Queen passed through the hall, offering a drink from the Cup to each of the women who was present. The Cup held the distilled wisdom of the world through all the ages past, and as each woman drank she suddenly grew wise, and understood many things she had never known before. Some were able to see much, some were able to see little – but every one of them benefitted. And then the women feasted, and the next morning they went back out into the world again, filled with the wisdom and knowledge of the Otherworld.[4]

Here in Ireland, the Otherworld is as real as any other. This is a landscape steeped in stories, and those stories stalk us still. They have seeped into the bones of this land, and the land offers them back to us; it breathes them into the wind and bleeds them out into streams and rivers. They will not be refused.

Before there was the Word, there was the land, and it was made and watched over by women. Stories from almost every culture around the world tell us that once upon a time it was so. For many native tribes throughout America, Grandmother Spider continually spins the world into being. For the Andean peoples of South America, Pachamama is the World Mother; she sustains all life on Earth. In Scotland and Ireland, the Cailleach – the Old Woman – made, shaped and protects the land and the wild things on it. In these and other Celtic nations, Danu[5] gave birth to all the other gods and was mother to the people who followed. Women: the creators of life, the bearers of the Cup of knowledge and wisdom, personifying the moral and spiritual authority of this fertile green and blue Earth.

Do you remember those days?

Me neither. Other indigenous cultures around the world may still respect and revere the feminine, but we Western women lost control of our stories a long time ago. The story which I was given to carry as a very young child, the story which both defined me and instructed me about the place I occupied in this world, accorded no such significance to women. In this story, woman was an afterthought, created from a man's body for the sole purpose of pleasing him. In this story, the first woman was the cause of all humanity's sufferings: she brought death to the world, not life. She had the audacity to talk to a serpent. Wanting the knowledge and wisdom which had been denied her by a jealous father-god, she dared to eat the fruit of a tree. Even worse, she shared the fruit of knowledge and wisdom with her man. So that angry and implacable god cast her and her male companion out of paradise, and decreed that women should be subordinate to men for ever afterwards.

The stories we tell about the creation of the Earth and the origins of humankind show us how our culture views the world, our place in it, and our relationships with the other living things which inhabit it. And the key consequence of this particular creation myth is a belief, prevalent now for centuries in the West, that women are naturally disobedient temptresses who must be kept firmly in their place. We are weak-willed, easily persuaded to think or do evil, faithless, untrustworthy, mendacious, and motivated purely by self-interest. The story of Eve in the Book of Genesis is the underpinning for countless measures which have limited the actions, rights and status of women. No matter what women might achieve in the world, the fundamental message of the sacred texts of the world's largest religious grouping, which for 2,000 years have supplied the foundational beliefs of our Western culture, is that men should not trust women, and that women should trust neither themselves nor each other.

When I was a child, this cultural story about who we are as women made me feel small, insignificant, empty. As I grew older, it made me angry. Angry, because it justifies a world in which men still have almost all the real power over the cultural narrative – the stories we tell ourselves about the world, about who and what we are, where we came from and where we're going – as well as the way we behave as a result of it. Angry, because it justifies the centuries-old violence against women which threatens even in this 'enlightened' twenty-first century to spiral out of control. That violence was endemic in my own family. My mother, as a tiny child, picked up a poker from the fireplace and held it up to her father to stop him beating my grandmother. A couple of decades later, at just about three years old, I took hold of my own father by the kneecaps and pushed him, step by astonished step, out of the room to stop him hitting my mother.

Yes, I come from a line of strong and brave women – but I grew up feeling that the world was not a safe place for us. And even though most of the men I've known during my life – the men I've loved, the men who have been my friends – find this situation just as abhorrent as I do, the story is replayed over and over again at a cultural level. In the United Kingdom, where I grew up, one woman in four experiences domestic violence at some point in her life, and one woman in four experiences sexual assault as an adult. Worldwide, the figures are higher: around one in three.[6] Political scientist Mary Kaldor has reported that in the 'new wars' waged over resources, ethnicity and faith, 80 per cent of casualties are women and children. Rape and pillage, says Kaldor, are the modus operandi.[7] Today, sexual abuse, abductions, forced slavery and forced prostitution are commonplace, even – especially – in the heart of the fine capital cities of Europe and America of which our culture is so proud. And that's not to mention the daily harassment in public places, the deeply ingrained everyday sexism that so many of us are conditioned just to take for granted.[8] This is a world in which the cultural narrative informs us that women don't matter as much as men, and so it is okay for men to do these things to them.

So many of us today accept this state of affairs as just the way the world is. We're conditioned to accept it. We get on with our lives and treat it as old news. It's okay, we tell ourselves: during the last century, feminism was born and so equality is happening and everything is getting better now. And among liberal thinkers in the UK, feminist writer and activist Beatrix Campbell suggests,[9] the optimistic belief that men and women are on a cultural journey toward equality still prevails. But Campbell argues that not only has this progress stopped, in some cases it has actually been reversed. Even though awareness of the issues which women face is high, even though lip-service is paid to women's rights, new inequalities are emerging in our culture all the time. We are living, she writes, in an era of 'neopatriarchy' in which violence has proliferated, body anxiety and self-hatred have flourished, rape is committed with impunity, sex trafficking thrives and the struggle for equal pay is effectively at an end. It's hard to disagree with Campbell that a new revolution is needed; the only question is what form it should take.

As I grew older still, I grew angry about other things, too: things that might seem on the surface to have nothing to do with the story of Eve, or the disempowerment of women – but which in fact are profoundly related. The same kinds of acts that are perpetrated against us, against our daughters and our mothers, are perpetrated against the planet: the Earth which gives us life; the Earth with which women have for so long been identified. Our patriarchal, warmongering, growth-and-domination-based culture has caused runaway climate change, the mass extinction of species, and the ongoing destruction of wild and natural landscapes in the unstoppable pursuit of progress.

At six years old, knowing nothing but somehow understanding everything, I sobbed as hazy black-and-white TV news footage showed a bird futilely flapping its wings, slowly drowning in a thick soupy layer of black crude oil which coated the surface of the sea. Another bird landed next to it, sank below the surface, re-emerged for a final few flaps, then drifted into the growing mass of dead bodies lining up along the southwest coast of England. I was watching one of the first major acute man-made environmental disasters, caused by the wreckage of the oil supertanker SS *Torrey Canyon* – 32 million gallons of crude oil dumped into the ocean, and around 15,000 sea birds killed. The sea burst into huge sheets of flames as napalm was dropped in an effort to burn off the oil. I thought the world was ending. 'It was just an unfortunate accident,' people said at the time – but how often have we done it since?

Then there was MAD: Mutually Assured Destruction. You

couldn't make it up. You didn't have to; I grew up in the shadow of it, at the height of the Cold War. Russia and America, each side armed heavily in preparation for an all-out nuclear world war. Each with a nuclear 'deterrent' that was supposed to preclude an attack by the other, because such an attack would lead to immediate retaliation and the annihilation of the attacker's country as well as the attacked. The United Nations website says it all: 'Nuclear weapons are the most dangerous weapons on earth. One can destroy a whole city, potentially killing millions, and jeopardizing the natural environment and lives of future generations through its long-term catastrophic effects.'[10]

We all firmly believed it was going to happen, one day; the government even published leaflets to advise us what to do when it did. 'Protect and Survive' appeared in the UK in 1980 after a resurgence of the Cold War and, with nice little line-drawings, helpfully showed how to build your own fallout room, advising that you stock it with tinned food and a radio. It even showed how an improvised toilet could be built from a chair. You might want to do this now, was the implicit message, because when the bomb hits, it'll be too late. 'Protect and Survive' stimulated Raymond Briggs to write *When the Wind Blows*, a poignant and oddly shocking graphic novel which shows a nuclear attack on Britain by the Soviet Union from the viewpoint of a retired couple. 'Further instructions' do not come by radio, as 'Protect and Survive' blithely promised that they would; the book ends on a bleak note, as Jim and Hilda Bloggs cover themselves in paper bags, praying in their fallout shelter as death approaches and the room slowly darkens around them.

I was twenty-one when *When the Wind Blows* was published; I'm fifty-four now and in spite of all the fine work to achieve nuclear disarmament in the past couple of decades, nothing fundamental has changed. 'Although nuclear weapons have only been used twice in warfare – in the bombings of Hiroshima and Nagasaki in 1945 – about 22,000 reportedly remain in our world today,' declares the United Nations, in the enormous section of its website devoted to Weapons of Mass Destruction: not merely nuclear weapons, but chemical and biological too. So many ways not only to kill each other, but to destroy non-human life on this planet in the process. I grew up with the knowledge that there were men ready to do just that. *Dr. Strangelove* might have been funny, but it was no joke. Still, we were just women, and we were supposed to trust their judgement. 'The men know best,' said a school friend's mother after I told her I was joining the Campaign for Nuclear Disarmament because if we didn't do something about it, they were going to destroy the world. *The men know best?* I didn't know what to say.

Women might have been complicit – we had been well-trained for centuries, after all; a little bit of burning at the stake, incarceration in nunneries and lunatic asylums if we didn't do what we were told, and the constant threat of rape and violence: all of them do wonders for compliance – but the men were the ones with their fingers on the buttons. The men were the ones in charge. As a teenager I wanted that to change, but I couldn't imagine how. I couldn't even picture a world in which it might be different: a world in which women were respected and in which we got to create the cultural narrative too; a world in which men and women lived together in a balanced and sustainable way, respecting the planet which gave us life and the other creatures which share it with us. So, as so many of us do, I just knuckled down and 'got on with my life', going to university, signing up for a PhD, preparing to enter the system.

A year into my PhD, just after I'd read *When the Wind Blows*, I went with a friend to visit her aunt, an elderly retired lecturer in history. Over tea in her Hampstead flat I talked about Briggs's book, bemoaning a Western civilisation in which the men had all the power, and women had never been able to influence the way the world was. I lamented the complete lack of stories from my own country which might offer us examples of, or even just inspiration for, women who were respected and could lead. She shook her head, levered herself slowly out of an ancient, dusty armchair and sifted through her bookshelves until she found the thick paperback she was looking for. 'Read this,' she said, putting it into my hands. 'It wasn't always so. It doesn't have to be so. Women could be leaders once, in this country; there were strong women, who influenced the way things were. It was long ago, but that doesn't mean it can't happen again. You're young; read about those women, and then decide what you are going to do to change things.' The book she gave me was called *The Eagle and the Raven*, and it was a historical novel by a writer called Pauline Gedge.[11] It was in good part about Boudica: the woman who fought the Roman patriarchy in the first century AD, and almost won. I left, devoured the book in a single weekend, and then tracked down everything else I could find about her in the library. There was virtually nothing; most of the history section seemed to contain books about men.

Boudica[12] was a member of the Iceni, who occupied an area of England roughly equivalent to modern-day Norfolk. They were one of many tribes of Celtic-speaking people who lived in Britain from the Iron Age through to the coming of the Romans and the subsequent invasion of the Saxons.[13] 'In stature she was very tall, in appearance most terrifying, in the glance of her eye most fierce, and her voice was harsh,' Roman consul and historian Cassius Dio said of her. 'A great mass of the tawniest hair fell to her hips; around her neck was a large golden necklace; and she wore a tunic of divers colours over which a thick mantle was fastened with a brooch.'[14] Following the Roman invasion, Boudica's husband Prasutagus had ruled the Iceni as a nominally independent ally of Rome. When he died, his will – in which, contrary to protocol, he left his kingdom jointly to his daughters and the Roman Emperor – was ignored. His lands and property were confiscated; his nobles were taken into slavery. And, according to Tacitus, Boudica was flogged and her daughters were raped.

While the Roman governor Gaius Suetonius Paulinus was away leading a campaign against the island of Mona (modern

Anglesey) – a refuge for British rebels and a stronghold of the druids – the Iceni conspired with their neighbours the Trinovantes and others to revolt. Boudica was chosen as their leader, for, as Tacitus said in the *Annals*, 'the Britons make no distinction of sex when they choose their leaders.' Boudica and her people destroyed Camulodunum (modern Colchester), Londinium and Verulamium (St Albans). Suetonius returned and regrouped his forces in the West Midlands; before the battle against him began, Boudica spoke to her troops from her chariot, with her daughters beside her. If the men wanted to live in slavery, then that was their choice, she declared: but she, a woman, was resolved to win or die.

Sadly, this time around the Romans won the battle, and it was said that Boudica poisoned herself after the defeat. More was lost, of course, than just a battle. The Romans remained, and the people were weakened. There were no more tribal queens: the Romans considered female power to be a sign of barbarism. The Anglo-Saxons came, the country converted rapidly to Christianity, and the patriarchy took firm hold. And yet, and yet . . . Boudica may have lost, but still she fought, and still she led. A woman from my culture, out of my history. I allowed myself to develop a fantasy. What if women rose again? Not in battle, but what if we could reclaim, somehow, that power and respect which women had lost? What if we could somehow dismantle this planet-destroying patriarchy, and recreate a world in which we lived in balance?

It was a lovely fantasy, but I was young, powerless and poor. I slipped back, as we all do, into the needs and strictures of my own life. I slipped quietly into the system, settled for safety and security. It was a long time before I thought again about Boudica, and the lost power of Celtic women.

The world which men have made isn't working. Something needs to change. To change the world, we women need first to change ourselves – and then we need to change the stories we tell about who we are. The stories we've been living by for the past few centuries – the stories of male superiority, of progress and growth and domination – don't serve women and they certainly don't serve the planet. Stories matter, you see. They're not just entertainment – stories matter because humans are narrative creatures. It's not simply that we like to tell stories, and to listen to them: it's that narrative is hard-wired into us. It's a function of our biology, and the way our brains have evolved over time. We make sense of the world and fashion our identities through the sharing and passing on of stories. And so the stories that we tell ourselves about the world and our place in it, and the stories that are told to us by others about the world and our place in it, shape not just our own lives, but the world around us. The cultural narrative *is* the culture.

If the foundation stories of our culture show women as weak and inferior, then however much we may rail against it, we will be treated as if we are weak and inferior. Our voices will have no traction. But if the mythology and history of our culture includes women who are wise, women who are powerful and strong, it opens up a space for women to live up to those stories: to become wise, and powerful and strong. To be taken seriously, and to have our voices heard.

While the stories of Eve, Pandora[15] and other 'fallen women' may be the stories that have been foisted upon us for the best part of 2,000 years, they aren't the only myths we have inherited, those of us who have Celtic roots. Refusing to confine itself in the whalebone corsets of national borders, the 'Celtic fringe' – made up of specific regions of the countries which stretch along the western oceanic coastline of Europe – binds together richly diverse populations with a strong thread of collective cultural identity. That thread isn't founded on tribalism or nationalism, and nor is it about genetics. These entanglements emerge from shared history, mythology and common belief systems; they arise out of a common landscape and environment which brought about a highly distinctive pan-Celtic culture that is rooted in intense feelings of belonging to place.

And so, rising high up on the heather-covered moorlands of Cornwall, Ireland, Scotland, Wales, the Isle of Man and Brittany, seeping through our bogs, flowing down our streams and into our rivers and out onto the sandy strands of the rock-strewn Atlantic seaboard, are the old Celtic myths and stories. Our own stories, no one else's. Stories steeped in sea brine, black and crusty with peat; stories that lie buried beneath our feet, which spring directly out of our own distinctive native landscapes, and which informed the lives of our own ancestors. These are the stories we will visit in this book.

For women particularly, to have a Celtic identity or ancestry is to inherit a history, literature and mythology in which we are portrayed not only as deeply connected to the natural world, but as playing a unique and critical role in the wellbeing of the Earth and survival of its inhabitants. Celtic myths for sure have their fair share of male heroism and adventure, but the major pre-occupation of their heroes is with service to and stewardship of the land. And once upon a time women were the guardians of the natural world, the heart of the land. The Celtic woman who appears in these old tales is active in a different way from their heroes and warriors: she is the one who determines who is fit to rule, she is the guardian and protector of the land, the bearer of wisdom, the root of spiritual and moral authority for the tribe. Celtic creation stories tell us that the land was shaped by a woman; Celtic history offers us examples of women who were the inspi-rational leaders of their tribes. These are the stories of our own heritage, the stories of the real as well as the mythical women who went before us. What if we could reclaim those stories, and become those women again?

In this book, I'll share with you the story of how I reclaimed my native myths and traditions, for the stories of women today need to be told. We begin with the stories which tell of our sufferings, of the age-old violence that has been committed against us and against the planet. But the journey doesn't end there. Once our old stories have been told, we need to find and claim the new stories which will inspire us to move forward. It took me a long time to find my own guiding stories: stories which not only captured my imagination, but which reminded me that there are other ways of belonging to the world than those that were handed down to me. Each of us travels that road for ourselves, each of our journeys is unique, and all of our learnings and insights are valuable. For all my railing against the patriarchy, my own journey wasn't one which made men the enemy; it was a journey in which men and women could become allies, and the stories which guided me arose from a culture in which both men and women were valued for the different things they brought to the world. My journey was a pilgrimage: in making it, I discovered how it might be possible to become an authentic, rooted woman in these challenging times. During the long, winding course of it, I learned how to find my place in the world, and then take responsibility for it. I learned how to uncover and then employ the unique gift which I could offer.

Several decades ago, American mythologist Joseph Campbell developed his well-known and tremendously influential outline of the 'Hero's Journey'.[16] The basic plot of all the world's great stories, Campbell declared, involves a Hero who happens to be a person of exceptional gifts, which may or may not be recognised by his society. He and/or the world in which he lives suffers from a symbolic deficiency (in a fairy tale, for example, it may be something as simple as the lack of a specific golden ring); the Hero must set out on a great adventure to win the missing treasure and bring it back to the world. Campbell argued that there are three key phases of these symbolic journeys, beginning with the phase of separation, or departure, in which the Hero hears the 'Call to Adventure' and sets out. In the second phase, 'the trials and victories of initiation', the Hero passes along a 'Road of Trials' and is tested. During the third phase, 'the return and reintegration with society', the Hero brings back his gift to the world and so saves it, or himself, or another. Campbell believed that those three phases and the sub-stages which he outlined within them are common not only to the structure of the myths themselves, but also to the structure of our own individual journeys through our lives.

This model may well explain the features which many myths and fairy tales from around the world have in common, and may also, as many Jungian psychotherapists who followed Campbell have suggested, offer up a template for a real-life Hero's Journey and a metaphor for personal spiritual and psychological growth. But it has little to offer women. It does not reflect the full reality of women's lives, either inner or outer. In it, women appear either as the Temptress, there to test the Hero and lead him off-course (there goes poor Eve again . . .); or in the guise of the Great Goddess, who represents the 'unconditional love' which must be won by the Hero to give him the courage to go on with his quest. In other words, at their very best, women can be no more than the destination: we represent the static, essential qualities that the active, all-conquering Hero is searching for. Maureen Murdock, one of his female students, reported that Campbell told her: 'Women don't need to make the journey. In the whole mytho- logical journey, the woman is there. All she has to do is realize that she's the place that people are trying to get to.'[17]

I respectfully disagree. Women absolutely do need to make the journey; we do not, however, need to make the same journey which the Hero makes. Our journey is different; our stories are all our own. It's more than time we told our own stories, outlined our journeys for ourselves. We don't need Heroes to tell us who to be.

Campbell's Hero's Journey, along with later adaptations of it by a variety of Jungian therapists and other writers, is entirely focused on an individual's spiritual growth and personal transfor- mation – the process which Jung called 'individuation'. But the journey we need to make today is one which rips us out of the confined spaces of our own heads and plants us firmly back in the world where we belong, rooted and ready to rise. Yes, if we want genuinely to contribute to the world, if we want to change it, we need to do some work on ourselves first. We need to understand our dysfunctional ways of being, to confront the beliefs and values we have subscribed to which caused both women and the planet to be in this mess in the first place. We need then to discover our own authentic values and ways of being in the world, to wake up to our own creative power as women, conceive our own individual vision for what we might offer to an ailing Earth. But this work on ourselves is not an end in itself, and neither is it work we should do in isolation. We are not separate from this Earth; we are a part of it, whether we fully feel it in our bodies yet or not.

The Heroine's Journey we'll follow through this book is a journey to understanding how deeply enmeshed we are in the web of life on this planet. It is a journey which leads us firmly back to our own sense of belonging to this Earth – but after that, it is a journey which requires us to step into our own power and take back our ancient, native role as its guardians and protectors. The Heroine's Journey we need to make today is, above all, an Eco-Heroine's Journey.

It's an idea that has come of age. A growing number of contemporary women's movements are focusing on a new and strongly felt desire to actively re-root ourselves in the land and in our communities, to take responsibility for shaping the future, to bring back awareness of and respect for deep feminine values in a world dominated by the masculine. It's a revolution of belonging, and it goes far beyond simple environmentalism.

More and more, women are taking the lead in the environmental movement. Nobel Prize-winner Wangari Maathai launched the Green Belt Movement,[18] which has planted millions of trees in Kenya and transformed women into powerful advocates for their rights, good governance and democracy, and natural resource protection. London barrister Polly Higgins founded the growing global Eradicating Ecocide movement.[19] Vandana Shiva[20] is India's best-known ecofeminist, environmental and anti-globalisation activist, promoting the idea that a more sustainable and productive approach to agriculture could be achieved through reinstating systems of farming that are more centred on women.

Even more radically, Canada's Idle No More movement[21] took the world by storm in 2013, when what began as a simple resistance campaign against a pending bill in Saskatchewan, spilled across the border to the United States and spread its influence across the world. The movement – which inspired solidarity actions around the globe – was founded by four women, three of whom were from Canada's Indigenous nations. Idle No More's vision 'revolves around Indigenous Ways of Knowing rooted in Indigenous Sovereignty to protect water, land, and all creation for future generations'. It is a vision that is deeply rooted in the old ways of being, the old Indigenous mythologies which reveal an inextricable bond between the living world and the feminine. 'It's time for our people to rise up and take back our role as caretakers and stewards of the land,' a spokeswoman for the Athabasca Chipewyan First Nations proclaims on the Idle No More website.

In our own Western societies we are seeing more calls for a return to native wisdom, but we cannot live by the worldviews of other cultures, which are rooted in lands and histories that have little relationship to our own. And yet, so often we try to: we look for our spiritual practices to the East – to Taoism, for example, and to Buddhism; we look to the West for guidance on how to live in harmony with the land – to indigenous stories and traditions from the Americas. But fine as all of those traditions are, we don't need to look to the myths of other cultures for role models, or for guidance on how to live more authentically, in balance and harmony with the planet on which we depend. We have our own guiding stories, and they are deeply rooted in the heart of our own native landscapes. We draw them out of the wells and the waters; beachcombing, we lift them out of the sand. We dive for them to the bottom of deep lakes, we disinter them from the bogs, we follow their tracks through the shadowy glades of the enchanted forest. Those stories not only ground us: they show us what we might once have been, we women, and what we might become again if we choose. 'The world will be saved by the Western women,' the Dalai Lama once said.[22] And, if we stand with our powerful and inspiring native sisters from around the planet, together we all might just have a chance.

If women remember that once upon a time we sang with the tongues of seals and flew with the wings of swans, that we forged our own paths through the dark forest while creating a community of its many inhabitants, then we will rise up rooted, like trees.

And if we rise up rooted, like trees . . . well then, women might indeed save not only ourselves, but the world.

2

Wells and Waters

The Wasteland

Clootie tree, Madron Well, Cornwall

'That'll put the jizz back in you,'
said old Brid, her eyes glinting,
as she handed me a bowl of real water
from the purest well in Gleann an Atha.
A well kept sweet and neat
by her people's people, the precious
legacy of her household,
tucked away in a nook,
a ditch around it for protection,
a flagstone on its mouth.
. . .

But for a long time now there is a snake
of pipe that leaks in from distant hills
and in every kitchen, both sides
of the glen, water spits from a tap;
bitter water without spark
that leaves a bad taste in the mouth
and among my people
the real well is being forgotten.

'It's hard to find a well these days,'
said old Brid, filling up my bowl again.
'They're hiding in rushes and juking in grass,
all choked up and clatty with scum
but for all the neglect they get
their mettle is still true.
Look for your own well, pet,
for there's a hard time coming.
There will have to be a going back to sources.'

from 'The Well' by Cathal Ó Searcaigh[1]

Just as I arrived at the start of the way to the well, the heavens opened. Setting off in search of water, I passed through a world suddenly saturated with water. Within seconds I was drenched. The narrow path was muddy, and the still-bare whitethorn and blackthorn trees which arched overhead spat enormous drops of rain down onto my head. Trees and bushes were densely crowded at either side of the track, and the leaf-covered floor of the wood was punctuated with stagnant pools of thick brown water. Blackbirds and crows, startled out of the trees at my passing, screeched at me in irritation and flew deeper into the wood.

A few minutes later, the monochromatic gloom of a waterlogged early-morning February wood was pierced. Ahead of me, just to the left of the path, a small wide tree was festooned with brightly coloured rags, or 'clooties'. There was bunting too, and bracelets and beads; there was a bright turquoise elastic hair band, and long thick blades of grass tied into a bow. This is the clootie tree which stands guard at the entrance to the well, and the rags and other objects which hang from it reflect the continuation of an ancient tradition, common throughout the Celtic world. Pilgrims have always come to sacred wells for healing. At clootie wells such as this one, they would hang a rag on a nearby tree after washing, bathing or drinking from the well. The illness would then be driven into the cloth, and as the cloth disintegrated, so would the illness fade. I might also be a pilgrim in my way, but today I had brought no clootie with me; so I bent and picked some sodden rushes from the ground below the tree, plaited them with freezing, fumbling fingers, and knotted the plait around the tip of one of the branches closest to me.

The track I was following leads to the holy well which lies just outside the village of Madron, in a beautiful high-moorland Cornish parish which is home to a number of important Neolithic sites, including the iconic Mên-an-Tol stone and Lanyon Quoit. The Madron well, which bubbles up lavishly from an underground spring, is revered for the healing powers of its waters and has been a site of pilgrimage and ritual for centuries.

In the seventeenth century, a miraculous healing was described by the local bishop: a severely crippled man, John Trelille, told in his dreams to wash in the well and then to sleep on a nearby hillock known as St Madron's bed, 'was suddenly and perfectly cured'. But I hadn't come to this famous well in search of healing; I had come for insight, for my Celtic ancestors believed that drinking the waters from sacred wells could bestow the power of the Otherworld in the form of wisdom or poetic inspiration. And I had a book to write.

There was only one passable path which led beyond the clootie tree and, setting off along it, I very soon came to a small ruined twelfth-century chapel built of stone, which I later discovered had been torn down by Cromwell's men during the English Civil War. There was an altar along one side on which various objects had been placed: a tea candle in a jar, petals, leaves, stones and fragments of frayed cloth. On the other side of what remained of the chapel a continuous stream of water gushed out of a hole close to the base of the wall, and poured itself into a small baptistry. Its source is the original holy well, which is situated further into the wood, and so abundant is its flow that until the eighteenth century it was the only source of water for the entire parish as well as the town of Penzance. These days our requirements are greater, and so we must 'manufacture' our water, but the excess flow from the baptistry is still piped into a nearby reservoir.

I came out of the chapel and retraced my steps to the clootie tree, searching for a way to the source. But wherever I went, I found only water and bog. Somewhere in those woods there was a well – but I couldn't get to it. Later that morning, enquiring, I discovered that it can rarely be reached: the original drainage channels throughout the surrounding woodland are not maintained by the owners of the land, and so they are blocked; as a result, it is only possible to come to the well after prolonged periods of drought. At most times of the year the ground around it is so saturated as to be impassable, and besides, the well itself is neglected and is covered in stagnant water.

It is no longer tended.

I shook new raindrops from the hood of my sodden jacket, and I left. As I retraced my steps, thinking about unattainable wells, I remembered that a couple of decades ago, in my early thirties, in an old stone cottage near a river in the heart of Connemara in the far west of Ireland, I had depended on a spring well for water. At the time, the thoroughly impractical product of a life spent mostly in industrial towns and overcrowded cities, I had no idea what such a thing might look like, let alone how it might work.

On my first visit, I left the derelict cottage which my then-husband Len was sizing up, and headed off to the far corner of the field behind the house where the land began to rise up the hill. The farmer who owned the cottage we were thinking of buying had waved his hand vaguely in that direction. 'Sure, there's all the water you'll ever need in that old spring well,' he'd told us. 'A good well never runs dry.' I didn't know what I was looking for, and so was imagining the only kind of well I had ever seen: the archetypal storybook well which you might find in a cottage garden in some tidy English village. A stone wall encircling it at a safe height, with a little roof over it, and a tin bucket tied to a rope on a cross-beam so that you could carefully lower it into the well and then hoist up your water.

There was no such contraption in this field. Instead, by virtue of almost falling into it, I happened upon a miracle. Surrounded by winter-browned rushes and slimy decaying leaves, there in the ground – just right there in the ground, no infrastructure, no warning sign – was a gently bubbling pool of water, around three feet in diameter, draining away slowly along a slight slope and down into the burn which ran along the boundary of the field and emptied itself into the river.

I crouched down beside it, awestruck. I don't know what I thought might happen at the site of a spring well, but for sure I had never imagined this. A constant stream of water – fresh, drinkable water! – bubbling up freely and flowing out of the earth. The generosity of it took my breath away. In a sudden moment of clarity I understood that this was what I was looking for here in Ireland: a sense of abundance to heal the aridity of a life – my life – that somehow had gone wrong. I closed my eyes and listened for a while, and then, reverentially, I cupped my hands and dipped them into the water, and for the first time I drank the water from our own spring well.

The river had been the major draw, but the presence of the well sealed the bargain on the cottage. Several months later, in the middle of summer, we visited it again, to plan the renovation work which we would undertake over the next couple of years. Drained and brittle from the fallout of a high-powered job which I hated, soiled by the grime of life in the city and suburbs, I had spent the months since our first visit longing to go back to that well, to sit by it and listen to the music of it and drink from it again. It had become a symbol of everything I needed to heal the great gaping wound which occupied the space where my heart should be.

I climbed up the bank behind the house and began to set off across the long, rising field. After a hundred yards or so, I stopped in horror. The entire field ahead of me, stretching all the way along and then right up to the top of the hill beyond, was covered in bracken. The corner where the well was situated seemed to be clear, but I couldn't get to it without walking through the knee-high plants. And unfortunately, I had a phobia: an intense and oddly incapacitating fear of ferns and anything shaped like them. It had begun when I was a child, and over the years had proved completely resistant to any therapies I'd undergone. Between that well and me stretched a chasm containing twenty-five years of fear.

Shaky and disheartened, I turned back. And even in winter when the bracken had died back and the crisp, rusty deadness of it crackled pleasingly underfoot so it was no longer a source of terror, I never went again up to that well. Len built a pump-house, bought an electric pump, laid a long pipe across the field and brought the water from the spring well up into a black plastic tank up in the loft. And like everyone else I had ever known, I simply turned on the taps in my kitchen and bathroom, and water came gushing out. I never thought much about the source. Not until a couple of years later, when the life-giving wellspring inside of me once again ran dry. Then I would begin to understand exactly what it was that I had abandoned when I abandoned that well at the bottom of the hill – but it was going to be another couple of decades, and a long and winding journey, before I would find it again.

Wellspring. The word, like a good well, runs deep. It conveys so very much more than simply the source of a stream or spring: it says something about the source of life itself. According to the *Collins English Dictionary*, a wellspring is 'a source of continual or abundant supply' – which tells us why wells, along with certain rivers and lakes, have been recognised as sacred by nearly every culture on the planet, and throughout every age. There is an especially strong tradition of sacred wells in the Celtic nations; in Ireland, a survey carried out in the 1940s recorded as many as 3,000 of them. These wells once were thought of as gateways to the Celtic Otherworld. Magical fish which lived in them might sometimes appear to those who came seeking insight into the future; more often than not the fish would be a salmon, credited in mythology with being the bearer of *iomas*, a form of intuitive knowledge and wisdom which is the Otherworld's greatest gift.

These springs and wells which originated in the Otherworld would once have been dedicated to the goddess of the land: in Ireland, to the goddess Brigid; in the north of England, to Coventina. At Madron, both the well and the parish are, it is claimed, named for St Madron (or Madern), a local hermit of whom nothing now is remembered – but the women of this land have always known the truth, whispered it down the centuries from the shadows of their kitchens to the corners of their herb gardens. The name of the well comes from the name of the Celtic mother goddess, one of whose names was Modron.[2] In the nineteenth century an old woman, An Katty, used to attend the well in springtime and instruct visitors on the correct rituals to perform there. She understood that the connection of St Madron to the well had been relatively recent, and was known to complain about the 'new gentry', who persisted in giving new names to places they thought they knew more about than 'the people who have lived here since the world was created'.

An Katty was right, for sure; traditions associated with this free-flowing well, as with others, would have significantly pre-dated Christianity. But during its early days the Christian church, finding it impossible to forbid people to visit their sacred places, developed a strategy of taking them over. It built chapels and baptistries over the wells; it walled them in. And so there are many wells which, like Madron, are named now for the saints – but under their shallow surface ripples lie the deep, clear traces of far older stories. In those older stories, as in life, the wells were guarded and tended by women. An Katty at Madron well was probably one of the last in a long tradition of well-priestesses in Cornwall; at Gulval, the eighteenth-century chronicler William Hals wrote about the 'credulous country people' who visited the village well for healing and divination.[3] The well, he said, was tended by an old woman who kept the site neat and clean, and proclaimed the 'virtues and divine qualities of those waters', which she offered to visitors in return for a fee. She gave oracles to strangers, and could reveal the whereabouts of lost and stolen objects, including cattle.

Even those of us who take for granted a constant supply of water piped into our homes nevertheless understand the value of a good well. It's in our folk memory, an archetypal image in our collective unconscious. *A good well never runs dry*; you can always depend on it. And water is the source of life. But the source of life, like all things, must be cared for; a good well must be tended. A curious short tale, hidden within Chrétien de Troyes' medieval manuscript *Perceval, le Conte du Graal*, warns of the dire consequences which might befall us if we should fail to tend the wellspring, and if we should fail to cherish the women who offer the waters of life. It is entitled 'The Elucidation';[4] here is my own version of the story.

~

The Loss of the Voices of the Wells

Do you know the Tamar, the great river which once cut Cornwall off from the rest of the world, until they built a big bridge and let the others in? Do you know its story, the story of the water nymph Tamara, who was turned by her father into a stream and then grew up into a mighty river? I was looking for the source of the great Tamar one day, up among the willow trees by Woolley Barrows, when out of the corner of my eye I caught sight of a grey heron standing in the boggy waters from which the river is known to rise. At least, I thought it was a grey heron, but when I turned to look at it, in the place where I thought the heron had stood was a tall, skinny old woman, all dressed in grey, and with straggly white hair. I imagined at first that she hadn't seen me, but then suddenly she turned her head and began to speak to me.

'I don't imagine you remember,' she said, quite apropos of nothing, 'that once the court of the Fisher King could be found along the banks of the Tamar?' I was taken aback, but found my tongue and answered politely that I had never heard such a story. She laughed, a curious sound; more shriek than laugh, if truth be told. 'It's no story, girl,' she said. 'In the kingdom of Logres – for that was what this land was called, in those days – were all the riches of the world, and they all came from the court of the Fisher King. Gold and silver, splendid furs, nourishing foodstuffs and beautifully woven cloth – the people did not lack for health and comfort and beauty. But more than this: from the court of the Fisher King came falcons and merlins, goshawks and sparrowhawks; wolf and bear, badger and fox. All the beautiful wild things of the land. In those days, when the King's court could still be found, there was such an abundance of riches throughout this land that everyone was awestruck by it.'

I don't know quite how it happened, for I didn't see her move, but all at once she was standing very close to me, her face just a couple of feet away from my own. Her eyes were black, black and shining as pools of tar, and I felt oddly vertiginous, as if I were being drawn in. 'It's not like that now, is it?' Caught off-balance, I simply shook my head. 'You want to know what happened?' I nodded, of course; I've always loved a good story.

'Well, then, I'll tell you what happened. You won't like it.' She shrieked that strange not-quite-laugh again, head tilted up to the sky, and closed her eyes. She lifted her bony arms to the sky, as if to call on it as witness. And then she sighed, lowered her arms, and began.

'In the old days, as I was saying, the kingdom of Logres was rich and beautiful, and the land offered nourishment for all, for it was properly tended and cared for. It's a contract you see, people and the land. You care for it, and it cares for you. The source of the kingdom's life, the life-giving blood which surged in its veins, was the sacred water of the wells, which flowed up out of the deep potent waters of the Otherworld. The wells were tended by maidens, and these maidens were the Voices of the Wells. And this is how they served: if a traveller in need should pass by a well in those times, a well-maiden would appear and, if he asked reasonably, offer him the food he liked best, and a drink of well-water from her golden grail. This gift was given to all, freely given in the spirit of service to the land.

'But then there came a king in the land who did not cherish the old customs, or understand his contract with the land and the duties of hospitality, which travel both ways. That king's name was Amagons.' The old woman paused and shuddered as she said his name, and I swear to you that a tremor passed through the ground beneath our feet, as if the land shuddered too, to hear it spoken out loud. 'As king it was his duty to guard the land and those who lived on it; it was his duty to tend it and see that all was in good heart, for this is the sacred contract which maintains the balance of the world. It was his duty to keep the well-maidens safe, for they were the Voices of the Wells, and without the wells the land would lose its heart. But Amagons wasn't much of a man for duty, and the day came when he broke faith. On that day a well-maiden, seeing him pass by, offered him food and water, as was the custom. After eating the food and drinking the water, Amagons tore off her white dress, threw her across the stone wall which surrounded the well, and raped her while his men looked on.' Tears leaked from the old woman's eyes. 'Can you imagine? Can you imagine it, girl? A maiden from the sacred wells. Can you imagine how the Earth itself must have cried out in horror? How the waters of the wells would have stopped mid-flow, and recoiled from this evil which was visited on the land?

'But it did not stop there. After this violation, Amagons stole the well-maiden's golden vessel and kept it for himself – though it did not stay with him, for the well-maiden's grail might not pass into hands such as his. He carried the maiden off, and made her serve him.

'Then, seeing what the king had done, and taking their lead from him, all around the country his men began to rape the other well-maidens. So the maidens no longer came out of the wells, and withdrew from the land altogether. And so it was that the people of Logres lost the Voices of the Wells, and the services of the wells ceased. This is how the land was laid waste. The leaves on the trees shrivelled and died, plants withered, fields and meadows turned brown, and the earth lay barren and scorched. The waters of the land diminished and the rivers ran dry, and no one could find the enchanted court of the Fisher King, who had once made the land bright with his treasures.'

She look at me, long and hard. 'Do you think it was all long ago, girl, if it even happened at all? Do you think, because the land has grown green again, and the great Tamar flows strong and true, that we do not live in the Wasteland still? Have you seen the great scars that men have made on the face of the Earth? Have you seen the starving masses in the scorched lands, and the hungry hearts amidst the richness of the cities? Do you think there are no men like Amagons?'

And I could not answer her, for I knew that what she said was true.

'The green crept slowly back,' she whispered, 'but in its heart the land was still a Wasteland, for the Voices of the Wells were lost, and the maidens and their grails were gone, and along with them passed the riches of the court of the great Fisher King.'

With that, the old woman grew silent, and stepped away from me, staring back into the boggy morass from which the great Tamar sprang. I stood with her for a while and then I turned, and began to walk down the hill. After a little while I stopped to look back at her, but all I saw was a large grey heron, standing on one leg, perfectly still.

~

'The Kingdom turned to loss, the land was dead and desert in suchwise as that it was scarce worth a couple of hazel-nuts. For they lost the voices of the wells and the damsels that were therein.' So says the unknown author of 'The Elucidation'. They lost the Voices of the Wells, the source of the land's life, and the voices of the women who tended them. As a consequence they lost the land's spiritual heart: the court of the Fisher King. And so we came to live in a Wasteland, barren in body and soul.

The story of the rape of the well-maidens has immense potency, and just as I have never said the words 'the Voices of the Wells were lost' when telling the story without a crack in my voice, I have rarely told the story to a woman who has not shed a tear. The parallels are clear in our culture, which has for centuries suppressed those qualities (dreaming, creativity, openness, nurturing, community) which are perceived to be feminine. Much of the unique wisdom that women hold has been eradicated or driven underground, out of sight, away from the dangerous, damning eyes of men. It's no accident that this systematic suppression of the feminine has been accompanied down the centuries not only by the devaluation of all that is wild and instinctual in our own natures, but by the purposeful destruction of natural ecosystems. We long ago turned our backs on the planet which gives us life.

How did we end up in such a mess?

This state of affairs has its roots in the deeply dualistic world-view which emerged out of Western philosophy over the last 2,000 years: we have come to believe that we are separate from nature, and more than this – that we are somehow above it. Often, it's something to be feared, as anything which cannot entirely be controlled is to be feared. In the Western philosophical tradition, since Plato and before, reason and intellect are the unique and privileged domain of humans, superior to everything else in nature – everything which is physical, emotional, instinctual and wild. In this tradition, women are linked to those inferior qualities of nature, just as men are associated with the superior qualities of reason and intellect. And so it follows that if men are superior to nature, they must also be superior to women. And what is physical, emotional, instinctual and wild must never be embraced, but must instead be overcome by the uniquely human – masculine – force of reason.[5]

Early in the seventeenth century, French philosopher René Descartes modernised this old dualistic and hierarchical perspective, wrapping it up in the formal ribbons and tightly tied bows of mechanisation and reductionism, declaring that only humans are endowed with 'mind'; that matter is inert, lifeless and passive, and that animals have neither mind nor reason – they are nothing more than elaborately contrived machines. It was a message perfectly in tune with the sonorous preachings of Western religious authorities, who quoted their scriptures to demonstrate that God had indeed given humans dominion over nature – and over women. And so the way was perfectly paved for the nineteenth-century Industrial Revolution, which systematically laid waste to the planet on a previously unimaginable scale, and at an unprecedented speed.

In a culture founded on such beliefs, it follows that the natural world is no more than a backdrop for human activities, to be exploited. Wild places have become 'resources', and if they cannot be used for human benefit they are not valued. Nature is seen to have little agency of its own; it is empty of purpose or meaning. As for nature, so for women. And so the Voices of the Well have been lost, and now all is Amagons. Now we have lost touch with the ancient wisdom, with the old knowledge that we are thoroughly enmeshed in the web of life on this beautiful planet, akin to and bound up in relationship with the millions of other species who live on it. So much has been lost in devaluing the feminine, in wiping out the Voices of the Wells. We have lost the dark, dancing wisdom of women, our deep ways of knowing, our creative, life-giving fire. We have become separate from the world around us; we've abandoned our roots in nature and the land.

Our severance from nature leaves us feeling as if we do not belong in the world, and that can be a source of anxiety and deep despair. My friend Viv Palmer had a nervous breakdown when she was thirty-six. 'It had been stalking me for years,' she says, 'on its soft, padded feet.' This is how she describes it: 'Imagine sitting, all alone, in a room. You aren't quite sure where you are, and you know that you don't belong there, but there are table lamps, and candles: little bright spots that give you the illusion that everything is okay. And then, one of the lights goes out. You aren't too worried, but then you see that the sun is going down outside, and long shadows are creeping across the floor. You raise your coffee cup to your lips, and realise that it tastes of absolutely nothing. You put it down. The light fades some more. Another light flickers, goes out. A breeze blows up under the door, and the candles gutter. One of them is extinguished, and a trail of blue smoke meanders towards the ceiling. The darkness is a heavy presence, creeping towards you. You can hear your heart beating. Your body is so heavy that it is impossible to stand, but anyway, you know that the door is locked, so what would be the point? Another candle goes out, and then another. The darkness is sitting on your chest, crushing your lungs. There is one last candle, just a tea light, fragile. You turn your eyes towards it, just in time to see it waver, dance, go out. Now, all that is left is the green after-image of the flame, fading. You try to hold onto it, but it is hopeless. And then, there is infinite blackness, and just you, sitting.'

Viv is a city girl; she was born and raised in London, and it's her home. If you talk about someone who is closely connected to nature, most people will assume you must be referring to someone who lives in the country, or in the wilderness. But Viv lives in North Finchley, and yet she's one of the most 'connected' people I know. She's not a naturalist by profession, she's an accountant, but she sees the life around her with a clarity and a detailed knowledge that few of the people I know who live in the countryside can match. She is particularly passionate about bugs, and once she even managed to convince me once that cockroaches, of all things, were . . . well, not precisely cuddly and lovable, but a useful and necessary part of the cycle of urban life which she understands so well.

On her popular nature blog, 'Bug Woman – Adventures in London',[6] she describes herself as 'a slightly scruffy middle-aged woman who enjoys nothing more than finding a large spider in the bathroom'. Viv has always had a strong sense of the natural world around her. She remembers going to Wanstead Park with her parents and her brother when she was a small child. 'We were walking along a wooded path when there was a scuffle in the undergrowth, and a sharp thump. "Rabbit," said Dad. We bent down, and under a holly bush there was, indeed, a rabbit. Its nose was twitching, its whole body alert. Our eyes met, and for a minute there seemed to be a crack in the fabric of my world. I had such a sense of belonging that even today, fifty years later, it can bring tears to my eyes.'

To Viv, then, belonging was about being outside, and in the company of animals. But one day something went wrong. When she was nineteen she rewarded herself for completing her first set of university exams with a trip to Winchester. After a visit to Jane Austen's grave in the cathedral, she noticed a hill that was wooded on its lower reaches but bald on the top, like a monk's tonsure. Of course, she just had to climb it.

It was a hot day, and when eventually she made it to the top she flopped down onto the grass and dug around in her backpack for a soft drink. The can was cold, and she rolled it against her forehead before cracking it open and taking a gulp. The air was so still; she could hear crickets singing in the long grass. She put the can down, and lay back. She saw a ladybird making its way up the stem of a daisy. Above her, swifts were circling and screeching and as she watched them revolving, she felt as if she was looking into a deep pool. 'The whole world seemed to tilt, and I hung onto a handful of weeds, afraid that I would fall into the swifts and never emerge again. It's as if I didn't know what was up or down, in or out. I could have been a plant growing out of the soil, or a swift flying, or a ladybird climbing. For the first time in my life, I was truly happy.'

She felt his footsteps before she saw him. She sat up, shading her eyes. A balding, freckled man ambled up the path, walked past where she was sitting, then turned. 'Nice day,' she said, and he nodded and moved on down the hill, back into the woods. She noticed a torn condom packet under one of the bushes near where she was sitting, and a crumpled cigarette packet. 'Although the swifts were still whirling, it was as if a cloud had passed in front of the sun,' Viv says. And so she packed up her things and started to walk down the path, the same path that the man had walked along. 'Inside me a doe had raised her head, sniffing the air, fully alert to danger. I chose to ignore her.'

As she was passing through the woods, the man stepped onto the path in front of her, only this time he was completely naked, except for his shoes. She remembers that he was covered in freckles, that he had big, yellow teeth like a horse, that he was holding his penis in one hand. Even now, she didn't run. She went to walk past him, thinking that if she only kept calm everything would be all right. He shoulder-charged her and she fell, then he stood over her, masturbating. And, at last, she was up and running, scattering fallen leaves, thrashing through brambles, leaping over a stream, heart thudding, sides heaving, until she was back in the sunlight, scratched, bleeding, but safe.

Viv describes the impact this event had on her. 'It seemed to me, then, that I'd been punished for some crime that had no precise name. It seemed to be part naivety, and part presumption. Where had I failed to read the rule that women weren't supposed to go lazing around in public open spaces on their own? What had happened felt both deeply personal and completely random. It was something that would maybe have happened to any female who had been hanging around alone on the hill that day. I wanted to pull myself together and get over it. Instead, I grieved. I knew that I would never recapture that sense of freedom and possibility.

'Whenever I was in the woods, on my own, I would have one ear pricked for the sound of approaching footsteps. I would always make sure that I knew what time sundown was, how to find the path back. I started to carry a pepper spray. I was full of impotent rage. When I saw men jogging through the trees I envied them their freedom, and this is in the full knowledge that men, too, can be attacked in quiet places. But the men I saw seemed to think they were invulnerable, just as I had on that summer day; the women, on the other hand, were more like me, all too aware of how "the great outdoors" can be a dangerous place for a lone female, even in broad daylight.

'There are many threads that braid together to make a life. Who is to say which ones are the most important? But this single incident severed me, for too long a time, from something that I needed as much as I needed to breathe. If I can't walk, alone, amongst trees and grass, birds and insects, I feel estranged, dissociated, lost. Although there were other things that contributed to it as well, it was no wonder to me that I fell prey to anxiety attacks and depression. I need access to somewhere where I can feel the earth, feel that I really belong to the world. And when I lost it, everything seemed to fall apart.'

The world we occupy is one in which women, as a matter of course, live with fear. 'I can't believe we live like this in 2015,' columnist Daisy Buchanan wrote recently in the *Guardian*.[7] 'Women should be enjoying more freedoms than ever before, but many of us are frightened, and we're running out of options.' More than that, the world we occupy is a Wasteland in which too many men and women are cut off from the source of life: from the planet we live on, the ultimate source of all our belongings.

The Heroine whose stories and whose Journey we will explore throughout this book begins her life in this arid, patriarchal Wasteland, obeying its rules, locked into its systems. The chances are that, for lack of obvious alternatives, she has embraced the male Heroic Journey, an action-based model which repudiates her feminine instincts and values, and which often runs counter to her sense of who she is as a woman. But when women seek success and 'equality' in a male-dominated world, then in order to achieve it we must act like men, play by their rules and, if they deign to allow us, join their societies and institutions. We are judged by masculine criteria for success – and inevitably we fall short, because we are not men. The best we can ever hope to be is not-quite-men, not quite good enough.

We live, then, in a culture by the standards of which most women are doomed to fail. But it is easier by far just to go with the system, because this world values women who do: women who stick to the rules, women who do not rock the boat, women who do not push for more. Women who are like men, or women who become what men want them to be. But in becoming what we are not, in colluding with the patriarchy, we are cut off from the source of our own creativity, from the wild mystery and freedom which makes our hearts sing. And in following this path, we prop up and perpetuate the system which destroys us and the planet. In living like this, we embrace the Wasteland.

The Wasteland is a rootless place, and its ground is infertile. I inhabited it for decades. If I close my eyes I can take myself back there in an instant. Let's try 1989.

I see a slim young woman, around twenty-eight years old, who is standing on a platform at London's Fenchurch Street station. She is waiting for a train. It seems as if she is always waiting for a train. Today, the train is late again. She holds a black briefcase in one hand; a black leather handbag which she bought on a business trip to Columbia is slung over her shoulder. She is wearing an impeccable beige designer business suit; her red-blonde hair is simply but expensively cut. She is the image of everything she never believed she could be as a child, growing up on the fringes of a small-town council estate in the industrial north-east of England. She is a Success. She works in a senior advisory role for a major international corporation. She has a first-class honours degree in psychology; she has a PhD in neuroscience. She has achieved a long list of publications in scientific journals, and in her early twenties was awarded two competitive and highly sought-after mental health research fellowships which took her to the Hôpital Pitié-Salpêtrière in Paris, and the Institute of Neurology at the National Hospital for Nervous Diseases in London.

She is often told that she should be proud of herself, but today she is just waiting for a train. She is waiting for a train, and trying hard to push out of her head the lines from T.S. Eliot's 'The Hollow Men' which she read over the weekend. Hollow men, stuffed men, valleys of dying stars . . . She lives among those people; she inhabits that world.[8] The truth is, she isn't proud at all, she's just a little confused about how she got here. The train she stepped onto a few years ago to reach the place she's now in wasn't late; it ran precisely according to schedule and it ran away with her. No, she ran away with it; she knows how to take responsibility for her own choices. This wound runs deep.

This wound is festering. It's festering because she is not who she intended to be. Not even remotely. At sixteen she dreamed of working for Greenpeace and manning the *Rainbow Warrior*; instead, she now works for a tobacco company. A global, multi-national tobacco company, the third-largest corporate entity in the UK. She was employed to manage their external medical research programme, researching the effects of smoking on health; and she does so assiduously, aided by first-class train tickets and air fares, and from the sanctuary of five-star hotels around the globe. She applied for the job out of a curious mixture of anger and desperation, when the academic life she had once longed for turned out to be as arid and heartless as any other. When she found herself inside a Machine – a great publication-producing Machine, in which your value to the world was measured in the number of articles you could publish in the *Journal of Neuroscience* or *Brain Research* and in which it mattered not a whit whether your work would do anything at all to make the world a better place. When, in spite of all her accolades and successes, academic tenure (conveying job security) was an impossible dream and all she could look forward to was a future lurching from one year-long post to another three-year fellowship . . . if she was lucky, and played the numbers game.

Why did she think that working for a tobacco company might be a better option? She didn't, but it was safe, and it was easy. And she was frightened. It seems she has always been frightened, but it'll be another long decade before she comes either to acknowledge that fact, or to understand the reasons for it.

Her irritation is rising; it's been a long day. On a good day, her commute takes her about an hour and forty minutes each way. She is trying not to wonder why this ever seemed like a good idea. She has already fought her way through the rush-hour streets of central London, sweltered in the stale trains of the over-crowded Underground. When this train eventually shows up there'll be a forty-five minute journey to the small-town Essex station where her husband will be waiting impatiently in the car to drive her home: there is no public transport which can take her there. Once she walks through the front door, the first thing she'll do is throw off her business suit and put on some comfort-able old clothes in which she can breathe. She'll choose not to read the daily message in this urgent and violent shrugging-off of the trappings of her Success. She'll cook a quick meal. There may be time to read for an hour, then it will be time for bed. A snatched seven—eight hours and she'll be up at the crack of dawn, quick shower, skipping breakfast (a recipe for midday heartburn), gulping down tea, off to the station, ready to do it all again.

She is a Success. Why then is her heart so hollow, and how can something so hollow be so heavy? She knows there is no sense in what she is doing, but at the moment she can't imagine a way out. This husband doesn't contribute to their joint income, and she is solely responsible for an enormous mortgage on a small house, rapidly approaching negative equity in a property market which has been stagnant for some time. In the area where she lives, houses are simply not shifting. Even if eventually she sold up and managed to pay off the mortgage, she would be left with nothing. 'Nothing' is a black hole, uncontrolled and chaotic, and she has been ill-equipped by a turbulent childhood to handle situations defined by either of those adjectives. And besides – what then? What is she qualified to do? More to the point, what does she want to do?

She doesn't have time to think about it.

Truth is, she chooses not to think about it. She lives for the weekends, but they are spent in a state of near-exhaustion, cleaning the house, fighting her way through supermarket crowds to prepare for the coming week. She longs for holidays and time in the wild. In her weaker moments she allows herself to dream of a life outside the Machine, and goes to bed with an aching heart and a sense of desolation so deep in her core that she cannot imagine how she might not someday soon die of it. She dreams of a small stone cottage in the Irish hills, of work that has heart and meaning, and time to simply be. She dreams of a night sky from which the stars have not fled in horror, and of wild-pawed, stinking foxes yapping in a moonlit wood. She can see it; she can almost taste it.

The train arrives, heaving with people. She gets on.

The Wasteland is the hollowness inside us, for we are reflections of the hollow world we live in. To embrace it might mean that we spend our lives doing work we hate in order to feel secure, defining ourselves by that work which we're paid to do for others, wondering then why our hearts are breaking. To embrace the Wasteland might mean that we hunger for ever-grander houses and ever-smarter cars and all the latest versions of all the latest gadgets, as we try to fill the hollowness inside us with 'stuff'. It might mean that we wrap ourselves tightly in busy-ness and noise and never-enough-time and anxiety and panic and wonder why eventually our bodies break.

I had another friend who broke. She was a colleague in that company I worked for, and when she first arrived she was full of fun and laughter. Over the course of a couple of years, day by day, she became more and more stressed, frangible, touchy. Her skin turned dull and her hair grew limp and her eyes grew desperate. One day someone walked into her office and found her on the floor, rigid, unconscious, collapsed behind her desk. She couldn't take any more; she had simply come to a full-stop. There was no complicated medical diagnosis; it was put about that she had simply had what once upon a time was referred to as a 'nervous breakdown'. It was six months before she could summon the energy to walk down the street.

The Wasteland burns us up and burns us out. Instead of

following our own instincts, instead of discovering what it is that gives us joy, what makes our heart sing, we spend most of our lives trying to make other people happy, squeezing ourselves into their boxes, living from our head rather than our instinct for what is good and healthy. And following these conventions, living these lives of arid appropriateness, kills all that is alive and vibrant inside us. We can possess all the fine goods that our civilisation has to offer us; we can have important jobs, and social status, and tone our bodies on all the latest machines – but without a sense of belonging to the world, we feel empty and our lives lack meaning.

Yes, something is rotten at the mechanical heart of the Wasteland and, whether or not we fully acknowledge it, whether or not we know what to do about it, something in us feels it. So many of us suffer from the stresses of living in a world that inflicts on us an excess both of connectivity and complexity, ties us to machines and gadgets, keeps us forever moving, forever doing. There is no time or place to develop community, no time to develop a relationship with the planet which sustains us, no time to think about, let alone act upon, spiritual values. We inhabit a world which locks us indoors for the greater part of each day, and which alienates us from the wider ecosystem of which we're a part.

We are bleeding at the roots, because embracing the Wasteland means that we are out of touch with the seasons and the cycles of the year, with the natural world to which we have forgotten we belong. And when we lose our relationship with the land and the other creatures around us, then in the deepest sense, we lose ourselves. This is what happened to me; it is what happened to my friend Viv. If we no longer feel nurtured by the Earth, we no longer belong to it, and because we do not belong to it, we do not feel responsible for it. We read the statistics in the newspapers, watch the scenes of devastation on the TV; we shake our heads and say that it's terrible, and something ought to be done about it. And then we just get on the train.

★

We all know the Wasteland; we've all heard its stories. It is an idea at the very heart of Arthurian legend: the quest for the Holy Grail, one of the foundation stones of Celtic mythology. It has inspired writers for centuries: writers like T.S. Eliot, whose famous long poem *The Waste Land*, published in 1922, interweaves fragments of the Grail myths with depictions of the fractured and alienated British society that followed the First World War. In the poem, the polluted rivers and canals which run alongside smoke-spewing industrial estates in the edgelands of our cities are the contemporary parallels of the barren landscapes of Grail mythology, which were devastated by fatal wounds and a failure to ask the right questions. To Eliot, then, the modern world was a ravaged place in which neither the land nor the people who inhabited it could conceive of new life. He was right. The Wasteland is not just something that happens in mythology and literature: we are living in the Wasteland today.

Exhibit One: In November 2014, during a pre-Christmas sale known as 'Black Friday',[9] fights broke out at stores all over the UK as throngs of shoppers who had queued for hours struggled to grab the biggest bargains. Scenes of 'mayhem' were reported as police in Greater Manchester were called to at least seven Tesco stores; the Metropolitan Police said that officers were called to at least four large supermarkets in London. The first fights in the Asda store in Wembley broke out at 8 a.m., minutes after the store opened. As cheerleaders in black bikinis welcomed and encouraged shoppers, crowds rushed to the widescreen TVs stacked beside the door, grappling with each other and with supermarket staff to secure one. Two men had to be separated after one was said to have hit the other's fiancée on the head with a TV. Later, a woman who thought she had escaped the scuffle with a large TV in tow was knocked to the ground.[10]

Remember *Brave New World*?[11] In Aldous Huxley's 'utopia', failure to sufficiently consume was a crime against society. The authorities tried gunning down the 'Simple Lifers' who wanted to live differently, but that was neither popular nor effective. And so instead they developed 'the slower but infinitely surer methods' of conditioning: immersing people in advertising slogans from infancy. In Huxley's day, it was still a fiction; today, it's our reality.

We are bombarded by advertising which exhorts us to acquire more and more 'stuff', because global economic systems are founded on a requirement for continually rising consumption in order to avert economic collapse. Growth is the meaning of life, we are told, and progress is measured by the speed and efficacy with which we destroy the ecosystems which sustain life on this planet. We do not think about where the materials come from to fabricate the things we buy and so carelessly throw away, or the industrial wastelands where they are produced, or the fossil fuels that are burned during their manufacture. We do not think of the vast toxic landfills into which we pour them when we have had enough of them. We just keep on consuming, because that is what we are told we must do. Having the right 'stuff' gives us status and so we imagine consumption makes us happy – but a large and increasing body of psychological research shows that materialism is a cause of anxiety, depression and broken relationships.

Exhibit Two: Zoom in on Canada, in the vast wild forests of the province of Alberta, through which great rivers drain down from the Rocky Mountains and out into the watershed of the Arctic Ocean. There's enormous diversity of vegetation and wildlife here, and a number of now-endangered species depend on this natural boreal ecosystem for their survival. But a vast programme of oil and gas exploration and development, which has been endorsed by the Canadian government, has left vast toxic scars across this otherwise unspoiled environment. This is a consequence of exploitation of 'tar sands': the name given to land which contains a combination of clay, sand, water and bitumen – a heavy black viscous oil which, when extracted and processed, is a much-desired source of fuel. But the bitumen in tar sands cannot be pumped from the ground in its natural state; instead it must be mined. It is sometimes extracted by underground heating, but most usually by strip-mining or open-pit techniques. Once the sand has been dug out of the land, it is hauled to an extraction plant where it is mixed with hot water and chemicals to liberate the oil and then release it into pipelines, or into tankers to be transported to refineries.

But not all of the water which is used during the extraction process can be recycled, and what remains is a thick liquid waste which is toxic to aquatic organisms and mammals. This is held in open man-made 'ponds' which currently cover a surface area of around 170 square kilometres, and which contain around 720 billion litres of toxic waste. It is estimated that by 2040 the toxic ponds will cover 310 square kilometres.[12] Pollutants from these ponds are known to migrate through groundwater into surrounding soil and surface water, into the Athabasca River, and from there into the ocean. They are also released into the air. Some First Nations communities who live downstream from tar-sand sites are reporting increased incidence of respiratory and cardiovascular diseases, multiple sclerosis and rare types of cancer which are believed to be due to the toxic waste which is leaching into waterways. So we are left with one of the bleakest and most devastating scenes of man-made destruction on the planet – and yet, today, development in tar sands continues to expand and to be actively encouraged by the Canadian government.

Exhibit Three: Cut to Europe. Here as elsewhere, the philosophy of growth and the pursuit of 'progress' means that we are resorting to ever more excessive methods of energy extraction. In 2015, a law was passed in the UK which gives energy companies an automatic right to frack deep beneath homes, without the owner's consent, in pursuit of shale gas or oil. 'Fracking' is the word commonly used for an extreme approach to oil and gas drilling known as hydraulic fracturing. Natural gas occurs in shale rock, one to two miles beneath the surface of the Earth. Fracking refers to the process of injecting highly pressurised water, mixed with a soup of highly toxic chemicals and sand, into a 'well', thereby creating a chemical reaction which opens up fissures in the rock. Natural gas escapes through these fissures and is drawn back up the well to the surface, where it is processed, refined and shipped to market. A fracking minefield generally contains thousands of wells, all using different chemical compounds. Toxic wastewater, called 'flowback water', returns to the surface after the fracking process is completed. There is no known way to effectively dispose of it. Fracking has been associated with surface, ground and drinking-water contamination, with serious air pollution and with earthquake threats.

Exhibit Four: Ireland. We turn on the television to watch the early-evening news. An advertisement for Concern Worldwide with a soft Irish voiceover shows video footage of a starving child. 'Just seven euros,' the voice exhorts us. 'Just seven euros could save her life.' Just seven euros, to 'fill painful, empty tummies'. The next advertisement is for Burger King. A special 'King Deal', for just €5.50. An enormous double-layered 'Big King' super-burger, complete with an enormous portion of fries and a bucket of fizzy drink. 'Every day at Burger King.' Somewhere in the offices of Sky TV, an advertising executive thinks it is entirely appropriate to schedule these two ads to run next to each other. How many viewers will notice this irony while they are eating their dinner, likely obtained from a chain supermarket full of over-processed food wrapped in an excess of unnecessary plastic? And if they do, how many will do anything about it? Meanwhile, the UN Food and Agriculture Organization (FAO) estimates that about one-third – 1.3 billion metric tons – of all food produced for human consumption goes to waste each year. It also estimates that nearly 870 million people of the 7.1 billion people in the world, or one in eight, were suffering from chronic undernourishment in the period 2010–2012. Today, statistics suggest, over one billion people go to bed hungry.[13]

Exhibit Five: According to a 2014 report from the World Wildlife Fund,[14] the number of wild animals on Earth has halved in the past forty years as humans kill them for food in unsustainable numbers, while simultaneously polluting or destroying their habitats. This is the 'Holocene Extinction', sometimes called the 'Sixth Extinction',[15] a name commonly given to the extinction event of species that has occurred during the present Holocene epoch (since around 10,000 BC) and which is known to be mainly due to human activity. The large number of extinctions affect numerous families of plants and animals including mammals, birds, amphibians, reptiles and arthropods. Although several hundred extinctions occurring between 1500 and 2009 have been officially documented by the International Union for Conservation of Nature, the vast majority are undocumented. According to a 1995 study, the true present rate of extinction may be up to 140,000 species per year.[16]

There are so many more examples that could be given; two-and-a-half centuries of industrialisation and explosive population growth have left the biosphere in a perilous state. The oceans are warming, the glaciers are disappearing, and large-scale habitat destruction, massive soil depletion and extensive deforestation have led to a worldwide disruption of natural cycles. Climate scientists worldwide are using increasingly apocalyptic language. Even the carefully conservative United Nations website, in summarising *Climate Change 2014: Impacts, Adaptation, and Vulnerability*, from Working Group II of the IPCC, declares that 'Observed impacts of climate change have already affected agriculture, human health, ecosystems on land and in the oceans, water supplies, and some people's livelihoods. The striking feature of observed impacts is that they are occurring from the tropics to the poles, from small islands to large continents, and from the wealthiest countries to the poorest.'[17] In 2011, the International Energy Agency (IEA) issued a report projecting 6 degrees Celsius of planetary warming by the end of this century rather than the usually quoted figure of 4 degrees.[18] And, as the IEA's chief economist Fatih Birol bluntly stated in an article in *The New Yorker*: 'Everybody, even the school children, knows that this will have catastrophic implications for all of us.'[19]

In the summer of 2015, James Hansen, the former NASA climatologist who brought climate change to the American public's attention in the summer of 1988, reported that he and a team of climate scientists had identified a new feedback mechanism off the coast of Antarctica which suggests that mean sea levels could rise ten times faster than previously predicted: ten feet by 2065. The authors included a chilling warning in their statement: if emissions aren't cut, 'We conclude that multi-meter sea-level rise would become practically unavoidable. Social disruption and economic consequences of such large sea-level rise could be devastating. It is not difficult to imagine that conflicts arising from forced migrations and economic collapse might make the planet ungovernable, threatening the fabric of civilization.'[20]

But in spite of the strength and consistency of the warnings, and the clear evidence that human activity is primarily responsible for this runaway climate change, reckless consumption and pollution continues in all corners of the world. Meanwhile, global population is growing by 80 million people a year.[21]

There is a collusive madness here, irrationality on a planetary scale. A civilisation which can do this much damage to the planetary fabric on which it depends, and which can continue to do so in spite of unambiguous signs pointing to the catastrophic direction in which we're heading, is nothing less than pathological. But our insanity springs from the fact that we have constructed an exclusively human world for ourselves, and in so doing, we have cut ourselves off from the source of our belonging: the land, and the non-human others who occupy it with us. We have lost touch with the sense which our ancestors had of being a part of the natural world, of living in our bodies, embracing the cycles of the seasons, fully present in time. We do not recognise ourselves any longer in their stories. Something essential has vanished from our consciousness. We are caught not only in an industrial wasteland, but in a Wasteland of the heart and the spirit. The Wasteland is not just outside of us, a sickness in the system, in our culture: the Wasteland is in ourselves.

Polly Higgins[22] has a word for what humans are doing to the planet: she calls it 'Ecocide'. Polly is a barrister, and is probably as far away from your image of the average barrister as it is possible to get, describing herself on her website as 'a Celt and a free spirit'. After talking to her I came away feeling as if I'd experienced an hour-long hug; you can be sure that I've never felt that in a lawyer's presence before. But Polly describes herself as a lawyer who loves the Earth, while noting wryly that it's not often you hear lawyers talking about love in the course of carrying out their professional duties, either. And her love for the Earth isn't just a nice feeling: it's an intrinsic part of her life and the sole focus of her work, because Polly is the lawyer who proposed to the United Nations in 2010 that Ecocide should be the fifth 'Crime Against Peace'. In recognition of that work, she was named 'the Earth's Lawyer' by the 2010 Change Awards, and 'one of the world's top ten visionary thinkers' by *The Ecologist* magazine.

Nothing about Polly is entirely expected, including her office: a large annexe to her Gloucestershire house which conveys an overwhelming sense of clarity, of warm, light space and pale, restful furnishings. 'It doesn't look like an office on purpose,' Polly tells me. 'And that comes out of wanting to create my own intimate space, rather than a homogenised workspace. A place which can reflect the creativity and fluidity in what I'm doing. Because what I'm doing isn't a job: I'm on a quest, and a quest which is deeply in alignment with my values. A quest in which who I am informs what I do.'

And what she does is remarkable enough: Polly is pushing for the UN to adopt an international Ecocide law because she believes that the destruction of the Earth's environment is a crime, and one for which those responsible should be held accountable. In her view, a law of Ecocide could end many destructive environmental practices which currently seem unstoppable.

'Law can be life-affirming or life-destroying,' she says: 'it just depends on where you align it. At the moment the law instructs a company to put its shareholders' interests first, which means maximising profits. A law of Ecocide would shift those priorities. It will say: first and foremost do no harm, and then think about making profits. That's the key driver for my work – can you imagine a world in which the law would prevent corporations from investing in business practices that cause harm to people and the planet? It's important to understand that this isn't about closing down companies; it's about giving them a legislative framework which allows them to reinvent themselves. What we need is encouragement for business leaders to demonstrate moral courage, to stand up and say this has to stop; it's not working. Because no matter how we look at it, commoditising the planet and destroying it for short-term profit makes no sense. To raze forests and ancient peatlands and wetlands, for example – natural carbon sinks that have taken thousands of years to create – for short-term profit and to enjoy unlimited energy for a few decades just does not work, and therefore it must stop.'

The concept of Ecocide has been around for a while, and the possibility that it might be made a Crime Against Peace was examined within the United Nations during the 1970s, 80s and 90s. Unfortunately, the idea was shelved in 1996 without it being put to the vote, despite a number of countries objecting to its exclusion. Ecocide is already classified as an international crime during wartime, Polly tells me: according to the International Criminal Court's Rome Statute, it is a crime to 'intentionally launch an attack in the knowledge that such attack will cause . . . widespread, long-term and severe damage to the natural environment . . .' But during peacetime no such crime exists, and the work of Polly and her team is focused on trying to close that legal loophole.

'To create an international law of Ecocide, it would only take one State Party to call for an amendment to the Rome Statute, and then eighty States would need to agree.' ('State Parties' are countries which have signed and ratified the Rome Statute, and there are currently 121 of them.) 'Once an amendment to the Rome Statute to include Ecocide was agreed, there'd be a transition period of five years, to allow for subsidies to be redirected from dangerous industrial activity which was causing Ecocide, to clean and green business. This would ensure that economies didn't collapse, and would turn businesses which are currently the problem into the solution. They would then become leaders for change.'

Polly was born and raised in Scotland, and there is still a hint of a Scottish accent in her voice, despite the fact that she's lived in England for many years. Her strong identification with her Celtic roots has informed her deep sense of attachment to the Earth which she is so passionate about protecting. 'I feel a strong connection to my native land,' she says. 'It all starts from there.' Her 'spiritual home' is Kilmartin Glen, on west coast of Scotland in Argyllshire, and she enthusiastically describes the cup and ring markings on its ancient stones, suggesting that they look like an ancient wifi sign.

'That place – my native place – is where the Eradicating Ecocide campaign first began,' she tells me. 'When I was approaching my fortieth birthday I had a huge yearning to get back up to Kilmartin, where I'd spent my childhood holidays. I had a sudden and strong need to connect with that old source of inspiration. At the time I also badly needed peace and quiet, so my husband and I rented a cottage up there. We spent lots of time brainstorming, sitting on the rocks where those old cup and ring marks are. And during that time, among those ancient stones, I had my big idea: that just as we have a universal declaration of human rights, we should have one for Earth rights. My husband is a lawyer too, so we spent some time drafting out the first twelve rights and freedoms to get an idea of what the declaration might look like. Then we talked about the need to get support from the United Nations. Towards the end of that week we were walking up among the rocks again and my mobile phone rang (it was a huge surprise, as we'd had no reception at all around Kilmartin until then) and it was a young woman from the UN, passing on an invitation for me to speak at an upcoming conference on women and the environment, and to do a workshop. And I said no, I have something far more important to talk about! Something about a far bigger woman: the Earth herself. I told her that I wanted to come and speak about that. I asked her to write down what I was proposing, and to take it to highest level she could. She did, and she phoned me back fifteen minutes later with an invitation to address the UN, at their top climate change conference, on the possibility of a universal declaration of Earth rights. And so I think of being in Kilmartin, among the stones with their ancient wifi signals, as intrinsic to that process of coming up with a plan to protect the wider Earth. Because the important thing, and the root of it all, was my connection to that place.'

Kilmartin is known above all for its 350 ancient monuments – rock carvings, standing stones, burial cairns – 150 of which are prehistoric. There's a strong sense there of the long history of humans in the Scottish landscape, and it's this ancestral past which Polly speaks about most enthusiastically. 'For me that particular place represents my indigenous roots. It speaks to me like nowhere else can. It nourishes me. It's such a deep thing, stretching out into the story of my ancestors, generations back.'

Polly has a strong attachment to her native land, and yet her work means that she lives away from it. 'I don't think you have to live in a place for it to matter to you,' she says. 'Your sense of your own roots grounds you. And you can take it with you, that sense of your own roots, and then you can ground yourself anywhere. For me, for example, it's important to be able to physically touch the Earth with my feet. When I travel, one of the first things I do when I arrive somewhere is to take my shoes off, or swim – in some way to connect energetically with that place where I am. It's a very conscious intent on my part. Like plugging in, gaining an energy source from the Earth. It makes me understand why so much harmful decision-making is made by men working at the top of skyscrapers, surrounded by concrete jungle. They make poor, damaging decisions because they're literally disconnected from the Earth.'

Her mention of men in skyscrapers raises the question of whether women's sense of relationship might differ from the ways in which men relate to the natural world. 'I do think that men and women have a different approach and a different energy,' Polly offers, 'but the critical thing of course is to find the right balance of both masculine and feminine energy in each person, in each situation. We need both perspectives, both energies in balance, to make whole decisions. And the suppression of feminine energy is a huge part of the problem in the world right now. It pushes down our ability as a civilisation to feel, and especially our capacity to feel great pain. Women give birth, one of the most painful experiences humans routinely endure. We know how to feel that pain and allow it to pass through us with love, and that's an utterly remarkable thing! But we need to take that ability to feel outside of us, to put it out there in the wider world.

'Political and corporate decision-making is based on a numbing out. And that's how corruption sets in: *coeur-ruption*, a rupturing of the heart space. So we need to bring in that feminine quality, the capacity to feel. If we allow it to come through in ourselves, as women, to manifest it honestly in our lives, then we give permission for it to come through in men, and that very necessary rebalancing of male and female energies can take place. Of course the intellectual and the rational is also important – but there is way too much of that in the world right now. It feels deeply unbalanced. If we were to allow ourselves properly to feel pain, to feel the Earth's pain, we wouldn't be able to make the decisions we do, which lead to tar sands, fracking, deforestation. To Ecocide.'

Her Scottish background means that Polly is especially taken by the idea that Celtic mythology positions women as guardians and protectors of the land. 'Yes,' she says, nodding vigorously, 'and that makes me think too about our Western concepts of power, which seem so very masculine, and which insist that we must have rulers, governors who centralise decision-making and power. This creates a dependency situation, a situation based on control rather than trust. Whereas feminine energy produces a much softer kind of power. That idea of soft power means that you don't necessarily have to sit in a parliament and dictate and put lots of laws in place – we have far too many laws, and most of them are born out of fear and control, rather than trusting communities to choose how they are governed – or how they might govern themselves. This is exactly what happens in many indigenous communities around the world. Where those communities are thriving, I think it's because of their more balanced and inclusive approach to decision-making. Even if women often don't take the most overt roles, their covert roles are deeply necessary, and deeply valued. Also, there is fluidity between the two, and a lack of pigeon-holing which is important.'

This valuing of women's roles is critical precisely because we have been so deeply devalued in the West over the past 2,000 years, and I often find myself wondering whether perhaps the biggest mistake made by early feminists might have been in the translation of equality for women into fighting for the rights of women to walk men's paths: for the Heroine to take the Hero's Journey. Polly agrees. 'Rather than try to outdo men at their own way of being, we need to focus more on our own. I saw this when I first started practising as a barrister – there were a lot of women who believed that the only way to succeed was to out-man the men. And maybe that was the case back then; this was their way of trying to carve out their own niche in that very male-dominated space. But the younger generation I was part of – we wanted something more harmonious, which drew on our different ways of being.'

Given that women lawyers are fighting for change within a

justice system which is very patriarchal, Polly acknowledges that finding the way isn't always obvious. 'The legal system in the UK is definitely energetically unbalanced, very masculine. There's a space opening now for something new to emerge, but the system itself is caught in a pattern of control. You end up being coerced into its ways of being, of operating. Good people end up getting compromised; people go in with great aspirations but end up jumping out after just a few years. And so as part of my work on Ecocide, I am asking how we might reinvent that system. How do we stop these wheels from turning and turning, and allow a new way to emerge?

'One way is through restorative justice, which is part of the Ecocide law we're formulating. It offers a safe space for a CEO, company director, whoever, to accept responsibility for decisions they have made which lead to Ecocide, and then to step into a restorative justice circle. There, they come together with others who represent the beings who've been harmed, and collectively they decide what can be put in place to restore the land, to mend the damage. That's the really radical part of the Ecocide law, offering up the tools to allow those who have made decisions which cause harm to face that harm in a healing space. Yes, accountability is essential – but it's no use just locking people up, or perpetuating a culture of blame. It's about finding ways of healing, and so changing things – and people – in a more mean-ingful and enduring way.'

Looking at Polly, eyes shining, enormous smile, talking so passionately about changing the world, and so clearly a source of inspiration to many women, I find myself wondering why it is that we're seeing more and more women coming out as envi-ronmental leaders, and more women-led activist movements. Polly is clear that the environmental 'establishment' is just as male-dominated as the legal system: conventional environmental conferences are still predominantly full of men. But if you move away from the conventional, from the establishment, then you begin find more women stepping into that space. 'I think women are being called upon to become a voice for the Earth,' she says. 'I think we can pave the way, show how using a softer, more inclusive collaborative narrative can work.'

Polly's work has obviously driven the direction of her own personal journey, and changed the way she chooses to live. She recently moved out of London, she tells me, and makes her home now just outside of Stroud, in Gloucestershire. 'I needed to be connecting with communities who care, and there is a deep ecological, caring community here,' she says. 'I don't have to justify my values here as I do in the city; it seems as if everyone I meet cares for the Earth and is somehow constructively engaging in helping to co-create a better world.

'For me, it's not enough to be connecting with land; I also need to connect with a community which cares for the land and for the Earth as a whole. I have a very large appetite for that. And also, I needed to be able to return after travelling – I have to do a lot of travelling – to a base which deeply nourishes me on those many levels. When we moved here, my husband had been saying for fourteen years, "Let's go and live up a Welsh mountain!" But I said no, because I need community. And it's also about tapping into creativity: music, the arts – it's about being able to celebrate and come together. It's so easy to be pulled down by life's challenges and the awful things that are happening to the planet, but it doesn't serve any purpose to stay in that place. It's not what the Earth requires right now. The Earth is calling on us to change things – but also, while we're doing it, to have fun! Fun – maybe that's the most radically feminine idea of all.'

If women want to change things, we need authority, and authority comes in good part from inside ourselves. It comes from conviction, from understanding and owning our stories, from a strong sense of who we are and what our place is in the world. The story of the rape of the well-maidens seeps out of an old Celtic tradition in which women held authority as well as men: a different kind of authority, more often than not, but one which exercised a moderating influence over the power of men. Men might have wielded social authority more often than women (though women could clearly be rulers and tribal leaders too), but Celtic mythology depicts a society in which women – almost exclusively – held a form of moral and spiritual authority which not only rose directly out of the land itself, but which carried all the weight of the Otherworld.

Although Celtic society was not fully egalitarian, and although over time – with the strong cultural influences of Greece and Rome and then the rise of Christianity[23] – it became increasingly patriarchal, historical sources suggest that, unlike their Greek sisters, who were idealised in myth but had no power in the world, Celtic women enjoyed a social standing which their contemporaries in most other European cultures did not share.[24] In Ireland and Britain especially, women were able to rule and played an active part in political, social and religious life: Boudica and Cartimandua, prominent tribal leaders, are the best-known examples. Women were physicians, judges and lawyers, poets, astronomers, artists and priestesses. They could own property, and retain ownership when they married. They had sexual freedom, were free to choose their partners and divorce, and could claim damages if they were raped or assaulted. Celtic women could, and often did, lead their men into battle and warrior training was often undertaken by women. Diodorus of Sicily reported that 'the women of the Celts are nearly as tall as the men and they rival them also in courage'; the Greek historian Ammianus Marcellinus stated that 'a whole troop of foreigners would not be able to withstand a single Celt if he called his wife to his assistance'.

Celtic mythology is highly goddess-centred:[25] the creative essence of the universe was female, not male; women represented the spiritual axis of the world. The Celtic divine female in her various incarnations was deeply grounded and rooted in place, indivisible from her distinctive, haunting landscapes. In the story of the coming of the Wasteland, the well-maidens are manifestations of Sovereignty, a quality of the goddess of the land who was its guardian and protector. Sovereignty was the spirit of the Earth itself, the *anima mundi*, a deeply ecological force.

But she's been treated badly over the centuries, this old goddess of Sovereignty. She began to lose her power when stories from the ancient oral tradition of the Celts were committed to paper by Christian monks; their written words formed the new and only permitted truth. A goddess could not be tolerated in this brave new world: theirs was the only god. These powerful, complicated divine women who carried with them all the authority of the Otherworld, and the fertile and creative power of the land in all its ambiguity and complexity, were reinvented as saints. And if the qualities they embodied in their specific incarnations didn't fit the new image of what a good woman should be, they were portrayed simply as 'fairy women', or remodelled as promiscuous, pseudo-historical queens. By the seventeenth century, when a woman could no longer be accepted in any significant position of influence, all that remained of the story of the powerful goddess of Sovereignty were the dreamlike visions in which she appeared to inspire the poets — a weak, melancholy maiden, romanticised and unreal.

In the days when our native traditions predominated, the power of Sovereignty was also the power to determine who should rule the land. In the old myths, Sovereignty's power was paramount. If the power she bestowed was abused, then we invited disaster. During the reign of a king favoured by the goddess, the land was fertile and prosperous, and the tribe was victorious in war. But if the king didn't match up to her expectations, he didn't last long. And what she expected more than anything was that the king, and through his example, the people, would cherish the land. So it was that the ancient rites of kingship in Ireland included a ceremonial marriage, the *banais rîghi*, between the king and the land, and those rites lasted into the sixteenth century.[26]

In this sacred marriage, the king swore to uphold the land and his people and to be true to both; in return Sovereignty granted him the gifts which would help him to keep his oath. Inaugurations might take place by a well; the new king would receive a drink from it to demonstrate his dependence on the Sovereignty goddess, and to show that he recognised her as the source of the kingdom's life. But the source of life must be respected. While there is mutual respect between the two partners – between the goddess and the king, between the land and the people, between nature and culture, between feminine and masculine – then all is in harmony and life is filled with abundance. But when the contract is broken, the fertile land becomes the Wasteland. The story of the well-maidens is the story of such a fall from grace: the balanced and harmonious union between male and female, the king and the land, was shattered forever. And so it is that the Wasteland, which came into being as a direct result of the abuse of those women, becomes a metaphor for the world we have inherited today.

The Heroine's Journey for these times is a journey out of the Wasteland. Each of us has our own unique set of stories to tell: the story of the years we spent in the Wasteland, the story of our awakening, and then the story of the path we took out of it. Telling those stories helps us to understand ourselves – not just the place that we've come from, but where we might now be heading. Similarly, telling our stories to others can help them to work through problems they are facing in their own lives. We all look to the real-life stories of others for guidance, just as we are often influenced by myths and novels. My own journey was inspired by listening to the stories of people I knew, as well as by reading the stories of historical figures and several compelling works of fiction. But the particular path I found myself on was also deeply inspired by those Celtic myths and stories which showed me a way of belonging to my own native lands, and which offered an image that I hungered for of what it might be to be a woman.

Today, after many comings and goings, I live again in a small stone cottage on the banks of a fast-flowing river in the Irish hills. But this is a different river, and a different county – a couple of hundred miles to the north of that first house in Connemara. The cottage sits in a grove of native trees, near a waterfall. Water, the old stories tell us, flows up from sources in the Otherworld and gushes out into the rivers. Like wells, rivers are closely identified with divine women who are present in the water's flow. My river winds through a green valley in north-west Donegal, and as it flows, it sews together many scraps of cloth – fields, bog, heather moor, scree slopes; stands of trees, birds, fish, sheep, people. On paper maps the river is called the Tullaghobegley, after a male Christian saint – but I name her Riverwitch, for somehow, she holds together this elaborate habitat: magical and ordinary, ancient and subtle, robust and harebell-delicate.

It's her voice which catches you first as you step out of this simple old house: a raucous, joyful clatter of sound as she tumbles down the waterfall, somersaults across the stepping stones and plunges down through the lush green valley to the sea. Her voice is everywhere. In full spate, she is glorious. Always she flows on, and there is no stopping her: she is everywhere and nowhere; she travels on by and still she remains. The land thirsts for her; the sun sees himself reflected in her. She is the Earth's laughter, her accompaniment the whispers of trees, her stories the dreams of fish. The river is the flow of all of our longings, the flow of all of our journeys. You can follow her if you choose; she'll lead you to the court of the Fisher King; she'll lead you out of the Wasteland.

Yes, the good news is that there are ways out of the Wasteland, paths through the hinterlands of the heart. My own journey has been far from straight, but I found the river and I followed it, and here I am finally, in this place I once dreamed of, doing work which has heart and meaning, this patient work of remaking the world. In the old stories, it is women who make the world; why then shouldn't we remake it? Women are the spinners, and the weavers; no matter how deeply we lose ourselves in the dark woods, we can always picture the shining thread of the river, far off in the distance. Women know how to find the way out of the woods; we have only to remember that we know it.

We are wild creatures still, at heart, and if we listen to our hearts we will remember how to listen to the song of the fierce-beaked, wild-winged little wren who, hopping from tree to stump, shows us the way home. When we stop, when we let ourselves see, when the torn veil of this broken civilisation lifts away from our eyes – we can find our way back home. And when we find our home in our distinctive, iconic Celtic landscapes, and connect there with our stories, it is from that strong place of belonging that we can begin the unravelling of the Wasteland. The Voices of the Wells were lost, long ago – but the Voices of the Wells were women. We were the Voices of the Wells. We can take up that old mantle. We can take up our golden grails again, and offer their life-giving drink to the world.

3

Islands of the Heart

Embracing the Call

The headland, Breanish, Isle of Lewis

Peregrina

O mother of the sea
lend me a wave that is strong and true
to carry me from this Age which unbinds me.

I do not need a ship, mother,
but make it a buoyant swell
to bear me up and float me on the sea's dreaming
then beach me on some lighter shore.

When I land there, give me warp and weft again,
and an urchin quill to remind me
how the prettiest barb can lodge under your skin
and leave you undone.

Only lend me a loom and I will
take up the threads of this unravelled life.
I will weave a braid from three strands of seaweed
I will wind it three times around my finger
I will dig my salt-encrusted hands into the soil
and wed myself to the thirsty
brown roots of a new beginning.

Sharon Blackie

If you have ever driven the road through the district of Uig to the farthest south-western corner of the Isle of Lewis in the Outer Hebrides, you'll know Mangurstadh Beach. It sits almost out of sight, well below the road, just as you reach the top of that rise, three miles or so before you come to the crofting township of Breanish. You'll recall the rise, where the road you have been confidently riding falls away from you like a breaking wave – I'd bet you'll never forget it – the place where you suddenly fall forwards into the open jaw of the Atlantic, where the sea and the sky rise up to ambush you. Just there, when you think that you are going to pitch headlong into so much space and distance, Mangurstadh Beach is waiting to catch you. If you allow yourself to be ensnared by its curving white sands and the bright turquoise and emerald green of the shallows, you'll forever be a haunter-of-edges. If you don't watch yourself you'll turn to stone down on that beach, a sea-smoothed rock-creature with eyes that are holes where the sky shines through.

Pass by it if you can. Drive another four miles and, as if losing heart, overwhelmed by so much wildness and beauty, the road gradually peters out into bare stone mountains on the border between Lewis and Harris. It ends just beyond another white-sanded beach in the abandoned village of Mealista, one of many casualties of the Clearances. On this far section of the coast the prevailing gales are so strong that every few winters an especially violent storm will blow all the sand off the beach. After a year or two it creeps back, slowly, as if hoping that the wind won't notice.

I lived there for a while not so very long ago, just two miles up the coast from Mealista beach – and I can tell you that the heart gives out along with the road there on the edge of the world, overwhelmed by so much wildness and beauty. Some edges cut through you like a knife. If you are lucky, though the cut may be deep, it will also be clean.

We are all edge-dwellers, those of us who inhabit this long Atlantic fringe in the far west of the continent of Europe. I have always been drawn to the edges of things, the places where two things collide. Where bog borders riverbank, where meadow merges into forest. Where you stand in the margins of what is behind you and look out across the threshold of the future. The brink of possibilities – will you cross? Edges are transitional places; they are also the best places from which to create something new. Ecologists call it the 'edge effect': at the convergence, where contrasting ecological systems meet and mingle, life blooms – life, diverse and various, unexpected, abundant and unique.

The shore is the greatest edge of all. Sometimes it seems gentle, on a still summer's day when the sun warms the shallows and the soft sand cradles you. But you must also be able to face the storm. I have stood on the rocky shoreline by my old island house, facing into the ocean, arms stretched wide; I have closed my eyes and fallen forwards into a wind so strong that it held me up, my face encrusted with salt and globs of sea-foam caught in my hair. Those of us who live here must be comfortable with storms and with change, for it is on these unsettled, unsettling edges that we will hear the Call which launches us on our journey. And though we can never quite be sure what that journey will involve, we know that new possibilities may be created only if we surrender to uncertainty.

Whatever your cultural background may be, to stand on the dramatic shoreline of any of the Celtic nations looking westwards over the Atlantic is somehow to participate in the recognisable, powerful and curiously timeless experience of Celtic identity. Roiling seas, mist, constant shifts of light, ever-changing weather – all of our coastlines are edgelands, and for the most part we may come to them or retreat from them as we choose. On an island, though, edges are inescapable. As island-dwellers we are surrounded by them – bound by them or freed by them, according to inclination. Edges define an island . . . and yet an island's edges are not strictly defined. They shift with the tides, in an ongoing, fluid, co-creative partnership between land and sea. They are in an unending state of becoming, and we are like them: we ebb and we flow; we soften sometimes, merge into the ecosystems of others, then retreat into the safety of our own sharply defined boundaries. We are gentle, and warm, and then we are storm. Perhaps this is why islands fascinate us so; perhaps this is why, at certain times in our lives, they draw us to them.

On Lewis, these apparent contradictions were both the geographical and the existential terrain I inhabited. On an island, nothing is fixed, and yet everything is fixed. Nothing is possible, and yet everything is possible, and both things are true at the same time. It creates an oddly vertiginous way of being. I came to Lewis – though I did not know it at the time – to test myself on the wildness of its edges, where the elements meet head-on. To stand and face a sea so capricious that one day it may shower you with fish and the next it may threaten death. Could I be equal to it? To stand steadfast under a thousand stormy skies and walk each day into incessant wind? Could I hold myself together in the face of it? To inhabit the remotest of places, to find its wildness reflected in myself. To find out what is left when those elements strip you down to the bone, and to let the rest fall away.

It was unboundedness which first drew me to this island in 2010, at a time in my life when all my stories seemed to have failed me, when every Heroine's Journey I had embarked upon threw me back to the same starting point: the same state of mind I had been in when I first left the Wasteland for my small cottage in Connemara, almost twenty years earlier. The same lessons, still unlearned. This was far from my first journey; by now I had lost count and I had also lost heart. Did I have the energy for another?

I didn't honestly know. So I was biding my time on the edge. From the salt-smeared kitchen window of our old stone croft-house I looked directly out over the sea to the St Kilda archipelago, getting on for forty miles away. It was all that lay between me and the coast of Canada, 4,000 miles across a great and formidable ocean. The small isle of Hiort and the great bird-cathedral of Boreray would flicker in and out of view on the far western horizon as the light shifted from moment to moment, and legends of hidden, magical islands like Tír na nÓg and Hy-Brasil seemed suddenly far less fanciful. On a good day the world – all deep blue waters and vast blue skies – seemed infinite; but on a bad day those seas held me there, trapped me.

Over the four years that I lived there, I grew to know my three-kilometre section of the coastline intimately, and I grew to know its stories. Like all of the islands strung along the Atlantic seaboard of Europe, Lewis and Harris – together known as the Long Island, the largest of a small cluster of islands collectively called the Outer Hebrides, or sometimes the Western Isles – are awash with myths and legends of the sea. On such a narrow island, deeply cut with sea lochs, it is impossible ever to be far from the sea; the village of Achmore is the only one on Lewis from which the sea cannot be seen. Throughout the past few centuries, almost all local families will have had at least one fisherman among them.

The sea dominated our crofting township: tiny Breanish, the last inhabited village at the end of the road which runs south-west through the district of Uig on the Isle of Lewis. None of its crofts is especially well sheltered from the full force of Atlantic storms and prevailing salt-ridden sea gales from the south and west. The soil is mainly peaty, and wet. Except for a tiny amount of low cover (mostly *Rosa rugosa* and scrub willow) in the more protected areas of one or two crofts, there are no trees or shrubs; the surrounding land is blanket bog. To the east is Mealasbhal, the highest of the ancient range of walnut-like mountains which run along the spine of Uig. To the north, and running along the border of what was then our land, is Loch Greibhat: a long, shallow loch which attracts large migrating flocks of whooper swans in spring and autumn. Humans are secondary inhabitants there: herds of thirty or more stags freely roam the village in winter; sea eagles dominate the skies.

On an island like this the sea is part of you, both outside of you and in you. Every day's sea is different, and every new sea washes up new stories. You find them in the sheltered coves and the deep-cut geos. You find them in the rock-pools, hidden under red-fringed dulse. Turn over a stone on the sandy beach, and a story will escape, briny and encrusted with barnacles. So come out of the house; brace yourself against the wind which always is waiting to lift you off your feet. Turn right out of the big deer-proof gate and walk down the small track which runs down to the *àird*, the headland. Go through the gate, past the fencepost capped by a lone upturned weathered wellington boot, hoping someday for a mate. A little further and stop right there, just on the top of the small green rise where the path subsides.

Look at it. Look out at the world. It opens its arms and offers you only emptiness. The St Kilda archipelago may be seen ahead of you in the west; the isle of Scarp dominates the horizon to the south. If you should find yourself walking in the darker hours, you'll see the light on the tiny island of Gasker pulsing to your left, just north of the Monachs, and the lighthouse on the Flannan islands will be flashing to your right. All of these islands are uninhabited. From time to time, you may see the light of a distant solitary voyager in the shipping lanes which run far out west. Otherwise there is only you, and the sea and the sky.

Walk west, in a straight line, keeping the small humpbacked look-out mounds to the south, keeping the tall stone cairn to the north. The grass is green here, and if you should be walking in spring you'll find it scattered with dog violet, milkwort, lesser celandine, bird's-foot trefoil, spring squill and tormentil. Jump over the natural channels which now are filled with water, and just over that last small green rise you'll find yourself at the edge of the shore. Large smooth rocks and pebbles pass for a beach, and such treasures it holds for sea scavengers. Bright, battered plastic floats, plastic bottles and plastic fish-boxes. Fragments of cerulean blue rope, of green fishing net hopelessly entangled with seaweed. A vast array of single shoes, boots, wellies, flip-flop sandals. There is little that is shiny or beautiful, here among the washed-up detritus of the modern world. But if you are lucky you will find a shell, or a feather, or a very occasional piece of sea-smoothed driftwood.

Stop there for a while. Look out to a sea which is continuously in motion; watch the ebb and the flow, the shifts of the tides. Doesn't it make you believe that any sort of metamorphosis is possible? Metamorphosis, the core of so many Celtic myths and stories; so many of our sea stories are about shape-shifting. See that dark line of seaweed, thrown up by the tide, which gathers on the pebbles there, between sea and land? That dark band represents the threshold between one world and another, for at the water's edges, so the old Celtic stories say, you can cross over into the Otherworld. Myth is born here, cast up out of the waves, there for the taking by any beachcomber.

Between sweeping Mealista beach to the south and curving Mangurstadh beach to the north, this coast is all wilderness: jagged rock and smooth pebble, sea-stack and cliff and geo. But treasure always hides in such places, and if you should turn north here, just here at the point where the land surrenders to the sea, at the right time of the day, you will find (if you are lucky) a hidden sandy beach: a tiny thing which vanishes completely at low tide, set on the edge of a small calm bay protected by an arc of high rock on both sides. It is there that you will find the seals. More often than not, you will find just one, her grey head popping up from the sea, bobbing in the waves, large dark eyes staring straight at you. She's waiting for a song, so sing to her. Above all songs, she'll love to hear 'The Sealwoman's Sea-Joy', written to express the delight of the Selkie who finds her lost skin.

~

The Selkie's New Skin

There is an island to the far west of these lands, close to the end of the world; somewhere in your dreams you've seen it. Long white beaches, rocky coves, stormy seas. From the cliff-tops on its western-most shores, you might sometimes catch a glimpse of Tír na mBan, the Isle of Women, way out on the horizon. When the sky is blue and the air is still – which happens rarely enough in those parts. Here, the wind blows hard and long through the dark days of winter, and summer is precious and fleeting. Somewhere along the storm-iest section of that westernmost coast is a high, inaccessible cave where they say the Old Woman of the World lives still, with her companion Trickster Crow – but no one I've met has ever found that cave, though many have searched, and many have drowned in the process. Maybe she's still there, stirring the soup which contains all of the seeds and all of the herbs and the essence of all the growing and living things in the world. Maybe she's still there, working on the most beautiful weaving in the world, with its fringe of sea-urchin quills.

The island's beaches are haunted by seals. Neither common seals nor grey seals; I've never seen their like elsewhere. But then they're not just ordinary seals: they're Selkies. And for one night every month, on the night of the full moon, they can take on human form if they choose, and it is said that on those nights they slip off their sealskins and dance on the beach under the moonlight.

On this island, once there lived a fisherman. He was a handsome man with coal-black hair and bright blue eyes, and he stood tall and strong. Although many of the local girls mooned over him and dreamed of being his wife, he never seemed to find anyone that represented the qualities he wanted. He was something of a dreamer, you see. They said that it was a miracle that he managed to catch any fish at all, for all the time he would spend staring out to sea when he took to his boat. He believed that love would come upon him like a clap of thunder or the crashing of the waves on the rock. And he never had that feeling with any of the girls he had grown up with: they were all too familiar, somehow. He wanted mystery. He yearned for something that he couldn't name.

One night he was feeling restless, and so he took a barefooted walk along the beach as often he did. The sky was midnight-blue velvet, the stars shining brightly, and the full moon smiling down on him as he stared out into the waves. His eyes rested on a large smooth rock that lay in the far shallow waters of the bay, and it came to him that he could see movement on and around that rock. As he paddled slowly and quietly towards it, he saw a small group of women dancing in the sea. Their hair shone like the moon, their eyes glistened like the stars and their skin shimmered like milk in the water. Their bodies were long and graceful, their voices soft and lyrical as they called and laughed with each other. They were so beautiful that he stood quite still, drinking in the sight of them as they drifted farther away from the rock, playing in the shallow water.

After a while he noticed a pile of what looked like animal skins lying on the top of the rock. Chilled to the bone and yet strangely excited, he recalled all the old tales about Selkies. They could change into women, he remembered, by slipping off their sealskins. Without those skins they would remain human and trapped on the land, unable to return to their home beneath the waves. The man was overtaken by a strange yearning as he watched the women in the sea, and a feeling crept over him that this was the mystery he had been looking for, all his young life. Somehow, these women personified his love of the sea and her beauty and mystery, and he wanted one of them for his wife. So he crept quietly to the rock and stole one of the sealskins, folding it tight and tiny, and pushed it into the pocket of his jacket.

After a while the women called to one another and began to swim back to the rock, each one finding and putting on her sealskin, transforming herself back into a seal in the wink of an eye, and then slipping away into the water, disappearing beneath the waves. All but one of them. She searched high and low, clambering over the rock and diving into the sea around it, but she failed to find her skin. Seeing her distress, the man stepped out from where he had been hiding behind the rock.

'I have your skin,' he said to her. 'But I don't want to give it back to you. Won't you stay with me, and be my wife?' The sealwoman shook her head and shrank back from him, but slowly and carefully, as if he were gentling a wild animal, the young fisherman stepped closer to her, and as he looked into her eyes he saw hers change, widen, soften.

'Seven years,' he whispered to her. 'Just seven years. Give me seven years, and then I'll give you back your skin. After that, I'll let you decide. If you still want to leave after seven years, then I'll let you go.' And at that moment the first light of dawn crept into the sky, and the glow of the moon began to fade. Reluctantly, then, the woman went with him, understanding that without her skin she could do nothing. She had no choice. But he seemed to her to be a handsome young man, and strong. And his eyes were kind, for all that he had visited this fate upon her. With one last yearning look over her shoulder, she waved goodbye to her sisters, their seal heads popping up from the sea, their eyes glinting like dark jewels in the fading moonlight.

The young man was happier than he had ever imagined might be possible. As he lay beside his wife in bed at night, he fancied he could smell the sea, and as he listened to her breathing beside him, he fancied that he could hear the whisper of the waves. He was content.

As for the sealwoman: she bore him a daughter, nine months after they were wed. At first she seemed happy enough with her life and with her child. Mara, she called her, after the sea. She would take her daughter down to the shore and teach her the ways and the lore of the waters, telling her stories of her people and of other mysteries beneath the waves. The child loved the sea with all her heart, but she was half-human, and so she loved the land too, and could not imagine ever forsaking it. She was at home in her skin and knew her place in the world. But then so had her mother been, when she was her daughter's age.

The Selkie did her best to look after the child and care for her husband, but as the years went by things began to change. He went away from the house more often – either fishing, or drinking with his friends in the local inn – and she was left alone. She began to creep out by herself at night, stealing down to the shore, looking always for her sisters. But they had abandoned that beach on the night she was taken, fearing that the same fate would befall them. So she watched and she wept and as all hope began to fade she became more and more sorrowful. Her skin began to dry up, and her eyes and her hair grew ever more dull. When the seven years were up, hating herself for needing to leave her daughter, but knowing that she must find her way back to herself, which could come only with finding her way home, she asked her husband if he would return her skin. But he simply laughed and refused. She was still the most beautiful woman on the island, and she was his. Why ever would he let her go free?

The sealwoman grew slower and sadder. Frightened that she might lose her, Mara asked if she was ill, and finally her mother told her that she was fading from yearning for her lost home beneath the sea. Fading, because although she loved her husband still and loved her daughter even more, she was stranded in this place where she could not find a way to belong.

Mara feared the blank emptiness that had begun to reside in her mother's eyes. And so she started to search for the Selkie's lost skin. She searched every part of the house and every part of the land, but she couldn't find it. She searched and searched until she exhausted herself. Then eventually, one night, after she had spent hours searching again while her father was out and her mother asleep, she found herself yawning in the boatshed and crept into her father's boat to take a nap . . . and there under a heap of fraying ropes and soiled sailcloth she finally found the sealskin, hidden still inside the pocket of the old jacket that the fisherman had been wearing on the night he stole her mother away. As Mara pulled at it and the skin rolled out, she caught a faint whiff of the sea – the smell of her mother. But as she picked it up from the floor where it had fallen, the skin began to disintegrate in her hands. It was old and desiccated. It had not been used for a long time, and now it could never be used again.

Mara hurried home and wakened her sleeping mother, and with tears in her eyes brought her down to the shore where she presented her with her old shredded skin. She watched as her mother sank to her knees and wept. She saw the hope and then the life begin to drain out of her eyes – and then she acted. She half-carried, half-dragged her mother down to the sea, where she rolled her into the shallows and let the seawater cover her body. Slowly, slowly, the Selkie woman began to revive, but as she walked back to the house with Mara, there was nothing but emptiness in her eyes.

For many weeks the Selkie woman stayed in her bed. Her heart was a black hole; there was no help to be found, and her life stretched ahead of her, endless, dark and hopeless. She would never find her way home, never find her place, never again find a way to belong. But Mara would not let her mother die. And so she went to visit the wise old woman who lived in a small stone cottage, up in the hills at the far end of the village. She asked the old *cailleach* what she should do to help her mother – whether, indeed, anything could be done.

'Your mother must help herself,' the old woman told Mara. 'You cannot do it for her. And though I know the ways of herbs and moss, and the paths that animals take through the old woods, I do not know the ways of the sea. But there is one who does, and if your mother can find her way to her, it may be that she will tell how she might be saved.'

And so Mara went home, and told her mother that she must find the Old Woman of the World, who was sometimes to be found in those days, still – if you had endurance enough to make the journey, and courage enough to face her in the darkness of her cave. At first the sealwoman said that she could not possibly follow this quest. She was too tired, and too ill. The way would be too difficult, and there was no guarantee of success. But Mara would not let the subject go. She pleaded with her mother and pleaded some more and then she wept, until finally, one morning, the Selkie could bear her daughter's despair no longer, and she roused herself from her bed and put on her strong boots and wrapped herself in a warm cloak. She took nothing else with her, for the old *cailleach* had told Mara that the journey must be made while unencumbered with unnecessary things of the world.

The Selkie did not know where to go; not really. All she knew was that she would find the Old Woman of the World somewhere on the high westernmost cliffs of the island. And so, pulling her cloak tightly around her, she began to walk north. She walked in the rain along beaches with the wind so strong in her face that every step took twice as long as it ought. She clambered over rocks so slippery that she fell constantly into the water and had hardly the strength to haul herself back out. Her boots were cold and wet and heavy, and her heart was heavier still. At night she shivered in geos and cowered in coves. She drank from icy burns and ate seaweed for her only nourishment. It was hard, and she was weak, and when one wild day the storm raged more fiercely than ever and the wind finally whipped away her cloak and carried it over the cliff top where she was walking and on down to the sea, she sank to her knees and lay her forehead on the ground, and began to despair. But as she knelt there a strange rumble in the ground below her set her body vibrating, and she threw back her head and listened. And it seemed to her that, carried on the wind, in snatches, she heard a woman singing a song, somewhere down below, somewhere deep inside the cliff. And it seemed to her also that the strange shuddering rumble she had heard sounded something like the noise a spinning wheel might make, if pedalled furiously by someone who was skilled in the art.

She stood, and looked around her, and walked and peered and poked until finally she came upon the first step of the long stairway which was cut into the face of the cliff, seemingly ending in the sea, narrow and slippery, precipitous as could be. She closed her eyes and took a deep breath and slowly, carefully, down the stairs she went. And at the bottom, she found the cave: the cave of the Old Woman of the World. The Old Woman herself sat there, spinning a fine thread shining with all the colours that ever existed, on a rich golden wooden wheel in front of an enormous frame on which was displayed the most beautiful weaving that had ever been created, fringed with sea-urchin quills. The Old Woman turned, and looked at the Selkie.

'So you've come to find your skin,' she said, and it was all the sealwoman could do to hold herself erect, to lift her chin and stop her teeth from chattering, and to nod a faint yes. The Old Woman beckoned her over to a glowing fierce fire at the back of the cave, over which an enormous cauldron bubbled, and it seemed to her that the steam rising up from the soup in that cauldron contained the scent all of the seeds and all of the herbs and the essence of all the growing and living things in the world. She sat, and the warmth began to creep back into her bones, and she listened while the Old Woman spoke.

'So your old skin was no use any more,' she said, looking long and deep into the fire and nodding, as though she could see pictures in the flames. 'That's the way it goes, often enough. I've heard all the stories they tell of Selkies who find their old skins and slip them back on, and away they go, out into the ocean, and live happily ever after, just as if nothing had ever happened to them, and nothing had ever been learned. That's all well and good, but it doesn't always work out that way, and sometimes it shouldn't.' She passed the Selkie a cup of something hot and herbal and sweet, and she took it gratefully and sipped, and it seemed to her as she sipped that all the strength and vitality she had lost began flooding back into her bones. 'You've done well to make it this far, Daughter,' the Old Woman said. 'But there's more for you to do before you're done.'

And she told the Selkie what she must do.

The Selkie set off again when her tea had been drunk, fresh and fit as the day her husband had first discovered her, there on the beach. The sea was calm now, and the air still, and she found the curragh at the base of the cliff just where the Old Woman had said she would find it, and she climbed in and slowly she rowed across to the tiny island a mile to the north, and a mile to the west. She brought the curragh to rest on a long white strand in a calm sandy cove on the north side of the island, and there too she found the cave that the Old Woman told her she would find. And as she entered into the cave she saw what she had been told she would see, and her hands flew to her mouth and it was all that she could do not to turn and flee and throw herself into the sea and wait to die of grief. For there in the centre of the cave were the skeletons and skins of eleven dead seals. These were no ordinary seals – neither common seals nor grey seals; they were Selkies. They had been killed and then skinned, and left so that their flesh had disintegrated and all that remained of each of them was a pile of bones, and a skin beside each pile, shining silver in the dim light of the cave.

Eleven skeletons, and eleven skins.

The Selkie crept close, dread in her heart, but there was no help for it, for she knew her eleven sisters – she knew them in her heart, and recognised the markings on their beautiful silver skins. A seal-hunt, the Old Woman had said, and the corpses abandoned by the men in the storm, ready to be picked up some finer day. But the hunters had never returned, and the bones and the skins of the Selkie sisters had rested in the cave ever since.

But there was more to be done before she was done, and so she did as the Old Woman had told her. She lit a fire in the darkening cave, and she sat vigil over the skins and the bones. And as night fell she began to sing the old lament over the bodies of her kinsfolk. No one knows the language now, and nor is it a language that is usually written, but here are the words she sang:

> Ionn da, ionn do
> Ionn da, od-ar da.
> Hi-o-dan dao, hi-o-dan dao
> Hi-o-dan dao, od-ar de.

And as she sang on she heard a rustle out in the cove beyond the cave, and through the growing gloom she peered out and saw an old grey seal crawl up onto the sand and make its way into the cave. And the grey seal, who she saw was an old, old Selkie, began to sing the song too. And as the old Selkie sang, throwing back her seal head (for the moon was new, and she could not take on her human form unless the moon was full) a wondrous thing began to happen in the cave. Slowly, slowly, the flesh began to reform on the bones of the dead seals – all but one: the smallest, and the youngest. And little by little, the skeletons began to reshape and to seem more like seals, and they grew fatter and then they shuddered and breathed, and finally, when they were strong, rolled over and slipped into their skins – all but one: the smallest, and the youngest. And ten of the eleven seals formed a circle around the sister-child who could not live again, and they lifted their heads up and sang a song of mourning. When they were done, they crawled out of the cave on their bellies, and came again into the ocean, beckoning to their sister to follow.

The Old Woman had told the Selkie that she would know what to do when the time came, and it seemed to her now that this was the thing that must be done: she reached for the skin that remained and held it to her breast, inhaling the faint scent of a lost sister. The old seal nodded, and then turned away and followed the younger ones back into the sea.

It would have been easy for the Selkie woman to go then. Her sisters were waiting for her, and if she followed them, they would lead her home. But there was one thing more she must do, one thing that could not be abandoned so lightly. So she folded the skin tiny and tight, and tucked it safely into the belt of her gown, and she found the curragh on the beach and, taking up the oars, she began her long return.

She came to Mara when her husband was away fishing, and she took her down to the sea and told her all that she needed to know. Mara was young still, but there was something in her that understood that she must let her mother go. She could see that the sealwoman wanted to stay with her, but something called to her, something so deeply a part of her nature that she could not – and must not – resist it. The need to find her place, to find her element, to find her way home.

And so the time came for them to part. Taking her daughter's face in her hands, the Selkie looked deeply into Mara's eyes and breathed her breath into her lungs, three times. Turning to the sea, she began to sing a strange song in a high voice. She pulled out her sister's skin: newer than her own, younger, less marked by the cares and woes of the world. But it was the sealwoman's bones that this skin covered now, and which shaped it; the two merged together, old and new, and in this merging a new form was created. With one last long look at her daughter, the Selkie slipped into the sea and vanished beneath the waves.

The daughter and her father mourned long and hard. Mara would often go down to the shore at night, hoping to catch a glimpse of her mother – but she never came. And then, exactly one year later, on the anniversary of her disappearance, Mara's patience was rewarded. A seal was sitting on the rock and as it saw her approaching, it slipped off its skin and there she was: her mother. And yet somehow she was different. Her eyes and hair and skin were shining; and something in the way she held her body told Mara that she was at peace and at home with herself once more.

And so it happened ever afterwards that once a year, on the same anniversary of her departure into the sea, on the night of the closest full moon, the Selkie woman would come to the beach and talk with her daughter and tell her stories. She taught her to sing the song that she had sung in the cave: the song that would call to her Selkie kinfolk. She taught her the song so that one day, if ever she should so choose, she also could take to the sea. She taught her the song that would sing her soul back home. 'The Sealwoman's Sea-Joy', the Selkie called her song, though it had once been known as a song of mourning. For all mourning may be transformed into joy if you have endurance enough to make the journey, and courage enough to face the Old Woman in the darkness of her cave.

~

Stories of shape-shifting seals are told all along the west coasts and islands of Scotland and Ireland. In these places, the people of the land have always lived alongside the people of the sea. They occupy the same world, and compete for the same fish; it's not surprising that we should find in story the two merged into one. Such a commonplace story soon becomes legend, then legend is told as history, and so we have the MacCodrum clan of the isle of North Uist, who became known as the 'MacCodrums of the seals': they were descended, it is said, from the union of a fisherman with a Selkie. This explained the hereditary horny growth between their fingers which made their hands resemble flippers.

These Selkie tales resonate strongly with women, for the Selkie's song is our song. It is a song of yearning – yearning for a part of ourselves that we feel we have lost – or maybe a part that we feel we might once have had, but never knew. How many of us have lost skins to this super-rationalistic world in which we cannot feel at home, in which we cannot feel as if we belong? No matter how furiously we pile on the trappings of the Wasteland, no matter how cleverly we shed our own fragile skins and clothe ourselves in the coarser skins of men which do not fit us, or the thick, traditional female skins which suffocate us, we cannot hide the fact that it does not work. We do not thrive. Sometime or other, we will know it. Sometime or other, we will break.

The Selkie story is the story of a woman who breaks. Taken literally out of her element, trapped on the land, where she cannot find a way to belong. She has lost her place in the world, and consequently has lost her stories. Like the Selkie, so many of us lose our skins, and all too often we lose them early. This can happen in so many ways: it may be stolen by another who does us harm; we might give it away to someone we trust, who then betrays us; or we might hide it for safekeeping and then forget where we hid it.

I do not remember a time when I was a child when I felt as if I were in my element, when I felt at home in my skin. I lost it too soon. It was not stolen: I hid it away, so deeply and so cleverly that it took me decades to remember that I'd ever possessed it. My early childhood years were rarely a time of open, joyful wildness such as others might experience; often I felt unsafe. My father's violence towards my mother didn't ever quite spill over onto me, but it didn't need to for me to hold it as a distinct possibility in my head.

One day, coming home with him from someplace, walking down the street to the cockroach-infested terraced house we rented at the time, I listened with growing fear to his spitting rage, his mutterings about all of the ways in which he was going to beat me when we got home. I can't begin to imagine what I'd done to offend; I was such a quiet and obedient child. A 'paragon of virtue', as my first school report later proclaimed; it was safer that way, for sure. He opened the front door and I burst through it, running up the stairs and into the bedroom, pushing the door closed, putting all the weight of my three-year-old self behind me, listening to his footsteps pounding after me up the stairs. He burst through the door and I fell to the floor. He looked down at me, watching him with what must have been terror in my eyes, and he crumpled. He sat on the edge of the bed with his face in his hands, and he cried. I picked myself up off the floor and I sat down next to him and put my hand on his knee and told him that it would all be all right.

I was a strange little animal; how could I not be? Watchful, cautious, hiding underneath a tough new skin I manufactured for myself little by little over the years. Never let anyone see you're afraid; never let anyone see you cry. Always be strong, because you can't rely on anyone else to be. It wasn't till I reached my thirties that I realised that this skin I was wearing – the skin I had adopted because it seemed stronger, safer, more appropriate for the hard-edged world in which I found myself – not really a skin, but a protective, impermeable shell – wasn't my real skin at all. And then the stripping away of the old, and the search for that true skin was long, and hard, filled with stops and starts and twists and turns and unexpected dead ends. Sometimes, even today at fifty-four years old, I wonder whether the search is over. It seems there's always a new layer to uncover.

This skin which we lose is our power: our unique, authentic power as women. The power to create, to guard, to transform. We become disconnected from our female body-wisdom and instincts. We lose that power to the Wasteland. We lose it in so many ways. It is taken from us, with threats and violence. Or we follow the wrong path in life, a path without heart. We leave behind what sustains and nourishes us. We turn our back on the plight of the planet, out of fear, or out of ambition, or simply out of a refusal to see the situation for what it is. We might not have been responsible for making the world this way, but for sure we have been complicit in its creation, and in the maintenance of a civilisation which has caused so much damage.

But sooner or later, no matter how cleverly we try to hide ourselves, to turn away from the truth, we are called to change. To wake up, and to see, and so to take responsibility. To reclaim our power, and to participate in the remaking of the world. Joseph Campbell named it the 'Call to Adventure' – but it should be so much more than merely an adventure. It is a Call to Life – a full, authentic life. It is a Call to rise from the half-sleep of our existence, and take up our part in the great unfolding of the world. To become a Voice of the Wells. We must answer the Call, or forever be lost in the Wasteland.

For many women, that Call occurs at midlife. Dante expressed it perfectly, in the opening lines of *The Divine Comedy*: 'Midway upon the journey of my life I found myself in a dark wood, where the right way was lost.' Most women experience major change in these middle years: physical change or professional; social or psychological; changes in our family and our relationships. Our children leave home. We are overtaken by disillusionment and dissatisfaction. We find ourselves unhappy in our jobs, in our marriages. We develop physical illnesses, anxiety or depression. Rage and grief threaten to overwhelm us. We begin to contemplate our own mortality. We question who we are, who we might have been, who we might yet become. We question our spiritual values and our material values. We begin to wonder what we are doing with our lives, what meaning we might find. We open our eyes a little wider, and take in the world beyond ourselves. For the first time, we see the Wasteland for what it is.

Like so many women, I have found myself lost in that dark wood. Picture the scene: it is 1991, and I am thirty years old. I am sitting in a car outside an ugly office building in a small town in Surrey for which I have absolutely no affection and whose edges blend and blur into other small towns on all sides and eventually into London to the north. I have no affinity for this part of the world; my internal compass points north and west, and my feet literally feel as if they are in the wrong place. I am working in this building as a scientific adviser for a tobacco company – a large multi-national company which I dislike, in which I am surrounded by people who are far from the 'merchants of death' portrayed by anti-smoking activists and pressure groups, but who nevertheless share none of my values. I shouldn't be in this job; I should never have been in this job. It bears no relationship to the person I think I am or ever have been or will ever want to be. I have felt this way for a good three years, but recently the iron band around my stomach and the hollow fluttering in my chest and the dread that I awaken to each day has grown and become intolerable. I can't breathe; I'm constantly on edge.

This morning, I have battled my way north for the best part of an hour to drive no more than fifteen miles through the pre-rush-hour traffic which hurtles headlong towards London. I have stopped, started, stopped again. Stopped, stopped and stopped some more. Once, I sat in the queue at a traffic light for twenty minutes, edging forward one or two cars at a time, my entire body clenched, and at some point during this torture I floated out of my body and up through the roof of the car and looked down on myself from above. The person I was looking at inside the car wasn't anyone I knew or recognised; the world in which she seemed to be living was insubstantial, dreamlike.

By the time I get to the car park outside my workplace half

an hour later, I am afraid, and I have no idea what to do. I feel powerless to do anything. I'd like to pretend it hadn't happened, but I know this sign all too well. Psychologists call it 'depersonalisation': a change in your perception or experience of yourself so that you feel detached from, and sometimes as if you're an outside observer of, your own mental processes and your body. It makes everything seem unreal. It's a proper psychiatric symptom; it occurs in the American Psychiatric Association's *Diagnostic and Statistical Manual (DSM-IV)*, which most professionals in Western countries use to diagnose mental health disorders, and it means that I can no longer ignore the fact that I have a problem, or continue to hope that I'll just wake up one morning and find that it's miraculously vanished. The origin of the problem? It's big enough to be going on with: I don't belong in this place, in this job, with these people; I'm not even sure I belong in this Age. I lost my way a long time ago, but long before that I lost my skin.

I find a parking space as far away from the building's entrance as I can, and turn off the engine and sit there. I am incapable of moving. I simply can't bear to get out of the car, to walk into that building, to live one more day in this state of . . . well, I can only describe it as chronic fear. I'm afraid of everything. Of being alive, of not really being alive. Of failing at being alive.

This shouldn't be happening to me, I tell myself, as I sit with my hands still clenched around the steering wheel. How embarrassing, for a psychologist to find herself with a psychological problem. How incompetent of me, because during my PhD in neuroscience I specialised in the brain mechanisms underlying anxiety and panic. It seems like the ultimate irony, as if with one wave of some great cosmic wand I've suddenly found myself transformed from the master of a problem to its grovelling victim, and for a moment I want to laugh, but I don't quite manage it because all of a sudden I'm drenched in sweat, and my breathing is beginning to quicken, and there's a terrible clutching at my throat, as though someone has his hands around my neck and is squeezing and letting go, squeezing and letting go . . . and it's a vicious cycle, of course: now I'm afraid of the symptoms of being afraid. My head knows perfectly well that this isn't a heart attack, it's a panic attack, but my body is nevertheless experiencing the symptoms of utter terror, and what I do or don't know becomes utterly irrelevant as the age-old fight-or-flight mechanisms kick in.

Finally, after what seems like an eternity, but probably is no more than five minutes, the panic subsides. And yet that fiercely pulsating sensation of choking, of an enormous lump that I can't swallow, remains in my throat, where it will continue to reside for two years more. Paul Simon's 'Still Crazy After All These Years' is playing on the radio, and as I listen, suddenly, inexplicably, something settles into place: I need to get out of this job and away from this godforsaken town, before I too 'do some damage' – most likely to myself. Whatever it takes, whatever might be lost along the way, I need to cut myself loose from this increasingly meaningless life, and find another path.

So at thirty years old, in a car park in a small Surrey town, I heard the Call which beckoned me to change my own life, to search for a new skin to replace the one I had lost. I didn't respond immediately; I had no idea what I might do with the rest of my life. I didn't want to go back into academic life, even if it would have been possible, and it was apparent that I wasn't cut out for corporate life. As far as I could tell, I had no other skills. I had an obsessively jealous older husband and no close friends. I had no tribe, I had no place. And so I parked the problem along with the car, and I walked into the building and sat down at my desk and got on with my job.

The core of that problem was that I hated the world I inhabited. In those days there was so little awareness of environmental issues, and yet I knew that humans were choking the planet. I had known it since, at sixteen years old, knowing everything and nothing, I fell in love. While studying for an English Literature A level, I read D.H. Lawrence's novel, *The Rainbow*. It swept me off my feet. I had been brought up in a grey, heavily industrial town in the north-east of England; I was displaced at nine to another, larger, industrial city in the Midlands. In my early world concrete was king, and the air smelled predominantly of exhaust fumes and the chemicals spewed out from vast industrial chimneys. I felt no love for this world, no sense of belonging. I felt separate from it, closed in, claustrophobic. Some days, walking through identical grey suburban streets to school, I felt as if I were being buried alive.

Then I opened *The Rainbow* and fell head over heels in love with a world that had never been mine. But somehow, I recognised Lawrence's representation of the deep and instinctive connection between humans and the natural world, and all of the ways in which it was being obliterated by the industrial machine. Growing up as the son of a Nottinghamshire coal-miner, who taught him the names of plants and trees and how to recognise animal tracks, Lawrence was well aware of the head-on, bone-splitting collision between those two worlds. I had only ever inhabited a world that was dominated by that industrial machine, but I yearned for the slightly dangerous, often subversive, and above all overwhelmingly passionate pastoral world which he showed me in that book: a world in which the connection between humans, the land and the natural world is deep, vivid and, above all, visceral.

I had had only the smallest glimpses of such a possibility in my life. When I was a small child my mother would leave me with my ancient and notoriously crotchety great-aunt while she went out to work. Aunt Meg lived in a small post-war council house a little way down the road from my infant school, on the far fringes of town and a short walk away from the sea. From the windows at the front of the house you looked out, across unused fields and abandoned wastelands which were surprisingly full of flora and fauna, to the heavy industrial complexes on the River Tees. ICI chemical works, steel works, chicken-processing factories, sugar-processing plants. My free days were spent rooting in Aunt Meg's back garden, which consisted largely of an overgrown erstwhile cabbage patch next to an old Second World War bomb shelter, and a narrow, gravelly strip next to the house abundant with self-seeding wallflowers. I might fall asleep to nightmares of smoke-spewing chimneys and giant industrial pitchforks, and wake in the night to the sound of fog-horns, but in my daylight hours I learned about worms and snails and caterpillars; buttercups, pissy-beds (Aunt Meg's colourful name for dandelions) and Grandmother, Grandmother, pop-out-of-beds. In that overgrown cabbage patch, in the untidy wastelands on the edge of town, and on the long stretches of dune-covered sandy beach just down the road at Seaton Carew, I had a sense of openness, of space, and a very fragile feeling of wonder at the teeming life around me.

It was fleeting, and I didn't again experience that sense of connectedness which I yearned for until, when I was twenty-one and just about to embark on a PhD at the University of London, my mother suddenly decided to abandon the city; she moved to a tiny cottage in rural mid-Wales. Soon afterwards, she married a Welsh-speaking shepherd, and went to live with him in a small remote house up in the hills outside the small town of Machynlleth.

I took the train north at the weekend whenever I could afford a ticket, because for the first time in my life I was actually experiencing what it might be like to live surrounded by fields and mountains, rather than just reading about it. I would sit outside at night on top of the hill behind the cottage watching the stars, listening to the call of owls, wondering if there might be beauty and magic in the real world after all, rather than just in my imagination. The longing for that feeling never left me, but sitting in that car park not quite a decade later, I realised that I was facing the consequences of living with its antithesis.

There is a hollow desperation which, from the inside, borders at times on madness in living a life which you know is the wrong life, while not being able to see a way out. When all of your childhood conditioning tells you to stick with it, keep yourself safe, always vote for security and certainty. But I knew that I was not who I was supposed to be; I knew in my heart that I didn't like my life; and my body was beginning to buckle under the strain. One weekend, shortly after that first panic attack in the car park of my workplace, I went to Wales to visit my mother. I didn't need to save up for the train fare anymore; I had a nice comfortable company car to ease my journey. Somewhere among the hills and valleys, we took refuge from the cold and wet in a café which also sold a random assortment of old books and antiques. We ordered a pot of tea and went to sit at a wooden table by the window, staring out despondently at the pouring rain. And then an object on the windowsill caught my eye: an old Devon Ware jug, creamy yellow on the outside and rich, dark brown inside. The inscription on it read:

No star is ever lost
we once have seen
We always may be
what we might have been[1]

I glanced past the jug to my reflection in the window, and caught the dark circles under my eyes and the hollowness on my face. Swallowing down sudden tears, I snatched up the jug. The sticky label on its side declared that it was just £8, but I would have wanted it if it had taken every penny I possessed, and if it hadn't been for sale I would have begged for it. I bought it, clutching it to my heart like a talisman, like the talisman that it has always been to me and still is today, and when I got home I placed it on the small desk where I sometimes wrote, sometimes read, always dreamed.

We always may be what we might have been. What was it that I might have been? All I knew was that it was anything other than what I now was. What was the star that I once had seen? All I knew was that it shone brightly in a place that wasn't given over to the Wasteland. It shone down onto the top of a grass-covered hill at night as I sat watching it, head back, gazing up into a sky undimmed by light pollution. I closed my eyes and I saw myself getting up from that hill and walking down through the brightly painted wooden front door of a simple stone cottage, sitting in an armchair by a glowing stove, reading a book or maybe even writing one. I saw myself waking up to the nascent promise of each new dawn, taking my morning tea outside, listening to birdsong and the bark of a vixen in the wood. I saw my hands in the soil, my feet cold and bare in a fast-flowing river. The person I saw wasn't anxious, alienated, brittle. It wasn't her job that defined her, but her way of being in the world. She looked as if she belonged. Not just to a star, and a hill, and a cottage; but to herself, and the calling owls, and the wider world she inhabited.

In September of 1992, a year after my panic attack, I spent two weeks in Ireland. This was a country I had longed to visit since I was four years old, a country whose name was synonymous with music and magic and to which I had always felt as if I might belong – and yet somehow I had never managed to get myself there. A week into that holiday, I made a decision. I made it at sunset, standing on an edge. The Connemara coastline was rugged, rocky and intensely beautiful. To get there, I had travelled through a land that, while hardly empty of people, was nevertheless still intensely pastoral, and free of the stench of industrialisation which characterised so much of the country I'd grown up in. I stood there for a long time, staring out west to the islands. For the first time in my life I felt as if my feet were in the right place. My place, my culture and the stories of my ancestors rising out of the hills and bogs of this land where they were living still. The Call came again, loud and clear; this time I answered.

I returned home, put our house on the market, and made plans to hand in my notice when it sold. I had no idea what I would do when I got there, but I was moving to Ireland for sure.

I imagined, at the grand age of thirty-one, that this move would represent the end of my journey: that this would be the place where I could dig in deep and find that new skin which I so badly needed. As it turned out, it was only the beginning, and by the time I had moved to Lewis eighteen years later and stood on another far western shore, looking out to other islands, hearing another Call, contemplating another journey, a long and complicated tale had already unfolded. I had come to Lewis because I imagined, at the grand age of forty-nine, that this move represented the end of that long and winding journey I had been on since I was thirty. I imagined that this would be the place where finally I could dig in deep, where finally I might find that new skin which might fit me. And indeed, that particular phase of my journey did end – abruptly, in ways I could never have expected; brutally, as I found myself slammed up against yet another dead end. And so it was that I was hearing a new Call, finding myself hurled over a new edge, plunging into the darkness, then finding my path and embarking on a new journey – one which finally would make sense of the old. Edges, it seems, breed edges; and journeys, like edges, are fractal. There is never just one.

The Call comes when we break, or are ready to break. Sometimes it may come in the form of a change of circumstances: a relationship ends; we lose our job; we become ill. A child leaves home; a loved one dies. Sometimes the Call comes to us in a dream. At a critical stage in my own journey I had such a dream: a dream more vivid than any I had ever had before in my life. I dreamed of a creature with the face of a fierce, ageing woman and the body of a large hound. I held out my hand to her and she smiled; her teeth were pointed and sharp. Then she bit me. I looked down at my open, bleeding hand, and found that each of my fingers had turned into a bat. I had no idea then what I was dreaming, but I knew that I needed to know. After much research I discovered that the Greek goddess Hecate was sometimes represented with the head of a woman and the body of a dog. Hecate, who holds the keys to the Underworld, who calls us to follow her there, whose Call is a call to transformation. And the bats? In almost all cultures, they are a symbol of rebirth.

Some of us may hear the Call sooner, others later. But whenever it happens, whenever it transpires that we find ourselves on an edge, out of our element, out of our skin, there is something in us still which hears, no matter how deeply buried. Like the first

August swallow fidgeting on the telephone wires, we know there is something we should be doing. We know there is a journey we should be undertaking. We cannot rest; we cannot sleep. Something in us knows that there is somewhere we should be going. And in the end, whether or not we think we can, we go because we must. We go, on a wing and a prayer, because to stay is to die.

The Selkie's skin is the source of her life-giving, creative power. The skin – this pelt that once smelt so wonderfully of home and of herself, in all her natural wildness, in all her instinct and heat and passion – represents her unique self, her singular gift to the world, and it was stolen from her. The consequences of the loss, of this disconnectedness, this separation from her true nature and what nourishes and empowers her, have become apparent only after many years. She is living an unlived life, estranged from her own sense of authenticity, dried up and disconnected from intimacy – with herself, with others, with the world. Now she has heard the Call. She knows that she needs a new source of nourishing moisture to quench her aridity. What can she do? How can she find her lost skin? Is it even possible? What is it anyway, this 'true feminine nature'? And what is she supposed to do with it once she discovers it?

And so, with such questions, the journey begins. On any quest, there may be dead ends; sometimes we can set off down the wrong path. When the Selkie's old skin is discovered, when she understands finally what was lost, she cannot wear it again, because it has disintegrated through misuse. She cannot simply pick up where she left off; she must set off to find a new skin. Nor can she be saved by her daughter: she must save herself. She must separate herself from the Wasteland, and from the rules and control of the patriarchy – represented in this story by her husband. She must find her own way. It takes a monumental effort, for she has grown tired and jaded. But the choice is hers: to lie in bed and die, or to rise up, and find a new way to live.

We may need to travel a long distance before we find the new skin that fits us, and before we can learn to be comfortable in it – but first, we have to commit ourselves to the journey. We have to awaken from our torpor, commit to life instead of the desiccated half-life of the Wasteland. We must shake off the false skins we've cloaked ourselves in; we must let the old die to make room for the new. We must be willing to detach from who we have been, what we have become, before we can discover who we are really meant to be and what our work is in the world.

And it is hard, to begin; to get out of bed, to close our eyes and cross this first threshold. To fall forward into the wind, to let ourselves topple off the edge, to get in the tiny, rocking boat. It's a big step, this first movement towards wholeness. It means leaving behind the safety of familiar social structures and supports. It's a leap into the dark, a massive letting go. And yet, looking at our own lives, looking at the fate of the planet – it is clear that we're all standing on an edge, whether we mean to or not. These are edge-dwelling times. We may accidentally fall over that edge, pushed from behind like a lemming, plunging to our death, numbed by the Wasteland. But if we want to live we must stand there consciously, aware of the troubled times and the endangered planet, and then of our own volition step out across this first threshold.

Sometimes a person may deliver the push that helps us over the edge. Someone familiar: a daughter, a friend; someone unfamiliar: an unexpected teacher, or guide. Often we need help, to set ourselves off on the journey. We need the young daughters, who will not let go of hope, who will not let us die; and the Wise Old Women with compassion enough to lend us their secrets, to whisper to us of the mysteries of life and death. We need help to set ourselves on the way that we have lost, to find our way to that deep knowing, and so to the fullness of our own power. Of course, there is always a reason not to go, always a reason not to change. Someone needs us too much, or we are too afraid, and besides how will we live? We have families and responsibilities, and we must eat and pay the bills. And so we stay in the Wasteland, and perpetuate the system that is crippling us and the planet.

But let's say we go. Let's say we not only hear the Call, but respond. Let's say we take that first step. We leave the job we hate, or the damaging relationship. We want to find our lost skins, the missing pieces of ourselves that we seem to have lost somewhere along the way. We want to find the old cottage in the hills, the fast-flowing river, the work that makes us feel useful, and fulfilled. The Selkie crosses the threshold; she sets out. After all that she has been through, she nevertheless has the ability to see beyond what is known, to believe in a new beginning – even if she isn't entirely sure what that new beginning might consist of. For she is between stories: the story she's been telling herself about who she is is at an end; she has no idea what the next story might be. She travels empty-handed; she leaves the 'things of the world' behind her.

It is reminiscent of a pilgrimage, and for sure the true Heroine's Journey resembles a pilgrimage more than an adventure, and edges – like shorelines – are the places from which pilgrimages begin. Step across that edge and it is a severance, a kind of death: we can never go back to what we were before. A pilgrimage asks that we give up everything so we might learn what is truly ours. A pilgrimage is a search for knowledge, a search for becoming. And pilgrimage begins also with longing: longing for deep connection; longing for true nurturing community; longing for change and the rich, healing dark. Pilgrimage involves a new way of travelling and seeing, and it is in our ancestry. The Celtic *peregrini* of the Dark Ages set off on great sea voyages to found their monastic settlements, travelling in large curraghs which were capable of sailing immense distances. And in the great *Immramas* and *Echtrai*, the wonder-voyages of old Ireland, heroes set out in boats to discover the magical islands which they believed to lie far away in the ocean to the west. The Celtic Otherworld sometimes was thought to be such an island, and one which remained outside the influence of patriarchal structure, for it was ruled by women. It was called Tír na mBan, the Land of Women; or Tír na nÓg, the Land of Youth.

There is no map for this pilgrimage we are on; there is no fixed path. And that is a good thing, because following the paths that others have set for us, the paths that the system confines us to – that is the cause of the problem. We have been too timid, too blind, too unthinking; now it is time to find our own way. There are no maps. When the Selkie obeys the call and sets out to find the Old Woman of the World, she doesn't really know where she is going. All she knows is that the cave is somewhere on the coast, to the north and west. But she sets off anyway. She points herself roughly in the right direction, puts one foot in front of the other, grits her teeth, and she walks.

It was a pig which, in 2012, first brought Karen Taylor and me together: a handsome and good-natured pedigree Gloucester Old Spot boar called Rufus. Our two sows, Edna (named after the poet Edna St Vincent Millay) and Doris (named after Doris Lessing) needed a man, and Rufus happened to be available for an adventure. And so, one morning close to Christmas, my husband David and I set off from the far south-west tip of the Isle of Lewis on a slow, winding hour-and-a-half drive to the far north-west tip, livestock trailer hooked up and sheepdogs in tow. Normally, loading a pig of any description into a trailer of any description is challenging, but on this occasion, as soon as we backed it up and opened the gate to his field on Karen's croft, Rufus just walked right in. He obviously had some foreknowledge of the pleasures that would be waiting for him at the other end of the journey.

As well as appreciating her pigs, I quickly became fascinated by the work that Karen (a former psychiatric nurse) and her husband Ron Coleman (a voice-hearer and former 'user' of psychiatric services) were doing through their company Working to Recovery, which provides resources for people working in the mental health field. They have a particular interest in the design of mental health services aimed at people who are classified as 'psychotic', and specialise in cutting-edge training courses for working with people who, like Ron, hear voices. They tell Ron's own story of recovery, encourage engagement between mental health services, carers and service users, and spread their message that recovery is possible for everyone.

Karen, Ron, their twelve-year-old daughter, Francesca, and sixteen-year-old son, Rory, have lived since 2008 on a croft in the small Gaelic-speaking kingdom of Ness, which happens also to be the most north-westerly community in the European Union. Ness is best known for its continuation of the ancient tradition of guga hunting: each year in late August, ten men from the community go out to the island of Sula Sgeir for two weeks to harvest around 2,000 young gannets, considered there to be a delicacy. I drove there on a typically wild and blustery winter's day, with heavy leaden skies which intermittently burst open to shower down icy rain.

Karen is a large, vivacious fifty-three-year-old woman with short dark hair, an enormous smile and beautiful eyes. She and Ron spend much of their time travelling overseas, and a certain amount of consequent chaos characterises the house – but this is a comfortable family home, where much living happens. Over tea and a bowl of butternut squash soup, I discover that after training as a registered mental health nurse, Karen worked for many years in the National Health Service in England, where she designed, implemented and managed innovative community care services. While she was managing a day hospital in Gloucester, she attended a MIND conference in Blackpool which changed not only the way that she saw the mental health system of which she was a part, but the future course of her life.

'There were patients there giving presentations about their anger with the system. There were radical psychiatrists talking about different ways to practise. It opened up a new world for me: a world of service-user involvement and of patient rights. I started to become more radical at work, more challenging of the system. And then, at a similar conference shortly afterwards, I met Ron. He was speaking about his experiences as a voice-hearer, about his journey from diagnosed psychiatric patient to trainer, consultant and recovery specialist, and I was enthralled and inspired. It wasn't long before we got married, and then we became involved in setting up the Scottish Hearing Voices Network, and soon after that we founded Working to Recovery together.'

The work that Karen and Ron do and the message they spread is, by design, revolutionary, intended to challenge a psychiatric system which they believe lacks heart. 'The medical model, with all its emphasis on pathology and biology, brings with it a reliance on medication to keep the problem – and the person – under control. There is surprisingly little focus on recovery, on becoming a whole and functioning person. In fact, there's an assumption that recovery is impossible: if you're psychotic, you're always going to be psychotic. It's what defines you. You're never going to be able to function. But that's simply not the case. Recovery is perfectly possible: just look at Ron.' And indeed, since Ron's own recovery from mental illness he has gone on to write numerous books and papers on the subject, and is a sought-after lecturer at conferences around the world.

Karen finds herself constantly travelling around Europe, America and Australasia to spread their message, and so a home in the farthest reaches of the Outer Hebrides isn't perhaps the most obvious place from which to embark on a jet-setting lifestyle. It wasn't Gaelic roots which brought her here: although her family is of Welsh ancestry, she was brought up in Gloucestershire without any trace of Celtic tradition.

'What brought us here is a bit of a long story,' she laughs, 'and unlikely as it may seem, it began in New Zealand. Ron and I were working there for a couple of weeks, delivering Recovery Champions training courses. There were quite a few Maori elders attending the courses, and I remember being struck by their strong sense of community, of belonging to their tribe. It was a kind of belonging that also connected them very deeply to the land, and it touched something in me that I hadn't thought about since I was very much younger.

'I was very close to my grandparents when I was a child, spending most of my school holidays staying with them in Frampton-on-Severn, a beautiful village in Gloucestershire. My grandfather was a labourer on the manor farm, and I would go to work with him, watching the milking, sheep-dipping and combine harvesting, and helping in his vegetable garden. My paternal grandfather also worked on a fruit farm, had a huge vegetable garden, and kept geese. And for a while my father ran a market garden and had free-range chickens. So I grew up with a strong sense of connection to the land, which I gradually lost as I became older and more focused on my career.

'I started thinking about all that in New Zealand, and also about my own "tribe", and what that might mean. While we were there something strange entered me: some wistful need to reassess myself and my place in the world, and to think about why I was doing this work, and where it might lead. At the same time, I was exhausted: we always worked incredibly hard, and although I loved the energy, I was increasingly feeling the lack of time for myself.

'The other thing that I remember from that New Zealand experience is that there were spirals everywhere – for example, the landscape was full of unfurling ferns, the national emblem of New Zealand. The Maori carve spirals out of New Zealand jade and call them koru, and I was so strongly drawn to that symbol. When we got home I began to explore what it was that the spirals were evoking in me. It's a dominant feature of Celtic art and imagery, of course, and so that led me back to the interest in Celtic culture which I had had very strongly when I was a child. Then, I was always doodling, and so many of my doodles were spirals; it's a symbol that's always held a fascination for me. And now, it wouldn't let me go.

'It represents the cycle of life and rebirth, and this seemed so relevant to the work we were doing with recovery, and with change. I kept thinking that the same sense of attachment to the tribe that I had found among the Maori in New Zealand had also been there for the Celts, as well as the attachment to the land. And the warrior culture, of course, and the fact that some-times warriors were women. I have always considered myself to be a warrior woman. You have to be, to survive in this world.

'I've also always been drawn to the west, and specifically to west coasts. We lived on the east coast of Scotland, and so it seemed natural that my interest in all things Celtic would eventually take me all the way west to Lewis. We went there on holiday in 2006, and I felt an immediate recognition. As if the island was calling me here.'

My own experience of coming to live on Lewis was very similar: a sense of being drawn, or called. In my case, drawn to the edge, to explore the wildest, fiercest and truest elements of my own nature. To let the wind and sea abrade all the rough edges of my life. Some of the same yearnings drew Karen to the island at that time.

'I suppose . . . on the one hand, yes, I was on an edge, but on the other hand, I felt safe here, and held. More than anything, I was drawn to the ancientness of the land. Lewis rock – the Lewisian gneiss – is some of the oldest rock in the world. The wildness of the coastline, the beaches, the weather, the wind – all of it spoke to me of depth and change, and that was something I wanted badly. When we got back to the mainland after that first holiday, I couldn't settle. Something was beginning to shift in my own life, as if one phase was ending, and another beginning. The sense of being drawn to the island seemed like part of that process. I wanted to embark on a new quest, a search for myself, for spiritual development, and a new way of connecting to the world and the land.

'It took me two years to make it happen, but we moved here in 2008. It was a selfish move in many ways, though the family went along with it – some of them kicking and screaming! – but it seemed essential to me. When we first moved, Ron was travelling a lot, so I took six months off to settle the family in. It was the first time for years that I'd had proper time for myself. Most days there was just me and the croft, and it gave me time to learn to breathe again. It was a lovely warm summer, and I remember being out on the land till 11 o'clock at night, digging. It was such a joyful time. I'd walk down the croft and if I heard a lark singing, I'd look up and I'd sing back to it. It was as if I was singing in praise of the place, of the land, out of the sheer love of being alive. I felt more intensely alive than I had for a long time, and it was all part of the reconnection to this place, to the land and the Celtic culture.'

The rain has stopped, and so Karen and I clear the plates away and then head off outside and down the croft: I'm keen to see again the four Hebridean sheep which we had sold her the previous year. As we turn the corner of the house, a sudden gust nearly blows us off our feet and I stagger back and steady myself against the wall. It's not as remote as you might imagine, here: other houses are close by, and all the crofts neatly lined up in a row behind them. The crofting and fishing villages strung out along this north-western coastline of Lewis represent one of the most densely populated rural locations in Britain, accounting for around two-thirds of the population of the islands which make up the Outer Hebrides. The sea is by far the dominant feature of the landscape; inland, as far as the east coast of the island, stretches a vast area of flat blanket bog.

We finally make it round the corner, only to be greeted by an extended family of excessively friendly kunekune pigs who have escaped from their field. Karen ignores them and they root around the garden happily; it's obviously a common enough occurrence. Even though she now travels frequently, the animals and the croft ground her here, and that sense of connection to the island which she felt in those first months has stayed with her.

'Living on Lewis, being outside watching the sea, watching the storms come in, feeling the energy of the wind, the light, the rainbows . . . looking after the pigs and poultry, engaging in those same routines every day, brings me back to this need for my feet to be strongly grounded in the earth so that I am nourished, so that I'm able to carry out the work that Ron and I do.

'When you sit on this small island and see the huge waves pounding against rocks millions of years old it gives a sense of perspective – how tiny we are in this world, how insignificant our lives are, yet every act of kindness, every moment of love, can make a difference for generations to come. Love is a dirty word in psychiatry, it's an embarrassment, never to be mentioned.

In that sense, I see the psychiatric system as a prime example of that "Wasteland" you're talking about.

'What is better? To fill someone with pills, then strap them to a bed and leave them alone? Or to sit beside someone in their "madness", to really listen to their pain, anguish, joy, their search for spiritual identity, peace, meaning? To listen to the messages of the voices that they're hearing, to help interpret, to hold a hand, give a hug, to bear witness to their story, to believe in them, to give hope, to help understand, to build resilience, to leave them with the possibility of transformation. So I can't stop this work I do, every day seeing another person begin to understand the sources of their pain, begin to want to live, begin to love themselves . . . It is worth every sacrifice, every bit of energy I have. But being here, developing this connection with the land and the culture – that's what gives me the strength to go on with it.'

As we stand and look down the field at the little black sheep, who are clearly fat and thriving, Karen talks about the draw of the old Gaelic culture here in the Hebrides, comparing it to the Maori culture which affected her so deeply in New Zealand. 'It seems to me,' she reflects, 'that these cultures hold a secret to parts of us that have been lost in the West: our ability to live in accord with nature and with spirit. And this is also at the heart of our work: there is a growing awareness in me that our mental health suffers because we do not have our feet firmly planted in the land.'

And the land is at the heart of it, for sure. 'Climate change' may be new, but our broken relationship with the land is old. It goes back centuries – in England, for example, it goes back to the Enclosure Acts in the eighteenth century, which effectively removed the right of access to and use of common land from English rural life. But one of the many inspiring things about Lewis is a sense of connection to the land which is so intense that it defied all attempts to dispossess the people. At various significant points in this island's history, its people were prepared to fight to resist the power of landlordism and to insist on the right to remain on the land which they had occupied for generations.

As we walk back to the house, Karen tells me that it seems right to her that she has gone through the menopause here on Lewis.

'In a sense, I feel as if the Call to come to the island was the beginning of a quest: a yearning to make some sense of my life. The menopause is a time of looking inward, I think. It's a powerful time, and working through that threshold phase – no longer mother, but not quite crone – is quite a process. Turning fifty made me stop and think about who I am and what I want from this life; so for me, this island has definitely been a place to begin a new journey – or a new stage in my larger journey. I've shed a number of sealskins over the past couple of years. During this time, I've been questioning myself and my way of being in the world, as a woman. I've especially been thinking about power. I suppose I am in some ways a powerful person, in the sense of being strong-willed, driven to succeed. When I was a child I always wanted to be a star, and when I was young I studied drama and trained as an actress. That sense of power is very good for inspiring people, for helping them along that very difficult path to recovery, but if you're not careful, it can become controlling. To me, that's one of the big problems with the world, with the systems we've created. I'm striving for a more authentic way to use my power, and for balance.'

All of this, she is quite certain, emerges out of living on an island. 'It's back to that edge again: I feel as if I'm always walking on an edge between getting it right and failing, but living here has taught me not to fear that edge. And not to try always to control it – living on an island teaches you that, if nothing else. You're not in control. The weather is out of your control, and even just getting off the island is all too often out of your control when the ferries fail to run! The age of the land teaches me something similar. It's not all just about that sense of strength, of the force of nature – it's about understanding that I am not the centre of the universe, but just one small part of it all, a blip in this land's history. I still want to change the world, but living on an island has also taught me humility. An island is a great place to deal with your Shadow. There's nowhere to hide, on an island. It's brutal.'

4

Deep Caves and Bottomless Lakes

The Cauldron of Transformation

Entrance to Oweynagat cave, Roscommon, Ireland

It's possible I am pushing through solid rock
in flintlike layers, as the ore lies, alone;
I am such a long way in I see no way through,
and no space: everything is close to my face,
and everything close to my face is stone.

I don't have much knowledge yet in grief
so this massive darkness makes me small.
You be the master: make yourself fierce, break in:
then your great transforming will happen to me,
and my great grief cry will happen to you.

Rainer Maria Rilke
Translated from the German by Robert Bly[1]

Battling through an unexpectedly fierce February snowstorm, I tracked down the portal to the Otherworld. At the base of a small mound in a farmer's field in Roscommon in the west of Ireland, partially obscured by a hedge of overhanging, snow-clad trees, was a sunken black maw. It would have been intimidating enough even without the stark contrast it presented to the white world around it. It was unmarked and inconspicuous, with only the presence of a stone lintel to alert the passer-by to the fact that this isn't just any old hole in the ground. It is the entrance to Oweynagat, Cave of Cats. The cave referred to in the early ninth-century tale 'Cath Maige Mucrama' ('The Battle of Mag Mucrama') as Ireland's 'gate to Hell'.

The hell-mouth of Ireland. Would you pass through its jaws?

Given that the opening is less than three feet high, you might approach your journey to the Otherworld with a little trepidation. You'd want to have a head-torch, for you'll need both hands and feet to scrabble down into the cave. It's muddy; a pair of waterproof trousers wouldn't go amiss. Get on your hands and knees, bend your head low, and ease yourself down into the dark. You are passing through a hole in what once was the roof of a partially collapsed man-made souterrain: a particular type of underground passageway associated with the European Atlantic Iron Age. You'll want to go slowly; it's wet and slippery. Crawl down for two or three metres, and you'll find yourself in a small opening, a kind of entrance porch to the cave. Look behind you; shine your torch up at the back of the old stone lintel, and on its bottom edge you'll see an inscription in Ogham, the ancient Irish alphabet. When translated, it reads 'Fraoch, son of Medb'. Once, a passageway would have led out of this 'porch' to the right of the entrance, but now it is blocked with collapsed debris, damage likely to be due to the construction of a small lane which comes to a stop directly overhead. The last capstone which is visible amidst the rubble also bears Ogham letters, but it is incomplete, and no translation has been made.

Turn left, then, into a small opening through which nothing but black can be seen. The faint beam of your torch will be inadequate to penetrate this shadow; trust that there is a place to go. Wiggle on your backside down a low, narrow, slippery passageway which descends steeply for about ten metres over crumbling, uneven stone. As the passageway opens up above you, stand now and look up at the rock. Your torch will pick out myriad tiny crystals shining on the wet, muddy yellow-brown walls. Taste them: they're salty. Taste the food of the Otherworld. Taste the sweat of the deep Earth. Or are they the Earth's tears? Look behind you (*never look back*); the path slopes upwards and only the very faintest hint of light can be made out, and only because you know it is there. Look up; the roof above you is ribbed. You are in a tunnel, a birth canal, and you are slipping down it into the silent dark womb of the Earth. Take a deep breath; walk on. All you can hear is the occasional drip of water falling from the walls into pitch-black puddles on the floor. The topography changes again: duck, and slither on downwards as the floor level drops sharply one final time.

You're there. Oweynagat, Cave of Cats. A long, narrow natural limestone fissure, just 2.85 metres at its widest point and about 37 metres long. Watch your step: at the centre of the cavern is a hollow filled with mud; it has been known to swallow boots. It looks like a pool of clotted, black blood. In the feeble light from your head-torch (you wonder vaguely about battery life), edge your way around the walls to the end of the fissure, where the cave ascends, narrows again, and terminates in a crack. Is this the door to the Otherworld?

You're in a womb. Yes, really a womb: you're in the birthplace of Medb. Medb, Maeve: spell it as you will. The goddess-queen of Connaught was born in this cave. Medb: 'she who intoxicates'. Is it the dark which intoxicates you now, and if not, why are you laughing? Whisper the story of Medb; Oweynagat remembers. How Étain, reborn as a mortal, was fleeing from her human husband with her Otherworldly lover Midir. How they stopped to rest at Oweynagat with all of Étain's companions, including her maidservant Crochan Crogderg, whose name means 'blood-red cup'. At the end of their stay, Crochan so loved the cave that she begged to stay. Étain and Midir agreed, and so it was here that Crochan's daughter Medb was born.

Inside Oweynagat cave

The birthplace of Medb; the womb of the Earth. Oweynagat remembers. Turn off your torch. Turn it off; you know your way out. Turn it off, and succumb to the deepest dark you're ever likely to know. Unaccountably, incongruously, words will spill into your mind: words which purport to describe the dark. Tenebrous, stygian . . . stay still, calm your breath, try them all on for size. But there is no word for this dark, a darkness so complete, so thick, that it is tangible. You'll realise then, if you have not learned it before, that darkness is not simply a lack of light. Darkness is alive, and its life is obscured by light. Darkness puts out its tentacles and touches your face; darkness licks at your eyes and grants you a different kind of sight. Darkness is the voice of the shadow, a voice which words can only fail. Listen. Is it the drumming of your own heart that you hear, or the long, slow heartbeat of the Earth? Reach out, and there is nothing there. There is only you, whatever *you* might be, face-to-face with the long dark.

Do you fear this? You should not. You should not, even when you remember that this was also the dwelling place of the Morrigan, the Great Queen, the crow-goddess of death, war and rebirth. From here she emerged each Samhain, and from here she once came in her chariot, crimson-cloaked, leading a heifer to mate with the famous brown Bull of Cuailnge. Can you feel it now, the soft brush of a black crow's wing?

Stay with the dark, even though you are thinking now of the other stories that are told about Oweynagat. A band of magical wild pigs which emerged from the cave and wreaked havoc and destruction on the surrounding land before they were banished by Medb. The Ellen Trechen, a triple-headed monster which rampaged across the country before it was killed by Amergin. A flock of small red birds who withered every plant they breathed on, before they were hunted down by the brave Red Branch warriors of Ulster.

Chaos comes from this cave, and you fear chaos. Do not fear it. Stay with the dark.

Oweynagat: Cave of Cats. Three magical wildcats came out of this cave and attacked three great warriors of Ulster, before being tamed by Cú Chulainn.

Chaos. Chaos comes out of the Otherworld, and you have always feared it. Stay in the cave. Stay, and remember that the Otherworld was also a place of protection and refuge. Think of Fraoch, son of Medb, whose name is inscribed in Ogham on the lintel of this cave. Remember that old Irish tale, the 'Táin Bó Fraich'? Whisper the story; Oweynagat remembers. Fraoch seduced

Findabair, the daughter of Medb. When he refused to pay an exorbitant bride-price for her, Medb sent him on an errand near to the dwelling-place of a water monster. He slew the monster with the help of Findabair, but was severely wounded. A hundred and fifty maidens of the *sidhe*, all dressed in green, carried him off into Oweynagat and bore him out again the following morning, fully healed. Think of Fraoch, son of Medb, and stay with the healing dark.

The Otherworld grants visions; remember that, too. Remember Nera, the servant of Medb, who saved Cruachan from an attack by Otherworldly forces with the assistance of a fairy woman whom he met in this cave and married. She warned him that Medb's beautiful palace would be burned to the ground the following Samhain, and that warning enabled Medb to eliminate the danger. But as for Nera . . . he was left there 'together with his people, and has not come out yet, and he will not come out until the end of the world.' Will you come out of Oweynagat? Will you find your way back out of the dark?

Remember the gifts of the dark; Oweynagat remembers. The great cauldron of abundance which once was kept at Tara, but later came through this cave to the Otherworld. Remember the gifts of the dark. Turn around, grope for the wall and lay your forehead on its wet, muddy surface. Smell the fluids of the Earth; inhale their spicy brown richness. Can you hear the Earth breathing, or is the rasping breath your own? It is warm in here, warmer than the distant snowbound world outside. It feels safe, and it feels terrifying. More than anything, it feels alive, and you are alive in it. You are alive *of* it. Remember that; Oweynagat remembers. Remember the gifts of the dark.

That is enough for this visit; you have introduced yourself to the cave. You know you'll be back; the Otherworld doesn't give up its secrets easily, and certainly not all at once. Turn on your torch, and make the slippery climb back up to the surface. When you emerge from the birth canal which leads from the womb of the Earth, you'll be smiling. You'll be smiling for most of the day. But you'd better wipe that mud off your face before you make your way back to town, to find a bowl of soup and a comforting pot of tea.

Caves: portals to an entire unfathomable world which is hidden from our view. No wonder they are both feared and revered. Mythologies from around the world offer up stories of the magical, uncanny energy which can be found inside caves, and once they were important locations for ritual, ceremony and rites of initiation all across Europe.[2] According to archaeologists,[3] Oweynagat cave may well have been a focus for similar cult practices in pre-Christian Ireland, practices which included sensory deprivation and the powerfully altered states of consciousness that are associated with divination and prophecy.

Caves are the black, chasmal mouths of the Otherworld; the gateways to transformation – the deep and enduring transformations which are delivered from exposure to the darkest of places. The night-filled, fecund womb-places of the Earth – out of them we are reborn. This rebirth is at the heart of the Heroine's Journey; it catapults us into new ways of seeing, new ways of being in and of the world. The journey begins at the threshold of the Otherworld. You could cross over in the dark entrance chambers of the hollow hills; you could reach it through a burrow or cave.

In Welsh mythology the way to Annwn[4] could often be found at the bottom of deep lakes, and one old myth[5] recounts the story of Ceridwen, an enchantress who lived at the bottom of Llyn Tegid – known in English as Lake Bala – in Snowdonia. The lake was named after her husband, Tegid Foel, and it is told that it formed when a well overflowed because the cover was left off it. And so the well flooded the original town of Bala, which is said to lie now under the four-mile-long lake, the largest body of water in Wales. The River Dee runs through it – though according to legend, its waters never mix with the waters of the lake – and Llyn Tegid once was famous for its deep and clear water.

But as with so many of our rivers and lakes, pollution has seriously impacted its water quality, and in the 1990s a severe outbreak of blue-green algal blooms led to concern about the excessive inflow into the lake of phosphates from domestic detergents, agricultural fertilisers and public sewage. Llyn Tegid has always been famous not just for its abundance of pike, perch, brown trout and eel, but because it is also the only known home of the gwyniad, thought to be a kind of herring, a curious relic of the last Ice Age. Sadly, this unique freshwater whitefish is now under threat both from the deteriorating water quality and from the introduction to the lake in the 1980s of another fish, the ruffe, which attacks spawning gwyniad and feeds on their eggs and fry.

If you visit Bala and Llyn Tegid today, you will find a neat and tidy lake whose levels and outflows are carefully managed. Its edges are busy with pleasure boats – kayaks, yachts and all kinds of other water-craft for rent, and the narrow-gauge Bala Lake Railway runs for several kilometres along its southern shore. It is hard to imagine that this was once one of the most magical and powerful places in Wales, home to Ceridwen and her magical cauldron, the source of transformation, wisdom and inspiration.

~

Ceridwen and the Cauldron of Transformation

Ceridwen was a powerful sorceress who lived at the bottom of Llyn Tegid with her husband, Tegid Foel. She became pregnant, and in time gave birth to twins. Her daughter, Crearwy ('Light'), was beautiful, but her son, Afagddu ('Darkness'), was ill-formed and grotesque. Ceridwen loved her son just as she loved her bright, shining daughter, and wanted to offer him a gift which would compensate for his ugliness. So she decided that she would give him the gift of wisdom. Ceridwen happened to possess a huge cauldron, and into it she carefully poured the herbs and ingredients for a potion of her own creation which she planned to offer to Afagddu. Once it was ready, only the first three drops of this potion would bestow the magical gift of wisdom; the rest would be a fatal poison to anyone who happened to drink it.

111

The ingredients for the potion were precious and rare, and Ceridwen gathered them carefully from all the secret places of the land – places which only she knew. Once the constituents had all been brought together in the great metal cauldron in Ceridwen's house under the lake, she lit a great fire under it. The mixture needed to be cooked for a year and a day, and must be stirred steadily throughout this time, day and night. And so Ceridwen set Morda, a blind man, to tend the fire beneath the cauldron, and a young boy, Gwion Bach, to the task of stirring the liquid. With promises of dire consequences and fatal retributions if it should happen, she made Gwion swear that he would never taste the liquid.

On the final day of the allotted timespan, just as the concoction was about to be finished, Gwion Bach in his excitement to be free of his burden stirred a little too vigorously. Three drops of the liquid spilled onto his thumb, burning him. Instinctively, without thinking, he put his thumb into his mouth and sucked it to ease the pain, and this is how it came to be that the first three drops of the potion which had been intended for Afagddu were drunk by Gwion Bach. So it was that, in a single moment which lasted for no time at all and for all of eternity, he gained the knowledge and wisdom which Ceridwen had meant to pass to her son. Realising that Ceridwen would know at once what had happened, and would be furious, Gwion fled.

He fled from the cauldron and from Ceridwen's house, but Ceridwen gave chase. Using the powers that the potion had given him, he shape-shifted into a hare, and he ran through the great long grass in the fields, as fast as he could. But Ceridwen became a grey-hound, and began to gain on him, her mouth wide open in a vicious snarl. Gwion found himself up against a river, and in a sudden flash of silver, he changed into a fish and leapt into it. She transformed herself into an otter. As she caught up with him and opened her mouth to swallow him, he burst up through the bright water and turned himself into a bird.

Away he flew, up, up as far into the sky as he could reach – but Ceridwen became a hawk, and hurtled through the air in his wake. Down, down she forced him, until finally, exhausted, he took refuge in a barn. But she followed him in, swift and all-seeing, and in one final burst of power, summoning up the last of his strength, Gwion metamorphosed into a single grain of corn and fell to the ground amidst a scattering of wheat and other grains on the floor. Ceridwen wasn't going to let him go. She turned herself into a black, glossy, red-crested hen, and she bent her head down to the ground and she scratched at it until she found him, and finally she ate him. Triumphant, she took her human form again and smiled.

But Gwion could not be destroyed; he had drunk the potion from Ceridwen's cauldron of transformation: the cauldron of life and rebirth. The grain that once had been Gwion lodged itself firmly inside Ceridwen, and she became pregnant. She knew who it was, this child that she was carrying, and in her fury she resolved to kill him after she had given birth. But when he was born, he was so very beautiful, and Ceridwen found herself unable to end his life. Instead, she decided to give him a chance; she sewed him inside a bag made of skin, and cast him adrift on the great ocean. The child did not die, but was washed up in his bag in a salmon weir near Aberdyfi; there he was found by a prince named Elffin ap Gwyddno. The reborn infant was raised by Elfinn, and he grew to become the legendary bard and prophet, Taliesin.

~

The story of Ceridwen shows us the cauldron – like the cave – as a symbolic womb, the source not only of rebirth and transformation, but of knowledge, wisdom and *awen*,[6] or inspiration. Celtic mythology abounds with tales of magical cauldrons – tales which are believed by many folklorists to be the forerunners of the later body of medieval Grail mythology – and old cauldrons have been found at the bottom of lakes and deep well shafts throughout the Celtic countries, left there as offerings to the goddess of the land.

Ceridwen is the keeper of the cauldron of wisdom and rebirth, and her story reflects the role of women, in these native mythologies, as the source of all life and creative power. In some retellings of this story, Ceridwen is often described simply as an enchantress or sorceress – but once she would have been seen as very much more than a mere witch. Ceridwen's cauldron transforms Gwion Bach, and her long pursuit of him after he drinks the three magical drops makes it possible for him to discover and draw on the new knowledge that he's acquired in order to shape-shift, to try to escape her. But the dark goddess in the Otherworld cannot be eluded; finally, after submitting him to these tests of his newly acquired prowess, Ceridwen swallows him up and rebirths him as Taliesin, who became the greatest of all prophets and bards.

The story of Ceridwen and Taliesin, then, is the story of an initiation, a rite of passage, and of the transformations which inevitably must follow. And so, in this Heroine's Journey of ours, after the stage of Separation – in which we listen to the Call, and sever ourselves from the old world we inhabited – then the second stage, the stage of Initiation begins. But when we heed that Call and step off the edge, thinking to firmly set foot on the path which lies ahead of us, to strike out confidently on our new pilgrimage – we may instead find ourselves losing our footing, plummeting down into the dark.

Scream if you will, but let yourself fall. We have to let ourselves fall. If we want to become Voices of the Wells, we need to plumb their depths. And in order to kick-start the process of transformation to which we've now committed ourselves, we have to destroy old ways of thinking, remove old limits. So grope your way blindly into the darkest cave, let yourself sink to the bottom of the deepest lake. Jump into the black, bottomless well. It is this Descent, in which we go down and face the dark goddess in the Otherworld, which destroys outmoded forms of being and prepares us to develop the wisdom we need to give birth to our most authentic self – the self that knows its place in the world, that has its feet firmly planted in the rich loam of the Earth. The self that can begin finally to act from that place of solid, grounded rootedness.

The journey demands that we make this Descent, because a sacrifice is required before we may continue on our path: the sacrifice of our old upper-world self; the sacrifice of that part of us which once was sustained by our attachment to the Wasteland. There at the bottom of the lake, in the impenetrable darkness of the cave, in the roiling depths of the black, scalding cauldron, the ego begins to be dismantled. We must be taken apart, broken into pieces, so that we can begin the long, hard work of putting the fragments back together again, rebirthing ourselves into a new pattern.

Here, in the long dark, we must also meet what Jung called the Shadow: all that is irrational, instinctive and hidden in our own psyche. We are forced to go deep into ourselves, so that we might first discover what it is that we must accept, know, and above all lose before we can find out what it is that we might become. Our Descent starts with disillusion and ends with dissolution. There is no escaping the process, and it can be hard. The Descent is a time of helpless wandering, of grief, rage and alienation. There is no quick way through. But the destruction which takes hold of us is required to initiate us into the mysteries, to set in motion the long, difficult game of transformation. In staying with the dark, we gather the strength which we will need to find the way back to our path and to face the rest of the journey ahead of us. In that place of destruction, gestation and rebirth, we begin to learn the answer to the biggest question of all: if we strip away everything we are told we must be in the Wasteland, what is left? When everything we once valued is taken from us, what then do we become?

Storyteller and yoga instructor Tracy Chipman[7] lives in a small town in north-west Wisconsin. I've known her for a few years now; we first came into contact because of a mutual love of stories, and a shared connection with the stories and landscape of the Outer Hebrides. During a long, dark time in Tracy's life she connected very strongly with Lake Superior, the largest freshwater lake in the world. Superior is dark, and deep: at its deepest point, it runs to 406 metres.

'I was pretty settled in my life in south-east Iowa when my father was diagnosed with cancer. Eventually I moved in with him to care for him,' she tells me. 'I came to Lake Superior on a whim, for a little break from the fray, and I was unprepared to feel such a strong connection with it. From miles away I could actually "feel" its presence. From then onwards I became utterly besotted with it. When I thought of the lake, that enormous body of water, so incredibly deep, I pictured it as a feminine entity, a woman. I saw her gathering herself together deep under the surface, filling the dark cave-space of basalt and sandstone, waiting there for aeons, beginning to know herself, somehow finally coming to light. The lake, and this image of it, seemed to promise something that I needed. After that first visit I posted a note on Craigslist, an online classified site, looking for someone I could write to who knew Lake Superior well. And so, through this interest in the lake, I met a man called Mike, and the course of my life forever changed.'

Tracy doesn't have any obvious Celtic ancestry; her ancestors came to America in the 1600s, and what little she knows of them suggests a Dorset connection – though she thinks there may also be a Scottish link. But she always felt a strong tie to Britain, she says, even as a small child. And so in her mid-twenties she bought herself a one-way plane ticket to London, and from there set off for Scotland, where she felt a sudden and unexpected sense of belonging. Tracy ended up staying for six months, living near Edinburgh and travelling around Scotland. 'I had to return to the US, but in 1995 I came back to Scotland. I was invited up to the Outer Hebrides with an ornithologist friend who was heading to the island of South Uist to do research, and words can't really convey the impact the islands had on me. I was touched, inspired and moved, and I left knowing somehow I'd be back.' She went home to Oregon, where she was living at the time, and started up a non-profit organisation called The Hebridean Folklore Project, with a mission to help keep the islands' folklore alive and accessible, and in the summer of 1996 she went back to Uist for the first of many extended journeys to the Hebrides. By day she hitched, walked, ferried and bused up and down the islands in search of stories, 'listening to the old people, listening to the sea and the curlew's call.' By night she pulled pints and poured whisky at The Dark Island Hotel in Benbecula. The islands drew her back, over and over again.

'The islands and how I engaged with the land and culture offered me a solid connection to place that I hadn't experienced before, as well as an unequalled soul education – instructions for living a wild and authentic life, if you will. I spent so much time doing fieldwork, walking and exposing myself to the wind, to the sluicing horizontal rains. At the same time, I was tipping headlong into the ancient cooking pot of oral tradition shared by the old people of the islands.

'It was a time of unprecedented heady and hearty feasting. I was waking up to a strong affinity for Celtic culture, which meant above all awakening to the culture of place. Insights spilled out to me from those old myths and stories. Life's highest truths seemed to blaze out of them, from South Uist folklore to the great epic Celtic myths – they all drew me further through the doorway of Celticity. The spinning tales of ceremony, the sacral ebb and the flow, the feral land, dreaming, speaking, and the trove of deep magic firing from the Gaelic language . . . all this began informing the tread of my day-to-day life. Of how I live this precious life of mine; the breath-by-breath choices I make about how I spend my time; where I find and create beauty; the direction I steer my livelihood and soul work as a storyteller, writer and folklorist; how and with what I feed or soothe myself; the way in which I listen to the elements and all living and non-living beings. The way I live now is directly derived from my experience of Celtic lands and culture. The islands taught me not only how to be in relationship with place, but also how to simply be.'

During Tracy's extended visits to South Uist, she struck up a deep friendship with Seumas, an elderly local man. He was her guide to the land and its stories, and when she returned to America they kept in touch. But Seumas passed away in 2002, and his death led to an experience of profound grief and loss. 'There was a strong heart connection between us,' Tracy says. 'He embodied the land and the Celtic culture of the islands for me in so many ways. His death also signalled the beginning of a long cycle of loss in my life.' And indeed, it was a time of many changes, upheaval and isolation. Her father's long struggle with cancer led eventually to his death. Her marriage had begun to fall apart and eventually she and her husband split up. Her beloved cat was hit by a car and died. Then came the sudden death of a close friend and mentor. To cap it all, Mike, the correspondent with whom she had unexpectedly fallen in love, had a massive heart attack on Samhain eve, just as they were falling asleep, and died in her arms.

Tracy looks younger than her fifty years; she has a wide, open smile that lightens the intensity with which she talks about these darkest of times in her life. 'Quite simply, I retreated,' she says. 'I went to live in a primitive cabin in the woods at Four Mile Creek near Washburn, in Wisconsin. It was near Lake Superior, the beloved lake that had first connected Mike and me. It was winter, and I was deep, deep into my grief. I was living in an altered state, because that's what grief does: it changes you. I was surrounded by this all-white world, listening to wolves and coyotes, following tracks worn by deer and bobcat, feeling so close and connected to the land. I felt as if I was shape-shifting, actually becoming the land and the wildlife all around me. There were times where I felt non-human. Not surprisingly, that made it hard to relate to other people socially. I spoke about death often as well, which didn't help. I had such a strong sense of isolation and alienation from society, and in some ways, that's still with me; I'm still recovering from it. But during this remarkably transformative time there was a strong sense of merging with that creative intelligence, the energetics underlying nature.'

Pushed to explain what it felt like, this sense of shape-shifting into the land, Tracy shakes her head and laughs. 'It's hard to explain. It felt like belonging to something safe, like I could trust the cycles and the beauty of the land, of nature and the elements, not to just disappear. Everything else that mattered to me seemed to have disappeared; the land was all that was left. Nature was this relatively benign yet hugely powerful energy to shift into when my own experience felt so crushingly grief-stricken and traumatic at times.' She hesitates, runs fingers through her hair, gropes for words. 'All I can say is that I felt a *part* of the rhythms of the land and nature: there was no separation. It was so much more than the purely human experience

I had known before. In the Hebrides I had experienced a strong connection to the land, to those islands, and that experience was a type of education, showing me how it – this shifting into land or place – might be done, giving me something to take home with me. But years later, carrying all this grief and loss, I was completely raw. My human life had been stripped away, and I was living in the woods in a way that was uncluttered by all the crap we usually surround ourselves with. It was a very mindful experience in the sense that the past was a complete bombshell for me, and the future utterly unimaginable, so I was forced to live in the present – that was all I could endure. And the present for me in that place was nothing more than the land, the elements of fire and ice, the trees, the animals, the seasons. It was a tremendously transformational period in my life, and there were such gifts that came from it.'

So great were those gifts, and so transformative her time in the woods, that Tracy recently purchased fifteen acres of boreal woodland a mile from the shores of Lake Superior, and close to the cabin she once lived in. She is clear that those gifts – involving above all a deeply embodied sense of belonging to the land – have utterly transformed the way she lives now. 'It's a sort of internal spaciousness, a simplicity, which isn't dominated by the agendas and concerns of society. In my work as a yoga instructor and a storyteller, some qualities of that knowing, that being present, are brought in and shared with others. More and more in all of my work I find the rhythm and flow which came out of that time with the land and its creatures, which is now part of me. I've learned how to show up and pay attention in a new more authentic way which informs my daily life.'

For Tracy, the two sets of experiences, first in the islands and then at home in America, are deeply connected. 'It's as if the islands gave me the gift of understanding what it might be to belong, to be in relationship with the land, which came with me back to America. To me, Celtic culture is a calling to belong to something greater, something luminous stitched throughout the horizontal and vertical realms of life. Celticity is an initiation, a coupling of my soul-self with the land and the elements and with the web that meshes, coils and weaves it and us all together. It's both a reverence and a sense of responsibility. My way of being in the world now has been birthed, cultured and tempered by that sense of Celticity, and deepened by that long stint in the dark.'

The necessary disintegration of our former selves forces us to clutch, in the depths of our extremity, at whatever it is that we believe to be the source of life. When we have given ourselves over to the dark, allowed it to work on us; when we can no longer think, reason or manage our way out of the crisis we find ourselves in – then what we are left with is instinct, the soft animal nature of our physical bodies, the songs our senses sing. The transformation that follows is for sure, as Tracy discovered, in some ways about shape-shifting: about taking on new forms, remembering that we are two-legged *animals*, learning a new way of being in the world, a new tuning-in to the rhythms and seasons of this planet. Only then can we truly become creatures of this Earth; only then can we begin to feel a sense of belonging to it.

But sometimes that disintegration of the old social self, that falling back into more physical, instinctual, animal ways of knowing, can turn into a process we can't control; sometimes it feels like the onset of madness. In this most 'civilised' of all cultures, madness is never something to be embraced – but in our old Celtic myths it occurs often enough, and it's a perfectly natural response to the unendurable. More than that: it's an initiation, a precursor to transformation.

Inside us, those old stories whisper, there might well reside a sleeping madwoman: a woman who cannot and will not tolerate the brutalities of the world around her. They suggest to us that one day, in the extremity of some great grief, or following the brutal rending of some protective veil, this madwoman within us might break out. More importantly – they tell us that, at some point in our lives it might be *okay* to let ourselves break, to run to the comforting dark of the cave, to flee to the simple white wildness of winter woods, to withdraw from the deodorised, civilised world around us. To express our rage and lick our wounds; to allow the wilderness to work on us. And so it is that Irish mythology offers us a great gift: the story of the madness of Mis.[8]

~

The Madness of Mis

Dáire Dóidgheal, the most powerful ruler in Europe, set out one day to invade Ireland. It wasn't just that he wanted to conquer that beautiful, fertile country: it was that he had a particular hatred for the greatest of all Irish warriors, Fionn mac Cumaill. Fionn had eloped with both the wife and the daughter of Bolcán, King of France, when he spent some time in his service; Dáire was utterly furious about this, and determined to seek retribution for this disrespect to his friend. And it had to be said, the fact that Dáire's sense of pride was dented by all the stories which were circulating Europe about Fionn's prowess and successes might just have had something to do with it.

So Dáire mustered a large body of troops from all across Europe, and they sailed over to the south-west of Ireland in a mighty fleet of ships. Fionn came to hear that the invading forces were on their way, and so he gathered both his own people and allies from all around the country, and they were waiting for Dáire when eventually he landed at Ventry, near the settlement of Dingle in County Kerry. A great and bloody battle ensued, which lasted a year and a day. Fionn's son Oisín faced Bolcán of France in combat, and defeated him. But Dáire's forces fought so fiercely that eventually Fionn had to call the Tuatha Dé Danann to come to his aid before the battle could be won. But then Dáire's son Conmhaol was killed, and in spite of his great skill as a warrior, Dáire Dóidgheal himself was finally slain by the mighty Fionn.

Dáire had brought to Ireland with him his beloved daughter Mis, for he could never bear to be parted from her. Mis was as beautiful as the night, with her long black hair and large black eyes and her pale, perfect skin. After the battle was finally over and the remaining warriors had dispersed, Mis came down to the beach with the band of men who guarded her, to look for her father – but after a frantic search among all the dead and dying bodies lying on the beach, all she found was his decapitated corpse stretched out on the sand. She ran to him, but when she saw what had become of her beloved father her grief overwhelmed her, and she flung herself across his body and licked and sucked at his bloody wounds to try to heal them, just as an animal might.

But nothing could restore him to life, and when finally she understood this Mis staggered to her feet and wailed and clawed at her ravaged, wet face and her blood-stained clothing. Finally, in the utter, unstoppable agony of her despair, she cracked. Taken by the extremity of her madness, she rose up into the air like a bird, and with a long high-pitched howl which shook those who heard it to the very core, she flew away into the heart of the Sliabh Mis mountains.

There it was that Mis came to rest, and she lived in the mountains for many years. She was a crazed creature in those days, was Mis; she grew long trailing fur and layers of feathers to cover her naked skin; she grew great sharp claws with which she attacked and tore to pieces any creature or person she met. She could run like the wind, and no living thing was safe from her. They called her the wild woman, and so dangerous they thought her that the people of Kerry created a great barrier around the mountains, a desert stripped of people and cattle, just for the fear of her.

Feidlimid Mac Crimthainn was the King of Munster in those days, and he offered a great reward to anyone who could capture her alive. He promised half his kingdom if Mis could be restored to sanity and society, as well as the gift of her hand in marriage. But so fearful were the stories about her that none of the warriors in the land dared to accept the challenge.

And so the people continued to live in fear of Mis, until one day, a gentle young harpist named Dubh Ruis[9] came to the court of Feidlimid Mac Crimthainn. He approached the king, harp in hand, and announced that he would take up the challenge – for he had devised a subterfuge which he believed might restore Mis, and bring her back into the world again. Mac Crimthainn's warriors laughed and jeered at the idea that this tall, handsome but gentle young man might succeed where they had not even dared to go, but for lack of any alternative plan the king agreed, and gave him the purse full of gold and silver which he requested, and which formed part of his plan to beguile Mis. And so Dubh Ruis set off with his harp, and he travelled deep into the place in the mountains of Sliabh Mis where she was thought to have her lair.

Dubh Ruis found a good dry spot in a clearing at the heart of a small oak wood, in the foothills at the base of the narrow mountain range. He took off his clothes, and set out his cloak on the ground; he surrounded it with a circle of gold and silver coins. And then he laid himself down on the cloak and began to quietly strum at his harp. After a while he heard a rustle behind him, but he didn't turn around, he just kept on playing. Then the rustling sound grew closer, and slowly, carefully, he looked up.

There she was, in all her fearsome glory: part-hag, part-wolf, wild-eyed, hardly recognisable as human. She looked dangerous enough to strike horror into the heart of the most ferocious warrior – but Dubh Ruis ignored her; he lowered his eyes and turned back to his harp and his music. After a few more minutes, Mis spoke, her voice rusty and cracked. 'Once at my father's court there were things like that.' And she pointed with one long-clawed hand at his harp.

'Were there, now,' said Dubh Ruis. 'Well, won't you sit down and listen for a bit, while I play?' But Mis shook her head, and took a long step back. Dubh Ruis said nothing, but turned back to his harp and his music. He seemed to take no further notice of Mis – except that he watched her, out of the corner of his eye. And then she suddenly noticed the gold and silver coins, and she stared long and hard at them, and then she took a step closer to him.

'Once my father had things such as that,' Mis said. And she pointed with a sharp-clawed hand at the coins.

And Dubh Ruis said, 'Did he, now. Well, won't you sit down and look at them for a bit, while I play?' But Mis shook her head, and took a step back again. It was then that Dubh Ruis shifted around a little on his cloak so that his fine set of genitals were on display to her, but all he did was continue to focus on his harp, and his music. He seemed to take no further notice of Mis – except that he watched her, out of the corner of his eye. And then she suddenly noticed his genitals, and she stared long and hard at them, and then she took a step closer to him. She stood quite still, and didn't speak. But Dubh Ruis saw a flush rise in the grubby, bare skin of her face and brow.

And Dubh Ruis said, 'Won't you come and lie here with me for a while?' And this time Mis did not step away, but instead took another step closer, and then another, and so Dubh Ruis slowly reached out his hand to her – and still she didn't back away. He took her long-clawed hand and pulled her down beside him, onto the soft, fine-woven woollen cloak. Quietly he said to her, 'You wouldn't be hurting me now, would you?' Blindly, seemingly entranced, Mis shook her head.

And so it was that Dubh Ruis the harpist made love to her, crazy Mis, wild woman of the Sliabh Mis Mountains. And once it was over, she asked for more, and more loving she received; and then she asked for more music, and more music she received; and she sat calmly with Dubh Ruis while he played, and she fingered the silver and gold coins. 'I remember . . .' she started to say, but then she shook her head and would not continue. But Dubh Ruis saw that a tear leaked from the corner of her eye.

Dubh Ruis grew hungry, and he took up his leather bag and brought out a piece of bread from it. He offered half of it to Mis. She took it from him carefully, lifting it to her nose, sniffing at it, and she said, 'I remember this!' And Dubh Ruis said to her, 'Yes, you do. It is called bread.' Mis nodded – but there wasn't enough of it to satisfy their hunger, and so she ran off into the woods to hunt for a deer. When she brought it back to him, though, slung over her strong, bony shoulders, Dubh Ruis would not allow her to eat it raw, or to tear at it with her long sharp teeth as was her custom. Instead, he built a fire and he roasted the deer over it, and he served her cooked meat.

Then Dubh Ruis took Mis to a pool at the edge of the wood which had been warmed by the sun, and he coaxed her into the pool with soft words and kisses, and there he bathed her gently, and he washed away the dirt of the forest. And then he took branches from the forest floor and built a shelter for Mis, and he made a bed of moss inside the shelter, and he covered her with his cloak, and he stayed with her.

Each day, gently, Dubh Ruis scrubbed at Mis's skin, so that over time the fur and the feathers fell away from her. He combed out her long black hair, and cut back her rending claws. Each day he spoke to her of the world she had left behind. And each day he made love to her, on their bed of moss in the forest. Each day, she changed a little more; day by day she slowly transformed back into some semblance of the young and beautiful woman she had been before her father was killed. And finally, after two months had passed, Mis asked of her own accord if they could leave the mountains and go back down into the world.

So Mis returned to court with Dubh Ruis, and they were rewarded handsomely by the King of Munster, and Dubh Ruis was given her hand in marriage. They lived together happily for a number of years, and Mis bore four sons.

But the warriors who had been made to look small by Dubh Ruis' success plotted against him, and planned their revenge; and one day, while he was out walking in the woods, they killed him. This time, when faced with the dead, maimed body of a loved one, Mis did not lose her reason to her pain and despair. Instead, she poured her grief into a poem: a lament for her gentle harper, Dubh Ruis.

~

Sometimes, madness seems like the only possible response to the insanity of the civilised world; sometimes, holding ourselves together is not an option, and the only way forward is to allow ourselves to fall apart. As the story of Mis shows, that madness can represent an extreme form of initiation, a trigger for profound transformation. Mis is portrayed as a typical *geilt* – an Old Irish word which means a mad person, or a lunatic. But the word *geilt* has a particular connotation in Celtic myth and literature: it is conferred upon people who go mad from terror, often as a result of their exposure to the extremities of battle. There are several such old stories, but the best-known, of course, are about men. A great deal of literary attention has been paid to the episode of Merlin's madness in Arthurian legend, which comes upon him after the Battle of Arfderydd, and to the old Irish tale of Suibhne Geilt (Mad Sweeney) who similarly goes mad in battle – but the story of Mis is seldom told, even though it is believed to be older than all of these others.

Mis is the original wild woman, that archetypal madwoman who lives deep within each of us. She speaks for us all: for the rage which we cannot express, for the grief which eats our heart out, for the voices we have suppressed out of fear. This old story shows us a brutal descent into darkness during which all illusions are stripped away and old belief systems evaporate, and in doing so it suggests that the extremities of madness or mental breakdown, with their prolonged, out-of-control descent into the unknown, might offer us a path through which we can come to terms with the truth. Like other legendary *geilta*,[10] Mis is driven to extremity in her grief, shape-shifting into bird form, flying away into the hills and woods, growing fur and feathers, eating wild and raw food, leaving the intolerable world behind her. But a *geilt* cannot emerge from her madness and come back to the world until she has achieved some kind of personal transformation. Through her ordeal – her removal from society and her time spent in the wilderness – she must find a way to reclaim a more authentic sense of identity and belonging. She finds it with the help of a man; she finds it in the union of the masculine and feminine.

In all the old stories, the *geilt* is hypersensitive to the sights and sounds of the civilised world, finding them unendurable. She finds other people unendurable too; only alone in the wild, in nature, can safety and freedom be found. In the same way, it is our sudden awareness of the horrors of the civilised world, the Wasteland, which not only leads to our Descent, but which accompanies us into the dark. That awareness, that inability to endure the unendurable, forces us to challenge our old values, and in particular, the materialism on which our culture is founded. We are highly likely to be left feeling isolated and bereft; we may sometimes be left falling apart.

Sophie McKeand[11] was born in north Wales, and still lives in the town of Wrecsam, close to the English border, with her partner Andy and her eighteen-year-old daughter Rhiannon. She feels a fierce attachment to her land, and its people. 'Even when I wasn't conscious of it, I realise now that I've always struggled with the idea of ever leaving here. The Cymraeg (Welsh) word *hiraeth* is the only way I can explain it. It doesn't translate well into English, but it refers to a kind of deep longing for home.'

She comes across now as funny, practical and supremely down-to-earth, but ten years ago, when she was twenty-nine, Sophie thought she was going mad. 'I was trying to be a Good Citizen, whatever that was, and a "good single parent". I was working as a field sales executive in media, I had just bought a house, I thought I'd done everything everyone had told me I ought to do to be a good and productive member of society. But conforming to all those expectations, living in that way, was killing me. I hated my life. My escape was a headlong leap into the all-encompassing weekend fog of drinking and taking drugs for release before crawling into the sick, empty heart of Monday morning. I remember one Monday morning in particular, a distinct defining moment, after a long weekend of partying while my daughter was away. I was standing in the shower, feeling like shit, and this internal voice which I'd never heard before said very loudly and clearly, *This is not who I am.* It was a side of me which had never spoken before. It was like thunder, or a lightning strike. I heard it, and then all at once everything started to unravel. I kept thinking about all that I'd bought into – the house, the smart car, the laptop. All the *stuff.* If those things weren't what life was about after all, then who was I, really? What was it for?'

What happened next was a series of experiences that at the time made Sophie worry about her sanity. 'But I didn't seek out medical help, because I never felt that was the answer. Somehow I knew that I needed to work it through rather than medicate it, to understand the new way I was beginning to look at the world. I thought, who is anyone else to tell me that I'm thinking in the right way or the wrong way? I'd been doing that all my life, and look where it had got me.'

Her experiences during this time were both shattering and transformative. 'It was all about connecting directly with the land, right here in north-east Wales. I had what I can only describe as a huge spiritual awakening. I remember, after that moment in the shower, thinking that we're broken people, all of us. Our roots are torn from the earth, fed into the Machine, chipped and moulded into sheets of MDF which are used to build things we don't need.' Sophie found herself developing an aversion to pavements, to tarmac and concrete, and so she began to spend more and more time walking in the hills, forests and lakes with her dog. 'I'd walk for miles up into the hills, literally for hours. That was my therapy, I didn't want anything else. Then . . . well, I started to connect and converse with the land. It was as if the world exploded into life. I started to hear the trees' voices, the mountains' thoughts. At the time it was quite scary. One night I dreamed of a fire dragon and when I awoke he was still with me and he stayed with me for days. What was that all about? A psychotic episode? A hallucination? What with that and the voices, I was convinced I was completely nuts. But the truth is, I knew that it was really the rest of the so-called civilised world which was nuts! And that was hard to deal with. This is what I wrote about how I felt at the time:

Fear of all that we are, of all that I am, becomes a soul-silencing black rat chewing the tongue from the paralysed Self. It is nails screeching down blackboards. It is waking in the night infested with demons that burrow beneath skin as old ghosts tramp through the bedroom vomiting appalling truths. It is the blackened grief of the illumined mind. I do not fear death. I fear life, and what we do with it. I am suffocated with horror. *We are one?* It hurts to look anybody in the eye. Being around people becomes a terrifying ordeal. I am afraid for *all* children.

'I kept it all to myself, of course,' she laughs. 'Whilst it was happening, there was complete psychological compartmentalisation. The bigger side of me was denying it all, saying, *This isn't me, I don't think like this, the natural world doesn't communicate! I can shut it off, just let it run like a film in the other room whilst I get on with my normal life.* I was striving for "normality". I would watch TV, read the newspapers, go shopping. I would tell myself, *No, this is the real world, this one you've always lived in.* Then at the same time, the other half of me was embracing all of these voices and visions, and I couldn't stop them any more than I could stop breathing. They were like waking dreams, only tangible, material, and they were effecting visible changes *in the real world*!'

Sophie is very clear that the experience changed her and, given the extent of her distress at the time, remarkably positive about the nature of transformation she underwent. 'It changed me; of course it changed me. That moment in the shower, the moment I call the epiphany – that was the start of it, the dark time. Since then it's been a long, long journey. It didn't all happen at once. It's been a tough process to get to where I am now. Eventually something began to come out of the fog, the things I thought I must do. Write, walk in nature, wild-swim, learn Welsh, work in my community. Big things, too: I quit my job, sold my house, signed up for university, stopped smoking. I began to look into what it was to be Welsh. I began to write poetry, and then to perform it. What was interesting is that throughout this whole process, painful as it was, I felt as if I were becoming a better person. As if I were being transformed into a better mother, partner, friend, writer. More involved with my place, with the local community. I wanted to drink less, write more. I thought, if this is madness, I'll take it.'

The transformation clearly was a powerful one. On Sophie's website, acclaimed nature writer Jay Griffiths, author of the best-selling books *Wild* and *Kith*, says that her poetry offers 'an allusive, restless sensibility turned outwards to the world; her words have heft, they grasp their way out of poetry into landscape.' Talking to Sophie, I am looking into the dancing eyes of a seemingly average woman, approaching forty, with a brown chin-length bob, clutching a simple black cardigan around her. She's sitting at a desk in a pleasant, ordinary-looking room in their perfectly conventional house which she shares as a working space with Andy. But on her website you'll find photographs of Sophie on stage with paint on her face and feathers in her hair, with heavily tattooed forearms, wearing tight short dresses of black or shocking pink. She has performed her poetry, usually backed by musicians, extensively across the UK: at the Green Man, Wilderness, Dinefwr and Uncivilisation Festivals, as well as at venues like the Pizza Express Jazz Club in Soho. She insists that the spoken word has power.

'Performance poetry exists as a primeval reminder of our oral traditions, of who we are. Spoken as part of the landscape, it becomes landscape. Spoken as part of the community, it becomes community. Community really matters to me. Now, more and more of my work is in my local community. I work full-time in the arts, and especially with groups of young children in schools around the county, focusing on poetry, and on language.'

Celtic mythology is the foundation stone of much of Sophie's work; she is particularly passionate about connecting people to the stories which spring directly out of the places where they live, out of their own cultural traditions. 'Recently I've been working with the Ceridwen myth, because it allows and builds on the possibility of transformation and inspiration, and I think that's so important for kids to understand. So I get the kids in my poetry workshops to make a cauldron of inspiration, and then I ask them what we're going to put into the cauldron. They go outside and come back with found objects as metaphors – bark, standing in for dragon's tongue, for example: something which represents wisdom. Or they use objects that I bring – marbles, and so on – and they're the ones who decide what those objects represent. Then they stir it all up and pretend to taste it, and I tell them they've been transformed by the potion. And also, like Gwion Bach, we shape-shift! I bring fur or feathers and they transform themselves into some animal or other. And then I ask them what they are going to say now that they're transformed, and they write. They write very freely, about how they have been changed, about how it feels to be that animal.

'Watching the kids devise their own symbols and metaphors from these items is amazing. It encourages them to engage not only with their own Welsh myths and stories, but with the land and its animals. Connecting with the land is an integral part of my work. And learning Cymraeg, because the Cymraeg language grew directly out of this land; it is the voice the land gave us, the one it resonates with most beautifully, and this is why I'm working so hard to learn it. I'm still the out-of-tune violin in the orchestra, but I'm working on it.'

Sophie's experiences of what might be thought to be madness, and the strong sense of connection to the land which both began it and emerged out of it, have influenced the way she views her place in the world, her sense of responsibility to her land, and her community. 'It's definitely about protecting,' she says, emphatically. 'And I feel that part of that protecting is in encouraging the next generation to think about myths and their connection – and our connection through them – with the land. Planting a seed so that sometime, when they need it, they'll remember these things. Because it's time for us to rise up and take back our role as care-takers and stewards not just of the land but of the children, too. I think a lot of women are doing this now, with more home-schooling, with community projects, with educational projects that operate a little bit outside the norms of our patriarchal education system. This is how we ensure the land has good future caretakers.

'I also feel that the land needs something from us, yes. We always think of what we need, but the land needs us now too. The trees need help spreading their seeds. There's a need for people to speak poems and songs to the land. To collect litter. This is one of the ways I connect and respond in an authentic way. It's inter-esting because I never see people picking up rubbish. We always feel it's someone else's job, that we're too important, that we don't have the time or a suitable bag to put the rubbish in. But it's not always the grand gestures that will change the world.'

★

The descent into darkness can take many different forms. It might be a mental or emotional breakdown, but it might also be a physical illness or disability. In her remarkable book *The Alchemy of Illness*,[12] Chronic Fatigue Syndrome sufferer Kat Duff has this to say:

> The well venture forth to accomplish great deeds in the world, while the sick turn back into themselves and commune with the dead . . . Space and time lose their customary definitions and distinctions. We drift in a daze and wake with a start to wonder: Where am I? On a train to San Francisco or at Grandmother's house? Maybe both, for opposites coexist in the underworld of illness . . . Defying the rules of ordinary reality, illness shares in the hidden logic of dreams, fairy tales, and the spirit realms mystics and shamans describe. There is often the feeling of exile, wandering, searching, facing dangers, finding treasures. Familiar faces take on the appearance of archetypal allies and enemies, 'some putting on a strange beauty, others deformed into the squatness of toads,' as Virginia Woolf noted. Dreams assume a momentous authority, while small ordinary things, like aspirin, sunshine, or a glass of water, become charged with potency, the magical ability . . . We drop out of the game when we get sick, leave the field, and desert the cause. I often feel like a ghost, the slight shade of a person, floating through the world, but not of it. The rules and parameters of my world are different altogether.

When we descend into the dark, we find ourselves literally losing the plot. We find ourselves between stories. All of the stories we have told ourselves about who we are have begun to disintegrate. Chances are, we are losing much that we once held dear, all that we once thought defined us, all the old dreams. It's hard to let go of dreams, no matter how dysfunctional. But once the process of disintegration has begun it must be properly worked through. The old stories are clear about this: we must die to ourselves, and to the world, before we can be reborn.

Sometimes, that dying takes a long time; sometimes, we can't imagine we'll ever be free of the pain of it. Stay with the long dark: it takes as long as it takes. We cannot shortcut our time in the dark – but so often we try to, because we are born into a culture which has prepared us poorly for waiting. Instant downloads via the internet save us from having to wait for books to arrive in the post; videos can be streamed online with a few brief clicks of a mouse. Fast food, fast service. We want everything now, including transformation and wisdom. In this culture, if something seems to be broken or defective, off we go at once, looking for a quick fix. We want to medicate our way out of the dark, to drink or drug our way out; we want to treat our way out with solution-focused therapies, how-to spiritualties. We go looking for a product, a practice, a technique. We want to know *now* what it is we might become, and we want to become it *now*.

But we won't find our way by running hell-for-leather towards the light; we will find it rather by embracing the dark. By exploring the fecund, loamy ground of our being – our own being, and that of the rich, wide world around us. For some of us, this might mean adopting a meditation or movement practice which forces us to be quiet, and listen to what our bodies are telling us; for others, insight might come in the real dark, sitting in the woods alone at midnight, merging into the trees, listening to the night sounds. Some women will explore their past and present feelings by keeping a notebook. Whatever form it takes, whether it comes easily to us or not, we have to be still, and trust; we have to resist the urge to view what is happening to us as a problem to be solved. We have to let ourselves hurt, release the old needs, let go of the old urges to become what we are not, what we were not meant to be. This is how we pave the way for rebirth.

There are dangers to be found in the dark; of course there are dangers. One of the greatest dangers lies in the fact that it is all too easy to get stuck there. We may focus in too tightly on the intensity of our grief, sinking into it, drowning in it. We may talk of little else, we may become self-absorbed, self-pitying, navel-gazing. This is another of the ways in which our society tricks us, for we have become a culture of narcissists, excessively focused on the perfection of our own pain. But this is a time to resist the urge to protracted self-pity, because it is all too easy to lose ourselves in tending our own emotional wounds; it is all too easy never to move on. It is true that we have to do a good deal of inner work before we have anything meaningful to offer to the outer world; it is true too that we must recognise our wounds and incorporate them into the ground of our becoming. But we need also to stop licking them. We are more than the sum of our wounds. We need to focus on coming back to our bodies, beginning to repossess our instincts, beginning to reclaim our deep connection to the land and its non-human inhabitants. This is how we heal.

Slowly, then, in its own good time, the darkness begins to fade. We can begin to move again, to grope for the way ahead; we can find it, finally, the path which leads us on through the Otherworld. We can go forward on our pilgrimage, walking, working our way to understanding what it is that we might offer to the world. This journey of ours, like all pilgrimages, is in some senses a journey out of time – a journey which takes us far beyond the 'normal' everyday world. It is a journey through the Otherworld, where the rules are incomprehensible, the tasks seem impossible, and the stakes are perilously high.

And yet, as Sophie discovered, the Otherworld is also a fertile place. In stark contrast to many other mythological and religious traditions, although the Celtic Otherworld is dangerous, with ample traps for the proud or unwary, it is usually envisaged as a land of abundance. It is a place of beauty and harmony, not of darkness and terror. Old age and death do not exist there, and no hell-fires burn. It is a country which exists outside the laws of time and space; home to deities, other spirits and supernatural beings, and our ancestors. It is a world which runs parallel to our own, and which might sometimes seep into it. It is elusive, accessible only at certain times of the year, at certain 'thin' or threshold places, or by invitation. However you think of it, for the Celts, the Otherworld was just as real as our own; today, some would say it still is. The

Otherworld and our world are simply two manifestations of the same phenomenon.

I have travelled several times to the dark entrance to the Otherworld, because whatever the monomythic plot structures might like to suggest, a Heroine's Journey is rarely, if ever, linear. My own journey has been more like a series of spirals – spirals which go both ways, leading me inwards and then back out again. Sometimes it has seemed more maze than spiral, as I've lost my sense of direction completely, and found myself slammed up against a dead end. If journeys are fractal, perhaps mine has been more fractal than most. And the truth is, I've made most of the mistakes I warn of in the pages above.

My first flirtation with the dark came when I was thirty, when the veil which had shaded my sight and protected me from full knowledge of the Wasteland was shredded piece by piece, and finally ripped away. Everything changed. That veil could never be worn again, no matter how fiercely I might have wanted to sew it up with trembling fingers and too coarse a thread. I saw my life for what it was, and I couldn't un-see it. I had failed to become the person I had wanted to be. I had taken the wrong path, the safe path, the path without heart. I had made my choices out of fear, for the choices we make are the products of old wounds, and of baggage from the past which we might carry around with us still. I hadn't even begun to address the baggage from my own past, though I was awfully good at advising other people about theirs. The lives we eventually live are a function of the choices we think we have, or the choices we believe we do not have. Suffering always from an excess of caution, I had a habit of imagining fewer choices than I actually had.

But no matter how coherently you might be able to express and explain the factors which brought you to this point, when you come to the mirror and see yourself clearly for the first time, and do not like what you see, all excuses flee. Only grief is left – the great grief which comes from knowing that you have failed yourself. Some people fall apart then; others simply cannot contemplate the possibility of falling apart. So it was for me when, at thirty, I tried to manage my way through the Call which I first heard at that time. No deep plunge into the darkness for me; no signs of weakness allowed. I bit down on my grief and set about controlling the situation I found myself in. That is what I had always done; that is what I would do now.

'Out of control' was not an option. It had never been an option. I clung to control because that was how I had survived as a child. After my mother found the courage to divorce my father when I was four years old, she dealt with her own pain by sinking into a years-long struggle with binge drinking. During the drinking days I learned to fend for myself, and I learned to cover the tracks – for what I learned above all was that *no one must ever know*. We must keep the secret, we must cement over the cracks. And more than anything – more important than anything else in the world – I learned that I must take charge of my own young life. I needed to keep control, because the people closest to me seemed to have lost it.

There is no 'off' switch for such deeply ingrained habits; they become a part of who we are. And at thirty years old I was still so very good at papering over the cracks, and keeping everything tightly under control. So I planned the journey which I imagined was ahead very carefully, and timing was the essence of it. I knew that I needed to leave my job; I knew where I wanted to go – but everything must be tied up neatly, for above all else I feared chaos. I had seen chaos in my beautiful, sad mother; I had seen what happened when you went down into the dark and couldn't find your way back out again. It was not going to be my path. And so it took me two tightly controlled years to extract myself from the situation I was living in, because I left nothing at all to chance.

I might not have allowed myself the full experience of Descent, but those two years weren't pretty. Perhaps that's precisely why they weren't pretty. Every day, I longed to be somewhere other than the place I was. I longed very specifically to be in a tiny tumbledown cottage in the Maumturk Mountains of north Connemara which we were in the process of purchasing for a song, and which Len was going to move into and work on while I remained in the UK, earning the funds to renovate it.

Staying in the UK for a while was a necessity. We had a large mortgage, and I had no way of paying it if I didn't have my salary, and the housing market was in a slump. We couldn't take any chances; the house had to be sold before we could do anything. As soon as we decided to move to Ireland, we put it on the market, but it took a year to sell. Once the house was off our hands, I could safely hand in my notice – but I was contractually obliged to work out a notice period of a full year before I could leave my job, and I worked it out from a small rented, furnished flat so that I could squirrel away every spare penny to tide us over for a while when I finally escaped. And so, for two years, what I thought of as my 'real life' – my life-to-be in Ireland – was on hold. I hated every second of every minute of every day that I spent in that ugly office building in the small Surrey town. Every day was a roller-coaster, over and over again climbing the crest of anger and then plummeting down into despair.

Those two years that I spent hanging around at the threshold of the entrance to the Otherworld weren't good years, and I don't think I was a good person during them. I certainly made some foolish choices, did some things that later I wasn't proud of. Looking back at myself with the wisdom and experience of another couple of decades, I see a curious mixture of brittleness and savageness. Disliking both the company I worked for and the people I worked with, at the mercy of two unpleasantly sexist bosses, surrounded by back-biting and politicking and by people who it seemed would do or say anything to 'get ahead', I became hypercritical of others, maybe even misanthropic. I held myself in too much esteem and others in too little. I see fractures too that I wasn't aware of at the time, as the chaos which I had planned so carefully to avoid began to break out in other, more subtle ways. I see someone desperately hanging on to the cliff-edge of control with bleeding, shredded fingernails and gritted teeth, wanting all the while to just let go and scream her tired heart out as she fell.

But as always, on the surface, to everyone around me, everything in my life seemed to be perfectly – and characteristically – managed. I did everything properly and (mostly) politely and did not rock any boats. I did not smash the gates of the citadel as I left; I simply slipped away, smiling slightly. Never burn your bridges: that was my motto. That was my motto, and because of it, it was all too easy to find my way back over those bridges when my carefully planned escape didn't work out and I found myself in retreat, just a couple of years later. So it was that I found myself repeating the process, making the same journey all over again.

And so now I have a different motto: always burn your bridges.

In the autumn of 1994 I packed up a few meagre possessions into a crumbling black Fiat Uno (the smart, large and comfortable company car handed back without an ounce of regret) and I headed west. I knew precisely what I was driving towards, and it was all that had held me together for the last two years, since I first had stood on a Connemara shore looking west. I was heading for grey mountains, brown bog and the salty scent of a not-too-distant sea. I was heading for a small shallow river along the lane and a holy well over the hill. I was heading for the clean, crisp silence of a Connemara morning and visible stars in the sky at night. I could hardly believe my luck; I could hardly believe that I'd done it. And finally, after several hours of driving, a ferry trip across the Irish Sea, and a few more hours of driving on quieter, slower, kinder roads, I passed through the unrendered new concrete block gateposts of a cottage that still wasn't fully finished (though it did at least, thanks to the random, peripatetic comings and goings of a couple of local builders, have a new roof and windows and damp-proofing and plumbing). I stepped out of the car, fell into my husband's arms, and I wept. I felt as if I had escaped from Death Row.

For the first time in my life I began to feel as if I was at home. It was an odd feeling. Though I didn't actually set foot on Irish soil till I was thirty, I had always loved Ireland with an intensity that I could never explain. I had grown up immersed in and loving

Irish culture. My great-grandfather, Jimmy Dunne, was an Irishman who had come to England for work. Jimmy, who died in 1937 at the age of eighty-three, was a family legend. He had, we were told, fathered thirteen children with his first wife in Ireland, who died giving birth to her final set of twins. He then had another thirteen children with his second wife, my great-grandmother, who made clothes for the local gypsy population in Hartlepool, the English town in which he eventually chose to settle. The youngest of that second set of thirteen children was my maternal grandmother.

But the intense attraction towards Irish culture that permeated my childhood wasn't just genetic: after my mother had divorced my Scottish father, she fell in love with a golden-haired, blue-eyed Irishman from County Tipperary. Sean moved in when I was four years old, and brought with him into our world a small but perfectly formed collection of Irish folk music LPs: a vivid miscellany of comic and cautionary tales, tragic ballads and fiery rebel songs. Those songs infused me with a strong sense of the landscape, history and culture of this vibrant, passionate country which seemed so different from the dour north-eastern industrial town where we then lived. And as an antidote to a drab and difficult world, I spent much of the rest of my childhood and teenage years engrossed in Irish folk and fairy tales, myths and legends, literature and poetry.

That music and those poems and stories began to come to life again in Connemara, in the land from which they'd originated. And, little by little, so did I. I crashed for three months, exhausted, nursing myself slowly back into the world. The simplicity of my daily routine was transformative – the ability to take my tea outside in the morning and sit on the giant stone by the doorstep looking out at the mountains; to wander down by the river when I felt the need or the call, rather than when someone else said I could have a break; to empty my head of rage and despair and to focus on how alive my body felt, squelching through the bog. Removed from the Wasteland, managing for a while to hold the world at bay, my symptoms of anxiety began slowly to disappear.

My healing began in the land, and this land was what I had left the Wasteland for – the only solid refuge I'd imagined and held onto when everything else was falling apart. I turned away from the safe but confining refuge of my own head; I spent more and more time outside. In the peaceful, empty spaciousness of the bogs and mountains I found not only the silence which I always seemed to have needed, but a curious and very freeing sense of humility. I was a mere speck in this landscape; I didn't matter. Paralysed by self-consciousness from my early childhood, more than anything now I seemed to have a need for invisibility as I slowly began to prepare for the long hard work of trying to uncover what it was that I might become, now all the trappings of the Wasteland had dissolved. The bright shining veneer of worldly success was all gone; what was left that was 'me'? What did I want? More importantly, what did I have to give? The gift of this place was that no one knew me here; no one was looking at me, no one was judging me. The land certainly had no expectations of me. For the first time in my life I didn't have to perform; I didn't have to excel. I simply sat among the other living things I shared the place with, paying attention, and began instead to catch a glimmer of what it might possibly be like to just sink seamlessly into the world around you – to really live as if you were a part of it.

So it was that I found the smallest beginnings of a way of being in the land which forever afterwards was to become my touchstone for all that was healthy, and which never left me. Whatever else I did over the next few years, I was always trying to work my way back to that deep sense of silence and spaciousness, to that more tuned-in way of living in the world, to that sense of my feet being in the right place. I knew they were there somewhere, the answers I was seeking but for which I hadn't quite, yet, formed the right questions. I was to stay for only two years in that little stone cottage in Connemara, but while I was there I felt as if it might just be possible to find a sense of belonging to this saner, wilder world. I was learning to listen – though I wasn't entirely sure yet just what it was that I was listening to. I was learning, painfully slowly, to understand the importance of place.

5

Finding the Path

The Pilgrim's Way

A witch lurks in the woods around
Sarn Helen, north Wales

I see her walking
on a path through a pathless forest
or a maze, a labyrinth.
As she walks, she spins
and the fine threads fall behind her
following her way,
telling
where she is going,
telling
where she has gone.
Telling the story.
The line, the thread of voice,
the sentences saying the way.

Ursula K. Le Guin[1]

I knew the road was there, but I couldn't find it. The way wasn't marked, and there were so many possible paths to take. The Ordnance Survey map should have provided a clue; I could just about see the name of the track, but I'd left my glasses behind in my B&B, and the print was so tiny that I couldn't make out in which direction I needed to turn at the start of this journey to find my way onto it. I find Ordnance Survey maps challenging at the best of times; maybe I've wrestled with too many of them. They seem to have a life of their own, and I can never get them to fold back up properly. I did my best and stuffed the crumpled map back in my little rucksack, and as a result, instead of going straight on as I later discovered I should have done, I headed with an entirely unwarranted sense of confidence off to the right. So it was that I found myself wandering up and down a seemingly endless network of deserted tracks in the beautiful Gwydyr Forest, which neighbours the village of Betws-y-Coed in the Snowdonia National Park in North Wales. Meanwhile, a small handful of kilometres to the north, old Yr Wyddfa himself looked down at me and laughed.

There was some irony in the fact that I was losing my way while looking for Elen of the Ways. Or, to be precise, I was looking for Sarn Helen (sometimes, Sarn Elen): Elen's Causeway, the old Roman road which runs through North Wales. This 260-kilometre-long road connects Aberconwy in the north with Carmarthen in the west – though there's still some debate about its precise route, as there are long stretches which have been lost over the centuries and are now unidentifiable. Many sections of it have been overlaid by the modern road network; other parts can still be seen in something very close to their original form. The road is named after the woman who is sometimes called Elen of the Hosts, sometimes called Elen of the Ways, and also sometimes identified with Saint Elen of Caernarfon. Elen is an elusive character, existing in the tangled, gnarly borderlands between myth and history. We find her most memorably in 'The Dream of Macsen Wledig', a story within the medieval Welsh manuscript, *The Mabinogion*, most of the contents of which emerged from ancient tales in the oral tradition. In this particular story, Elen is said to have ordered the construction of great roads through Wales.

I seemed to be intent on repeatedly heading off in the same wrong direction at the beginning of my journey: I had also veered off to the right on my first foray into the forest that morning. But this was such a lovely path that I followed it anyway, even when it became clear that it was taking me in a different direction from the old road which was marked on the map. I made my way along a couple of different tributaries, accompanied by the softest of rain, walking entranced through mysterious fairy-tale woods thick with gnarly logs covered in moss, and lichen-encrusted rocks cosy under thick blankets of shiny ivy. One particularly striking cluster of tree stumps in front of a large, dark crevice in a rock face looked for all the world like a pair of shaggy-haired, horned monsters emerging from a cave, arms outstretched, staggering towards me. A tall, dead tree reached out to me a thin arm with long thorn-like fingers; it had a crooked nose and tangled vines for hair, like an old witch of the woods. I began to see faces in the rocks. I passed dark pools and ditches gleaming with jewel-like frogspawn; tiny streams tumbled down from the mountains, finding the most unlikely paths, carving their way through ancient channels in tree-root and rock.

For sure this tiny road was magical – but it wasn't Sarn Helen.

And then it stopped, quietly petering out into the trees. I brought myself to a halt and stood there perplexed, for all the world as lost as the archetypical fairy-tale heroine in the dark woods. Looking for the right path, and failing to find it. Lost down another dead end.

It wasn't till that evening, back in my B&B and poring over the map with a magnifying glass, that I understood the mistake I'd made at the very beginning of the journey. So I set off for a third attempt the next morning, and this time I followed the direction the path had been pointing in all along. I passed through a small gate, and finally set foot on Elen's Causeway.

Unlike most Roman roads, Sarn Helen is not straight; it winds its way across north Wales over high moors and through hidden, wooded valleys. It is a remarkable piece of road-building through challenging terrain, and as you look at the remote mountainous landscape through which it passes, it is hard to imagine its construction in the first place, and harder still to imagine Roman troops marching along it. The road climbed steeply at first through this beautiful forest of Gwydyr, which stories tell us once was filled with great oaks. Now, after centuries of felling and of managed forestry, it is mostly coniferous, but in recent years there's been a resurgence in the planting of native broadleaf species. It spreads across an undulating landscape which rises to 300 metres above sea level and is divided by the various valleys of the rivers Llugwy, Lledr and Machno – all of which are tributaries of the River Conwy. Mostly, the forest's growth is quite open, so from time to time there were spectacular views over these valleys and up to the mountains of the Glyderau, the Carneddau and to Snowdon.

But I wasn't there for the views, I was there for the road. Its old surface was cobbled and uneven; I stepped carefully, always conscious of the texture of the ancient stones underfoot. I walked sometimes with my eyes closed, in deep awareness of the continuity I felt so strongly in this place, knowing that I was just one more among countless pairs of feet that would have trodden this path down the centuries. My steps overlaying theirs, never wiping them out, just joining them. Adding another layer of memory across this well-walked land. In places the road was bordered by banks a couple of feet high, thick with moss and lichen, studded with trees. Sometimes the banks would give way to a low drystone wall; at other times, heather fringed the edges of the road and spread out into the woods I was passing through. Close to the abandoned village of Rhiwddolion a rocky outcrop loomed over the path. I looked up to see a single sheep high above me, lying down on a narrow shelf cut into the sheer rock face. Unperturbed, it tracked me with its eyes as I ambled past, just following for a while the road which Elen made.

~

Elen of the Ways

The handsome and vigorous man who came to be known in Britain as Macsen Wledig was the emperor of Rome, where he was called Maximus. One day, at the end of a meeting he had called with the thirty-two kings whose countries were subject to Rome's rule, he suggested that they might all go hunting together the next morning. So at daybreak they set off together, Macsen and his kings. They rode through the cool, crisp air of the morning until they came to a green wooded valley through which ran the great river Tiber, and they hunted there till midday. By that time the sun was fierce and scorching, and so Macsen decided to stop and rest. His attendants gathered themselves around him and rested their shields on the shafts of their spears to shade him from the sun, and they placed a gold-enamelled shield under his head. So Macsen slept . . .

. . . and in a fine stone castle on a misty island far, far to the west, a weaver of dreampaths cocked her head to the east, and cast out a thread. As Macsen slept, he dreamed. In this dream he was riding farther on along the valley they had hunted in, following the Tiber to its source. After some time he came to a mountain, a mountain so high that it seemed to touch the sky. When he crossed over it and reached the other side, he looked down onto the most beautiful land that he had ever seen. Several mighty rivers flowed down the mountain and out to the sea, and Macsen travelled on along the banks of the largest of them. Finally, he came to a city by the coast, and in the centre of the city there was a vast and beautiful castle with high towers of many different colours. And he saw a great fleet of ships at the mouth of the river, the largest fleet he had ever seen. One of the ships was larger and fairer than all the others; half of it was gold and the other half was silver, and a bridge made of whalebone arced across the water from the ship to the land. Macsen dismounted from his horse and walked across the bridge and into the ship. As he stepped on board, the sail was hoisted and the ship began to sail across the ocean.

On they sailed, and eventually the ship came to rest on the shore of the fairest island in the whole world. In his dream, Macsen travelled along the length and breadth of this country, from sea to sea. He saw beautiful green valleys, great woods, towering mountains and rocky precipices. He had never seen an island so rich, so diverse in its landscapes. And then finally, approaching the rugged far western shore of this breathtaking land, he saw another island, a little way out to sea. Between him and this smaller island stretched vast green plains surrounded by high mountains, and from the highest mountain of all a great river flowed down through the land and spilled into the sea. At the mouth of that river stood a castle, the finest that Macsen had ever seen, and the door of the castle was open, so he went in.

Macsen found himself in a magnificent hall. Its roof was made of silver, its walls of glittering precious gems, and the great double doors were made of gold. Golden seats and silver tables filled the hall, and in the centre of it, two red-haired youths were playing a game which looked like chess. The game-board was made of silver, and the pieces on it were made of gold. The youths were clothed in jet-black satin; bands of red gold, encrusted with sparkling rubies and other fine gems, bound up their hair. They had shoes of fine new leather, fastened by buttons which also were made of gold.

Beside a pillar at the far end of the hall was a grey-haired, clear-browed man sitting in a chair of ivory, with two golden eagles carved into its back. The man, who gave the impression of immense power, had gold bracelets on his arms, many rings on his hands, and a golden torque around his neck; his hair was held back from his face with a golden diadem. A game-board was laid out on a low table before him, and he held a rod of gold in one hand and a steel file in the other. Macsen saw that he was carving out pieces which looked like chessmen for the board.

Next to him was a young woman, sitting in a great chair of red gold. She was so beautiful, so blindingly beautiful – she shone brighter than the midday sun – that Macsen could hardly bear to look at her. She wore a gown of white silk with gold clasps at her breast, and an overdress of gold cloth. The gold circlet on her head was studded with rubies and gems and pearls, and a girdle of gold was wrapped around her small waist. In Macsen's dream the woman rose from her seat; he walked towards her and took her in his arms, and then they sat down together in her great chair of gold. But just as he was turning to face her, into his dream crept the sound of dogs chafing at their leashes, and the sound of shields falling against each other, and the beating together of spear-shafts as the canopy constructed by his attendants collapsed, and the neighing of horses and the sound of men rousing themselves from sleep . . .

. . . and so the emperor awoke. But all he could think of was the beautiful woman in his dream, and the great love that he had felt for her. And so, with the saddest face and heaviest heart in the world, he returned with his hunting party to Rome.

For a full week, Macsen languished in his rooms. He didn't go out, or eat, or drink; no song or tale could interest him, and he couldn't be persuaded to do anything but sleep, for it was only in his dreams that he thought he might see her again. One day, Macsen's senior adviser told him that all the members of his court – indeed, all of the people of Rome – were whispering against him. 'Why are they doing this?' Macsen asked, and his adviser said, 'Because no one can get a word out of you, or an answer to a question, or a judgement on a matter of importance. And so they say you are no true lord.' And Macsen said, 'Bring to me the wisest men of Rome, and I will tell them why I am so sorrowful, and ask for their advice.'

The wise men of Rome were brought before the emperor. 'In a dream I saw a woman,' he said to them, 'and for lack of her there is neither life nor spirit in me.' Macsen told them the full story of his dream, and at the end of it the wise men answered, 'Lord, this is our counsel: that you send messengers to the three directions of the world to search for the land and for the woman in your dream, for surely they may be found. And the hope of good news will comfort you in the months ahead.'

So Macsen sent out messengers, and they journeyed throughout the world for a year, seeking information about the land he had sailed to in his dream, and the woman he had seen in the castle. But when the messengers came back to Rome, they knew no more than they had known when they set out. Macsen was filled with sorrow, and a great wave of hopelessness descended on him. Then his senior adviser spoke to him again. 'Lord,' he said, 'let us go out to hunt in exactly the same way you went on the day you had your dream, and we will see if we can trace the path that was laid out before you.' And so the emperor went out as if to hunt, and came again to the green wooded valley of the great river Tiber. 'This is the place!' he remembered, and then the details of his dream began to come back to him. 'This is where I was sleeping, and in my dream I followed the river westward to its source. This is where it begins, the path that was laid out for me in my dream.'

And so thirteen messengers set out from that place at Macsen's command. Soon they came to a high mountain, and on the other side of it were vast plains, and large rivers flowing through them. 'Look!' they exclaimed to each other. 'This must be the land which the emperor saw!' And as Macsen had instructed them, they travelled the full length of the greatest of the rivers until they came to its mouth at the sea, and there was the vast city, and the many-coloured high towers of the castle. The largest fleet in the world floated there in the harbour, with one ship that was larger and fairer than any of the others. And again they exclaimed, 'Look! This is the place that the emperor dreamed about!'

They took berths in the great ship and crossed the sea, and so it was that they came to the island of Britain. And they travelled across the island until they came to the great high mountain of Snowdon; then they journeyed on until they arrived in the territory of Arvon, and saw the Isle of Anglesey laid out before them. 'Look!' they said to each other in wonderment. 'Here at last is the island the emperor saw in his sleep!' They made their way finally to Aber Sain, and to a great castle at the mouth of the river. The door of the castle was open, and they went in, and entered into a marvellous, rich hall. And there in the hall were two young men playing a game which looked like chess, and a grey-haired man in an ivory chair carving golden chessmen, and a beautiful young woman beside him, sitting in a chair of gold.

The messengers knelt and greeted the woman, hailing her as the empress of Rome. She frowned at them and said, 'You look and behave as if you are honourable men, and so why do you mock me?' The messengers assured her that it was no mockery. 'The emperor of Rome himself has seen you in a dream, and now he has fallen in love and cannot live without you. So tell us: will you go with us to Rome and be made empress?' And the young woman laughed at the messengers and said, 'If it is true that the emperor of Rome loves me, let him come here himself to find me.'

So the messengers hurried back to Rome, and told Macsen what they had seen. 'We will be your guides, lord,' they said to him, 'over sea and over land, to the place where the woman you love lives. We know her name, and her kindred, and her race.'

And so Macsen set off at once, with his army at his back. They landed in the island of Britain and Macsen conquered it, taking it from Beli the son of Manogan and his sons, all of whom he drove back to the sea. After his conquests he rode on to Arvon, and at Aber Sain he recognised the castle from his dream. He hurried through its wide-open door, and on he strode into the magnificent hall, and there at its centre he saw Kynan and Adeon, the sons of

Euday, playing at *gwyddbwyll*, the ancient game of destiny and divination. And he saw Euday himself, the son of Caradawc, sitting on a chair of ivory, carving out golden men for his own golden game-board. And there beside Euday, sitting on a chair of gold, was his daughter, the maiden Macsen had seen in his dream. He knew now that her name was Elen.

Macsen knelt before Elen and said, 'Empress of Rome, all hail!' That night, she became his bride.

The next morning, as was customary, Elen asked Macsen for a wedding gift. He told her to name whatever she wanted, and he would see that it was done. So Elen asked to have the island of Britain for her father: all the land from the Channel to the Irish Sea. She asked for the three adjacent islands for herself, to hold under her title of Empress of Rome. And she asked finally that three great castles should be made for her, in whatever places she might choose in the island of Britain. To all of this Macsen agreed.

Elen chose to have the greatest of her three castles built at Arvon, and Macsen stayed there with her. So that he would not be home-sick, earth from Rome was brought onto the site of the new castle. After that, the two other castles were built for her at Caerleon and Carmarthen. When the castles were finished, Elen looked around her and declared that she would create great roads which connected one castle to another, and which crossed the island of Britain. So Elen it was who caused the great roads of the land to be built, and her army watched over her roads and used them to travel up and down the country to keep it safe. And that is why they are called Sarnau Elen: the Causeways of Elen. For Elen was a native of this land, and the men of Britain would not have built such great roads for anyone other than her.

~

Elen it was who built the roads, and so it is that some call her Elen of the Ways. It's not as unlikely an idea as it may sound: in his ground-breaking book *The Ancient Paths*,[2] historian Graham

Robb argues convincingly that many of the roads attributed to the Romans actually were founded on old Celtic tracks which already formed a great network across Europe. These long, straight roads were created after exacting surveys and precise geometric analyses, because the Celtic peoples were surprisingly sophisticated astronomers and engineers. And so it is entirely possibly that these old causeways which are known as Sarnau Elen, as well as other such roads, were founded on paths which had been constructed and used by native people long before the arrival of the Romans. In this respect, it's interesting that Elen has her road-building equivalents in other Celtic countries. In Brittany, for example, the giantess Ahès, the old goddess of the Osmises, the Gaulish tribes who occupied the land before the arrival of the British settlers, is credited with the creation of causeways. The Roman roads throughout Brittany, then, are called the Chemins d'Ahès, or Henchou Ahes (in Breton), and the stories say that Ahès built the roads herself, carrying with her the rocks and stones which were needed. Following the same mythical thread, we find that 'Chemin d'Ahès' is also a name given in Brittany to the Milky Way.

Elen, like so many other female characters in *The Mabinogion*, is a representative of Sovereignty, the goddess of the land, and Macsen's dream is reminiscent of an *aisling* – the Irish word for a mystic vision in which a *spéirbhean* (literally, a 'sky-woman', a woman of the Otherworld who personifies the country of Ireland itself) appears to a hero. There are two main features of an *aisling*: it offers a vision of a beautiful Otherworldly woman who the dreamer subsequently longs for, and it inspires the dreamer to set off on a quest to find and win the woman he has seen in his dream. This is what happens to Macsen, and Elen is the Otherworldly guide who reels him in along the thread of her dreampaths, bringing him to her so that he can serve the land as its king. The imagery in his dream is full of Otherworldly symbolism: Elen's two brothers are playing *gwyddbwyll* and Elen's father is carving new men for his own game-board. The *gwyddbwyll* board symbolises the land in Celtic mythology, and it is usually possessed by a king or a representative of Sovereignty. That Elen wields the power of Sovereignty is also clear from the fact that she summons Macsen to her; she will not go to him, even though he is the Emperor of Rome. As for Macsen: his worthiness to be king is determined not only by his success in the challenge that was set him in his *aisling* – to follow the dream-paths back to Elen – but in the way that he conducts himself, and so demonstrates his merit. Only Elen, as the representative of Sovereignty, can bestow the kingship on Macsen, and so the marriage between the two represents the ancient sacred marriage between king and land.

The old story is very clear on this: that it was Elen who caused the roads to be built, not Macsen. The story firmly states that the men of Britain would have allowed the roads to be built for no one but her, because she was 'native to the land': the land's representative. She might have determined that an alliance with Rome was appropriate for her nation at that time, but both the power and the guardianship of the land remained hers. It might be that the sites of the three castles were chosen by Elen because they were already linked by older pathways; the story does not tell us. But the building of these roads is the reason why Elen has now come to be associated in the minds of many with the ancient native trackways, and why she has come to be known as Elen of the Ways. In the same spirit, Elen can be seen as an ally on our pilgrimage, an indigenous guide who accompanies us and helps us to find the way, as we forge our own pathways to reclaim the sources of our native wisdom.

It's time for our Heroine to set herself firmly on her way. She has survived her Descent. Now, she emerges out of the darkness and takes the first hesitant, stumbling steps along the hard path which lies ahead of her. Joseph Campbell refers to this part of his monomythic Hero's Journey as 'the Road of Trials', which he defines as a series of discrete tests, tasks or ordeals that the Hero must undergo (and in which he sometimes might fail) in order to achieve transformation. 'Dragons have now to be slain,' announces Campbell – but slaying isn't the Heroine's way. She would rather engage with the dragon than kill him, entice him into her purposely diverse team, harness his unique skills. The Heroine's path is different from, perhaps complementary to, that of the adventuring, all-conquering Hero. In the Otherworld, the long, hard process of transformation has been initiated; fragmented and dismembered by her experience in the dark, she starts now by searching for the lost pieces of herself. She needs to reveal her strengths as well as to uncover her weaknesses, and one of the key purposes of her Journey is to break through what she perceives to be her own limitations, so that she can not only identify her unique gifts, but develop the resources necessary to use them. The Journey requires her to explore the source of her own belonging, find her centre, begin to recover an understanding of her own place in the great, connected web of the world. She is walking her way back into being.

As in any pilgrimage, the path winds its way across unfamiliar, uneven territory, and this long, arduous Journey requires endurance, stamina and focus. There is nothing for it but to keep walking. Step by painful step; one foot in front of the other. The path will vanish behind you: there's no way back now. It's hard, to come back out of the dark. It's harder still, when you emerge, to hold onto the learning, to the gifts imparted by that deep, rich cauldron of wisdom whose potion you tasted while you were there. It's hard, once you understand just how far you must travel, to face up to the long, challenging road ahead.

That is why we must look for help along the way. The most valuable allies are those who teach us that we cannot succeed alone – and more, that it is meaningless to succeed alone, for an essential feature of the Heroine's Journey is uncovering the power of community. There are many kinds of allies, and some of them are human. People who help us to find the path, or who help to keep us safe as we pass along it. People who offer us sanctuary or wisdom; who teach us necessary skills or set us challenging tasks which help us to grow.

Moya McGinley's work is based at Cosán Ciúin, or Tranquil Paths,[3] the name which she gives to her four acres of land in County Leitrim in the north-west of Ireland. From her home there she offers 'sessions and teachings to nurture body, mind and spirit — encouraging rest, renewal, growth, healing and transformation'. Cosán Ciúin represents a dream come true for Moya, a warm forty-two-year-old with prematurely white hair, who laughs easily and has a rare ability to make you feel perfectly at home as soon as you walk through her door. As do Luna and Chara, two beautiful and deeply enthusiastic dogs who Moya rescued from the local pound. 'For as long as I can remember I have wanted to settle in a rural space, surrounded by trees and wildlife,' she tells me as she pours tea ('a hot drop') and offers up some particularly fine homemade scones with jam. We're sitting at an enormous wooden table in the large open-plan kitchen/living room of her lovely old cottage. 'When I was young I felt very connected to the natural world — especially trees — and to animals. I think that, as a lost wee child who didn't fit in the world or among her peers, nature was what saved me. I always wanted to pass that gift onto others.'

Although she quibbles with the word, Moya seems to have been set on a healing path from a very young age. She wanted to train as a nurse when she left school, but was persuaded that she should go to university first; so she did a degree in social science. But nursing still called to her, and eventually she gave in to it, left her job in youth services, and began her training. 'I loved nursing,' she says. 'I was an A&E nurse at first, and I always felt that it was a real privilege to be with people in that space. Later, I worked with a local palliative care team, helping them to set up complementary therapy services. But throughout my nursing career, the problem came, as it always had and always would come for me, with the system. It was very patriarchal: hierarchical, rigid, rule-bound, and purely focused on treating symptoms. Although people were talking about holistic medicine, there wasn't really much sign of it being put into practice. We never got to look below the surface, it was all about just damping down the physical symptoms. And there wasn't much spiritual care, which seems to me to be such an important part of healing someone.

'This way of doing things didn't feel right to me, or safe. People had no freedom to be creative in their work, and all the time I felt stifled and suffocated. I began to feel as if, by staying within the system, I was condoning it. A few years before I'd begun to train in a few different complementary therapies and practices – meditation, shamanic practices, life coaching – and started looking for some land in the country where I could practise, and do the kind of deep earth-based work which mattered to me.'

As soon as Moya saw the land she now lives on, she felt that it was the right place. Carved out into four relatively flat fields, surrounded by woodland, it lies at the bottom of a lovely green valley which, she tells me, creates a strong and beautiful echo. I ask Moya what her vision had been when she first came here.

'It was simple enough,' she says. 'I just wanted to create a haven. Some little centre where people could just . . . come. Just that. Somewhere they could come to step out of time, begin to look beyond the rat race that most people are caught up in. I never really had any fixed ideas beyond that; I'd had quite enough of fixed ideas! My intention was simply to move in, and then to see what would emerge from being here, out of the land itself. I had to spend three months or so renovating the cottage, and then my focus turned outside. Two of the four fields had been grazed and weren't in bad condition, but the rest of the land hadn't been touched in around twenty years, and was overrun with brambles and rushes – you couldn't even get into it in places. And so I began to clear some of the tangles, spending a lot of time out there, just being in it. I walked every inch of the place, again and again. And as I walked the land the idea of forming a labyrinth took hold.'

'Why a labyrinth?' I ask her, as we walk along a green path bordered by long grasses and straggly wildflowers, and soon find ourselves in the large open field where Moya tells me the labyrinth is situated. Standing on the edge of the field, I can't see it at first; all I can see is more long grass and straggly wildflowers. But I'm trusting that there's something out there.

'I'd never really thought about it before, but when the idea came to me, it made sense. For some time I'd been organising walking meditations with friends. We'd walk in places all over Ireland, sometimes for a day, sometimes for a weekend. We thought of those walks as pilgrimages. And that idea of pilgrimage, of purposeful walking, has been so important to me, a real anchor in my own life. Walking slowly on the land, often in bare feet. Feet on the earth, massaging the earth. And a labyrinth is another, more contained, form of walking meditation.'

Triple-spiral labyrinth, Cosán Ciúin, Leitrim, Ireland

But Moya didn't just create a conventional labyrinth. 'To use a classical labyrinth pattern didn't feel right, because that pattern comes from elsewhere, from another culture. I think it's so important to reclaim our own Irish ancestral traditions. And that has been my inspiration and my guide for everything I've done here at Cosán Ciúin. We have our own traditions here right under our feet; we don't need to be going somewhere else to find them. It's all here. The land is steeped in it. Something which is ours, which comes right out of this land and our interactions with it, as opposed to something we've just been told about, which belongs to another place, another culture.

'And so I imagined a triple-spiral labyrinth, because the triple spiral is an ancient symbol strongly rooted here in Ireland. And the idea of walking it onto the earth seemed so significant. This image has been present for thousands of years at the ancient sites of our land, carved into the stones at sacred places like Newgrange, for example, and I believe that experiencing the triple spiral in this way creates a strong sense of linking with our ancestors. As a symbol, it's often taken to represent rebirth and transformation. Which ultimately is the purpose of any pilgrimage.'

We walk into the field which is alive with early morning insects, and as Moya points it out to me, if I stand on tip-toes I can finally make out an enormous triple spiral pattern mowed into the long grass, complex but perfectly formed. I find myself wondering how on earth she managed to get it right on such a scale. It's a *big* labyrinth. She has already told me that, if you walk the entire path, along the three spirals to the centre and then back out again, the journey is two kilometres long.

'To begin with,' she says, 'it was important to me that the labyrinth was as natural as possible. I feel it should be impermanent, just a path mown into the meadow. I wanted the land to be free to reclaim it, to return to being wild and natural if the time comes. So I wasn't imagining any great complicated infrastructure. But even so, I had no idea at all how to make it! Fortunately, when I was talking about it to a friend, she said that her husband would be great at figuring out such a thing, and the next thing I knew he'd sent me a design by email, very technical, telling me how I'd measure it, and all . . . I looked at it and it was all very impressive, but I still hadn't a clue how to get started, so Niall and Claire came down here, along with another friend, Marie, and we mapped it all out in sticks and tape in a single afternoon. And there it all rested, over the winter.

'In spring 2014 the land sprang to life with new growth and so I started mowing a path through the grass, rushes and wild-flowers that grew naturally in the field, following the pattern we'd staked out. And what I love most about this labyrinth is that it's not manicured. Some parts are boggy – like life, there are muddy patches which you can get stuck in! It truly is a living, growing evolving being – it changes week by week as the growth around it changes, and then it enters into a period of rest over winter. The only permanent thing I did was to plant birch trees on the turning points, to mark the spots.'

Moya chose birch partly for practical reasons, because it's a compact, narrow tree. But she chose it also because in the old Irish Ogham alphabet, which is based on native trees, the birch is the first letter. 'So, symbolically,' she says, 'birch is about new beginnings. And that is what the labyrinth is about. It's a rebirthing, as you spiral in from the edge towards the centre, and then walk the path back out again.'

The labyrinth is the perfect metaphor for the Heroine's Journey, and the beauty of a labyrinth is that it is not a maze. There are no dead ends, and you cannot take a wrong path – because although the path may twist or wind back on itself, it leads always to the centre. And there, at the centre of the labyrinth, no matter how many times you have been there, you might still discover new insights; you might uncover old wisdom or gain new know-ledge. Then you walk back out again, taking back out into the world the gifts that you have received in the centre.

Moya leaves me alone to walk the labyrinth, but her two black cats, Ash and Willow, follow me in and roll on the grass in front of me as I begin to walk. Turning back on myself at the centre of the first spiral, I am startled by a flash of warm brown as Chara hurtles past, completely unheeding of the nicely mown paths, resolutely and joyfully following her own bliss. The morning is bright and warm, and it is early enough in the summer that the midges aren't yet biting. The only sound in the valley is the song of birds. I set one foot in front of the other, walking slowly, sometimes closing my eyes and lifting my face to the sun, sometimes watching the ground under my feet. Going in and coming out again, circling around as if I am a partner in some strange, archaic dance with the land. At the centre of each spiral I stand still for a moment, wondering what I will take back out with me and then what I will bring to the centre. And so I come to see for myself that the process of meditatively walking a labyrinth is indeed reminiscent of a pilgrimage, and to understand why it was that during the Middle Ages the practice of walking the labyrinth at great Christian sites like Chartres became entangled with the pilgrimage tradition. Labyrinths created in the stone floors of the cathedrals often marked the end of the pilgrim's journey, and so became a symbol for the spiritual journey which they had undertaken, assisting with the process of integration. And as I emerge two kilometres later to the welcoming wag of Luna's tail, I am calmer, surer and smiling.

Although it was Moya's unique labyrinth which initially drew me here, I find other treasures at Cosán Ciúin. There is an 'Ogham wood', planted with representatives of each of the twenty trees in the Ogham alphabet – the old runic language which is often carved into ancient stones and pillars. 'Again,' Moya tells me, as we walk through a field planted with saplings, each section labelled with the relevant Ogham rune, 'planting an Ogham wood is about focusing on our old traditions and customs. And reclaiming those traditions is all about inspiring others. If someone comes here and has a sense of connection to our ancestral energy, to the long history of our belonging to the land, then we can pass it down to new generations who will learn something from us about how to be in the world. Ogham is about a connection to that older time and place, and to our ancestors. Like the labyrinth, it's about understanding and then keeping the significance of the old ways.

And they're all about connecting us to the natural world, showing us how to be fully part of it. Trees connect us deep, deep to the earth. There's a wisdom in trees. Each tree has a different energy and something to impart to us.'

As we walk back to the house, Moya talks about other projects she's working on, and her future plans. 'In autumn 2014 a large polytunnel was erected which will house home-grown produce – vegetables, fruits, herbs and plants. We created a fire pit at the site of an ancient *fulacht fia*, a Bronze-Age cooking pit. And in November 2014 the *culú* was dreamed into being beside the fire-pit. *Cúlú* is an Irish word meaning "retreat", and the *cúlú* will be used in many ways. It can be covered and used as the old sweat-houses were used for purification purposes; it can represent a cave, the womb of the earth, to allow retreat and contemplation. As with everything here at Cosán Ciúin, I have no doubt that it will evolve over time.'

'And for the future?' I ask. She stops and points to a thicket in a nearby field.

'There's an old well over there which is very overgrown – I hope to clear and renovate it. Ancient wells still hold a lot of significance here in Ireland. This one is close to the *fulacht fia* and was likely the source of water for it. Ultimately, I plan to create a learning space in one of the sheds. Looking at old maps from the 1800s, I discovered that there was once a schoolhouse on this site. So I'd like to continue that history of learning, offering workshops and retreats so that people can come and be immersed in nature. I see the land as a big healing force. I feel as if the land here is getting ready for it. So, to go back to your earlier question, I suppose my overall vision now is all about bringing people here to show them ways of reconnecting with the land, ways of remembering.'

I wonder whether Moya sees herself, along with the land here at Cosán Ciúin, as a kind of guide to help people find their own paths in life. Beautifully modest, she demurs, but eventually I extract her agreement. 'I guess so,' she says. 'My passion is teaching.

I suppose the way I work is all about path-finding, path-showing. And I think what I bring to this work above all is the ability to hold space for people while they connect, and learn. I want this to be a safe place that people can step into, and to keep them safe while whatever needs to happen for them, happens. I like to think I can walk with people for a little while, as they walk along the path of their life.'

We all need allies to help us on our journey. Our European folk and fairy stories are full of them, and many come in human form: the wise old woman in the woods who offers advice, the fairy godmother who offers gifts . . . The kind of allies we're talking about here are different from the friends and family who might support us as we struggle along our path: more likely than not, they are people who enter our lives only briefly, offering up a clue or two which points us in the direction we need to go.

I happened upon my first such ally when I was twenty-one, visiting my mother in those first few months after she'd packed up and moved to her tiny cottage in Wales. So fleeting was her presence in my life that the significance I assign her sometimes seems out of all proportion. But there she was: Lorna, a woman probably in her early thirties, who lived alone in a tiny, crumbling old cottage at the top of a hill. There was no road in, only a long, steep, narrow footpath, and the dark, damp house she occupied had no electricity or running water. My mother knew her well enough, but I didn't ever find out much about her; I knew only that she had once practised as a nurse, but was now practising astrology. I didn't make friends easily in those days; I was reticent and gave little away. And I was in awe of Lorna's strength of character, her solitary self-sufficiency; I was in awe of her simply because she could chop her own wood. Because she wasn't afraid to live up a hill by herself; because she loved living close to the land. Because she was free. There was a part of me that so badly wanted to be her – but I couldn't begin to imagine how. Lorna was everything I was not: clear about her own needs and boundaries, courageous, intrepid. She might refuse to be part of what she called 'the system', but I was still oh so young – and wouldn't it be a failure to live like that?

But Lorna was so obviously not a failure; she was living in precisely the way she wanted to live at the time – and then, after a couple of years, she moved on. I held on to the image I had of her for many years, an image of what it might be like to be a resourceful, resilient woman who seemed to be, in every way that has ever mattered to me, free. *If Lorna could do it*, I thought, wondering ten years later whether it was possible to survive without a regular salary in a very basic partially renovated cottage in the wilds of Connemara. *If Lorna could do it*, again, taking another leap of faith another ten years down the line . . .

There are human allies, for sure, but for women especially, so many of our allies in the old stories are animals – from the birds who sing of truths and secrets, to the ants who help sort the grain – and so it is in mythological and folk traditions from all over the world. In Celtic mythology, there is an especially close affinity between animals and women. Women are not just helped by animals, they are accompanied by them, and often (as in the case of the Irish crow-goddess, the Morrigan) take on their forms. The Ceridwen story, which we encountered in the last chapter, is in many senses a story about becoming animal. Ceridwen initiates the shape-shifting dance with Gwion Bach; in order to be rebirthed as the greatest of all bards, he himself must learn what it is to become animal, to understand not only the wisdom of humans, but the unique and very different forms of knowledge possessed by the non-humans who share the planet with us.

This is the real importance of animal allies in our native traditions: that by understanding what it is to become animal, we participate in an ancient form of knowledge – a knowledge of the body and the senses, rather than merely of the intellect. Animals are teachers, and more often than not it is women who mediate their teachings. The most common companions of divine women[4] are snakes, horses, dogs and birds, and each of these creatures offers a different kind of knowledge and wisdom. This ancient perception of animals as so much more than mere companions, so much more than just a source of food, can't be assimilated into the worldview of a society which sees animals as inferior to humans, devoid of emotion and intelligence, and lacking in spirit or soul. But coming to understand our kinship with them is an important part of truly seeing ourselves as part of the web of life on this planet, and our stories tell us that, above all, it is the gift of women to bring this understanding to the world.

Perhaps because we have the capability of giving birth, perhaps because of the intensely physical cyclicity of menstruation, women have a deep, intuitive understanding that we too are animals, belonging to a world filled with other living things which are like us in more ways than they are different from us. Women too have been declared to be inferior to men; we know what it is to be afraid, and to be hunted. It's only natural, then, that we should closely identify with animals, and embrace them as allies and as teachers on our journey. But with that kinship comes responsibility, and so perhaps it is time to reclaim our ancient role as Mistress of the Beasts, as their protectors; perhaps it is time to guard them as they have so often guarded us. To insist on recognition for knowledge and intelligence in all its forms, no matter how unlike us those forms might be. And by accepting animals as our equals and our allies, by helping and respecting them, we help ourselves: not only do we share in their knowledge and wisdom, but we make of the world a less lonely place.

Allies are there to help us during the tests we will inevitably face as we follow the path of our pilgrimage. Allies help us prevail. In all the old stories, the Otherworld was above all things a testing ground, and as we travel along our way we will find our share of adversaries and obstacles. They'll test our strength and resolve, and sometimes the obstacles which are presented to us will seem insuperable. Some will be internal – self-doubt, fear, negativity – and some will be external: there will always be those who try to trick us, to lead us down dead ends. But it is the testing which makes us strong; the testing which helps us to learn. The old stories teach us this, too, and so we find ourselves at Gorsedd Arberth, a mound in the green and gently wooded hills of Dyfed, South Wales. It is the place where the story of Rhiannon, a prominent and strong-minded figure in early Welsh mythology,[5] begins.

~

The Testing of Rhiannon

There was a mound near the palace of Pwyll, king of Dyfed, which had a strange reputation: anyone who sat on the mound, it was said, would either suffer wounds and blows, or would see visions. One day Pwyll himself decided to visit this mound to see which of those things would happen to him, and as he sat on top of it he saw a beautiful woman in golden robes riding below the hill on a shining white horse, with three birds flying around her head. She went past so quickly that Pwyll had no time to call down and ask her name, so he sent a rider to pursue her. But no matter how fast the rider went, he couldn't catch up with her, even though she seemed to be riding quite sedately.

The next day Pwyll returned to the mound, hoping to see the beautiful woman again. But although she rode past in just the same way, the rider who Pwyll sent after her still could not catch up. On the third day, Pwyll himself pursued the woman, but he did no better in reaching her, no matter how hard he pressed his horse. In desperation he abandoned his pride and called out to her, asking her to wait. 'I will gladly wait,' she said to him, 'though it would have been better for your horse if you had asked before!' She introduced herself as Rhiannon, the daughter of Heyvedd the Old, of the Otherworld, and she told him her story.

She was trying, she said, to avoid a marriage which had been arranged for her against her will, to a nobleman called Gwawl ap Clud. She said that she would rather choose her own husband, and as it happened, she was thinking she might marry Pwyll, if he would agree. Pwyll agreed wholeheartedly, and so Rhiannon told him that she would marry him in a year's time.

The year soon passed, and Pwyll journeyed to the palace of Rhiannon's father for the wedding feast. Pwyll sat next to Rhiannon, and together they greeted their guests. One of them, a large, noble, brown-haired man, approached Pwyll and asked if he would grant him a favour. Generously, and as was the custom at wedding feasts, Pwyll said that he would – but, too late, Rhiannon rebuked him for his foolishness. She had seen that the man was Gwawl, her former suitor, and indeed, the favour he went on to ask of Pwyll was the gift of Rhiannon herself. Pwyll could not break his word, and so a wedding feast for Gwawl and Rhiannon was set to be held in a year's time. But before the grief-stricken Pwyll left her, Rhiannon took him to one side and gave him an empty bag, and told him how he might use it to thwart Gwawl when the time for the wedding came.

Following Rhiannon's instructions, Pwyll came secretly to Gwawl's wedding feast, disguised as a beggar. He asked Gwawl for a bagful of food, and as was the custom, Gwawl granted his request. And so Pwyll held out the bag that Rhiannon had given him – but no matter how much food was put into the bag, there was always room for more. Exasperated, Gwawl asked whether it would ever be filled, and Pwyll admitted that it was a magic bag and would not, unless a nobleman were to tread down the contents of the bag with both of his feet.

Impatient to be done with it all, and encouraged by Rhiannon, Gwawl rose from his seat and stepped into the bag. Pwyll quickly pulled it around him and tied it up, trapping Gwawl inside. Pwyll then called to his men, who were waiting outside the palace. They quickly overpowered and imprisoned Gwawl's men, and then they began, each in turn, to deliver blows to the bag. Gwawl soon begged for mercy, and Pwyll released him after making him promise to relinquish Rhiannon, and to leave without taking revenge. And so the wedding feast continued, and Pwyll and Rhiannon were married.

Pwyll took his new bride back to Dyfed where they lived together happily and ruled well. But three years passed before Rhiannon became pregnant, and during that time the people had begun to mutter against her, saying that Pwyll should not have brought a stranger to be their queen. Nevertheless, he refused to set Rhiannon aside, and now there was great rejoicing throughout the land when she eventually gave birth to a baby boy. But on the night of his birth, the child disappeared while Rhiannon and her six handmaidens slept. Her women woke first, and were terrified to find the baby gone. Fearing punishment, they decided to make it look as if Rhiannon had killed and eaten him. And so they killed a young dog, and laid its bones by Rhiannon, rubbing blood onto her face and hands. So it was that Rhiannon woke to find her baby gone, and the women accusing her of infanticide and cannibalism.

Despite the advice of his courtiers, Pwyll would not send his wife away, but he set her a penance instead: she must sit every day by the gate of the castle at the horse block, to tell her story to travellers. She must also offer to carry them into the castle on her back, as a beast of burden.

The same night that Rhiannon was giving birth to her lost son, another birth was taking place nearby. Teyrnon, the Lord of Gwent Is Coed, had a fine mare, and every year on the first of May, the mare would foal – but the colt would immediately disappear. Annoyed by these disappearances, Teyrnon took the mare into his house to let her foal there. She bore a large and beautiful colt, but then there was a tumult outside, and a clawed arm came in through the window and tried to drag the colt away. Teyrnon jumped up and cut off the arm, and so saved the colt; then he ran outside to discover who or what had been trying to steal his colt. He could not see anything in the darkness, and when he turned back to his house, he found an infant boy lying on the doorstep. Teyrnon and his wife decided to raise the boy as their own.

The boy grew unnaturally quickly and was strong and golden-haired, and Teyrnon began to see in him a resemblance to Pwyll. Thinking back on the news of Rhiannon and her punishment, it came to him that this must be their child. He and his wife decided that the child must be returned, and so the next day they set out, with the child riding the colt that had been born on the same night that he had been kidnapped. Great was the joy of Rhiannon and Pwyll when they came to the court and told the story, and returned the child to his true parents. They named the child Pryderi, and he became king of Dyfed in his turn, when Pwyll died.

~

Rhiannon, another representative of the goddess of Sovereignty, rides out of the Otherworld to take Dyfed's king, Pwyll, as her husband. She is feisty and resourceful, and at first she sets the pace in their relationship and seems to hold all the power. But even Rhiannon cannot escape the need for testing: she is distrusted by the people of Dyfed, betrayed by her own women, and doubted by her husband. She must endure her penance in order to survive, while nevertheless telling her story to all who would hear it, and firmly sticking to her own truth.

Like Rhiannon, above all we must uphold our own truths as we set off along our new path; we must always insist on telling our own stories. Our stories come directly from a woman's heart and mind, from the real, lived experience of inhabiting a woman's body and occupying a woman's place in the world. Generally, our stories will stand in stark contrast to the ideas of womanhood that are imposed upon us by the patriarchal world we live in – and it's important to critically examine those cultural myths of femininity which, if we succumb to them, will prevent us from completing our journey.

There are so many stories that are told about us and against us, some of them so cleverly and so extensively interwoven into the fabric of our daily lives that unpicking them can be hard. For young women especially, one of the most pervasive and pernicious myths of all is our culture's insistence on romantic love as the pinnacle of life's achievement. This isn't just something that crops up in old fairy stories or romantic pulp fiction: the new, contemporary stories we are constantly fed in books, movies and other forms of popular media still insist that, whatever distractions we may meet along the way, the real purpose of our lives is the acquisition of the 'one true love' that we're told everyone is looking for. The soul-mate, the perfect love. Once we achieve it, that story goes – once whichever modern-day equivalent of Prince Charming we might prefer, human or vampire, comes along and rescues us – everything else falls into place. It's all downhill from there; all we have to do is live 'happily ever after'.

Another such myth tells us that the only way to belong and to be popular – and therefore to be happy – is to conform to whatever expectations society might have of us, whether we are suited to them or not. Those expectations often focus on bearing children, along with the creation of a stable family unit and a fine, well-managed family home. Another myth declares that possessing and cultivating beauty is the best way to get ahead in the world. That good, healthy female sexuality is dependent on youth, beauty and the acquisition of consumer goods. Above all, that we are weaker and less clever than men, and so we must be dependent upon them.

But the truth is plain: we are neither stronger nor weaker, neither more nor less clever. The very basis for comparison lacks validity: we are, quite simply, strong and clever in different ways, and in order to create a world which works for all of us, women's different ways of being and relating to the world must be valued too – and valued for what they are, rather than held up against a standard which we can never meet. The myths of masculinity must also be challenged before healthier ways of being can replace these outworn and damaging images of femininity – but we have to start with ourselves.

So, as we progress along the path of our journey and begin to actively challenge the stories that have been told about us, about our roles and our place in the world, we must also learn how to outwit the domineering masculine which is so prevalent in our culture. Only then can the authentic wisdom of the feminine be recovered from the dark places where it has been buried; only then can the Voices of the Wells be heard again. And through all of the tests we face we must hold onto our own truth – the truth that we each have been forced to confront in the dark, deep caves of the Otherworld.

During the course of each of our journeys, we'll for sure come up against at least one great temptation; it's one of the major tests we'll have to endure. We may encounter situations or people who will seduce us off the path, and lead us to make decisions which prevent us from completing the journey. Each one of these temptations will present itself with its own set of unique dilemmas, and the choices we will be forced to make are unlikely to be easy. At every decision point along the way, we will need to stop and ask ourselves whether the path which we are proposing now to follow is a part of the true journey we set off on in the first place – and, if it is not, whether that path is worth giving up the journey for.

All too often, the temptation which challenges us most is the lure of an easy life: a nice house, a well-paid job; security rather than uncertainty. Often it comes in the form of a possible partner who, while being very attractive, does not share the values we've now come to espouse. Sometimes we do not realise that we are being tested; sometimes it seems as if we have no choices about the path we take. But we always have choices, and if we do find ourselves straying significantly from the path, it may be years before we can find our way back – if, indeed, we ever do.

One morning, fists clenched tightly at my sides, I walked into the shed where my husband was whiling away the hours re-arranging his vast collection of old bottles, cereal boxes and other antique advertising material for the umpteenth time that month, and told him that I was leaving him. My heart was pounding fit to burst and there it was again, that old clutching sensation at the base of my throat, and I didn't know whether I was shaking with terror or horror or some poisonous cocktail made up of a good measure of both.

After two years in Connemara it had become apparent that I couldn't stay. There was no fault in the place and my relationship with it, no flaw in my original determination to forge a life there. Yes, I was still struggling to get to grips with how I might earn a living – but the main and insuperable problem lay in my relationship with Len, which had always been fragile and now was failing under the weight of an excess of proximity.

Len was twenty years older than me, and I'd met him when I was a PhD student, unhappy and desperately isolated in London. I'd always had difficulty making close friends – no doubt in good part a function of the way I'd grown up, of the secrecy and hiding – but once I left school and said goodbye to the built-in community that comes along with it, it became close to impossible. I found it hard to create intimacy, to open up to anyone, and that meant that I found it particularly difficult to enter into romantic relationships. I'd had a couple of casual boyfriends during my teens, but since I'd left for university at eighteen I'd found myself living like a nun. I felt as if in some senses I'd been an adult for most of my life, which meant that boys, and later men, of my own age all too often seemed impossibly young. I just couldn't find a way to relate to them.

Perhaps, having been abandoned by mine as a very young child, it was inevitable that I'd fall for someone who was almost as old as my father. But in so many ways Len was exactly what I needed at the time. I was so deeply locked inside myself, so very alienated from everything and everyone around me, that I've often wondered what might have become of me if he hadn't happened along. And happen along he did, the friend of a neighbour, as I was topping up the battery of my small motorbike with water on the street outside the Tottenham flat I was then sharing with a young woman called Angela, who was a newly qualified vet. It was a hot Sunday afternoon, and I was inappropriately dressed for the job in a floaty blue summer dress, long hair flying around in the breeze. He later told me that he found the incongruity irresistible.

Len was funny and loved to laugh, and he taught me what I

had never properly learned as a child: how to play. He made connections with others effortlessly and instinctively, and by watching him make easy friends of complete strangers I finally began to understand how I might engage more easily with people. And also, I finally learned about physical pleasure. It was the beginning of a brand new awareness of and comfort with my own body, of a more physical, sensual way of being in the world.

But although Len was a very charismatic and creative man, over the years he had been incredibly difficult to live with. He had always had obsessive tendencies. It showed itself first in an ever-growing collection of 'memorabilia' which gradually took over every room of every house we had ever lived in. Shelves and shelves of dusty old tools, bottles, jars and other 'ornaments' lined every wall. Almost every time he went out he would return from some car boot sale or junk shop bearing another box of 'treasures' for which display space had to be found. This small stone cottage had become cluttered and claustrophobic, not to mention bizarre, and over the past two years he had also managed to fill up a large purpose-built shed.

Over the years, his obsessiveness had extended into his behaviour towards me, and now that I was spending all of my time with him in a small cottage, it was getting worse. I felt as if I had exchanged one prison for another. I have always needed long, cooling draughts of solitude to be able to participate fully in the world, but now I could hardly get out of the house alone. He was suspicious, jealous, distrustful. Not only was I feeling trapped and stifled, but I was becoming increasingly concerned about where his behaviour might lead.

Sometimes, if you have grown up in certain ways, a fear of being seen to fail can outweigh the personal cost of continuing to live in impossible circumstances. It took me a long time to accept that I would not be failing by leaving this marriage – I would be failing myself by staying. I badly needed to let go. The trouble is, when you have spent a childhood trying to mend broken things, holding yourself and your immediate environment together when everything looks as if it might fall apart, pretending to the world that everything is fine and normal when it is not, then the idea that you might yourself shatter something – anything at all – is unthinkable. But it wasn't just the marriage which I felt I couldn't give up on: equally unthinkable was the idea of walking away from my dream, because that little old cottage in Connemara represented to me everything that I held true, an image of everything that I wanted to become, everything that stood against the Wasteland I'd inhabited for my entire life.

Finally one morning, startled awake out of a dream of dungeons and chains and torture chambers, I curled my toes into the rough coir-matted floor at the side of the bed and discovered that the decision to leave had been made.

It wasn't at all easy to arrange. Quite apart from the fact that I had nowhere to go, Len was not a reasonable man. I knew that my only safe option was to just pack up and go, leaving him in possession of the cottage and pretty much everything else we owned. I had grown up in a low-income family; although I had been fed and clothed and had a roof over my head, living on very little was a familiar skill. I didn't need much – and yet leaving behind what little I now had was a hard thing to do. Partly because this dream had been entirely mine, though Len had followed willingly enough; and partly because he hadn't contributed financially in any significant way during our entire ten-year marriage. There was still a small short-term loan on the cottage which he, unemployed as ever, had no means of paying, and which besides was in my sole name. I would need to continue to pay off that loan over the coming three years, and at the same time, to keep myself fed and housed. I needed a proper job, and I needed it fast.

Never burn your bridges. I hadn't burned my bridges, and so it was all too easy to play it safe, and to accept a job offer which coincidentally came my way just at that time, from the American branch of the tobacco company I had once worked for.

Sometimes along the path, temptation comes in the form of

an easy way out; and if that was an important test on my journey then you could argue (and oh, how I have argued) that I failed it. In so many ways I was taking a step backwards. When the going got tough I ripped myself away from the land and ran back squealing to the safe, smug, paternal embrace of the Wasteland, exchanging my much-loved wellie boots and shabby peat-soaked waxed coat for the old straitjacket of smart shoes and business suits. It's only with the benefit of many years of agonising and hindsight that I've come to understand how this seemingly wrong choice led me to places – both internal and external – that I might otherwise never have known. It's taken me the best part of two soul-searching, self-flagellating decades to come to terms with that choice, and to acknowledge the benefits of the insights and learnings which would set me back firmly on my path some years later, but in a much more sure-footed way, and with so many more valuable skills and resources.

At the time, America was far enough away that I thought I'd feel safe there, and I intended the job to be temporary – maybe a year or two to tide me over during this difficult time, until I could regroup and figure out what I was going to do with the rest of my life. Because I still didn't know what it was, the work I'd always wanted to do that had heart and meaning. I knew only that I needed to live in a place where there was space to breathe, where there was the possibility of solitude and the freedom to make my own choices. I had always imagined that I wanted to write, but what I really wanted was to be a writer, because I had no urge to write any particular thing; I didn't feel as if I had anything original or compelling to say. The truth was, my vision was blocked. The years of academia followed by corporate life had deeply undermined my sense of who I was or who I might be, and I couldn't see any way to use the skills I'd acquired in a meaningful way.

For now, though, the decision was made and the words were said. After an impossibly difficult few days, I got myself to Shannon airport and on a plane to Atlanta, Georgia, from where I would take a connecting flight to the small, friendly city of Louisville, Kentucky. Although I needed the work, if this job I'd been offered had been in a big urban centre, then I'd have had to turn it down. Two years in Connemara had taught me that my days of concrete jungles, of commuting and choking on traffic fumes, were long gone; I needed green places in order to thrive. But I'd been to this beautiful state before, and I remembered the thickly wooded hills and gentle rolling fields of the 'blue grass' country, dotted with white-fenced horse farms. I remembered above all the vastness of the wider American landscape, and the sense of elation and freedom that comes with access to so much open space. I promised myself that I would immerse myself in America's desert and mountain wilderness whenever I could.

Back in the familiar comfort of a first-class airplane seat, torn between relief at having escaped from an impossible situation and guilt at abandoning my husband and my much-loved place, I allowed myself finally to chew over the deep uneasiness I was feeling about going back to work for a corporate entity. I had never had any interest in the world of profit and loss, shareholder value and 'stakeholder' dialogue, and after two years in the wilds of Connemara, such curious concerns had become utterly foreign to me, seeming to belong in some parallel universe which I could hardly believe I'd ever inhabited. But here I was back again anyway, simply because I needed an escape route and I needed a job.

In spite of my disquiet and my grief, I arrived in Kentucky with an open heart, and I loved it at once; there was something about the greenness of the land and the friendliness and deep courtesy of the people which reminded me somehow of Ireland and made me feel at home. And to my great pleasure, it soon became clear that my new colleagues also were infinitely nicer and kinder than any I had ever worked with before. In contrast to the ultra-conservative head-office arrogance and vicious, back-stabbing politicking I'd experienced back in England, the culture of this American subsidiary was changing rapidly, becoming more open, forward-looking, radical. And yet . . . I was nevertheless working for a tobacco company, and it was impossible to feel good about it.

When I first arrived in Kentucky I lived out in the country, not far away from the much-loved, multiple award-winning American writer and environmental activist Wendell Berry. Berry is a second-generation tobacco farmer who has always strongly supported tobacco-growing programmes in Kentucky, while acknowledging what he has called a 'serious moral predicament' because of the known health consequences of using tobacco.[6] I was in a serious moral predicament of my own. Every day of the five years that I eventually spent in America was filled with inner conflict.

On the one hand, I had what most people would have considered to be a very nice life. I was really very comfortable – too comfortable, for sure. My old childhood needs for safety and security were well satisfied. I was paid well, and at work I was appreciated by my colleagues; I soon took out a mortgage on a lovely little house in a subdivision on the outskirts of the city. I went west on vacation whenever I could manage it, falling in love with the desert clarity of Arizona and the mountain wilderness of Montana. But on the other hand, I had known, and still longed for, something more. I was very much aware that I had stepped off the path I had dreamed of for so long, and lived for too short a while. I felt as if I had fallen by the wayside.

Then, little by little, my initial love affair with America began to wear off. Once the novelty of a new place and a new independent life began to fade, as the months turned into a year and then two, it became clear to me that I had landed in a country to which I could feel very little connection. It was such a remarkable, beautiful country – but I was learning a lesson which would be emphatically reinforced in the years to come: place wasn't enough. I couldn't relate to the culture. I loved the open-hearted friendliness of so many of the people I met, but I didn't belong in an America which seemed to me often to be focused on the acquisition of wealth and status, on acquiescence and conformity as the only acceptable way of being, with its remarkably conservative politics and the constant, sinister presence of the deeply patriarchal religious Right. I foundered on this continent in which I had no history or ancestral connection, and I couldn't find a way to transplant my own native Celtic traditions there along with me. I for sure had no connection with, let alone right to, the traditions of the people who were native to this land. This, quite simply, wasn't in any sense my place.

Above all, although the work I was doing was now focused on advising the company on the development of safer cigarettes, I didn't know how to handle the 'moral predicament' (and the sheer unpleasantness, in a litigious and savagely anti-tobacco America) of continuing to work for a tobacco company. I still wasn't living the life I'd dreamed of, wasn't doing the meaningful work I'd always longed for, and the years were slipping by. I began to feel trapped, as if once again I had no choices, no way to pull myself free. I felt as if I couldn't breathe. And so, inevitably, my symptoms of panic returned: this time, with perfect resonance, taking the form of hyper-ventilation: a constant gasping for breath. I was thirty-seven years old, and it seemed to me that I was right back where I had started, seven years before. The Wasteland was all around me, and I was living in it again. But beyond a vague yearning for wilderness and wide open spaces, and a longing for something called 'home' which I couldn't have begun to define, still I had no real idea about what I might become instead. It was about time for a serious midlife crisis.

6

Moor and Bog

Retrieving the Buried Feminine

Meenderry bog, Donegal, Ireland

They say we are just embroiderers
but when we are working well, our tower turns
into burnished fire and the mantle flows
from our fingers, tumbling through the air
in loops of delight. There are always men
trapped in our weave. The sky calls their names
and they climb, trying to reach back
through the clouds to our blue fingers.
They glimpse us over the Tibetan Plateau,
our needles flashing like nimbus.
Each dancing thread and singing stitch
must be precisely placed in its matrix.

from 'Creation of the Himalayas' by Pascale Petit
after the painting 'Embroidering Earth's Mantle'
by Remedios Varo[1]

Time works differently in the bog. Sometimes, in this disquieting liminal zone in which decay and decomposition are largely suspended, it hardly seems to pass at all. The wide, flat immutability of the landscape, the low horizon, the stillness and intensity of the silence – all of these qualities could persuade you that a bog is not just set outside of time, but set apart from life. I have always loved moors and bogs, in the same way and for the same reasons as I have always loved deserts. The austere clarity of a bog doesn't assault your senses, like a rainforest; a bog creeps up on you, teaches you to appreciate the subtle beauties it holds, offers them up to you one or two at a time so that you may come to know them all the better. There is little to crowd them out.

Moor and bog isn't for everyone; these landscapes remain unloved and unappreciated by large numbers of people. Environmental journalist George Monbiot, for example, has called Britain's moors 'a burnt, blasted and largely empty land with the delightful ambience of a nuclear winter'.[2] But such judgements are arguably a failure both of knowledge and of imagination, for both moors and bogs have a rich ecology and heritage.

If you choose to look closely, to probe beyond their initially barren and inhospitable appearance, our moorlands and peatlands reveal an abundance of colour and texture. Winter comes clothed in all the subtle colours of grass and reeds: purple-black, burgundy red, sienna brown, yellow ochre. The bright sunshine yellow of scented gorse in spring gives way to the vibrant purple of late-summer heather, each of them a blessing for bees and other invertebrates. These 'blasted lands' are full of plants and flowers, along with many varieties of moss and lichen. These 'empty lands' are teeming with wildlife: frog, toad, hare, deer and otter; badger and fox wander on its fringes. Birds haunt it: peregrine falcon, hen harrier, kestrel and merlin; raven and crow; golden plover and dunlin; eagle and buzzard. Meadow pipits and stonechats nest in its tiny hollows. Jewel-winged dragonflies vie for airspace with an abundance of moths and butterflies; bog spiders while away the nights weaving sheets of soft webbing in which to drape the land, morning dewdrops hanging from them like crystals from fairy chandeliers.

My first bog-love was in Connemara, my second in the Outer Hebrides, and still I can't seem to give them up: here I am now in Donegal, in the green hollow of a sheltered river valley which cuts through a large area of blanket bog. That bog sprawls out towards the fertile coastal lowlands to the north and west, and ranges up the mountains to the south and east. The Seven Sisters, the Derryveagh Mountains, are the guardian spirits of this place. They gather round the fringes of the bog like a semicircle of elders, enclosing and protecting the land as it stretches across to the sea. An Earagail, or Errigal, the oratory; Mac Uchta, son of the mountain-breast; An Eachla Mhór, the great horse; Ard Loch na mBreac Beadaí, the heights of the loch of the canny trout; An Eachla Bheag, the little horse; Cnoc na Leargacha, hill of the Larkagh, and old sow-mother An Mhucais, or Muckish, the pig's back. Every name tells its own story; every mountain holds its own secret; every secret whispered down the scree slopes and sinking into the bog below.

Meenderry, our township, in the original Irish is Min Doire: plain of the oaks. There have been no oaks here for centuries; only bog remains, and the buried stumps of ages-old oak and deal which conjure up the ghosts of long-lost ancient forests. Each morning at first light, while the sheep are still sleeping in the fields and the land is quiet, the dogs and I set out to walk the bog roads, or boreens. From the Irish *bóithrín*, 'little road': a narrow lane, unpaved. Boreen. Such a delicious word, lingering in the mouth with a hint of yearning, almost a keening; full-bodied for sure, bursting with abundant flavours of wildflower, turf and tree. In this river valley which spreads out to the sea from the foot of An Earagail the boreens criss-cross the bog like a fractured web, the threads never quite meeting, each of them weaving through its own segment of the landscape and then casting itself off in the extremity of its own unique and secret place. The light is in constant motion – shifting, then settling for a while before shifting some more – in that way that you only ever really experience in the far west. Sun over An Mhucais, mist over An Earagail, dark clouds in between broken by insistent rays of light which dance, tease and flash through every gap. The only sound across the glen is the nearby fluttering of stonechats in the heather. The dogs play chase-and-tumble among dry tussocks of purple moor grass, bog rush and heather, and in the green valley below a heron shrieks, flying high along the path of the river.

There is rarely a plan for these morning walks, just an easy setting of feet one in front of the other, and a turn to the left or to the right on a sudden whim. Some mornings I am called to the blood-red ford and the fairy hill; some mornings An Eachla Bheag beckons, and I follow the long, winding, rising and falling track which ends at a turf stack close to its base.

Turf; always the turf. For this is working bog, and these rough roads which pass through it have been carved out and maintained down all the generations of families who have inhabited this land, for the sole purpose of cutting and bringing home the turf. From late autumn to early spring, the silence deep in the bog seems absolute – save for the trickle of a fast-flowing stream, or the call of a passing crow. But in the months between it teems with cutters and stackers, gatherers and baggers, till finally the black gold is taken home by peat warriors who have made their sacrifices to the god of horseflies, and who bear the scars inflicted by hordes of blood-sucking midges.

I have no turbary rights over this bog; my purpose here is different. I am engaging in the process of walking myself into this land. Feet pounding the tracks, eyes and ears open. Every inch of this old, old country sings of story, and I am walking the mythlines. The stories of rocks, and streams, and trees; the stories of fox, and badger, and hare; the stories of heron, and crow, and sparrowhawk. The story of Lugh of the Tuatha Dé Danann, who killed his own grandfather, Balor of the Evil Eye, in the Poisoned Glen near An Earagail with a spear crafted by Gobhniu, the smith of the gods. And as I walk, my own stories begin to take shape and merge with stories past. So it is that we give birth to new stories each morning, the land and I, along these old bog roads. I set out as one creature and may return home another.

Out in the black wet heart of the bog, the ground shines like the richest of chocolate puddings. Step off the track and there is always the fear of sinking in it up to your knees. If you live in the bogs, you learn to recognise the firmer land; you come quickly to know it by the texture of the grass, its colour, the particular way in which it grows. If you live in the bogs, under-standing the land on which you live is a necessity. 'Deceptive', people may call it – but the truth is that this is land which requires to be known. *Pay attention*, the bog says. *Where exactly will you put your feet? What is holding you now?* You must learn to look down, to examine and evaluate the earth before you step onto it. This is the lesson of the bog, and to love a bog is to learn to love uncertainty.

There is a sense of loss here sometimes, as you walk among the ghosts of dead oak and pine. And the ghosts of people too, for throughout northern and western Europe, Iron-Age bodies have been dug out of bogs, perfectly preserved. Our memories are sunk deep into the bog; pieces of ourselves, biding their time, waiting to be unearthed. Bog is both an archetypal and a geolog-ical memory-bank, said Irish poet Seamus Heaney: a 'dark casket where we have found many of the clues to our past and to our cultural identity'.[3] Many of his bog poems focus on the ancient bodies preserved in peat, over eighty of which have been found in Ireland. They are believed to represent ritual sacrifices to the goddess of Sovereignty, who needed a new mate to bed with her each winter to ensure the renewal and fertility of the land come spring.

To Heaney, bogs are female, fertile, fecund. 'It is as if I am betrothed to them,' he writes, 'and I believe my betrothal happened one summer evening, thirty years ago, when another boy and myself stripped to the whit and bathed in a moss-hole, treading the liver-thick mud, unsettling a smoky muck off the bottom and coming out smeared and weedy and darkened. We dressed again and went home in our wet clothes . . . somehow initiated.'[4]

Somehow initiated. Dipped into the wetness of the Earth, the sticky black blood of menstruation and birth. 'The wet centre is bottomless,' Heaney writes in 'Bogland'.[5] The bog doesn't give up its secrets easily, but it calls you to uncover them nevertheless. The lure of a bog-pool, which beckons you over to look down on its mirrored surface, the perfect blue of the sky an antidote to the darkness of the peat. But when you stand over it, if you make it that far, all reflections disappear; you are swallowed up into the blackness. Reach down with your fingers if you dare. Who knows what you might touch? Who knows what mysteries you might uncover? To love a bog is to love what lies beneath, buried in the rich black butter. Will you go willingly, and sink into the welcoming dark?

~

The Buried Moon

A long time ago, the bogs were full of dark Things. Shadowy creatures and crawling horrors; scuttling, biting Things and wet, slimy sucking Things. Nobody knew much more about them than that. It wasn't so bad when the Moon was shining; then the dark Things would sneak away back into the crevices and hollows, and the people of the land could walk down the boreens unafraid, almost as safe as they were during the day. But when the Moon was dark and hidden in the night sky . . . well, then, it was a different story entirely, and the Things that dwelt in the darkness would come out and terrorise anyone who might happen to be passing by. Sometimes those people would not be seen again; sometimes they returned mad to the village.

It happened one day that the Moon heard about this: about the darkness that filled the bogs during her absence, and the dark Things associated with it. Being the good mother Moon that she is, she was sorry for the people of the land and wept over their pain. And then she dried her tears and decided that she'd better see what she could do about it, and so the Moon came down from the sky to the bogs to find out for herself what happened during the dark times. For the only bogs that she knew were those that were lit by her own beautiful light, with the reflection of her face in the pools and small lakes, and the pale beauty of wet rocks and the shining chandeliers of tears that dripped from the gorse bushes in the early morning dew.

At the end of the month, down from the sky the great Moon stepped, first wrapping herself in an enormous black cloak, with a big black hood over her shining white hair so that no one should know who she was. She trod the bog road and everything was dark, dark – dark but for the faint glimmer of stars in the pools, and the light that came from her own tiny white feet, peeping out of her enormous black cloak. The Moon drew her cloak tighter around her and trembled a little to see such dark, but on she went until the track ran out and she stepped as light as the wind from tussock to tussock between the greedy, gurgling waterholes in the deep, dark heart of the bog.

But just as she came near to an especially large dark pool her foot slipped on a flat wet rock, and she began to tumble in. She grabbed at a gorse bush to steady herself but the spiky leaves surprised and pained her and she let go and in she fell, deep into the still, dark pool. She looked up, trembling in the cold, and all around her she saw them – shadows and shifting Things, creeping towards her. She grabbed at a long bramble stalk to try to pull herself out, but as soon as she touched it, it twined itself around her wrists and held her fast. The more she pulled, the tighter it held, and its thorns bit into her pure white skin.

And as she stilled herself for a moment, wondering what she might do now, she heard a voice in the distance, calling out in a crusty old voice; and then she heard steps floundering along, squishing in the mud and slipping on the tufts; and finally through the darkness she made out a big white face with bright, frightened eyes. It was a man, and he had strayed off the path and become lost. Spotting the light that flickered out from her cloak as the Moon tried to free herself, he struggled on towards the pool, thinking that the light might mean help and safety. And when the Moon saw that he was coming closer and closer to the deep hole, she fought and fought to free herself, fearing that he too would fall and become trapped in the pool, and maybe even drown. So hard she fought that the black hood fell off her shining white hair, and the beautiful light that spilled out drove away the darkness and the terrors of the night.

Oh, the man cried with joy to see the light again, and to see the dark, shadowy Things fleeing back into the dark crevices of the bog, for they couldn't abide the light. And now finally he could see where he was, and where he needed to be, and so off he ran, back across to the boreen again, finding his way home. He was in such a hurry to get away that he hardly thought to wonder at the source of the light, or to look down at the brave mother Moon, who was so glad to see him safely back on his path that she forgot to call out to him for help.

And so again she struggled, thinking how fine it would be to be out of the bog again, pulling and fighting as if she were mad – but still the bramble held tight, and all that she succeeded in doing was spilling the black hood over her face again, so that the light went out and the darkness came back to the bog, and out again crawled the dark Things. With screeches and howls they crowded around the pool, mocking the Moon and snatching and beating at her, shrieking with rage and spite, swearing and snarling. They knew her for their old enemy: the one who drove them away into the dark corners, and kept them from working their wills. And so miserable was the Moon that she crouched down further into the dark pool, cold and shivering and lost.

The dark Things fought and squabbled about what they should do with her, till a pale light began to rise in the east, and dawn began to think about breaking. The dark Things saw that they were running out of time, and so all at once they caught hold of the Moon and shoved her even deeper into the pool, and two giant bogles went and found a huge heavy rock and rolled it on top of the pool, to keep her from rising again.

And there lay the Moon, buried in the bog, with no hope of help.

The days passed, and it was time for the new moon's coming – but the Moon did not come. And the nights remained dark, and all the evil Things ruled over the bog, wilder and madder than ever before. And so the people of the land went to the Wise Woman who lived in a small stone cottage in the old oak wood, and asked her if she could help them find out where the Moon had gone. The old woman looked in her book, and she looked in her brewpot, and finally she looked into her fire – but nothing could be seen of the Moon. And so the people went away, wailing.

The nights passed in darkness, and passed and passed until one evening, his memory jogged by a fleeting conversation he heard in the street, the man who had strayed into the bog began to wonder to himself whether the light that he had seen in the pool might not have been the Moon. But because he had been lost that night, he knew that he would not be able to find her again. So off he went with the other people, back to the Wise Woman in the old oak wood.

She listened to what he had to say; she looked in her book, and looked in her brewpot, and finally looked into her fire – and then she nodded her head. 'I see it now,' she said to them: 'I see where you will find the lost mother Moon.' And she told them how the men must go into the bogs, just before the night gathered, each one with a stone in his mouth and a hazel wand in his hand. And she told them the way that they must follow, and how they might recognise the place where the Moon was to be found.

The next night, off they all went together, the men of the village, led by a woman who carried a burning stick to light their way and to turn back the dark Things from the path. They travelled on through the growing dark, stumbling and fearful of the sighings and mutterings all around them, and the cold wet fingers which reached for them . . . but soon it was as the old woman had said, and they recognised the signs and came to the pool where the Moon lay buried. They stopped, amazed, for there was the huge stone, half in and half out of the water. But the lid did not fit tightly and through a crack they saw a sliver of light shining out from underneath, like a dying candle.

Taking the strength of all of the men together they lifted up the stone, and forever afterwards they were sure that just for a moment they saw a strange and beautiful face shining up at them out of the blackness of the water – but all at once they were blinded by the light which came so quickly and so dazzling, and they covered their eyes . . . and the next thing they knew, there was the full Moon back in the sky shining down at them, bright and beautiful and kind as ever, making the bog and its paths as clear as day, and stealing into all the dark corners.

~

What is it that lies buried in the bog? What truth is it about ourselves that we need to uncover during the course of our pilgrimage, and bring back out into the world? In many cultures, including our own, the moon is a symbol of women's ways of knowing and being: constantly waxing and waning, associated not just with the menstrual cycles of the female body, and so with motherhood, but with the wider sphere of death and rebirth. And so this very old tale from the Lincolnshire fens[6] is a story about the lost heart of the feminine, consigned to a grave in the black heart of the bog. The dark Things, trying to destroy the power of the Moon; hating her light and wanting to cover it up. The patriarchy, so afraid of female power – and shouldn't that give us hope? – that they went to extravagant lengths to suppress it, created new stories to cover it up. The witch-hunters, who long ago buried the Moon.

But nothing is lost forever in the bog, because the bog is no symbol of darkness and hopelessness: the bog is the power which preserves. The dark centre of the feminine, moist and sticky, holding all the secrets of sustaining life. The lost heart of our womanhood, deeply entombed by a culture awash with thorny brambles and vines which clutch at us to hold us down. Still, our light shines through whatever cracks we can prise open. The light of the moon, the qualities buried so deeply inside us that we have forgotten they even exist, let alone where to find them.

So at this stage of our journey, as we travel along this new and testing path, we must go deeply back inside ourselves and search for what it was which was lost from the world when it turned to Wasteland. We are searching for the buried Moon, for the lost Voices of the Wells. This is our core task in this part of our pilgrimage: to discover and then integrate into ourselves the feminine mystery which has been suppressed over countless centuries. Until we do that, we can't restore the balance which will lead us all out of the Wasteland.

What is this power? What is it, then, to be a woman? Perhaps more than anything, it is the wisdom of the physical, the sexuality and life-giving power of the female body which we must begin to reclaim. But we are fighting against a culture which has both denigrated and commodified the female body for millennia. Every day, in all parts of the world, women are confronted with myriad cultural and religious taboos about our bodies. Menstruation is a dirty secret, something to be sniggered at; menstruating women are somehow 'unclean'. We must cover our faces with veils; we must not breastfeed in public. We must conform to societal expectations of what the female body should be, and which are thrust in our faces over and over again. It is served up to us in the media, in advertising and marketing which offers up girls and women as little more than sexualised and eroticised objects, and in which women's bodies are portrayed as mere objects of desire, property for (male) consumption.

So it is that we are dehumanised. We become, like nature and its fragile, precious ecosystems, little more than objects of exploitation. We are packaged up and presented to the world in images of dismembered, fragmented and disconnected body parts; when we are offered up whole, it is in a role which requires us to cater to the needs and desires of others. Every day, we are confronted in the media with idealised images of a female beauty which is impossible to achieve precisely because it is air-brushed and artificial, and we are judged harshly when we fall short of it.

In her 1991 book *The Beauty Myth*,[7] Naomi Wolf argued that the situation has worsened as women have achieved greater liberation: 'During the past decade, women breached the power structure; meanwhile, eating disorders rose exponentially and cosmetic surgery became the fastest-growing specialty . . . pornography became the main media category, ahead of legitimate films and records combined, and thirty-three thousand American women told researchers that they would rather lose ten to fifteen pounds than achieve any other goal.' In a 1991 interview,[8] Wolf added, 'I contend that this obsession with beauty in the Western world – which has intensified in my lifetime – is, in fact, the last way men can defend themselves against women claiming power.' Twenty-five years later little has changed, and the rise of the internet has contributed greatly to the growing commodification of the female body, particularly in the context of easy access to pornographic material.

The damage to the female body, and to our sense of ourselves as healthy animals, extends beyond mere image: in every nation in the world, the exploitation is physical too. In many countries,

men control women's sexuality and our right (or not) to repro-
duce. We tolerate the intolerable, always at risk of rape, incest,
violence, abuse. Harassment on the streets is an ongoing problem:
nearly 90 per cent of women have experienced sexual harassment
by the age of nineteen,[9] and one in three have experienced it
in their place of work or study[10] – yet the vast majority of
victims never report it to the police. Being followed and leered
at in the street or groped on the train are considered such
normal daily occurrences that they aren't even spoken of, let
alone reported.[11]

I do not remember a time, especially when I was young, when
I ever felt safe in a woman's body. I learned early that being
female was dangerous, and to fear the night. *Don't look a strange
man in the eyes when you walk down a street, especially if there's no
one else around. Watch out for lonely places, don't let your guard down,
never imagine you're free from danger.* 'Take back the night?' A lovely
slogan, but we all knew it wasn't going to happen. We had no
power, and we lack it still, and words are never enough. And we
have been led to believe that this is just the way things are – yes,
such a pity, poor things – and that we are powerless – because
any power we might once have had has been systematically
stripped away from us, so thoroughly and effectively and over so
long a period of time that we can hardly even imagine what it
might look like. So where do we find it, and how do we reclaim
it, that deep generative wisdom of the female body, the wisdom
of our sexuality and the great gift of giving birth?

As always, the stories show us the way. The old stories, the
ones which tell us that women are the land, the body of the
Earth. The old stories, the ones in which the Earth is sacred, and
so women are sacred too: the force of creation, the givers of life.
The stories in which women are the bearers of the Grail, the
keepers of the cauldron of inspiration and rebirth. We are Mebd,
who offers the drink which intoxicates to the men who would
be kings. We are the Sheela-na-gig – no cultural taboos there,
just a vulva wide open and on full display, nailed to the wild

edges of the men's carefully constructed churches where they worship an inside god. Mebd, Sheela: the forces of creative ecstasy which are purely feminine.

This is the core of our task: to remake the world in the image of those stories. To respect and revere ourselves, and so to bring about a world in which women are respected and revered, recognised once again as holding the life-giving power of the Earth itself. We can reclaim that image in each of us: the creative, ecstatic, powerful feminine that each of us embodies in our own unique way. Lacking it, it is no wonder that we are grieving, alienated, imbalanced – that we cannot find a way to belong to a world which denies us permission to be what we are, and which teaches us to cover up not just our bodies but our feelings, our dreams, our intuition. There comes a point in each of our lives when we face a choice. Will we stay as we are, embracing the pale shadow of womanhood permitted us by the patriarchy? Or will we sink deep into the heart of the bog, and find out what it is to reclaim our creative power as women?

Lucy Pearce[12] is a thirty-four-year-old force of nature who runs an editing and proofreading business, offers popular online courses on creativity and self-publishing, and is the founder of Womancraft Publishing, which she describes as 'a revolutionary imprint dedicated to finding and sharing exciting new voices and powerful messages that are being overlooked, silenced or sanitised'. She's a writer – the author of four books about motherhood and creativity – and also an artist. She is also the mother of three young children. She manages all of this from her home in Shanagarry, on the south coast of County Cork, the village where she was born.

Being a mother is the frame of reference for Lucy's work and much of her life, and so she laughs uproariously when I tell her that not only is it an aspect of women's experience which I have missed out on completely, but that as a consequence I don't much think about it at all. Although there was a short period of time in my late thirties and early forties when I wondered whether I should have had children (the classic last-gasp ticking of the 'female fertility clock'?) the truth is quite simple: I never felt a strong enough urge. Len had two children from his first marriage (they were in their mid-to-late teens when I met him, so although we all got along nicely there was no need for me to take on the role of stepmother) and had had a vasectomy after his divorce, so the decision seemed to be out of my hands. And by the time I left him, I had learned enough about myself to understand that I would probably have subsumed myself entirely in motherhood, lost myself completely, if ever I'd had a child. I'd spent too much time worrying about my mother during my own childhood, always feeling that I was the one who had to take care of her. I was far too good at caring for others and putting them first; utterly conditioned to believe that no one I loved could possibly get along without me. If I'd been a mother, I'd have simply vanished.

We might not share the experience of motherhood, then, but what Lucy and I do share is a recognition of the immense importance of a sense of place and belonging in our lives. Although she was taken to live in England as a child, the longing for Shanagarry never left her, and she moved back here full-time as soon as her son was born, nine years ago.

'The call to come back has always been huge,' she tells me. 'This place is my heartland, soul-land; I'm so deeply rooted in this landscape. There's something about the beach, the scale of the sea, the flow of the waves and tides, the lighthouse . . . this coast calls me when the furies race in my head. I walk the strand and the wind blows the anger from my mind. And the bog too, a precious limbo-land of tufted grass, hidden pools and sinking mud, full of migrating birds and rolling mists. It's wild heaven. Without this place, I don't think I would know who I was. And the land seems to be necessary for my creative process, in some way. All my creative work has been done here, in this village. It began here, like me.'

At the heart of that work is Lucy's belief that creativity is fundamental to women's way of being in the world, and that creativity is a revolutionary act. 'It's about using human energy to shape things into form, to revision the world,' she says. 'At its most basic level, of course, creativity is about making stuff. Taking something like wool, and turning it into a sweater. Or creating less tangible things, like taking the germ of an idea and turning it into a reality. But more than all that, creativity to me is a way of thinking and problem-solving, an imaginative approach to living. Creativity helps us to be more fully alive on every level, asking that we engage with life in a visceral and interactive way.'

'Visceral' seems to be the key word here; Lucy is very clear that women's creativity is a deeply embodied phenomenon. 'It's not just in our arms, our hands – it's in our hearts, breasts, wombs and vaginas, in our hormones and cycles of fertility. There is a juiciness to creativity, a succulence or a sensuality which both produces and is soothed by creating something. I think that creativity is pleasing to women on a very deep level, whatever form it might take – whether it's the feel of clay in our hands, the colours that work on us as we knit or sew, the meaning that we find in the words that we write, or the energising feel of movement as we dance and the music moves through our bodies.'

I'm curious about the ways in which Lucy sees women's menstrual cycles as intrinsic to our creative processes. Having been afflicted with the severe and debilitating pain of endometriosis for three to four days every month for thirty-five years of my adult life, right up until the (consequently very welcome) onset of menopause, I'm one of those women who find it very hard to conceive of menstruation as something to be celebrated. She explains the process to me, hands constantly moving – pushing back mid-brown chin-length hair from her face, rising up and down to emphasise a point.

'I see it as a kind of spiralling inwards and outwards, as if you were going in and out of a labyrinth. So when we ovulate, our energy peaks: it's a "doing" kind of energy, expansive, a time during which we like to interact with the world and with others. It's a fertile time: we release an egg, our feminine biological creation, into the womb. If it is fertilised by a sperm, our creative energies are directed towards it and our mothering energy is focused around the gestation of a new human life. If it isn't fertilised, our mothering energy remains full and expansive, and that energy can be turned towards creative projects. At this point in our menstrual cycle, then, we are outside the labyrinth, fully in the community, in the world.

'But as our hormones shift, we are called slowly back into the labyrinth, back towards our centre. This is the premenstrual phase, the beginning of a turning away from the world. Our mood can darken, our energy levels get lower, our patience shortens. And then, during menstruation itself, the "visioning" part of the creative process emerges. Our intuitive powers are greater, we have heightened sensitivity – for example, too much noise can take us away from our centre. We are sitting now in the dark heart of the labyrinth, resting, dreaming, shedding what's old and outworn. Gradually, the hormones shift again and our energy levels begin to rise along with our libido, and our desire to be back out in the world gets stronger, and so we spiral out of the labyrinth and re-engage with the world.'

The problem, of course, is that most women's lives don't allow them the opportunity to engage fully with those natural cycles. And so menstruation is something that most of us feel we have to ignore, trying to muddle through and stick to whatever daily routines we've become locked into. Our lives are too automated, too managed to allow time out. But that ability to take time to turn inwards for a while is nevertheless something that most women recognise as intrinsic to their wellbeing. This phenomenon is recognised by the rapidly growing, grassroots Red Tent movement,[13] which encourages the creation of 'Red Tents' in local communities: places where women can gather together, take time out simply to be, rather than to do; a place to incubate, dream, slow down, and share stories, laughter, songs and food.

The movement's focus is on honouring the cycles of womanhood: not just the monthly cycles of menstruation, but larger life cycles and transitions such as puberty and menopause.

And, of course, pregnancy; and Lucy is particularly fascinated by the burgeoning creativity which occurs during pregnancy or in the early stages of motherhood. When I first began to seriously explore what it might mean to be a woman, in my late thirties, I kept coming up against one question time and time again: if the most significant feminine archetypes relate to motherhood, especially in the context of the natural world – Mother Earth being the most obvious of them all – then what do they have to do with me? If my womb-space is 'broken' – those dysfunctional, painful periods as well as my failure to put that womb-space to the use for which it was intended in order to bear children – then by this society's reckoning, do I have the right to claim those archetypes of physical, creative womanhood at all? Can they ever belong to me, in any meaningful way? It took me a long time before I stopped feeling excluded from a true sense of woman-hood by my lack of experience of giving birth or mothering children, and there is still a tiny something in me which resists – and maybe sometimes resents – the focus on it in talk about what it is to be a woman. And yet, when Lucy describes the process, it seems both right and magical.

'For many women, something miraculous happens when they become pregnant or give birth. It sets off a creative renaissance which is the result of an incredibly complex shift of the woman's hormonal, emotional, physical and psychological states, along with a total shift in her social role, responsibilities and daily routine. She is blasted from her previous existence into an entirely new self. As a culture we hardly acknowledge what a massive shift simply becoming a mother is for any woman, let alone recognise or explore this creative renaissance that so many women experi-ence. Again, the problem is that once her belly has been filled with the life of another, her own inner creative life is expected to end. She is never told that she should follow her instincts and her heart – which means both to honour her children's needs for a mother's care, and her own need for a meaningful, creative life and work.'

Lucy believes that creativity is at its peak during pregnancy – though the exhaustion which most women feel during these long months might often argue against its practical expression. Nevertheless, she says, the real problems with most women's creative processes begin to arise just at this point, precisely because of this overwhelmingly powerful set of societal expectations which kicks right in.

'The world says you should have a nice tidy house, live only for your children. But as a creative woman, I can't live like that. I say, sod the washing up, go and get your hands dirty, write at this moment, because it matters, and the children can eat some crackers for now. That's so hard for most women, because we've been socially conditioned to do what is expected of us. And if I put my own desires, dreams, visions and priorities ahead of those laid down for me by our culture, if I follow my creativity, and the wisdom of my body, I might not look like what I'm supposed to look like in your eyes. And you'll judge me harshly for it. The pull and tie of children can be challenging, and society says all your energy should be focused on them. The Earth Mother is the archetype that women are supposed to be in our culture – someone who is self-effacing, deeply nourishing, who puts herself aside in order to give all of herself to nurturing others. This is the archetype which our culture deifies, which tells us what a mother should be.'

In Jungian terms, the Earth Mother is a reflection of the Good Mother archetype: the source of abundance and protection who stands in opposition to the archetypal Terrible Mother: the witch, siren or whore who is associated with sensuality, danger, darkness and death. 'The trouble with all of this,' Lucy continues, 'is not every woman is an Earth Mother, or can cope with living like that. So I was excited when I came across, in a book by Lyn Andrews, a second maternal female archetype which she says comes from the Mayan tradition: the Creative Rainbow Mother.'

I can see why the image resonated; if ever there was a Creative Rainbow Mother, I'd say it was Lucy. Everything around her is colourful, from her paintings which swirl and shimmer with layer upon layer of vivid colour, to her popular Pinterest boards, alive with vibrant art and photographs – her own work and that of others.

'The Creative Rainbow Mother is drawn by the ecstatic, and is often perceived, either in her own mind or those of others, as a bit of a misfit. She regularly needs to descend into her creative depths; she can't live, otherwise. She has the energy of the seer, the priestess, the artist, the poet. That sort of woman, in order to be a mother effectively, *inspires* her children rather than doing everything for them and living through them. Whilst the Earth Mother finds immense comfort, safety and satisfaction in marriage, domesticity, growing food and children, and enjoys order around her, the Creative Rainbow Mother regularly feels the need to fly free. And if she can't . . . well, the flip side of her is the Crazy Woman: depressed, unable to touch her power, tied, numb, self-medicating, addicted. Crazy Woman breaks out if we try to spend all our time out in the world, or serving others.'

The focus of much of Lucy's work and writing is in making women aware that there are these other, perfectly valid ways to mother: ways that aren't understood by a rigid and controlling society which doesn't allow women to be who and what they really are. 'I want to tell other women what it took me so long to find out,' she says, leaning forward for emphasis, all of her passion for her work evident in her voice. 'When I first came across it, that archetype of Creative Rainbow Mother made a lot of sense to me. Everyone used to call me an Earth Mother – I think because I wear hippy skirts and I breastfed my children, and I like cooking! But I'm really not, and this helped me to see there are other types of women and other ways to mother. It helped me to feel less judged, to feel okay about the deep pull I had to create and to do things sometimes away from the children. It's a real challenge to balance that dual pull. And it's so easy to feel judged against this other standard, and feel as if you're falling up short.'

Reclaiming our own particularly female forms of creativity is a critical part of reinstating the undervalued feminine principle in the world, but it's not as easy as it sounds to do that – the societal conditioning which pushes us in other directions can be so complete. 'Most of us women are, if truth be told, afraid of power: of truly engaging with our own creative power, or being seen to be powerful,' Lucy says. 'And that's completely understandable, because for most of history the only creative power women have had is that of creating, and sustaining, the lives of others.'

And this fact, of course, lies at the heart of my own equivocal reaction to archetypes of womanhood which focus on pregnancy and giving birth – because for centuries, that has been one of the few activities for which women have been valued, and the only source of their power. For centuries, every other form of power was actively withheld from us, denied on moral, political or religious grounds. If we don't choose to give birth, then, what are we for? Women like me would have been valued little, if at all.

Lucy agrees. 'And history is scattered with women who had to adopt male names in order to work or be published, women who wore britches just to be allowed a voice, to be someone in the world. There's been a long history of keeping women's power and creativity down either through physical violence or by threatening to remove her children, income or social status. Big and small acts which have taught women not to raise their voices.'

Today, I suggest to her, it's often argued that this is all a thing of the past: men no longer have the rights they once had to lock uncooperative wives away in asylums, for example, as they still did in countries like America and Britain less than a century ago. And it's true that the things which threaten women in Western countries today are usually more subtle than the things which silenced our ancestors – though in other parts of the world very little has changed. But the tools of control remain the same: guilt, shame and fear.

Lucy nods. 'Whether we have experienced this personally, or heard about it in history books, on some level we feel it in our bellies, in our bones. Consciously or unconsciously we know that to be a creative woman can entail huge risk. And this is what we have to overcome,' she says emphatically. 'This is why my driving passion is to empower women and inspire them to get their work out there, so that the world is full of our vibrant voices, creations and dreams. Our world needs all the colour and innovation we can give right now.'

It's not as easy as it might sound, this business of reclaiming the feminine; we have to dig deep. The problems we face in doing this are compounded by a sore lack of relevant female role models who inspire us, and who can offer up an image of someone that we might actually want to become. As a child, I never found such a creature among the unseen, powerless, dissatisfied women of my mother's generation, strangled as they were by the patriarchy. Later, as a young woman, the contemporary role models I was offered were all women who had found ways to become 'equal' by remodelling themselves on men, and working in the heart of the Wasteland. The first female judge; the first female head of an old-school old-boys' political party. Women who 'did well for themselves' in a consumption-driven world, or women who simply, for some other reason, had earned the title of 'celebrity'.

Sitting in Kentucky, approaching the end of the fourth decade of my life, I realised that not only had I never found a contemporary female role model I could relate to, but I didn't even know what a healthy woman looked like. What did it mean, really, to be an empowered woman? I had absolutely no clue. Where were her stories, and who spoke with her voice? It seemed as if the only women I'd ever found to admire had all lived long ago, and their challenges and breakthroughs were no longer open to or relevant to my generation. Those women more often than not were creative types, writers and artists who had broken the rules of the patriarchy and survived. But my attitude to and relationships with contemporary women were deeply troublesome, stemming for sure from my complicated relationship with my own mother. Psychological research shows that difficult mother-daughter relationships may mean that we struggle to feel nurtured, fail to fully nourish our bodies, emotions and instincts. We become unearthed, ungrounded; we have a poor sense of relatedness to the physical world.

All of those things applied to me. I was an only child, and I loved my mother deeply. But over a decade or so during my childhood and teenage years, as she struggled with regular bouts of binge-drinking, I in turn often struggled with a deep sense of abandonment. She had always been honest about the details of her own life, so that even at a very young age I understood and empathised with her longing for oblivion – but I nevertheless often felt lost, and anxious about the times when I was left to cope alone.

I had no cause to doubt my mother's love for me; I was clothed and fed and had a roof over my head. My mother was – and still is – an immensely strong and courageous person, with many admirable qualities, including an absolute determination never to give up, never to moan or complain or become bitter, and an unflagging and mischievous sense of humour. But nevertheless, the ambiguity of my experience of being mothered, this most critical and fundamental of all the experiences we ever have with the Feminine, had its consequences in other aspects of my life. I didn't relate at all to the broader cultural and mythical archetype of Mother; I didn't much trust other women, and I found it hard to make female friends. The truth is, I'd hardly ever thought about what it was to be a woman; I'd shied away from any consideration of it and set about becoming a good daughter of the patriarchy, forging my own unique way along someone else's defined road to success.

So, back in America, I was struggling again. I had achieved my freedom from Len; now we were divorced and my feelings of relief were immense. Although I was still paying off the loan on the Connemara cottage and (foolishly, out of guilt and that over-developed sense of responsibility I'd had ever since I was a child) supporting him financially, I was earning enough that I could start saving a little, after covering my bills and new mortgage, for whatever future I might finally come to imagine. But that was still the crux of the matter. What future, and where?

Alone, finding it hard to make meaningful friendships in this country and culture to which I could find no sense of belonging, I felt adrift – both physically and emotionally. I began now to look back at my own life, to think not only about what had brought me to this place, but what had made me the way I was. I began to wonder about the sources of my anxiety, and my fear. I began to wonder why I was so alienated from my own sex.

It was a strange business; I had been an introspective child and I was an introspective woman and I had always considered myself to be very self-aware. And I was a psychologist. So I was confident of being very clued in to the kinds of situations and issues which can lead to psychological dysfunction. I was the one that my friends had always turned to for insight and advice. But somehow or other I had managed to avoid ever really thinking about many of the consequences of my own childhood, and the ways in which it might have shaped me. I had always been aware of, and grateful for, the ways in which it had probably made me strong and self-reliant; I had completely failed to address all of the ways in which it also weakened me. I had certainly never even acknowledged, let alone thought of delving into, my difficulties in finding a true sense of my own embodied womanhood.

One day, out of the blue, sandwiched in an enormous pile of junk mail, a beautifully produced large-format catalogue from a company called Isabella landed in my mailbox. 'Gifts for awakening the spirit' was its subtitle, and if ever a spirit needed awakening, it was mine. Suddenly overcome by a hunger I had never before admitted to, I began to leaf through it. It was filled with the kind of books I never read, and products relating to activities I would never have indulged in. Books that were environmental, psychological, 'inspirational'; music for meditation, and chanting; symbolic jewellery, and all kinds of spiritually oriented gifts and accessories for the home. And then a book title caught my eye: *My Mama's Waltz: a Book for Daughters of Alcoholic Mothers.*[14]

I had hardly ever spoken to anyone about my mother's drinking. Len had known, of course, but I had only ever disclosed it to one or two other people in all the years that had passed. That was how it was: *keep it hidden*, I was always told; *don't tell anyone.* The need to keep the situation a secret made it seem like something that was shameful, something that made us – me – different from other 'normal' people. Somehow I had carried that burden with me into adulthood, because self-disclosure had always been anathema to me. Without even realising that it was happening, I had walked around for thirty years as if I still carried around some shameful secret, as if I still expected that other people would find me strange, as if I could only ever be an outsider – and that was my going-in position, in any social situation. I had closed myself down, because for sure if I opened myself up to anyone else, they would see right through to the heart of me, and the heart of me was something they would never understand and would almost certainly reject if they did. Now, reading through the description of this book, I was hungry to know that there might be others out there who felt the same. More than that – I badly wanted to know what they'd done about it.

I ordered *My Mama's Waltz*, and when it arrived I devoured it over the course of a weekend, reading some sections over and over again. And suddenly the world – and me – began to make sense. I began to understand why I had always found it so hard to make female friends; why I never trusted anyone else to take care of me – or of anything else, for that matter; why I always felt responsible for caring for everyone and everything. I began to understand why I couldn't tolerate chaos, why I couldn't even acknowledge, let alone cherish, the madwoman who lived inside me as she lives inside all of us.

Through all of this, I began also to understand the source of my anxiety. Early losses or abandonments, in whatever form they may come, or early failures of nurturing – all of these things make it difficult to trust: either people, or the world. The world becomes an uncertain place, a place which is separate from you and doesn't necessarily wish you well. I might have loved the land and its wild places, but a nurturing Mother Earth? The idea made no sense to me, at any level.

I had never trusted that there was a place for me in this world, and that I was an intrinsic part of it, because I had only ever felt like an outsider. And in such circumstances, instead of trust, you learn self-reliance – but also you learn anxiety, because you have come to believe that you are the only thing on the planet which can be counted on, and that is too great a burden for anyone to bear without sagging somehow under the weight. But more than anything, I began to understand why, because of my deep and determined dissociation from all that is perceived to be feminine, I always felt so disconnected from anything real and physical, and so readily locked myself away inside the perceived safety of my head. Why I had always struggled with a sense of belonging to the physical world; why I had always lacked a meaningful sense of embodiment, of genuine kinship to other animals.

I was now well aware that much of what was holding me in America, in this job, was fear. Fear of failing at things I could hardly even define. Fear, it seemed, was beginning to characterise my life, and I didn't like it. Now, bursting with all of these new insights, I wanted to get right to the heart of the things that made me anxious, rather than avoiding them. I was thirty-eight years old, and I wanted finally to find out what it was to burn, to risk, to fully live. I wanted to find out what it was that I'd buried so deeply inside of me for all those years. I wanted to feel connected to the world, to be physically present in it. I wanted to know what it was to be a woman. I wanted it all. I wanted to push myself, to test myself. And one bright, humid Kentucky summer morning, waking up screaming after a long, nightmarish dream of falling through the sky and crashing into a hard, unwelcoming earth, I thought I knew how.

Three days later, I turned up at the local airport for my first flying lesson.

It seemed to come out of nowhere, this decision to learn to fly, and it was a perplexing thing. Not just because I believed that people like me – physically timid working-class women from small industrial towns – didn't take up flying, but because flying was another of my fears. It wasn't a debilitating thing, but it was unpleasant, and the smaller the plane, the greater the anxiety. And now here I was, standing next to a frighteningly boyish nineteen-year-old from Montana into whose inexperienced hands I was about to place my life, watching a tiny two-seater Cessna bob up and down in the wind on the tarmac to which it was tied down. *Tied down?* As insubstantial an object as that?

I went through my introductory lesson in a state of sweat-soaked terror. But there was some bright, hard diamond at the core of me which I had never seen before, and which I certainly didn't under-stand, but which was absolutely hell-bent on carrying on. I half-fell out of the plane at the end of the thirty-minute flight – the longest thirty minutes of my life – because my legs had turned to jelly under me; but I staggered straight back into the flying school and I booked my next lesson there and then. I had become completely incomprehensible to myself; I had no idea what I thought I was doing. I only knew that I had to do it anyway. I drove home cackling like a mad creature, trapped in that uncomfortable, ambig-uous zone which occupies the territory between elation and terror.[15]

At every new stage during the several-months-long process of learning to fly, I was convinced that soon I would have to give up, certain that any day now I would come up against a challenge that I couldn't break through. Learning to stall the plane? Utterly impossible. Simulated engine fire which has us hurtling towards the ground at break-neck speed while we look for a safe place in which we might land, if we had to? You have to be joking! But somehow I made it through them all, absolutely sure during every new trial that I was going to die.

Until one morning, a long and testing five months after I took that first introductory lesson, I found myself alone in the two-seater Cessna from which my instructor had decamped. Sitting at the beginning of the runway, I was waiting for clearance to take off on my first solo flight.

In the early days the thought of flying solo had loomed ahead of me like a monster: a three-headed guardian at the threshold of paradise who'd laugh in my face and forbid me to pass. More recently I'd quite simply blocked it out, my focus firmly fixed just on getting through the lesson and trying to put the plane down on the ground in one piece. So many lessons; so many struggles. Lying in bed at night, dreaming about the shape of the runway at different altitudes. Hour after hour of touch-and-goes; practising landings, over and over again. Days when I'd thought I would never get the hang of it; days when I'd wanted to weep with frustration. A perfect set-up and the airplane within fifty feet of the runway – and then I'd blank out. 'Flare,' my instructor would bark, as it looked as if I'd forget to pull up on the yoke altogether and just crash head-long into the asphalt. 'How about you fly it down to the runway rather than driving it, next time?' Or I'd pull up too soon and float down the runway for a while before the airspeed bled away and we'd drop down with a bang. So many hurdles to overcome. And now, the biggest hurdle of all.

Alone. I'd never been alone in a plane before. The silence was oppressive, and the usually cramped space stretched out to infinity. The late January morning was cool, light and crystal clear: perfect flying weather. My mind was completely empty. When the clearance came for take-off, I didn't think at all; I just pushed the throttle in firmly and the plane hurtled down the runway. I can still taste the feeling; it was a moment of perfect purity. I was calm, I was clear, I was doing what I had been trained to do. And now that little plane wanted so badly to fly: freed from the burden of one more body she leaped from the ground, thrusting herself through the air, rising effortlessly, purring her pleasure. Airborne. I cleared the field and banked to the left, ascending all the while into a sky which had never been so blue. Time didn't just slow down: time simply was not. Suspended between heaven and earth, I could have been there for seconds or minutes or hours or maybe even for the whole of my life. Part of the plane, part of the sky.

In spite of the strange calm I knew there was terror, lodged there somewhere at the back of my mind. Elation still grappled with fear whenever I flew. But I became the fear and the fear became me and there was never any other option than to travel on through it: the only way back was to die. So I'd clench my teeth and hold tight to the yoke, and fly that little plane right into the cold blue fire of my fear. As it burned me, it changed me, and here was the result: I was more alive than I had ever been in my life. I was so . . . clear, so bright, so *vivid* that I feared I would catch light, burst into flame. I felt as if I had been asleep for forty years. This is what I needed: this risk, this wind rocking my wings. This is what I had been missing. This is what it meant to be alive – up there, balancing on the edge of death.

And so, after several months of twice-weekly lessons followed by two weeks of back-to-back lessons and cross-country solo flights in the New Mexican desert in spring 2000, I obtained my pilot's licence. It was and still remains the high point of my life, and I emerged from the long process transformed in ways that I never imagined possible. Above all, I emerged from it trusting not only that the air would support me, but that the Earth would welcome me home when I came back down. In the face of this activity which was so patently unsafe, I emerged feeling safer than I had at any other time in my life. I felt nurtured and supported and vividly connected to a world in which I was truly, physically, participating for the first time. And once I had that much-longed-for pink slip of paper in my hands, I never again suffered from all those old dreams which had plagued me since childhood: dreams of trying to fly but never being able to get more than an inch or two off the ground, always sinking back down and scraping it with my toes.

There were so many dimensions to flying. More than anything, it was a lesson in learning to let go, in relinquishing the tight control which I'd kept over every aspect of my life. And this was the fundamental change through which I weaned myself finally away from the safety of the patriarchy. For me, as for so many women, the way back out of the Wasteland could only begin with the relearning of instinct and what it was to truly inhabit my body. Strangely and unexpectedly, it was learning to fly which taught me how to do that. At this level of flight training you don't acquire the skills to fly on instruments alone through cloud: you fly under VFR, or Visual Flight Rules. You have to watch, to judge the plane's attitude while always looking down at the ground to see where you are going; you learn to feel the vibrations and motions of the plane around you, and to judge the currents and moods of the air you are flying through. You have to be aware of the cues coming from your body and to trust the evidence of your senses. You may be protected by the metal skin of an airplane around you, but, for me at least, flying was an intensely physical and sensory experience. I flew with my whole body. I had always deeply mistrusted the physical, but now, precisely because I had chosen to risk it, and believed that I risked it every time I stepped up into that tiny plane, I was fully alive in my body for the first time in my life.

But what happens, then, when you come back down to Earth, brimming over with new-found lightness and courage? Where do you go from there? And the old, old question: what kind of person will you now become? More to the point, what kind of *woman* will you now become? One humid morning in early summer, curled up on the white-painted wooden swing on my back porch, somewhere in some book that I was reading I found a poem entitled 'The Blanket Around Her'[16] by a writer called Joy Harjo. I also found an answer:

> oh woman
> remember who you are
> woman
> it is the whole earth

As I read the words, something in my heart split open. The whole *earth*? Woman? Me? I wanted to know who she was, this poet, that she could know such things, that she could have such a powerful sense of womanhood and value it so. How could I learn to value it in turn? How could I develop that certainty, that feeling of being the whole earth? That would be a sense of self-worth indeed; that would be a sense of belonging. And now that I had finally seen the possibility, I wanted it more than I'd ever wanted anything.

I discovered that Harjo was a member of the Mvskoke/Creek nation, and that many of the ideas and images in her writing came out of the traditions of her people. I found, and began to devour, other books by Native American women writers: Linda Hogan, Louise Erdrich, Leslie Marmon Silko. And through those writings I found myself turning back to my first loves – to myths and stories – to see where it came from, this beautiful sense of woman as the Earth. In those Native American traditions I found so many stories of women as creators: Changing Woman, Sky Woman; Grandmother Spider, who wove the world into being. Always, women as the bright, burning force of creation, women as the givers and sustainers of life.

I loved those stories that I found, but I was acutely aware that this wasn't my mythology, that it derived from a land and a culture that I didn't belong to. Where would I find such stories in my own traditions? Were there any such stories at all? As a child who devoured every book on mythology she could find, I had grown up with an encyclopaedic knowledge of Greek and Roman myths, but fascinating as they were they too sprang out of countries that I had no connection to; they didn't seem to say anything about my land, or my life.

Nevertheless, I found myself remembering that in the Greek tradition it was Gaia, the great Mother, who created and gave birth to the universe and to the Earth, and who was also the mother of all the other gods. The great Mother? . . . and yet I had been brought up in a Christian tradition in which there was no Mother – there was only a great Father, and in the creation story that he dealt out, women were merely afterthoughts, created for the benefit of men. Worse than that: those Christian stories taught us that it was Eve, the first woman, who destroyed the Garden of Eden, who let evil loose into the world. But then I remembered that the Christian traditions and the Hebrew traditions out of which they had grown didn't originally spring out of my native culture, either; they were imports from the desert lands, far away in the Middle East. And so what, really, were my own native traditions, the ones which grew out of the ground beneath my feet? What did they tell me about what it was to be a woman? Did they show me an image of woman as creator, of woman as the whole earth? Could they offer me that?

I retraced my steps, went back to the old Celtic myths which I had also glimpsed as a child in books of Celtic fairy tales, hero tales and Arthurian legends. And here I found it, after all, in the pages of books by Lady Gregory and W.B. Yeats, in *The Mabinogion*, and so many other classic texts.[17] There it had been, all along. Woman, the personification of the land; woman, the life-giving, creative power of the Earth. Danu, the great mother goddess of the Tuatha Dé Danann in Ireland; Dôn, the mother goddess of Wales; in both Scotland and Ireland, the Cailleach Bhéarra, the divine hag, the old woman who shaped the land. The goddess of Sovereignty, the *anima mundi*. This was more than just an interesting intellectual discovery, more than a mere revelation: I had finally found my place in the world. There in the Celtic and pre-Celtic traditions, there among so many other prehistoric cultures which had also looked to mother goddesses to explain the creation and nurturing of the Earth. Long before God the Father, there she was – God the Mother. Where did she vanish to, this great mother goddess? How did we women become so completely dispossessed? It wasn't that I wanted to replace a male god with a female god; it wasn't that I wanted to find a religion at all. I was simply looking for some sense that women might have worth. And I found it: there in the old stories of my own native land, I found it.

Filled with images of women creating, women weaving the world into being, I took up knitting. Thread by thread, stitch by stitch, I began to knit *myself* back into being. I had never thought of myself as being a particularly creative soul, but I discovered that creativity was a wide-ranging affair. I simply thought about what brought me joy, and I began to cultivate it. I dug my hands into this strange foreign soil, and I began to grow things. I began to reacquaint myself with the soft animal object that was my body. Slowly, spending more and more time outside, focusing on the wisdom of my senses rather than on what was going on inside my head, I began to weave myself back into the fabric of the Earth.

Some months later, I handed in my notice for a second time. I needed to go home, and home was the land of my ancestors. Home was simply the land. I was a woman, and I had begun to remember who I was. It was the whole earth.

When we uncover the buried feminine, we will always find there a strong creative element. But the important point about this creativity isn't just that we can harness it to sit around making nice things, however fine and nourishing an activity that might be. Creation, and so creativity, is the act of giving life, the nourishing and enhancement of life, in whatever way you choose to do it. And when we find our individual creative power, we can harness it and use it to fight for what we care about, to remake the world in our own image. But what might such a creative woman look like, and how might she do such a thing?

Some years later, I found a powerful example in the person of Alice Starmore, a textile designer who is internationally renowned for her richly illustrated books of knitting patterns based on Celtic and other traditional designs. Her work is inspired by the intricate patterns and rich colours of Celtic manuscripts and stonework, as well as by the landscape of the Isle of Lewis where she grew up. Alice's company Virtual Yarns[18] produces beautiful skeins of wool named after features and inhabitants (both real and mythic) of the Lewis landscape to which she is so deeply attached: Bogbean, Mountain Hare, Storm Petrel, Kelpie, Dulse, Selkie, and many more. 'My first language is Gaelic – one of the few remaining living fragments of Celtic heritage – and it was perfectly natural that I should create work rooted in my own language and culture,' she tells me. Alice comes from a long line of crofters and fishermen, generations of them who have lived in the same place, and she feels those roots very strongly. And so when she returns from her travels around the world, she comes home to a working croft in the tiny township of Gress, on the east coast of Lewis, where she cares for and breeds from a small herd of pedigree Highland cattle.

On a bright spring morning I drove across the island to Alice's modern but traditionally styled house, which looks out across the green fields where the cattle graze to the long pale sands of Gress beach. I was there to talk to her about her love of, and activism in support of, Lewis' bogs, and I discovered a woman who seems to be so inextricably connected to the huge moor on which she grew up that it would be hard to imagine her removed from this land. 'Oh, the land, of course,' she exclaims as she hands me a cup of tea and joins me at a long wooden table under the window in her elegant, understated living room. 'I know every hill, glen, loch, stream, here on this land. I can shut my eyes any time and be there. I can see the detail and the grand view; I can smell it. It's a comfort to me when I'm away. I can't imagine what it would be like to not feel a sense of belonging. To be adrift. But a sense of belonging for me is also about culture, not just the place. It's about the continuity of our culture. Each generation is another layer of this moor. My experience of it is shared by countless generations of people who've inhabited this land throughout the centuries. People who, hundreds and thousands of years ago, saw what I see now.'

Another name for the Isle of Lewis is Eilean na Mille Lochan – the Isle of a Thousand Lochs – but that number is an understatement, Alice tells me, because there are well over a thousand lochs of every shape and size, linked by networks of burns and rivers, and separated by jigsaw pieces of moor dotted with innumerable boggy pools. The view from any hilltop reveals an immense, intricate water system in which the land seems to play a supporting role. This great blanket bog stretches almost unbroken across the entire island, covering an area of roughly 450 square kilometres, over 70 per cent of the island's land mass. 'Northern Lewis is the largest undisturbed blanket bog left in Europe,' Alice says, 'and its importance as a rare and special habitat is equivalent to that of the Serengeti or the rainforest of Brazil. It is designated as a European Special Protection Area, and recognised by the United Nations as a special area of conservation.'

And yet not everyone can find it in themselves to love a bog. Echoing George Monbiot, former *Granta* editor Ian Jack said of Lewis' moor: 'What a vast, dead place: dark brown moors and black lochs under a grey sky, not a tree, hedge or house in sight, and all swept by a chill wet wind.'[19] But to Alice it is a landscape of intense beauty. 'I spent my childhood summers on the Lewis moors, and this unique landscape has been at the heart of my work for over thirty years. It's immensely rich. The rocks are patterned with crotal, cudbear and various *Cladonia* lichens; dog violets grow in the crevices along with grasses, sedges and ferns – it is an amazing panoply of colour and texture. In summer it whirs with life – moths, butterflies, damselflies . . . I simply don't see how you could ever call it dead!'

Alice's deep knowledge of and love for the moor derives in good part from the fact that, for six weeks during each summer of her childhood, her family moved from their house to their *àiridh* – a bothy or sheiling made of dry stone and thatched with rushes – on their ancestral *gearraidh* (pasture) on the moor just south of the main island town of Stornoway.

'In order to provide enough fodder for the cattle to survive the winter and early spring, it was necessary to take them away to moorland pastures for the summer months, so that the village pastures could be harvested for winter feed. Our summer hill grazing was on the far side of Stornoway, and so we had to undertake a long march with the cattle through the centre of the town and then over the hill and burn to the *àiridh*. It was a great way to spend your childhood.' Alice, now an articulate woman with long wavy grey hair, strong beautiful features and a quiet confidence which comes from being quite clear about her place in the world, belonged to the last generation to take part in this traditional form of transhumance.

She fears that the old intimacy with the moor has now been lost. 'When I was growing up, almost every feature, from hill and loch to tiny burn and hummock, had a name which bore testimony to the intimate knowledge and regard that Lewis people had for their moor. We knew those names and we knew the landscape, and that knowing gave us the freedom of it. Our parents could get on with their day and trust that we wouldn't get lost or drown in that vast network of lochs, burns and bogs. A respect for the bogs was instilled in us with stories of how, if you weren't careful, you could be sucked down to the centre of the earth and never seen again. This was a horror to which I responded with fear and fascination in equal measure.

'I always found the bogs terrifyingly beautiful and I spent many hours crawling as close as possible to the edges of the deep pools to catch a glimpse of the exotic life within. I might see two ferocious dragonfly larvae fighting to the death, or the flash of gold on the side of a great diving beetle as it barrelled up out of the depths to grab an unwary water boatman, or – best of all – a dragon or damsel larva emerging from the pool to climb up a bog bean or moor grass stem and start the metamorphosis in which it burst out of its skin, all pale and fragile. I would be spellbound as I watched it slowly pump fluid into its wings and colour into its body to become one of the most spectacular creatures on earth.'

Those long childhood days living on the moor connected Alice deeply to the land. 'I feel like it's part of me, and I am part of it. I belong to the very Earth itself. To us, out there on the moor for weeks on end, the land was real. Alexina, the oldest member of our community, was an expert sky reader, and one day, when we were packing up to go, she admitted that she was feeling very sad at the thought of *fàgail a' ghearraidh na aonar*: "leaving the pasture in loneliness". To us, the moor had a spirit, a heart and a soul, just as we had ourselves.'

That strong sense of the land as a living being inspired Alice's role in trying to defeat a 2005 planning application for a large-scale windfarm on the north Lewis moor, which would effectively have obliterated the larger part of this unique landscape. Lewis Wind Power Ltd had applied to the Western Isles Council for planning permission to site on it 234 turbines which would then have been, at 140 metres high, among the highest onshore turbines in the world. The resulting development would have constituted the largest wind farm in Europe, involving 200 kilometres of new roads and a vast number of overhead pylons to carry the generated electricity off the island. When the proposal was made public, local people led massive protests with the support of the Royal Society for the Protection of Birds and Scottish Natural Heritage, on the grounds that large-scale developments in such a fragile and important peatland would cause huge and irreversible damage to the area, altering the water pattern and the soil make-up, as well as causing the permanent loss of important habitat for wildlife.

In its comments on the proposal, the RSPB noted that the moor contained 9 per cent of the entire British population of red-throated divers, 8 per cent of the population of black-throated divers, 37 per cent of the population of dunlin, 8 per cent of the population of golden plovers, 10 per cent of the population of greenshank, 20 pairs of merlins and 5 pairs of golden eagles. Active peatlands aren't just unique landscapes from an ecological perspective: they act as both carbon sink and store, and have an important role in regulating climate change. Wetlands, including bogs, store over three times as much carbon for a given area as tropical rainforest. But when peatlands are disturbed, carbon dioxide is returned to the atmosphere.

The value of peatland is internationally recognised, and there is strong guidance towards preservation and restoration of bogs. In spite of this, peatlands, together with their unique mix of plants and animals, are a seriously endangered western European habitat. In Ireland, for example, over 80 per cent of their former extent has been lost. The idea that such landscapes are 'dead' places or 'blasted heaths' simply encourages people not to value them, and increases the threat of development.

Alice Starmore was one of the most vocal local protestors against the north Lewis windfarm proposal. She put together an exhibition of her own work[20] which was her response to suggestions by supporters of the development that the moor constituted 'Miles And Miles of Bugger-All'. Alice reclaimed the acronym and called her exhibition 'MAMBA: Miles And Miles of Beauty Astounding'. Her images incorporated photography, watercolour and drawing, blended with tapestries which included colours hand-dyed from the mosses, lichens and plants of the moorland. Her ultimate aim was to raise awareness of the moor and its rich and unique ecological and cultural heritage.

'I wanted to teach people to value the bog and the moor again. I think I succeeded to an extent: mainly with children, who learned something new from the exhibition, and then with the older generation, who were reminded of things they once knew intimately. That was good and encouraging. There are so few places in the developed world where people can live intimately with nature in its most elemental and awe-inspiring forms; where there really are no beaten tracks; where you can be alone with wildness and where every footstep is a journey into a world of colour, texture and life.'

But Alice's face is sad as she talks of how, in the 1960s, everything began to change as the effects of 'progress' hit even the remote Outer Hebrides, devaluing the moor in the minds of many Lewis people. 'Increasing affluence meant that more people had cars, and a crofter with a car could take a weekly drive to check on his stock. There was no need to live out on the *àiridh* with the animals. Why go and live there and wipe your backside with sphagnum when you could stay home and enjoy all your new conveniences? Those who clung to the old ways were just not "modern"! So, times have changed and the *àirighean* lie in ruins. Yes, there are now those – not only visitors, but islanders too – who find the moor a desolate place.'

A sense of responsibility for the land is a natural consequence of this deep sense of place, Alice argues, and that's why she fought so hard against the big windfarm proposal. On this occasion the protesters won the battle, and the proposal was refused by the Scottish Executive. But other, smaller windfarms have been constructed, and the land is still under threat. 'Now people have lost their connection with the land. Turned their backs on it. When did the moor become so devalued in a community where it meant so much and for so long? Many islanders now consider the moor to be a useless, featureless wasteland fit only for industrial development. They'd trade it all for money, street lights and hanging baskets. Such islanders no longer know their moor – and it is hard to care for something you do not know.'

7

The Enchanted Forest

Restoring the Balance

Huelgoat forest, Brittany

The Creel

The world began with a woman,
shawl-happed, stooped under a creel,
whose slow step you recognize
from troubled dreams. You feel

obliged to help her bear her burden
from hill or kelp-strewn shore,
but she passes by unseeing
thirled to her private chore.

It's not sea birds or peat she's carrying,
not fleece, nor the herring bright
but her fear that if ever she put it down
the world would go out like a light.

Kathleen Jamie[1]

Brocéliande: the word itself is captivating, evocative, conjuring up images which rise fully formed out of medieval legend and Arthurian myth. The original vast, ancient and enchanted forest which once covered the whole of Brittany, scattered with beautiful castles, punctuated by magical springs and fountains frequented in stories by fairy women, haunted by knights questing for the Holy Grail.

Little of Brocéliande now remains; we cut down this Otherworld centuries ago, tree by groaning tree, Western civilisation burning and slashing its way through the great wooded wilderness. Only patches endure, here and there: dense woods of oak, ash, chestnut and beech, criss-crossed with paths and tracks, dotted with ancient burial mounds, with menhirs and dolmens erected during the Neolithic. Fragmented it may be, but enchantment can be found in this old forest still, if you know how to see.

Although it was a lovely place, I didn't find the greatest enchantment of all in the privately owned, heavily managed and relatively young forest of Paimpont, which claims to be the last remaining fragment of Brocéliande. I found it in the smaller but wilder old forest of Huelgoat, farther west at the end of the world, in the region of Finistère. Huelgoat: 'high wood', scattered with immense granite boulders; teeming with lush ferns, strange moss-covered root formations and clear, dark pools.

Sometimes, when you wander through the forest with an open heart in search of enchantment, you find it. I found it off the trail, clambering and sliding a good fifty feet down a steep muddy bank slippery with old leaves, my attention caught by a glimmer of water far below. At the bottom of a narrow green valley I picked myself up and wandered through thickets of tall, tangled trees, stepping carefully over crumbling trunks festooned with ferns, along the overgrown fringes of a beautiful little river which hardly seemed to be flowing at all. All at once a string of pools opened up, one after the other, shining and still like silver charms on an antique bracelet. I sat there on a warm moss-covered rock in the eerie silence of the wood for an hour and a half, entranced and cross-legged, watching the light change as the sun played among the clouds and rays of sunlight skimmed across the surface of the water, spotlights searching for who knows what. Once I looked up to see a single crow gliding slowly past, just above the water. Following her path with my eyes, I thought I saw the figure of a reclining stone giant in the shadows, hidden in the trees on the far side of the river. Old Moss Woman: soft green hair, staring eyes and wide dark maw.

To enter into any wood is to enter into a realm in which transformation seems inevitable; the particular brand of transformation you're heading for depends heavily on the nature of the wood. In our imaginations, the fairy-tale forests of northern European stories are shadowy, dangerous places, thick with dark conifers, immensely tall and tightly packed together. Pressing in on the fringes of the village, representing another world which lies outside of normal human experience, these forests are the homes of witches and monsters, places in which you're more than likely to be eaten by a wolf dressed up as your granny. All the fears of the collective unconscious, perfectly personified. But the Celtic broadleaf forests – dense in a friendlier, leafier kind of way, though often perilous, and never to be taken for granted – offer light to offset the shadow. They are places where the sun still shines through, where fairies and enchanted damsels might be met, where entrances to a beautiful and magical

Otherworld might be found. The ancient wildwood of Brittany is such a place.

Brittany, once called Lesser Britain: the far western outpost of a region once known as Armorica. Celts from Devon and Cornwall settled here in the fifth century, fleeing those chaotic war-ridden times which followed the departure of Rome. The migrants brought with them their old Celtic traditions, and a bagful of myths and stories which adapted easily to this new land. The dense, shadowy forest of Brocéliande seemed an ideal setting for the Arthurian legends which travelled across the sea with the British settlers.[2] New stories soon came to be formed, arising directly from the topography and natural features of this wild and mysterious country which nevertheless felt like home. The Val sans Retour, a beautiful valley which gave rise to the story of an enchanted land in which the powerful sorceress Morgan le Fay, half-sister of Arthur, imprisoned unfaithful lovers. Lancelot once passed through this place, and his love for Guinevere was so perfect and true that his presence alone was enough to release every faithless man who had been trapped. It's a lovely spot, bright with wildflowers, with rocky outcrops looming high above wide green woods. On moonlit nights the waters of a small lake hidden in the folds of the hills will reflect, it is said, the face of the person you're destined to love. There's the Fontaine de Barenton, a mineral spring known for its healing properties. When a piece of copper or iron is thrown into it, the water begins to bubble. If you take some of that water and pour it onto any of the rocks in the forest, so the story goes, a terrible storm will blow in, summoning Esclados le Ros, the knight who defends the forest.

According to the Breton Arthurian tradition, the Fontaine de Barenton was also the place where Merlin the magician met the love of his life, the beautiful, clever Viviane. Brocéliande was Merlin's home; it was also the site of his death. 'A storm was coming, but the winds were still,/ And in the wild woods of Brocéliande,/ Before an oak, so hollow, huge and old/ It look'd a tower of ivied masonwork,/ At Merlin's feet the wily Vivien lay . . .' So wrote

Tennyson in the 'Idylls of the King', a characteristically Victorian retelling of Merlin's story in which Vivien (called Viviane in Brittany; in some works also called Nimue) seduces and then betrays him, traps him in a tower and steals his knowledge and his power.

There are several versions of this legend, but in most of the older stories Viviane is no wicked enchantress intent on betrayal and theft; rather, she is Merlin's student and lover. He teaches her voluntarily, wanting to share and pass on his power, and at the same time understanding the pulls and necessities of his fate. One local Breton story tells that he built for her a crystal palace, surrounded by beautiful gardens in which apple trees with silver blossoms grew, in front of her father Dyonas' castle at Comper. He then created the illusion of a lake to hide the palace, so perfect an illusion that no one other than Viviane and her servants could see it unless she allowed them to. In that beautiful crystal palace Merlin and Viviane spent a year and a day together, before he was obliged to return to Arthur's court to fulfil some outstanding duties. But Merlin was a prophet as well as a magician; he knew fine well that his fate was bound up with Viviane and the wildwoods of Brittany. He returned willingly to her arms, and granted her wish to learn the secret of eternal imprisonment. Once she had learned it, wanting to keep her lover beside her forever, Viviane cast a spell on Merlin and imprisoned him in a tree in the heart of Brocéliande. It is said that still they live there together, bound together in perfect harmony in the heart of the forest, invisible to the human eye.

Where legends of Arthur and members of his court and entourage go, so go stories of the Holy Grail. An understanding of the importance of the Grail stories to this part of Brittany, and a lesson in the ways in which the legends have crossed traditions, can be found in the tiny and remarkable church of Tréhorenteuc, which lies to the west of Paimpont forest. It was built in the seventeenth century and was originally dedicated to St Onenne, but in the twentieth century it was restored, rededicated to the Holy Grail, and redecorated accordingly: around the church are many scenes from the Arthurian romances. The stained-glass window at the rear of the chancel depicts Joseph of Arimathea kneeling in front of Christ to receive the Grail, which is shown beside Christ's head. Another window shows Arthur and his knights seated at the Round Table, staring at a vision of the Holy Grail. A third window shows the Last Supper, with the Grail set on the table in front of Christ. A mosaic shows Christ as a Brocéliande forest stag, and one of the framed paintings on the wall shows him prostrate at the feet of a decidedly buxom Morgan le Fay.

Of all of the myths which sprang from the Celtic nations, those involving the Grail have had the greatest traction over the centuries, and have most vividly captured the popular imagination. They've captured the attention of scholars too: the volumes written on psychological and mythic approaches to the Grail quest, from Emma Jung and Marie-Louise von Franz's seminal work, *The Grail Legend*, to the writings of later mythologists like Joseph Campbell, would fill a small library. Both the Grail itself and the stories of quests to attain it have become metaphors of astonishing power. For psychotherapists, they have become road-maps for our personal journeys to individuation; most Jungians view the Grail quest as a metaphor for the quest of the animus (the masculine principle) to find the anima (the feminine principle) – a joining of opposites which results in the healing of the inner Wasteland of the soul. But the antecedents of these popular medieval romances were never focused so simply on the individual and (if he is lucky) his salvation; their province is much wider than that. They concern, quite simply, the world: a world in which feminine power and wisdom has been lost, in which nature has been violated and an Otherworldly treasure stolen; a world which, as a consequence of these circumstances, has become a Wasteland. The quest for the Grail, the female principle, the giver and sustainer of life, is not merely a quest to restore ourselves: it is a quest to restore the world.

The Grail myth is one of the foundation myths of Celtic culture. It advances a potent narrative which explains the schism between masculine and feminine qualities in the world and the resulting coming of the Wasteland, as well as offering up some inspiring and cogent clues for how the situation might be healed. For that reason, it's worth spending a little time to examine its complex origins.

The legend which most people would now recognise as the quest for the Grail first found written expression in the writings of the French poet Chrétien de Troyes towards the end of the twelfth century, where it appears under the title *Perceval, le Conte du Graal*. It was one of the last of a number of courtly romances that he wove around the ancient 'matière de Bretagne', an extensive oral tradition relating to the exploits of Arthur and his Knights of the Round Table. No one knows precisely how old this oral tradition is, but Chrétien states clearly that he is retelling the Grail story, not inventing it. After Chrétien, various other written versions appeared – by Robert de Boron, Wolfram von Eschenbach, Sir Thomas Malory and others – which differ in their plots and their detail. But most of the tellings have some features in common: the Grail – a mysterious, life-preserving vessel – is guarded by a king, usually called the Fisher King, or the Rich Fisher, who lives in a castle that is difficult to find. The king is either very old or suffering from some mysterious wound, usually as a result of being stabbed by a spear in the thigh or genitals, and his kingdom (either as a consequence of his wound, or because of some other circumstance such as the rape of the well-maidens) has become a Wasteland. The king, 'too ill to live but not ill enough to die'[3] – a metaphor for our own contemporary Wasteland if ever there was one – can only be restored to health if a knight of great virtue (usually Perceval, sometimes Gawain, occasionally Galahad) succeeds in finding the castle and then asks a certain question.

In all versions of the myth the Grail is in the possession of women; usually a spear accompanies it or appears at the same time; the spear is borne by a man. It's worth noting that the Grail is referred to as 'holy', so acquiring the trappings of Christian symbolism and its association with the Holy Chalice used by

Christ at the Last Supper, only in later versions of the story. In de Troyes' poem, the spear is accorded as much significance as the Grail itself. Folklorist Jessie Weston[4] suggested that the spear represented the masculine principle and the Grail the feminine principle, and that the myth was about uniting the two in order to restore the Wasteland – an outcome which she describes as 'the restoration of the rivers to their channels, the "Freeing of the Waters".' In this account, the Grail represents the golden vessels that were stolen from the well-maidens when they were raped by Amagons and his men; it represents the loss from the world of the life-giving gifts of the feminine, a symbol of Sovereignty. The spear, dripping with blood, is the spear which struck the 'dolorous blow': the stroke which wounded the Fisher King. And so the spear represents the wounded masculine: the masculine principle which cannot flourish in isolation, when the feminine principle which both balances and nourishes it is taken away. Jungian analyst Robert Johnson[5] describes that wound in this way: 'The fisher king wound is in the male, generative, creative part of a man's being. It is a wound intimately connected with his feeling function and affects every sense of value in his psychological structure. This is the price we have paid for the cool, precise, rational, and scientific world we have won at so high a cost.'

Although the medieval Grail myths are always presented as a Heroic quest, women are central to Grail mythology: they are the Grail bearers, the Grail messengers, and it is invariably a woman who directs the Hero on his road to the Grail castle, or reproaches him for his failure there. In many of the medieval Grail romances, the question which must be asked before the Grail can be attained is 'What ails thee?' Perceval, confined both by his conventional training as a knight and by cultural expectations of what it is to behave like a man, fails at first to ask the question – a question born of compassion and care – which would heal the wound of the Fisher King and begin the restoration of the Wasteland. But our task as women in these challenging times is focused precisely on healing what ails us, both as individuals and as a culture.

What ails us is the dominance of the dry, wounded, merciless, over-extended masculine. What ails us is the loss and violation of the feminine. The quest for the Grail, then, is the quest to restore the lost feminine to the world. Women are essential to this task, and so in this sense our Heroine's Journey is also a quest for the Grail – but our path to it is a different route, for we *are* the Grail. Our weapons are not swords and spears but the fertile, creative, life-giving energy of the universe which is contained in the vessel itself: the energy we need to find within ourselves and bring out into an ailing world.

The compelling imagery and enduring themes which are given full expression in the medieval Grail romances can be traced back to Welsh and Irish mythology: the Wasteland as a concept, for example, first occurs in early Irish literature.[6] John Carey,[7] Professor of Early and Medieval Irish at University College Cork, argues that a series of early Irish stories which contained central elements of the Grail mythology influenced later Welsh stories, which in turn subsequently influenced medieval French literature. These old stories relate to life-giving cauldrons, and cups or grails, which serve up the gift of Sovereignty.[8]

One of the legends cited by Carey is the tale of Bran, the king of Mag Febail, which is likely to have inspired the story of the rape of the well-maidens in 'The Elucidation'. Bran, learning from a druid that a treasure of great value was guarded by Otherworldly women at the bottom of a spring well in his territory, set out to discover it and to take it for himself. Chances are, Carey suggests, that Bran and his men also abused the Otherworldly women of the well. Whether or not they did, their aggression against the well resulted in disaster: the waters of the spring burst forth in a deluge, engulfing the whole of Bran's beautiful and fertile kingdom and leaving it drowned, lost forever at the bottom of the newly created Lough Foyle. There are clear parallels here with the theft of Otherworldly treasure from the maidens of the wells, with their rape, and with the coming of the Wasteland which followed. It is interesting that, among a group of gold objects dating to the first century BC which were found on the east shore of Lough Foyle, is a small vessel, similar to a cauldron.

Once we have uncovered and embraced the feminine energy buried inside each of us, the next stage of our Heroine's Journey is to bring ourselves into balance – to integrate and harmonise the masculine and feminine qualities we all possess. Those qualities of the female principle, the anima, are the instinctive, feeling, relational qualities traditionally associated with the heart and the soul; the qualities of the masculine principle, the animus, are the active, rational, goal-oriented, structuring qualities traditionally associated with the intellect and the spirit. This harmonising of the energies within ourselves, this appreciation of what should be cherished and valued in both the archetypal feminine and the archetypal masculine, is a prerequisite for the work of restoring balance to an outer world which has lost its equilibrium. This particular concept of balance is comparable to that expressed by the ancient Taoist symbol of yin and yang, in which masculine and feminine energies flow and curve around each other, together creating a circle of wholeness.

While we're looking east, it's also interesting to bear in mind that Celtic culture has Indo-European origins,[9] and scholars have pointed out a number of intriguing parallels between Celtic and Indian belief systems and mythologies. In the current context there are clear parallels with Hindu mythology, in which a male divinity can do nothing alone but must be complemented by the female – and vice versa. Shiva is consciousness, the male principle; Shakti is the activating, creative force and energy, the female principle. Until creative energy (the feminine principle) is impregnated with consciousness (the masculine principle) it is lacking in knowledge, disordered and aimless. Creative energy alone can produce nothing; consciousness bestows upon it content, form and direction. Conversely, consciousness without energy remains dormant, and on its own is unable to achieve anything. Only when Shiva and Shakti combine, then, can creation arise. We can only hope to be effective by beginning from a place of balance inside ourselves; and we can only hope to do so in partnership with men. This is the marriage between Sovereignty and the king, the alchemical *hieros gamos*, the sacred marriage between masculine and feminine.

~

What Do Women Want?

One day King Arthur was hunting in the forest with his men when a deer briefly stepped into view and then just as suddenly vanished into a tangle of trees. 'Stay here, everyone,' said Arthur, 'I'll stalk this one myself.' With his bow in one hand and his arrows slung over his shoulder, the king crept after the deer until, deep into the forest, he slew it finally with a single shot. But as the animal fell, a tall figure, all dressed in black, well-armed and strong, stepped from the shadows and stood in front of Arthur.

'How fortunate for me that we meet this way, with your arrow already released from your hand,' a deep voice boomed. 'Arthur, once you did me a great wrong by giving my lands to your nephew, Gawain. Now I will repay you with death.'

Thinking quickly, Arthur said, 'To slay me here, armed as you are and I clothed only in my hunting greens, would bring you no honour. Shame will forever follow you. I'll grant you anything – name it – land or gold, to spare my life.'

The Black Knight nodded, slowly. 'There is no land or gold that I desire,' he said, 'and so I'll give you the chance to solve a riddle. One year and a day from now, you must come to me here in the woods, without friends and without weapons. If at that time you're unable to solve this riddle, no man will object if I take your life. But if you answer the riddle correctly, you may go free.'

'I agree,' said Arthur, hastily. 'And what is the riddle?'

'You must tell me what it is that women desire most, above all else.'

Arthur frowned, but then nodded, and gave his word of honour that he would return as asked, a year and a day later. And so the Black Knight slipped back into the trees and was gone. Arthur blew his bugle, and his hunting companions soon found him with the slain deer at his feet; they returned at once to Camelot. But Arthur shared what had taken place only with his friend and nephew, Gawain.

'Sir, don't worry,' said the young knight after he heard the story, 'let's ready both your horse and mine. I will go in one direction and you the other, and so we will ride into every town in the country. Wherever we go, we will ask each of the women we meet for the answer to this riddle, and we'll go on until we find the response which seems to be correct.'

And so the king and Gawain rode away. Everywhere they went, they asked what it was that women desired above all else. All the women who answered were certain that their answer was the only true response, and yet each answer was different. Some said that women loved to be well clothed; others said they wanted never to be scorned. Some said women wanted a husband who was handsome and strong; others that they wanted a man who would never try to prove them wrong. And so Arthur and Gawain collected many an answer . . . yet neither of them found one that rang true. Soon only a month remained, and they each turned back to Camelot, downhearted.

As he rode through the forest not far from the castle, Arthur met a woman. Though she was clothed in gold and wore precious stones, she was as foul a creature as ever a man saw. Her face was red and covered with snot, her mouth huge, and all her teeth yellow, hanging over her lips. Her eyes were bleary and protruded, each larger than a ball, and her cheeks were as broad as women's hips. She had a hump on her back, her neck was long and thick, and her hair was clotted into a heap. She was built like a barrel, with shoulders a yard wide and enormous hanging breasts.

The lady stepped up alongside Arthur as he stared. 'Godspeed, King Arthur,' she said. 'You may speak with me or ride on, but either way, your life is in my hands.'

'What do you mean, lady?' asked the king. 'What business have you with me?'

'I know of your quest,' she said, 'and of all the answers you have been told, I know that none of them will help you. Only I know the correct answer. Grant me just one thing and I'll tell it to you – or else you'll lose your head.'

'What is it that you want?' said Arthur. 'If I can, I shall grant it.'

'You must grant me a certain knight to wed. His name is Gawain. Either I marry him, or you will meet your death here in the forest in a month's time.'

Alas! Arthur thought to himself. *What a terrible thing, that I should be the cause of Gawain marrying such a creature!* He said aloud, 'I cannot promise that Gawain will marry you; he alone can decide. But in order to save my life, I will do what I can. And so for now we must part, lady. But tell me, before I go, what is your name?'

'I am the Lady Ragnelle,' said the loathsome hag.

Arthur returned to Camelot, where the first man he met was his nephew. Arthur told Gawain everything except the request of the loathly lady to wed him, saying simply that the Lady Ragnelle would only share her secret in return for the promise of a husband.

'Is that all?' said Gawain. 'I'll wed her, and would even if she were a fiend, otherwise I would not be your friend and kinsman. You are my king, and have honoured me in many a battle; I will not hesitate.'

And so, a few days later, Arthur rode out of town, and returned to the spot where he had met the Lady Ragnelle. He told her that Gawain had agreed to marry her. 'So tell me now, and quickly, my lady, the answer to the riddle.'

'Sir, you will now know, without further digression, what women want most,' Lady Ragnelle responded. 'It is a simple enough answer: the one thing that we desire above all else is to have Sovereignty. So go on your way and tell this to the Black Knight, who will for certain be angry and curse the one who taught it to you, for all his labour is lost. I assure you that your life is now safe, and ask you to remember your promise.'

Arthur rode on as fast as he could, alone and unarmed, to the place where he had met the Black Knight a year and a day before. There he found him, waiting. The king began by offering an answer that he had been given by one of the women he'd encountered around the country . . . and then another, and another, and yet another. And after each answer the knight shook his head with glee.

'No, no,' he said. 'Obviously you have no idea. You are as good as dead. Prepare to bleed!'

'Wait a minute,' Arthur said. 'I have one answer left to offer you.'

'Very well, then,' said the Black Knight, 'but know this: after that answer, there'll be nothing left to you but your death.'

'Here is the answer,' said Arthur, 'and there will be no death. For above all, women desire Sovereignty.'

'And who was it that told you this?' roared the Black Knight. 'No doubt it was my sister, the Lady Ragnelle! May she burn alive on the hottest of fires! Yet now I am compelled to release you – so go, before I change my mind and break my word!'

Arthur quickly turned around his horse, and sped back to the Lady Ragnelle to bring her back to Camelot for the wedding. So unpleasant was the prospect of holding a public wedding with such a bride that he told her the ceremony would be an early morning affair, knowing this meant that there would be few or none to attend. But Lady Ragnelle would not agree to this.

'No,' said she, firmly. 'I must be wed openly, with a full wedding feast and plenty of guests in attendance.'

When finally they met, Lady Ragnelle carefully watched Gawain, her future husband. Was he disgusted by her? Would he turn his back on her and ignore her? Strangely, he did none of these things. Gawain behaved as if he cherished his loathsome bride. And so they were married, with great ceremony, and in a hall filled with guests. The queen and her ladies wept for Gawain, and the king and his knights mourned, for the Lady Ragnelle was so ugly. She had two long teeth on each side like boar tusks: one grew upwards, the other down. Her wide, foul mouth was covered with grey hairs and her lips lay lumped on her chin. But all the while, Gawain treated her with great affection, courtesy and respect.

After the wedding came the wedding feast. Lady Ragnelle sat at the head of the high table, and everyone gasped at her bad manners. When served, she ate as much as six people might. She used her nails, which were three inches long, to break up her food. She ate and ate; nothing came before her that she didn't eat. And so she ate until the meal was done.

Later that night, as they arrived in their bedchamber, the Lady Ragnelle turned to her husband, and said, 'Sir Gawain, now that we are married, show me your love with a kiss. If I were fair, you would not delay. But even though I am not, I pray you do this at my request, and with all due speed.'

Gawain said courteously, 'Indeed, my lady, I will at once, that and more!' But as he turned to kiss his bride, standing there before him was not the appalling creature he had married, but the fairest woman he had ever seen.

'Oh!' he cried out. 'What are you? A witch?'

'I am your wife,' she said. 'That is all.'

'Ah, lady, then I must not be in my right mind,' said Gawain. 'Earlier today you were the foulest sight that ever I saw – pardon me for saying so – and now, I cannot believe my good fortune!' And he kissed her with great joy.

'Sir,' said she, pulling away for a moment, 'there is more you must know. Several years ago I was deformed by an enchantment caused by my brother, the terrible Black Knight. He put this spell on me because I would not give him my treasure, and my land. And because of this curse my beauty, as you see it now, will not hold. You need to choose whether you will have me fair by night and foul by day, or else have me fair by day and foul by night. With the enchantment, it cannot be both. What do you choose?'

'Alas!' said Gawain. 'The choice is hard. To have you fair by nights and no more, that would grieve my heart right sore. And if I desire by days to have you fair, then nights I'm sure I could not bear. So I must put the choice in your own hands. Whatever you choose – well then, as your husband, that choice will also be my own, and I will be glad of it.'

'Oh, most honourable and compassionate of all knights!' cried Lady Ragnelle. 'Now the enchantment is released completely! You shall have me fair both by day and by night. For the only thing that could release me from this evil curse was the granting to me by my husband, and of his own free will, the Sovereignty which is mine by nature. And now, courteous Gawain, you have done just that. You have granted me Sovereignty, that which every woman wants above all else. Kiss me, and be glad!'

And so it was that the Lady Ragnelle remained beautiful all day and all night, and she and Gawain lived happily together thereafter.

~

The story of Gawain and Lady Ragnelle is an old one; the motif (in which the question 'What do women want?' must be answered in order for a king or a knight to survive a threat to his life) appears in numerous tales throughout the medieval period, including 'The Wife of Bath's Tale' in Chaucer's *The Canterbury Tales*. The answer to the question is always 'Sovereignty'. Some of the stories go on to interpret this as women wanting sovereignty in the simple sense – that is, control over their own lives, the right to make their own choices; others go on to interpret it as women wishing to have power over men. But at another level, the answer is plain enough: women want Sovereignty – to take up their ancient role as the moral and spiritual authority of the land. In our native myths and stories, Sovereignty represents the creative, regenerative, life-giving feminine principle; when it is balanced by the good masculine – when the goddess of the land enters into a sacred marriage with the true king of the people – then the land is fertile and the people safe from harm. In this story, then, Gawain, representing the masculine principle, doesn't need to resort to domination and control over the woman who represents the land. He has compassion, courtesy and honour enough to allow Lady Ragnelle to make her own choices and follow her own path; he feels no need to impose his choices upon her.

The story shows the feminine principle of Sovereignty being honoured; it also shows the 'good masculine' in practice. The 'good masculine' is essential to the functioning of a healthy, balanced world. In decrying the repression of the feminine in our culture, it can be all too easy not only to blame men for the mess the world is in, but to set ourselves against them. Men – our brothers, fathers, lovers, friends – are not always the enemy, and to think of them as such would be like placing ourselves against half of nature, half of our own souls. Men too have cultural expectations foisted upon them, and, increasingly, they are speaking up about all of the ways in which Western rationalism has distorted their image of themselves.

American poet Robert Bly, who spearheaded the 'mythopoetic' men's movement in the 1990s, was one of the first to openly acknowledge the pain of contemporary men: 'The grief in men,' he wrote, 'has been increasing steadily since the Industrial Revolution and the grief has reached a depth now that cannot be ignored.'[10] In this context, figures released by the UK Office for National Statistics in 2014 showed that the rate of suicide in men was three times that of women; astonishingly, suicide was the leading cause of death for men aged between twenty and thirty-four in England and Wales. Speaking about those figures, a senior manager at The Samaritans suggested that the deaths occur because 'society has this masculine ideal that people are expecting to live up to', and because men are increasingly unable or unwilling to do so.[11]

In seeking to restore the feminine in our culture, then, it's critical not to lose sight of the fact that the cause of our problems isn't the presence of masculine qualities in the world, but rather the fact that those qualities have been allowed to become dominant and, because they are not moderated and held in balance by appropriate feminine qualities, they often become pathological. The masculine striving towards achievement, production and domination takes hold and spirals out of control, while the feminine qualities of relatedness are suppressed: relatedness to other humans, to the non-humans who share the planet with us, to nature and the rhythms of nature, as well as to the rhythms of the physical body and the stages and passages of our lives.

The mythopoetic men's movement coined the phrase 'toxic masculinity' in an effort to contrast 'normal, healthy' masculinity with more negative manifestations of manliness. What we need to focus on, then, is encouraging the 'good' or the 'deep' masculine:

> . . . he who wields the sword of discrimination, distinguishing between right and wrong. This is the glorious ability to focus, to question, to find out, to be precise, to get things done. It is the pioneering spirit that's willing to go out and take risks and explore. It invests selflessly in the protection and support of nature, of women, of children, of the feminine. The deep masculine is the courage in the heart of every one of us, able fearlessly to confront the challenges facing the planet.[12]

But it is also important to understand that just as the masculine principle can become toxic if not balanced by the feminine, the reverse can also apply. The pathological or 'monstrous' feminine which is not balanced by the masculine principle can manifest itself in an excess of emotion and neediness, a tendency to manipulation, an over-focus on relationships, and a refusal to apply reason to a situation. We need both kinds of qualities in ourselves and in the world, and we need them in appropriate balance.

Old-growth forests like Brocéliande, whether enchanted or not, are complex, diverse ecosystems which seem to embody the idea of balance and harmony. Here, too, we find ourselves at the centre of a community of beings which survives and thrives through a network of interconnected relationships. In these ancient woods the vegetation has reached its fullest development, and death is balanced by reproduction; a state of dynamic equilibrium exists, which gives rise to a high diversity of trees, plants, birds and animal species. In mature forests, trees and plants communicate and interact with each other through a vast underground web of fungi which connect the trees and plants.[13] Resources are shared through this network – carbon, water and nutrients – so helping the whole system of trees and plants to flourish.

At the heart of such forests stand the majestic 'Mother Trees': large, older trees which stretch high up into the canopy, and which are connected to all the others in the forest by this complex web of fungal threads. Mother Trees manage the resources of the whole plant community, and when a Mother Tree is cut down, the survival rate of the younger members of the forest is substantially diminished. Mother Trees, holding together an entire, enchanted woodland world.

Brocéliande, though, isn't the only enchanted forest which remains alive in the Celtic psyche. The great Caledonian Forest of the Scottish Highlands, sometimes called the 'Great Wood of Caledon', is an archetypal forest deeply rooted in the Scottish imagination – even though, like Brittany, much of the Highlands and Islands have had little or no tree cover for centuries. The Caledonian Forest was more akin to the dark woods of northern European fairy tales, and once formed the western-most outpost of Europe's boreal forest. Although its true extent has been disputed, once it might have covered as much as 1.5 million hectares: a vast wilderness of Scots pine, birch, rowan, aspen and juniper. Many species of wild animals which now are long gone would have flourished in those woods, including the European beaver, wild boar, lynx, moose, brown bear and wolf. And inevitably perhaps, given its location in a Celtic nation, the great Caledonian Forest also has its place in Arthurian mythology: stories say it is the site of one of King Arthur's Twelve Battles, the Cat Coit Celidon, and Myrddin Wyllt (Merlin) retreated to these woods in his madness after the battle of Arfderydd in the year 573. According to two poems in the *Black Book of Carmarthen,* he was fleeing the wrath of the king of Strathclyde, Rhydderch Hael, after the slaying of Gwenddoleu ap Ceidio, the king of an area which included parts of south-west Scotland and north-west England.

The Caledonian Forest, like so many others, started to disappear when significant amounts of land began to be cleared during the Neolithic period to make way for agriculture. Trees were cut for fuel and timber, and over the centuries the forest continued to shrink as the human population grew. More recently, large areas of Scottish woodland were felled for industrial purposes, particularly once the timber supply in England had been exhausted, and the widespread introduction of sheep and a large increase in the numbers of red deer ensured that once the forest was cleared, it did not return. The charitable organisation Trees for Life,[14] established to renew the Caledonian Forest, reports on its website that only a tiny percentage of the original forest survives today, and this in small, isolated remnants. Gone with the trees are all the large mammals, with the exception of red deer. The brown bear and the wild boar had become extinct by the tenth and seventeenth centuries respectively, and the final species to disappear was the wolf: the last of its kind was shot in 1743. And so, as a result of these human-created imbalances in the ecosystem, the remnants of the Caledonian Forest have become 'geriatric' woods, filled with old trees that are reaching the end of their lifespans. No new trees are naturally growing to take their place. As the trees die, the forest continues to shrink, and without protection from overgrazing, Trees for Life estimates that most of what remains will disappear during the next few decades.

Mandy Haggith is a writer[15] and forestry campaigner who lives on a woodland croft in what she calls Scotland's 'wild west': the stormy coast of Assynt in Sutherland. The croft is affectionately named Braighlinne (brae, or hill, of the sea-loch), and it stretches steeply down to the shores of Loch Roe. Mandy and her partner,

Bill, pursue a unique lifestyle here: instead of a house, dotted about the croft are two twelve-foot caravans, seven sheds and an upturned boat. Each has a distinct function; for example, one shed serves as a bathroom, another as a kitchen, and one of the caravans is the bedroom. 'One visitor described it as "an exploded house" and another as "radically detached",' Mandy laughs as she shows me the layout of the land one sunny afternoon in early spring. It is for sure radical: Mandy and Bill's desire to live a simple life means that they don't have many of the things that most people hold to be necessary for a 'proper' twenty-first-century domestic life, such as flush toilet, shower, oven, fridge, washing machine or television. 'We don't have mains electricity at all,' she tells me as she points out a tiny wind turbine at the highest part of the croft, and a few solar panels here and there. 'We don't have insurance or a mortgage or proper jobs, either. But we do have eleven hectares of paradise, and a bed with a view over the sea-loch from where we can watch curlews, black-throated divers, otters and seals.'

Mandy hasn't always lived like this; once upon a time she was an academic, developing software tools for land managers and foresters. But in the mid-1990s she quit academia so that she could spend more time writing and campaigning for the world's forests. 'I had been working with people in world forest conservation,' she says, as we sit for a while in her working space, a lovely new wooden shed with enormous windows to the front, looking out – of course – over trees. 'But over time it became very clear to me that there were no technological solutions to the global environmental crisis. Anything I could do as an academic working in the field of computing wasn't going to help at all – we needed political solutions and human solutions, not technocratic solutions. I'd met Bill at that time, and we'd fallen in love. So we decided we would build a life around working together to help save the world's forests.'

Mandy's partner Bill Ritchie, who received an MBE for his services to the environment and sustainable development, is a well-known activist in his own right: he was one of the prime movers behind the historic community buyout of the 21,000-acre North Assynt estate in 1993, and then the Assynt Foundation's subsequent purchase of the 44,000-acre Drumrunie and Glencanisp estates in 2005. He's a former chairman of the Taiga Rescue Network,[16] and a long-time member of the board of Caledonian Forest organisation Trees for Life. Together, Mandy and Bill see their stewardship of their own land as a part of that wider work to care for the world's forests, because what makes Braighlinne remarkable is that, even on this windswept, salt-ridden western shore, about half of it is native woodland. Here, rowan, birch, aspen and willow grow right down to the high-tide line, a reminder that, in contrast to the forbidding Caledonian Forest further east, a more temperate rainforest type of ecosystem would once have predominated here on the west coast – one rich in ferns, mosses and lichens.

'Ever since Bill got the croft in the early 1990s, he has wanted to manage it with the aim of restoring the ecosystems to something closer to their wild state,' Mandy explains as we wander through a wilderness of small but well-established trees which are just beginning to come into leaf. That old phobia makes me relieved to be here in spring: it's clear from the dead undergrowth that the bracken grows thickly here – 'Up to your waist in places,' she tells me, and then laughs as I shudder. 'We mostly let the plants grow which want to grow, and let wildlife do their own thing. The croft is fenced to keep sheep, cattle and horses out, while being permeable to wild animals like deer. Apart from a small patch of herbs and vegetables, we don't till the ground. We don't use chemicals, and we don't burn. We don't cut trees, or collect deadwood. We contribute by enhancement planting of native trees, but otherwise we try to minimise our impact on this particular piece of land, allowing it to rewild itself in its own way while we live as lightly as possible.'

The idea of living in sheds and caravans as they do, she tells me, didn't begin as an active choice; it came about originally because they couldn't afford to build a house. 'But once we got to the point where we might have been able to think about having a house, we realised that we liked not having one. A fundamental thing to me is having a different kind of lifestyle and different habits depending on what time of year it is. In a house you have all your paraphernalia around you and so you behave more or less the same way all year round. We spend the winters sleeping in a shed tucked into the woods, and in spring-time we migrate down to the shore, spending most of our time in a little caravan there. But then by the time midsummer comes around, the midges make living full time in a small caravan intol-erable, and so we shift our cooking activities to a cool shed at the top of the croft. In autumn, as insects decline, we revert to the spring pattern, and then in winter we retreat to the shelter of the woods, and so the cycle begins again. It's a form of trans-humance. These seasonal changes are an acknowledgement of one of the most basic rhythms of life. I think of it as my own rewil-ding.'

Although I'm entranced by the idea of this way of living, after having spent several years enduring the wild, cold winters here on the far north-west coast I'm considerably less enamoured by the outdoor open-air compost loo – a kind of lean-to contrap-tion with a thin curtain across the doorway to keep out the worst of the weather. But Mandy just grins, enthusiastic as ever about the benefits. 'Every trip out here is an opportunity to bump into a shrew or an owl. It's true that if I want a cup of tea, I have to walk 250 metres from my studio to the kitchen caravan, which is tucked into the woods at the east side of the croft. But in summer I'll pass five species of orchids surrounded by butterflies, and on winter evenings the torch might just pick out the eyes and white rumps of roe deer. Sometimes I'm in full waterproofs and wondering if I'm mad to live like this. But then along comes a sparrowhawk and I remember why we do.'

It's rare today to see people living full time in the woods, although Scotland has a long history of occasional hutting which involves not just construction of the odd solitary bothy, but the development of more extensive woodland communities. This form of hutting is a working-class movement that developed early in the twentieth century, when clusters of small holiday huts began to be built on land close to the country's main industrial cities. In 2011, Reforesting Scotland launched a campaign called A Thousand Huts[17] to promote a resurgence of interest in hutting. As poet and hutting campaigner Gerry Loose explains in a recent article,[18] the campaign was born out of a concern about 'an increasing and urban dis-connection to land, from an uneasy certainty that there are better ways to use and own land, that we are not nurturing ourselves nor our local environments'. The campaign aims to promote access to woodland in 'a sustainable way' – but is it sustainable, I wonder, as we clamber down a steep track to the rocky, seaweed-strewn shore of the sea-loch where Mandy and Bill's summer caravan sits. It seems to me as though an influx of human activity would disrupt the natural processes which exist, but Mandy firmly believes that the woods benefit from people living physically within them.

'Some of the reasons are practical – for example, we move the deer on, so they're less likely to stay in one place and cause major damage. We don't have running water or toilets, so just like the birds we're giving our nutrient contributions directly back to the environment. But it's more than that: it's a sense of appreciating, of witnessing the place. We observe very closely every flower as it opens in spring, we are breathing in the same air as the trees, greeting them every day, greeting the birds . . . I can't help but think that this has some regenerative usefulness. There's a real feeling of truly inhabiting this environment and being a genuine part of it.'

We climb back up to the main body of the croft by another route, at one point hauling ourselves a few feet up the cliff-face using a rope permanently tied there for the purpose. The views out beyond the sea-loch to the open sea are stunning, and offer a perfect antidote to the sense of enclosure among the trees up top. 'All of this – this living as we do, among the trees – links directly into the work I do as a forest activist,' Mandy tells me as we make our way past a small polytunnel filled with thriving strawberry plants, and back to the main cluster of caravans and sheds. 'All the great forests of the world are inhabited by people, and when governments hand over forest rights to corporations they're almost always doing that over the head of indigenous peoples. Where indigenous peoples can live undisturbed, the forests tend to be more diverse and in better shape. Corporate tenure tends to lead to destructive forestry practices like clear-felling. Humans make it better. There's evidence of this from tropical forests where human activity – the planting of fruit tree seeds, and so on – increases biodiversity. When they harvest a plant, seeds can get discarded in new places, so just like birds we can be big seed distributors. Forests are places to really remember that we're animals.'

Bill is working away at something on an open piece of land behind the caravans as we walk back to my car. Although he is several years older than Mandy, for as long as I've known them I've always been struck by the closeness of their relationship, which seems to be founded on a deep mutual respect as well as shared values. 'Bill and I have been working and loving together for almost two decades now,' Mandy tells me, 'so the dynamic has changed a lot over that time. We share values – trying to consume as little stuff as possible, living off-grid, reducing our carbon footprint. We totally share love of the woods, a spiritual sense of being part of nature, a need to be awed by living things bigger than we are, a passion for fierce creatures. The truth is, though, I think we're not very representative of our genders – I am goal-driven and Bill does the laundry! I know I'm very lucky to live with a man who is not at all macho, though I guess there are plenty of times when he has his overalls on and his head in the boat engine while I'm floating about reading poetry. Somehow, it all balances out.'

★

I've always found balance to be a challenge, in all its aspects. Maybe because it's such an over-used word, and I'm not sure I've ever really known what it would mean anyway, to live in a state of balance. In some ways it seems such a static idea – maybe even a little dull. Either way, back there in Kentucky I might finally have unearthed the feminine principle which had been buried in my own life, but bringing it into any kind of harmony with the masculine ways of being in the world which I'd been learning and living for four decades was going to prove to be rather more of a challenge. In spite of my new-found appreciation of the feminine, it was going to take a while before I could wean myself away from the habits I'd acquired during the course of a lifetime. And what I had internalised more than anything was the message that achievement was the answer to everything; achievement was the only goal, and you should collect accolades and stack them on your mantelpiece like Oscars for best actress in the fine art of living. The idea that I might not go on achieving was unthinkable. It was true that now I had reached a major turning point, and arrived at a new level of insight about my own life and my relationship with the world around me. But insight is one thing; wisdom is quite another and doesn't descend on you fully formed overnight – irritatingly, all the problems don't just disappear because you happen now to understand them a little bit better.

So, now I was going home. Such a big word, 'home'. What does it really mean? All I thought I knew about home was that it existed somewhere back in my native lands: Ireland, Scotland – the places where my ancestors came from. But Len was still alive at the time and living in our old cottage in Connemara and, irrational as it may have been, it seemed to me that the country was too small for the two of us. So instead of returning to Ireland, I decided to head back to Scotland. Although I'd never had the same sense of passionate attachment to Scotland, it seemed, after six years of living in an alien country, like a place that was at least *mine*. The place from where my name originated (Blackie, a Scottish name, is my birth name; I'd returned to it after I was divorced), and where much of my father's family were still living. And after all those years of loving America's empty spaces, of hankering always after the clear skies and clean air of the Rockies, I was very much aware that Scotland was probably the only place in Ireland and Britain where I might find something approaching a similar sense of physical freedom.

One rainy weekend in early spring, I bought a travel map of Scotland from the local Barnes & Noble store. I spread it out on the kitchen table and stared at it hungrily, feasting on the wild, mountainous country captured on the map, wondering where I might focus my search for a new home. My eyes kept slipping to the left: although I spent my early years on the north-east coast of England, some strange internal compass in me has always pointed north and west. And so, after hours of weighing up this place and that, the place I finally decided on was a large village called Ullapool on the shores of Loch Broom, a west-coast sea-loch about fifty-five miles from the Highland city of Inverness. Although I'd never been to Ullapool I'd once spent a summer vacation from university working at a hotel on the shores of Loch Ness, so I knew roughly what I would find, and a couple of hours' worth of web searches showed me a beautiful, wild land-scape which perfectly combined sea and mountains.

And then came a strange coincidence: an old friend and colleague from the UK arrived on a business trip, and I mentioned to him over lunch that I was thinking of buying a place in Scotland. He asked me where I wanted to be, and I told him that I thought I probably wanted to be near Ullapool. He smiled, and said that he had recently bought a house in Ullapool which he planned one day to retire to. What kind of a place was I looking for? So I described the image I was carefully guarding in my heart. I wanted an old cottage by the water – sea or loch – and I didn't care how much work needed to be done on it. I'd like a little land to keep hens and grow vegetables, and to have a little privacy – not to have neighbours too close. He laughed and said that he knew just the place: a derelict croft-house owned by the son of the elderly couple from who he'd bought his own house. He wasn't sure whether it was for sale, but there would be no harm in asking.

I asked, and within a month I'd flown over to Scotland and made an offer on that dilapidated croft-house, which sat on a fertile seven-acre croft on the shore of Loch Broom, twelve miles from Ullapool. All of the reading and self-examination I'd undertaken since I'd discovered *My Mama's Waltz* had caused me to settle on one thing: I was going to return to my vocational roots as well as my ancestral roots, and practise psychology. Ullapool, a compact but bustling village which was the main centre for quite a large area of the north-west coast, seemed like the perfect place to set up a therapy practice.

No star is ever lost/ we once have seen/ We always may be/ what we might have been. That old Devon Ware jug sat still on my mantelpiece, and as I looked at it now, it seemed as if I might finally be going to act on its message. I might finally be going to get it right. No more backtracking; no more failures of will. This time, I was going to pass all the tests – and this time, I would burn all my bridges. And so, after a few months of frantic saving and scraping together every penny I could, I packed my bags again and returned to the UK. A major renovation project on the croft-house ensued, and during the eighteen-month period while it was happening, I undertook professional training in clinical hypnotherapy and other creative imagination techniques. At the end of June 2003, on the day of my forty-second birthday, I moved in.

I could hardly believe my good fortune. Each morning when I woke up, I stood in the kitchen of that fine, sturdy old croft-house, staring out through wide windows filled with water and mountains. Here was the place I knew I would stay forever; Connemara had just been a practice session for this. The location was perfect: I had plenty of space and privacy on my seven acres, but delightful neighbours. Ami, the seventy-year-old crofter next door to me, who had always lived in that house where he had been born, took me under his wing; Mary, his friend, who lived alone a little further down the road, inducted me into the mysteries of poultry-keeping. I planted native trees and hedges, dug out a flower and herb garden, created a vegetable patch, and acquired beautiful rare-breed hens, glossy black ducks, and a trio of elegant, white Roman geese. I was a crofter. A little black cat called Fingal moved in, and then an enormous boisterous golden retriever called Frodo, and I imagined that this was how my life was always going to be.

For a while, work went well; a stream of people came to be treated for everything from smoking to panic disorder. Still brimming over with all the insights I'd gained from learning to fly, I decided that I now had something to write about, and I enrolled for an online master's degree in creative writing and began to work on my first novel. As a result of that course, and my ongoing re-immersion in the study of story and mythology which I'd been steeped in ever since I was a child, I developed a successful specialism in narrative therapy. I put together a training course for an organisation which provided continuing professional development to clinical psychologists and other mental health professionals. I continued to work with individuals, helping them to understand and tell their own stories. Life was full and rich. It was well balanced, too; my work might have required me to be indoors and to use my head, but the croft required me to spend time outdoors and to come to understand how the land I was living in actually worked.

The only cloud which began to loom ever closer on the horizon was the slow-dawning understanding that it was going to be hard to make a living over the longer term if I wanted to continue to work from home. Ullapool might have had a large catchment area, but the resident population was small and at the time there was very little turnover. There was nothing remotely resembling a therapy culture; people came to be 'fixed', and once they'd been fixed they moved on. Referrals flooded in – but nevertheless I soon began to exhaust my client base, and it became clear that I was going to have to think again about future sources of income. I expanded my work area, now offering courses and individual work in creative imagination techniques for writers – but I was struggling to make it enough.

One Sunday morning, in February 2006, almost three years after I'd moved to the croft, a stranger arrived on my doorstep. He brought with him all the glory-bound glamour of a fast-jet pilot in the RAF, and all the midlife angst of a man who knows in his heart that it isn't enough. It was an irresistible combination. Earlier that week I'd received an email from this man, who was based a couple of hours to the east at the Tornado base in Lossiemouth and was recently divorced. He had been writing poetry for years, but somehow it felt as stuck as the rest of his life, and he was interested in the creative imagination work I was offering. Intrigued, I invited him to come and see me; and so here he was, clutching a selection of Sunday newspapers and some very fine poems.

By the time he had told me the story of how, once upon a time, fresh from a philosophy degree at Oxford, he had had to remove his earrings and dye his bright green hair brown again so that he could look 'respectable' for his interview to join the RAF, I was hooked. He left, clutching a biography of Ted Hughes and Sylvia Plath which I'd just finished reading, promising to return it 'next time he happened to be passing by'. Which happened to be the following weekend . . . and so it began.

After I left Len I'd imagined I would never want to live with anyone again. I was unutterably happy to regain my independence and, after the constraints of the eleven years I spent with him, I loved living alone and having the freedom to do what I wanted to do with my life, to grow into the person I wanted to become, rather than being controlled by someone else's incompatible needs, expectations and values. But I often missed the intimacy – both emotional and physical – which is so much a part of committed long-term relationships, and sometimes wondered what it might be like to be in a more functional marriage. I had never been much suited either to casual relationships or to casual sex, and throughout those years I simply never found anyone I came close to falling in love with – no one remotely compatible. But in David I found a companion whose intellectual curiosity matched my own, whose sense of honour and bravery I could admire, who had a remarkable way with words, and with whom I found a physical pleasure which seemed somehow, indefinably, to be all tied up with my deepening relationship with the land and the natural world around me since I had moved to this croft. I closed my eyes, and jumped. Eighteen months later, one sunny day in July, and under a tree at Ullapool's Ceilidh Place, surrounded by family and friends, I married him.

David's income was a welcome addition to my own, but after twenty-six years in the RAF, and after a life filled to the brim with flying – he had spent most of his spare time during those years hang-gliding – he had come to recognise that he badly needed a change. I'd now completed my creative writing MA, and received into the bargain a pretty good education on the challenges being faced both by publishers and authors in a competitive and price-driven book market. I had begun to hanker after setting up a small literary press. I wanted to provide a home for marginal work: the kind of literary fiction that wasn't commercial and formulaic, that wasn't a product of the Wasteland and its values, but that said something important about the world and our place in it. Or at least, which asked the right questions. I wanted to publish the kind of book that I could rarely seem to find any more on the shelves of bookstores.

One Sunday, on a working trip to Edinburgh, I sat in a café and jotted down a few rough and appallingly uninformed ideas. I took them back to David, and in a fit of rash enthusiasm, we decided we'd go into partnership together. It was the excuse he'd been looking for to leave the RAF and, like me, he had a deep love of literature and words. It seemed to be the perfect solution:

we would do what we loved, and make a living in the process. And so, in very short order, Two Ravens Press was born.

We had absolutely no idea what we were doing. None at all. I had no clue about how you got books printed on a relatively small scale; I imagined at first that we'd have to kit out the conservatory with a small printing machine. It was such a relief to discover that you could simply upload a typeset book file to a printer via the internet, and a few weeks later your books would arrive, neatly boxed and ready to go. But there was a small problem; we didn't know how to typeset, and we were doing this on absolutely no budget at all. Not even a shoestring. Although David had left the RAF with a small pension, I'd given up my own meagre income from therapy work to take this on, and we needed to be careful.

So we learned to typeset. And then to design covers. And to create our own website, because we couldn't afford to pay anyone else to do it. I could edit and proofread; David could do sums, and so he became the company accountant. We spent an intense few months trying to figure out how the publishing industry worked, from scratch. How to get your books distributed. How to get them reviewed. How to market them; how to get publicity. How to get them into shops. All of this, and more, we did ourselves, and from a baseline of absolutely no knowledge at all.

It was impossible, but neither of us could contemplate the idea that we might not make it work. If my default position was an excess of bright ideas combined with a tendency to over-achievement and a need for perfection, David brought with him the military motto that 'the mission must be accomplished'. If someone sets you a task, you make it happen, and it doesn't matter what gets broken in the process.

The mission was accomplished, but as the years slipped by, many things were broken. And yet, we had much of the recognition we had hoped for: just a year into its life, Two Ravens Press was described by *The Herald* newspaper as 'a quiet publishing revolution', and by *Publishing News* as 'the most talked-about publisher in Scotland'. We published twelve books during our first year and by 2008 we were publishing twenty-four. We had taken on many debut authors, but also acquired books from a few established, bestselling or prize-winning writers. Several of our books came up for major literary awards.

But in spite of the accolades it was outrageously hard to actually sell books, and impossible to make a living from it. In all the apparently successful years of its existence, Two Ravens Press just about covered the costs of publishing books, paying royalties to authors, and the costs of establishing the business – but it paid us virtually nothing. We lived off David's pension, a few typesetting and book design jobs for other publishers, and dwindling savings. We received little moral support and minimal funding from a Scottish Arts Council which really didn't know what to make of us. It became clear to us over the years that the grant-giving culture in the arts is designed for particular kinds of companies and particular kinds of people: people who like to network and go to big-city publishing parties; people who are good self-publicists and enjoy the limelight; people who are comfortable within the constraints of the establishment. Good people – but not us. It was not designed to support and encourage two people who came out of nowhere, who lived on a croft in the north-west Highlands and wanted to stay there, and whose publishing manifesto declared, 'This is not a game. This is the Alamo. We want ideas, we want . . . language as a rallying flag, as a sanctuary, a bayonet, a broom. . . . [W]e won't compromise for profit. We won't hesitate to publish books which barely make a profit – if we believe in them and believe that they need to be published.' That wasn't what the publically funded grant-giving establishment had in mind at all.

Because we had neither personal fortunes nor wealthy backers, and so couldn't afford to employ anyone to help us, we did everything ourselves – from reading all the submissions in the slush pile to sticking the books in envelopes to be posted to those customers who ordered directly from our website rather than through bookstores. We worked every day, all day and usually into the evening, hardly ever taking holidays or weekends off, falling into bed exhausted and bad-tempered. We ran the business from home, and so could never close the door on it; the computers were always switched on and the computers controlled our lives. Everything was down to us, and each of us in our very different ways and for very different reasons had an over-developed sense of responsibility. Neither of us knew how to give up. It was an accident in the making.

While all of this was going on, we were still trying to keep the croft going. I still kept hens, ducks and geese, though growing vegetables was increasingly hard to squeeze in, and because David really wanted to keep sheep, we bought a small flock of ten beautiful black, horned Hebridean ewes. The trouble was, although I had moved to this croft so I could spend time out on the land, now I had no time to appreciate it; the small beginnings of a relationship with the place which I'd enjoyed at first had all but vanished. There was only ever time for the chores, and in between the chores I was tied to a desk.

Over a two-week period during Christmas and New Year of 2009, three years after we'd started Two Ravens Press, three challenging years of constant hard grind (and yes, sometimes a lot of fun), we crashed. But we weren't just exhausted, we were also heart-sick. All around us, crofting was dying out as people moved in from the far southern suburbs looking for cheap properties to 'retire to'. The property market was booming and crofting land was being sold off for house sites and holiday chalets, and what once had been a remote, five-mile-long narrow cul-de-sac of a road with four tiny, scattered but close-knit crofting communities along it had become a sprawling five-mile-long suburb of the increasingly overcrowded village of Ullapool.

And then came the sudden, acute and profoundly transformative onset of what ecologist and activist Joanna Macy has called 'environmental despair'.[19] Our love for and engagement with the land and the vanishing crofting culture around us had led us to slowly drift into publishing books which celebrated people's relationships with the natural world. Now, little by little, we were beginning to understand for the first time in our lives the true scale of the environmental crisis facing the planet. The extent of the damage astonished me.

I had been aware of the ugliness of industrialisation and the pollution it caused since I was a child. I had been aware of a few other odd things which happened to get media attention – that there were problems with cutting down the rainforests and that there was a hole in the ozone layer – but I had never properly focused in on the notion that humans were, quite simply, killing the planet. Like so many people, I had been existing in some strange kind of bubble. The world seems to work, you think, so it can't be that bad. And you're so busy, and besides, what can you do, and anyway, the politicians will take care of it, or the scientists and engineers . . . But now I was beginning to understand the real nature of the problem, and to see that the world didn't actually 'work' and the politicians didn't give a damn and the solution could never be technological – and I began to grieve, profoundly.

Philosopher Glenn Albrecht[20] calls this phenomenon of environmentally induced distress 'solastalgia': 'As opposed to nostalgia – the melancholia or homesickness experienced by individuals when separated from a loved home – solastalgia is the distress that is produced by environmental change impacting on people while they are directly connected to their home environment.' I was solastalgic for sure, in pain for the whole world. 'Environmental despair' was now added to the despair I had felt for most of my life at the aridity and hollowness of our Western civilisation, at the Wasteland which so many people around me seemed to inhabit.

This grieving for a world which might soon be lost was compounded by a growing awareness of the frenetic lunacy of my own life. I couldn't imagine how I had let it happen. Two Ravens Press had become the proverbial runaway train, and I didn't know how to get off. Each morning, I would walk down the field to the lochside and lower myself down onto a large flat rock, holding tight to my big old dog, looking out hollow-eyed at the solitary seal who would come each morning, as she always had, to pop her sleek grey head out of the water and stare at us – and I despaired. Once, I had sung to that seal whenever she appeared; now I hadn't the heart. I was bone-tired and fractious. Somehow I had managed to take a life that had finally seemed so promising, that was heading gently but firmly precisely in the direction I had always wanted it to go, and I had ended up back in the Wasteland. But this was a Wasteland I'd created all by myself, and I didn't know how to make it go away. I couldn't just leave this job like I'd left the others; I'd created an entire company, an entire infrastructure; I had *responsibilities*.

Old habits might sometimes die hard, but my old habits had delusions of immortality. They clearly planned to live forever.

When the breaking point comes, it rarely comes in a form you might have anticipated. But it comes. Sometimes it comes when you are confronted with the one thing that, at the time, is most likely to break your heart – and which makes you understand, finally, that you cannot bear to live in a world in which that happens. It might be a real event – or, sometimes, just the idea or image of an event. Often, it comes as a surprise to you, and if anyone had told me that the one thing I just couldn't tolerate in the world at that time would be found in the pages of a novel by Cormac McCarthy, I'd have laughed.

One week just before the Christmas of 2009, taking some rare time out, I read *The Crossing*, the middle book in McCarthy's 'Border Trilogy'.[21] It is the story of a boy who lives on a cattle ranch, and rescues a she-wolf from a trap he himself has set. The boy decides to take her back across the border to the mountains of Mexico, where he believes she came from. He travels with the injured and wary wolf, developing a deep bond with her, but once they're in Mexico she is captured by officials who impound her and hand her over to a group of local men. They take her into an arena, where she is going to be made to fight every one of the town's dogs in turn.

The boy, knowing that she will sooner or later be torn apart, tries to rescue the heavily pregnant wolf, but he doesn't succeed. He leaves the arena, fetches his rifle, returns, and shoots the wolf in the head. He then trades his rifle for the wolf's carcass, and takes her to the hills astride his horse, to bury her:

> He squatted over the wolf and touched her fur. He touched the cold and perfect teeth. The eye turned to the fire gave back no light and he closed it with his thumb and sat by her and put his hand upon her bloodied forehead and closed his own eyes that he could see her running in the starlight where the grass was wet and the sun's coming as yet had not undone the rich matrix of creatures passed in the night before her . . . He took up her stiff head out of the leaves and held it or he reached to hold what cannot be held, what already ran among the mountains at once terrible and of a great beauty, like flowers that feed on flesh . . . But which cannot be held never be held and is no flower but is swift and a huntress and the wind itself is in terror of it and the world cannot lose it.

The world cannot lose it – but if I understood anything now, I understood that the world was going to lose it. *We* were going to lose it, we humans, and we didn't seem even to care.

I broke down completely. I didn't know quite what it was that I was weeping for, but I felt as if my heart was caving in. For the wolf, for all wolves, for all the pregnant females who are beaten by men, for all wild things, for the cruelty of humans, for the heartbroken boy, for my dogs, for the future death of my dogs, for the beauty of words, for my life, for all our lives, for the whole world which we were turning into a Wasteland. For all the Wastelands of the human spirit, for the Wasteland that I was creating out of my own life.

I was heartbroken and I was angry. After a while I was more

angry than sad. I didn't know where it would end, my rage against this Machine which passes for civilisation, which values life and the planet so little; which seeks only to kill and especially to kill anything that is wild and free. Which seeks to kill wolves, and women, and which is now killing the planet. I wanted to set myself apart from it, and David seemed to share my despair. I wanted to be somewhere wilder; somewhere that wasn't turning more and more suburban with every passing year.

Neither of us was much good at hanging around once it was clear something was irretrievably broken. And so, shortly after the New Year dawned in 2010, the decision was made. We would abandon these lives that were becoming so intolerable, this Wasteland which was encroaching on us again. And, unthinkable as it was, in the process we would abandon this beautiful place into which I'd poured my heart and soul. We would leave.

We each had our own vision of what a better life might be, and we didn't understand at the time how different those visions were. While David was happy enough to head into the wilds, civilisation and all its trappings – and in particular the status associated with running Two Ravens Press – still had some hold. We couldn't possibly close down Two Ravens Press. We had *responsibilities*; we couldn't just give it all up. And besides, he argued, what would we be, if we gave it up? Who would we say we were?

I, in contrast, had had more than enough of publishing by then; I'd had enough of everything and everybody. I wanted to be *nobody*: that's precisely who I wanted to say I was. I wanted to stop. I wanted to sit for a while and lick my wounds, to re-examine my view of the world and my sense of my own place in it. I wanted to know what you did when that world was falling apart as a consequence of your own species' actions, and when there was little or nothing you could do to prevent it. I wanted to know how you still got out of bed in the morning.

I longed for peace, and a wild and quiet place to find that peace in, and the time to sit and listen to the land as I once had begun to do. To find my connection again, to plug back into the Earth, to remember what it was to begin to belong. And so I looked for, and then I found, the house at the end of the world. One day, browsing on the web for an escape route from civilisation, I happened upon a house with a croft for sale, right at the end of what was described as 'the longest cul-de-sac in Europe'. It was on the far south-west coast of the Isle of Lewis in the Outer Hebrides, sandwiched between a vast, wild ocean and bleak, rugged mountains. It seemed to be perfect. The house needed some work, and there wasn't a fencepost on the croft that wasn't rotten or crooked. But we were beginning again, and we were young enough still, and surely we had the energy for that?

My much-loved house and croft on the shores of Loch Broom sold in a flash, and just five months after the unspeakable had been spoken, we had packed up the house and Two Ravens Press, and off we went, across the Minch to Lewis. The Calmac ferry from Ullapool for a while took on the appearance of Noah's Ark as little by little we transported dogs, sheep, geese, hens, ducks and a hive of bees. Amid the exhaustion, excitement was in the air. We were starting again, and everything would be different this time around.

8

The Fertile Fields

The Heroine's Return

Llyn-y-Fan Fach, Brecon Beacons, Wales

Curandera

They think she lives alone
on the edge of town in a two-room house
where she moved when her husband died
at thirty-five of a gunshot wound
in the bed of another woman. The *curandera*
and house have aged together to the rhythm
of the desert.

She wakes early, lights candles before
her sacred statues, brews tea of *yerbabuena*.
She moves down her porch steps, rubs
cool morning sand into her hands, into her arms.
Like a large black bird, she feeds on
the desert, gathering herbs for her basket.

Her days are slow, days of grinding
dried snake into power, of crushing
wild bees to mix with white wine.
And the townspeople come, hoping
to be touched by her ointments,
her hands, her prayers, her eyes.
She listens to their stories, and she listens
to the desert, always, to the desert.

By sunset she is tired. The wind
strokes the strands of long grey hair
the smells of drying plants drift
into her blood, the sun seeps
into her bones. She dozes
on her back porch. Rocking, rocking.

At night she cooks chopped cactus
and brews more tea. She brushes a layer
of sand from her bed, sand which covers
the table, stove, floor. She blows
the statues clean, the candles out.
Before sleeping, she listens to the message
of the owl and the coyote. She closes her eyes
and breathes with the mice and snakes
and wind.

Pat Mora[1]

Just the other side of the full moon, a few days after summer solstice, the sun finally shines. It's been the coldest and wettest spring in living memory, the temperatures barely rising above 10 degrees Celsius all the way through June. Friends in California and Brazil tell of land ravaged by record droughts, but here in Donegal the rain and wind have been ceaseless. What would we do, if summer never came? What would we do, if the old reliable cycle of the seasons failed?

We don't worry about that now, just breathe long sighs of relief. The trees are finally in full leaf, the grass is long enough to need cutting. We throw off our sweaters and are fallen upon by biting insects desperate to make up for lost time. A friend's bees swarm; the next one will be ours, and the hive is sun-warmed, waiting. Can we imagine a day when the bees might not swarm? The branches of the ash trees sweep the surface of the river, green enough now to obscure the budding fuchsias on the far bank. The ancient elder scrapes up a tired blossom or two, and the fields are tangled into a tight weave of weed and grass. The verges of the lane are teeming with blue geraniums and red clover; cow parsley pops up everywhere, and vast swathes of fragrant meadow-sweet are starting to bud up, down by the river. The brambles are flowering, clambering over all the drystone walls, pushing through cracks, and I'm dreaming of blackberry jam and autumn pies. The swallows have arrived and are building a nest in the turf shed. What would we do if the swallows didn't come?

Summer is here. How can the world contain so much life? Water tumbles down the waterfall, across the stepping stones, rushing by and tickling the feet of the grey heron fishing on a stone down-stream. The long winter's sleep is over, the capriciousness of spring is past, and the world shouts out its fullness. This world is so full of gifts. This abundance! Can we bear to see it die?

It is dying, nevertheless. We know it; we seem to be resigned to it. Our institutions reflect the truth of it. According to a recent article in the *Guardian*,[2] words for elements of nature have been systematically removed from the *Oxford Junior Dictionary*: 'almond', 'blackberry' and 'crocus' made way for 'block graph' and 'celebrity' in the 2007 edition, and instead of 'catkin', 'cauliflower', 'chestnut' and 'clover', today's edition of the dictionary, which is aimed at seven-year-olds, features 'cut and paste', 'broadband' and 'analogue'. Travel and nature writer Robert Macfarlane called it:

> ... an alarming acceptance of the ideas that children might no longer see the seasons, that all childhoods are urban, that all cities are denatured, and that what exists beyond the city fringe or the edge of the computer screen need not be named ... We do not care for what we do not know, and on the whole we do not know what we cannot name. Do we want an alphabet for children that begins 'A is for Acorn, B is for Buttercup, C is for Conker'; or one that begins 'A is for Attachment, B is for Block-Graph, C is for Chatroom'?[3]

A recent book by Michael McCarthy, former environment editor of *The Independent,* is entitled *The Moth Snowstorm.* It powerfully and evocatively summarises what has taken place in the United Kingdom, almost without people noticing:

> It's the loss of abundance itself I mourn ... people over the age of fifty can remember springtime lapwings crying and swooping over every field, corn buntings alert on each hedge and telegraph wire, swallow aerobatics in every farmyard and clouds of finches

on the autumn stubbles; they remember nettle beds swarming with small tortoiseshell and peacock caterpillars, the sparking pointillist palette of the hay meadows, ditches crawling and croaking with frogs and toads and even in the suburbs, song-bird speckled lawns and congregations of house martins in their dashing navy-blue elegance . . . but most vividly of all, some of them remember the moth snowstorm.

What McCarthy calls the 'moth snowstorm' refers to the times when, driving at night on a dark road, you would see so many moths caught in your car headlights that it resembled driving through a snowstorm. No longer. 'The country I was born into,' McCarthy writes, 'possessed something wonderful it absolutely possesses no longer: natural abundance . . . Blessed, unregarded abundance has been destroyed.'[4]

Who will ensure that what is left of the Earth's abundance isn't destroyed? Who will stand up for the Earth, if not the women who are of it and mirror it? We women are so full of gifts, containers for so much life. We are part of the Earth's abundance – what is left of it. An abundance which is still there, in the wild places – but only just. Still now, even in the bleakest of bogs, on the saltiest and rockiest of shores, there is abundance if you know both how to see it, and what to do with it.

The wild and exposed south-west coast of Lewis to which we moved in 2010 had no fertile fields, no hay meadows, no lush gardens, and few opportunities for food foraging – but it had its own great treasures, which I gradually came to know. On that wildest and rockiest of all headlands, and around the shallow freshwater loch at the bottom of the croft, grew a profusion of wildflowers. Plants which once were used for dyeing: tormentil, bog asphodel, marsh marigold, butterwort, lady's bedstraw, various lichens. Plants which had herbal medicinal uses: bogbean, self-heal, eyebright, sundew, dandelion, plantain, sphagnum moss. Seaweed galore: kelp and bladderwrack to fertilise the garden, and beautiful red dulse, packed with vitamins and minerals, to eat. Flowers to feed the hive of honeybees that we cherished, out there at the end of the world, on the farthest edges of their possible habitat.

When the land offers up relatively little, you come to treasure what gifts it gives, and during the years we spent on that croft, I came to know the plants intimately. I knew when they would appear, and in what sheltered pockets: sundew in June, down by the burn that fed the loch; self-heal on the verges of the road in July; wild thyme out at the rocky place, hidden in cracks of the cliffs. Each morning and afternoon, as I roamed a land empty of humans with only the dogs by my side, my walking was teaching me. As time went by, more and more plant-strangers became friends, could be greeted by name as I passed along my way; now each day I walked not through uncharted territory, but through a brave new world of magic, medicine, folklore and food with which I was growing unexpectedly intimate. I harvested carefully, dyed the fleece from our own sheep, made herbal tinctures, gathered and dried seaweed for use in the kitchen. In short, I became a 'weed wife'.

'Something has happened this year . . . Those of us who have loved the plants since childhood and dreamed of a cronehood stalking the fields with a basket, kitchen windowsill a stained glass apothecary of sunlight falling through bottles of herb-infused oils and tinctures − a Church of Weeds − have heard the hedgerows calling, clearer and more insistent than ever before.' So wrote my artist friend Rima Staines in the summer of 2013 in a post on her popular blog, The Hermitage,[5] and when I read it I shivered a little, because that was exactly what had been happening to me. In my case, the newly arising plant-longing could be traced back to an old yearning, stemming in good part from a figure from the folk tradition of a land half a world away: the Hispanic folk figure of the *curandera*. A *curandera* is a traditional Hispanic healer, herbalist and all-round Wise Woman, and I became acquainted with her history while learning to fly in the south New Mexican desert in the year 2000.

I was inspired by the figure of the *curandera* in good part because a poem that I read during that time by one of my favourite poets − New Mexican poet, Pat Mora − slipped right into my heart, lodged itself there and never left. When I first read it I felt a jolt of recognition: a very definite 'Yes – that is it; that is what I am supposed to be'. This image of the Wise Woman, connected to the land and its plants, communing with the desert and its animals, was something that translated perfectly.

The Wise Woman – the *bean feasa*, the 'woman of knowledge'; the *bean leighis*, the 'woman of healing' – is a key figure in Celtic folk traditions. There has always been a thriving tradition of powerful local female healers in Ireland[6] and Scotland, and their remit included but then transcended the practices of herbalism which they shared sometimes with male healers. In mediating people's relationships with the Otherworld, the role of the Wise Woman incorporated elements both of spiritual guide and modern therapeutic psychologist. The power and authority of these women derived from their close association with the native Otherworld, and the knowledge, wisdom and skill which that association conferred. In many ways, the Gaelic tradition of the *bean feasa* was shamanic in nature, involving visits by practitioners to the native spirit world in order to return with gifts and knowledge.[7] Crucially, the *bean feasa* was implicated in the wider health of the community, as well as that of individuals: she was consulted to repair 'breaches of communitarian or cosmological harmony'.[8]

The Wise Woman as herbalist, spiritual guide and psychologist – I recognised at last that this was the ultimate journey I was on, its goal a way of being in the world that I had longed for all my life. I wanted to become a Wise Woman, grounded and rooted in the Earth, listening to its stories and mediating the wisdom of the Otherworld – the old ancestral and spiritual wisdom which shows us how to live in balance in the world, how to live in harmony in our communities. That was my journey: the weed wife's version of the courtly Grail quest – moss-encrusted, grub-infested, infinitely more feral. No knights, no unearthly longings, just an ear to the Wells, and the nourishing beauty of the rich brown earth.

The Wise Woman is the Heroine, returned from her Journey, belonging finally both to herself and to the land where she lives.

She is ready to offer up her knowledge and her gifts in service to the community. The Wise Woman, the weed wife, the *curandera* – whatever you call her, she is my inspiration. I recognise in her the need which each of us has to find strength from within ourselves; the need which each of us has to delve deep inside to uncover and develop the sources of our own belonging. To come to belong to this wide, wild Earth.

This is the work we must have done before we can ever hope to bring our newly birthed wisdom, our skills and our love, out into the world. Those gifts are hard won, and take a long time to cook before finally you get to serve them up in a thick, nourishing herb-scented stew. But once the stew is ready, the Wise Woman is a critical and integral part of her wider community. Her gifts are the gifts of the land to which she completely belongs; her voice is the voice of the Earth, the voice of the Otherworld which echoes from the depths of the Wells. Her gifts are the gifts which heal; she can use them to heal the Wasteland, reweaving it back into fertility, one thread at a time.

'Women have always been healers,' scientist and alternative medicine pioneer Jeanne Achterberg[9] tells us. 'Cultural myths from around the world describe a time when only women knew the secrets of life and death, and therefore they alone could practise the magical art of healing. In crises and calamity, or so some of the stories go, women's revered position as keepers of the sacred wisdom was deliberately and forcibly wrested away from them.' Women have always been the keepers of the Earth's healing wisdom, and from the beautiful mountain lake called Llyn-y-Fan Fach, in the Brecon Beacons National Park, comes the story of one such woman.[10]

~

The Lady of Llyn-y-Fan Fach

A widow-woman lived once with her son in the Black Mountains of Wales. Her husband had been a farmer who was killed during the troubles which plagued the land in those times, but despite this, fortune seemed to smile upon the woman and her son. Their cattle prospered and grew fat, and increased in numbers so much that she had to send her son away out over the hills with a portion of the herd to graze the fertile lands near Llyn-y-Fan Fach. The son tended the cattle well, and as the years passed and the herd thrived, he grew into manhood.

One morning, as the young man was walking by the shore of Llyn-y-Fan Fach, he saw a beautiful woman sitting in the centre of the lake, seemingly floating on top of its calm waters. It came to him that she was one of the Gwragedd Annwn – the wives of the Otherworld – who are known to live at the bottom of such remote mountain lakes. She was the most beautiful woman he could ever have imagined, and as he stood there with his mouth open staring at her, she lifted her head and looked right back at him. He lifted his hands to offer the woman some of the bread and cheese that his mother had made him for his lunch, and she rose, and glided over the surface of the waters towards him. She gently refused the food, and as he stretched out his hand to touch her, she eluded his grasp, singing out: 'Hard-baked is your bread! And it is not so easy to catch me.' With these words she immediately vanished beneath the surface of the waters, leaving the young man yearning and love-lorn.

On his return home, he told his mother what had happened. She told him that he should return the following day to the lake, and instead of the hard-baked bread, he should take unbaked bread dough with him, in case the woman might like it better. And so the young man rose well before dawn the following day. He placed bread dough in his pockets and made his way to Llyn-y-Fan Fach, reaching its shores just as the first rays of dawn peeked over the nearby crags. He walked and walked, his eyes straining over the waters so that he might catch sight of her when she came. And when finally she appeared there in the centre of the lake, just as before, his hand went into his pocket and he offered her the dough. Again, she floated over the surface of the waters towards him, and before he could stop himself, his lips moved and words came pouring out and he found himself offering her his undying love. She gently turned away, saying:

'Unbaked your bread! And you I desire not.' And once more she vanished beneath the waters. But this time, before she slipped away, she turned to him with a smile playing upon her lips, and the sight of this gave the young man some hope that he might still have a chance to win her. Again he went home, and told his mother what had happened. This time his mother suggested that he take with him part-baked bread, and that this might please the mysterious lady.

At the crack of dawn the following morning, the young man once again made his way towards Llyn-y-Fan Fach. With renewed hope in his heart, he reached the shores of the lake and resumed his walking and gazing. But the morning sun climbed in the heavens, and eventually noon came and went, and still he had seen no sign of the lady. By the time the day cooled to evening, he still had not caught sight of her. Then, just as he was about to give up as the sun fell in the sky and the shadows lengthened, the lady appeared and glided over to the land. She smiled at him and, emboldened, the young man reached out to her.

This time she accepted the part-baked bread he offered and did not shrink back as he took her hand. She listened to his marriage proposals and agreed to wed him. But there was a condition, she said: if ever he were to strike her three undeserved blows, then she would vanish and leave him forever. He readily agreed; he was in love and of course would have consented unthinkingly to whatever she requested of him. Then she released his hand and began to call up from the lake a flock of sheep, and then a fine herd of fat cattle, many goats and several horses, while the young man looked on, unable to believe his good fortune.

He returned home with his lady and her animals, and they were married. They settled at the farm known as the Ridge of the Milk-Parlour, close to the village of Myddfai. They lived there in happiness for several years, and were blessed with three fine sons. Then, one day, there was a christening in the neighbourhood to which they had both been invited, but the lady was reluctant to go, saying that it was too far to walk. Her husband said that she should fetch one of the horses, and she agreed to this, as long as he would fetch her gloves from the house. He did so, but when he returned, he found that she was staring into her herb garden and had not yet fetched the horse. Playfully he slapped her on her shoulder with a glove, crying, 'Go on, go on,' but she turned on him and reminded him of the promise he had made, that he would not strike her without provocation. It was for her, she said, to decide whether time taken to ponder a cure from the plants in her garden was more necessary than arriving early at a christening. Now he had struck her the first blow, and she warned him to be far more cautious in the future.

On another occasion, they were attending a wedding, but in the middle of the wedding party the lady of Llyn-y-Fan Fach looked at the bride and groom and then burst into uncontrollable tears. Her husband slapped her on her shoulder and demanded to know why she was weeping inappropriately in the midst of such a joyful occasion. She replied: 'I am weeping because these people are entering into a life of trouble, for they do not love each other well; and now your own troubles have been doubled, for you have struck me a second time without cause.'

The years passed and their sons grew up to be handsome and accomplished young men. The times had been good, but still the man was watchful and his wife reminded him to be careful that he did not inadvertently lay upon her the final causeless blow, for then she would be gone from his life. But one day they were attending a funeral, and while the assembled mourners were overcome with grief, his wife seemed full of mirth and high spirits. On occasion she would smile, or burst into fits of laughter. And because of this, her husband tapped her on her shoulder, imploring her to hush and not to laugh. She replied that she was laughing and joyful because, when people died, no more earthly concerns could trouble them. But the final blow had been struck. 'Now the marriage contract between us is broken. Farewell!'

And immediately the fairy woman set off towards the farm and there she called her sheep, her goats and the horses to her. And she called her cattle to her: 'Brindled cow, white-speckled, spotted cow, blood-freckled, four-filed sward-mottled, the old white-faced, and Geigen the grey; with the white bull from the king's court, and

the little black calf suspended on a hook, come you all safely home!'
They all responded to her command, and even the little black calf,
though it had been slaughtered, came back to life and leapt off the
hook and trotted towards her. This was the springtime, and four of
her oxen were ploughing a nearby field. To these she sang: 'Four
grey oxen upon the field, come you also back safely home!' Then
the lady crossed Myddfai Mountain with all of her stock behind
her, and they came to the shores of Llyn-y-Fan Fach, where they
entered the waters and vanished beneath the surface.

Her three sons were left disconsolate, and often they could be
seen wandering the shores of the lake, in the forlorn hope of catching
a glimpse of their lost mother. For in his sorrow, their father had told
them the tale of their mother and her magical origins. Then, one day,
as they were walking near the place called Dôl Hywel, near the
mountain gate known today as the Physicians' Gate, their mother
suddenly appeared to them. She called her eldest son Rhiwallon to
her, and told him that his appointed mission on Earth was to relieve
his fellow man from suffering and pain through an ability to heal all
manner of diseases. To this end, she gave him a bag full of instructions
for the preservation of health. She told him that by strict adherence
to the methodologies here, he and his descendants, for several generations, would become the most skilful practitioners of the medical
arts in the entire realm. Then she vanished, but her voice lingered
and she promised to meet him whenever her advice was most needed.

On several occasions after that it is said that she met her sons.
Once she met them at quite a distant place known as the Dale of
the Physicians, and from there she walked with them all the way
back to Llyn-y-Fan Fach, pointing out to them all the healing and
medicinal plants that they encountered on the way. The knowledge
that their mother had imparted to them, along with their own natural
skills, soon made them the country's most notable physicians. And
so that their knowledge would never be lost, they had it committed
to writing and so preserved it for all successive generations.

~

A converted stone church in the village of Coachford, a few kilometres outside of Cork city, isn't the kind of setting in which you'd
normally expect to find a place of learning focused on disseminating
indigenous herbal traditions. And yet, as well as being the home of
Nikki Darrell and her two teenage children, the church is also the
premises of Veriditas Hibernica,[11] an organisation which Nikki
founded to teach the reclaiming of Ireland's native herbal heritage.
It's an unpretentious and beautiful conversion, and although the
rooms are dark – the old church windows are small, and the walls
thick – they're large, the ceilings are high, and there's a liberating
sense of space. Evidence of Nikki's herbal practice is everywhere;
one wall in the huge, decidedly unfitted kitchen is lined with
shelves filled with herb vinegars: 'We're testing them out, as alternatives to alcohol-based tinctures,' she tells me, as she pours a
measure of something into a pan of bubbling bean stew.

Fortuitously I've arrived at lunchtime, and am offered freshly
baked bread and a bowl of that gloriously aromatic stew, which
also contains a variety of herbs foraged from her compact garden.
'There's such a big interest in foraging now,' she tells me as we
sit down at a large wooden table, 'which is good because wild
foods have been shown to contain all sorts of micro-nutrients that
aren't present in our diets normally, and which can protect against
lots of diseases. It's all part of the desire that so many people are
feeling to return to living in harmony with what is around us.'
That desire to connect back to the cycles and rhythms of the
natural world is the origin of Nikki's vision for Veriditas Hibernica,
which came into being about eight years ago. 'It was born out of
a desire to help people in Ireland reclaim their relationship with
plants, to remember the rich cultural heritage of this land, where
people came to learn plant medicine and lore many centuries ago.'

Nikki has had a strong relationship with plants ever since she
can remember, and was always drawn to work with them. 'I bought
my first packet of herb seeds when I was about nine, and my first
herbal when I was eleven. I used to help out in the garden at
home and we did a bit of foraging among the weeds that grew

alongside the vegetables. We pickled, made cordials, jam and wine, and I loved it. In my teens I helped out at summer Woodcraft camps for kids and rambled through wild places, always loving to discover new plants. All I ever really wanted to be was a herbalist, a gardener, a grower – to tend plants and make good food and medicine with them. When I left school, I studied horticultural and plant science at university and spent five years as a research scientist, because as far as I knew then there was nowhere to study to be a herbalist, and questions about pursuing such a path didn't meet with much support in a middle-class grammar school environment focused on academic competition and achievement!'

Although it wasn't what she'd originally intended to do, Nikki's scientific training gave her a good grounding for the rest of her work, and now she is glad to have pursued that initial path. But when she came across some people who were actually training professionally to be herbalists, she left the research world and signed up for Herb College. But by the time she graduated as a Medical Herbalist, she was feeling that something important was missing from all that study she'd undertaken.

'I became angry,' she tells me, 'because people in the herbal profession were declaring that it was necessary to have at least a BSc and probably an MSc in order to practise, and that the proper place to learn to be a herbalist was in the lecture theatres and laboratories of "real educational establishments", to the exclusion of all other routes. Now, I have a long string of letters after my name, and lots of academic qualifications; I've worked as a lecturer in third-level institutions and sat on all sorts of fancy boards. But this is not what made me a good herbalist. In fact, I had to unlearn quite a bit of what I was taught. And that journey to finding out what it is that was missing from most of the professional training that's on offer has been fascinating, and led directly to the approach to herbalism I'm offering here.'

Nikki's diverse and comprehensive training is very much in evidence: after we've finished that delicious lunch she gives me a tour of the premises, and I am utterly entranced by an enormous library of books on plant science, herbalism and related subjects in the high-ceilinged living room, which also happens to be the room where she holds many of her classes. Shelves and shelves of them, and so many titles which leap out and beg to be picked up. I linger, but there's more that she wants to show me and so we move on; if I could ever find a way to be left alone in this place for a couple of days, I'd leap at the chance. But in the meantime, I'm interested in that alternative approach to learning herbalism which she champions at Veriditas Hibernica.

'Well, I had a little epiphany in the midst of my anger at the system,' she says, 'which related to the fact that community herbal practice has existed ever since people joined plants in the world, and for thousands of years people grew up learning the traditional healing arts from their mothers and grandmothers (and sometimes their fathers and grandfathers). They learned to recognise the plants, to grow them and tend them, to prepare food and medicine from them at the kitchen table or in the community house. Every woman was taught how to do this work for her family, and sometimes for the wider community. It is part of our heritage.'

I come to a halt again, thoroughly captivated by a beautiful little white-washed chamber with a massage table where she carries out her consultations. The walls on one side of the room are lined with shelves and cabinets filled with jars and an extensive selection of large bottles of neatly labelled herbal tinctures. I flick my eyes over them to see which ones I recognise, which plants I've worked with myself, as Nikki explains how she set about turning that epiphany into a vision for how herbal practice might be brought back into the community. 'I started by running short introductory courses on herbs for use at home as food and medicine, on setting up a herb garden, on making natural skin care products. And then some of my friends and acquaintances began to ask me to teach them more, so that they could use herbs for their friends, family and community with confidence.'

It's clear from everything she says that Nikki strongly believes that community empowerment is the critical ingredient that's lacking in traditional herbal training. That, in refusing to acknowledge the long traditions and great strengths of folk medicine and community herbalism, it runs the risk of becoming – like conventional medicinal training – both exclusive and excluding. 'Yes,' she says, nodding emphatically, 'I do feel very strongly about the value of empowering people to take care of their own health issues where possible, and also about the importance of community in our wellbeing. So I took hold of that thread and set about devising a longer training in community herbal medicine. It's been incredibly successful; last October we had our seventh intake of herbal apprentices, and in March we started a second intake for this teaching year, as there were about twenty people on a waiting list for next autumn.'

We head outside and walk around the gardens, and Nikki explains how they evolved over time, just as the philosophy here at Veriditas Hibernica evolved and clarified. The garden area around the church is a small plot, mostly consisting of gravel. Initially, Nikki laid out a few neat potager rows, but as the focus of her teachings turned to foraging and recognition of wild plants both as food and medicine, she began to develop larger beds in the middle and at the edges of the gravel, with wild forage plants growing freely alongside cultivated vegetables and exotics. From a distance the beds look chaotic, but when you step closer and begin to sift through the mass of green and identify individual plants, it's easy to see how it might work beautifully for teaching purposes.

'We bring the forage plants to live beside us, or often they just show up and then we tend them. We teach people how to cook, garden, clean, make medicines in a simple ordinary grounded way – the "ordinary sacred", which is what we believe feminine wisdom is about: grounded and earthy and full of fun. We encourage the apprentices to sit with the plants, to spend time with them, to learn to tune in to what they are saying or expressing through their form and colour and taste and texture and smell. We also teach them about the plants as chemists and alchemists, and how to use their sense of taste and smell to recognise the different molecules which the plants manufacture.'

As well as working in the gardens, the large rambling building is now tended by Nikki's growing community of herbalists, who use natural products made of vinegar, oil, salt and herbs to rejuvenate the wood and clean the windows and floors. 'Often they'll light incense or smudge as they work, playing music, or singing and dancing,' she says. 'We aspire to get to the point where people take this as commonplace, the normal and natural way to live: in healthy sustainable community, with the humans and the other beings in our local habitats supporting and encouraging each other to be our most authentic selves. And above all, caring for the plants that clean our air, our water, provide food, fuel, medicine, shelter and help us to remember who we are.'

For Nikki, whose original roots are not in Ireland but in the Caribbean and in London, the core of this work is about being local, becoming native to a place. To be native in this sense is to know, as well as to cherish, the place you are in. Native wisdom is the foundation of a lifestyle which is grounded, in harmony with the land and the specific place where you live, and she bemoans the fact that native plants are often seen as second-class citizens in the herbal world.

'Our native plant allies have been discarded in favour of the exotic and scientifically validated. Plant medicine has been given over to academics and scientists and dissected, its spirit nearly extinguished. At one time the people of this land saw themselves as part of the web of life, understood the sacredness of the natural world and the part that humans need to play in order to make a healthy ecosystem. They saw the need for working together with the other living beings in their local habitat, and knew that they had to be in a sustainable relationship with them in order to be care-taken by their environment. Nowadays, so many people have lost touch with the knowledge and wisdom that was once commonplace, common sense, innate, almost instinctive: that indigenous knowledge and wisdom which allows us to recognise plants, to know how to gather and harvest them sustainably, how to encourage them to grow well, which ones are good food and medicine.'

It seems that it's taken us so little time to lose the rich knowledge that was built up over thousands of years by our ancestors in this land – the kind of knowledge which, in most of the remaining indigenous cultures around the world, is the foundation of their daily lives, as they live in ways which are intimately and vitally connected to their wider ecosystems. Nikki agrees. 'My vision at Veriditas Hibernica is to do my part to help restore that state of affairs here,' she says. 'And especially, to work with the feminine energy that I think relates so well to plants and to our other allies in nature. My own personal journey has taught me so much about the need to honour feminine community in particular, to offer a space where women can gather together to reclaim their identity and strength and wisdom. Traditionally, women have always come together to plant seeds, gather herbs, cook soul food, share stories and make medicines, and to pass on their wisdom and knowledge. Women are the core of a healthy community, and also at the core of a healthy community and world is respect for women, their voices, their medicine and their work.

'So my work here has shifted into alignment with the journey which many women are now making: a journey back to authenticity, to respect for the feminine, and to a good grounding in traditional wisdom – our own indigenous wisdom. It seems to me that the next step is to learn to bring together that indigenous wisdom and all the valuable learnings and technologies of the last centuries – while discarding those that are not healthful – to create a reality in which we can live sustainably on this planet, in harmony both with our own species and all the other species we share it with.'

It is easy to sink into the magical Otherworld of the journey, and for some of us the temptation to stay withdrawn from a challenging everyday world can be strong. As Joseph Campbell writes, 'The first problem of the returning hero is to accept as real, after an experience of the soul-satisfying vision of fulfilment, the passing joys and sorrows, banalities and noisy obscenities of life. Why re-enter such a world?'[12] And it is always possible to refuse the

Return, to go into permanent retreat, or to make the search for personal enlightenment and self-illumination your lifetime's work – but if you do, chances are that, sooner or later, the world will come knocking. For others of us, as the world (and our own species) lurches from crisis to crisis, as we listen to the cry of a grieving Earth, the call to Return is strong.

As in Campbell's model, when the Heroine returns from her Journey she always brings back to the world a unique gift. But the wisdom which Campbell's Hero has achieved on his Journey is 'transcendental' and 'cosmic'; our Heroine's wisdom may spring in part from her association with the Otherworld but above all else it is grounded, rooted and earthy. It is the wisdom of this world and the Otherworld combined: the creative, regenerative power of life. Campbell declares that, 'Not the animal world, not the plant world, not the miracle of the spheres, but man himself is now the crucial mystery.' But for us, for women, there has been more than enough focus on 'man'. For the planet, there has been more than enough focus on humankind. And in our endless self-obsession we have clearly lost sight of the 'crucial mystery' – which is not man, and is not humankind; it is an understanding of our place in the wider web of life on this beautiful and mysterious Earth.

And so the Heroine's task on her Return is to bring humankind back in its place in the world: to bring about a re-enchantment of our relationship with the Earth. The Return, then, is about what Jungian analyst Marion Woodman calls 'conscious femininity'[13]: bringing the wisdom in nature to consciousness, as we position ourselves with nature against a destructive and dualising culture. This is the true task of the Wise Woman: to offer again the fructifying, land-healing, life-giving drink from the Grail. To reclaim our ancient authority: to restore to the world the Voices of the Wells.

Each of us returns from our pilgrimage changed, because sometime during that long process of transformation we've undergone, new insights and strengths have been uncovered. The first question which arises on our Return is what we are going to do with them. According to Jungian Robert Johnson,[14] the wounded feminine in women is associated above all with helplessness, so that a woman feels incapable of acting – 'What can I do? What can I do?' is her cry. Now that we have discovered and uncovered the buried feminine – in ourselves and in our culture – and now that we have walked the long path of our pilgrimage and endured, we must each begin to decide how, using our own unique gifts, we can work to restore the fertile feminine principle to the world, to reclaim our lost power, and so take responsibility for the healing of this Wasteland. To speak for the Earth itself.

One of the wounds dealt to us by the coming of the Wasteland is our severance from the land, the rupturing of the relationship between people and their places. The healing of the Wasteland requires a healing of this wound. Our Return, then, requires a place in which we can be grounded, rooted; a place in which our particular gifts and wisdom can flourish; a place in which we can fully embrace the natural world around us, and our part in it. A place from which we can speak.

Whether it is permanent or temporary, attachment to a place is intrinsic to the formation of a healthy, ecologically aware identity. We all need a sense of belonging – but sometimes it seems as if this is the most difficult thing in the world to achieve. If you ask people what it is exactly that so many feel is missing in their lives, what it is that creates the daily sense of dread and dislocation that so many of us live with, they'll very probably talk about belonging. 'I don't know where I belong,' they'll say, or 'I can't seem to feel at home.' Sometimes, 'I can't seem to put down roots.' This is the ailment which lies at the heart of the Wasteland: so many of us – and especially, so many of our young people – are alienated because we feel as if we can't belong to the world.

Belonging: from the Middle English *be* (an intensifier) and the archaic verb *long*, based on the Old English *gelang*, 'together with'. There are two ideas caught up in most dictionary definitions of the word: the idea of belonging to or fitting into a group of people, and the idea of belonging to a particular environment – or, as the *Shorter Oxford Dictionary* puts it, 'not be out of place'. For sure, belonging is about people, and about community, and this is the way the word is most commonly used. Our tribe matters. But place is important too, and it's unfortunate that so often in contemporary intellectual discourse the idea of place is considered to be an unfashionable, outmoded concept – a fixed concept, when the fashion is for fluid. Place, we are frequently told, is rather a static idea, whereas movement and mobility are inevitable and essential consequences of the 'Modern condition'. And rootedness apparently is passé; we're supposed to have moved beyond it. Rootedness to place often seems to be associated with closed-mindedness, even poverty; with lack of education and ambition. So the implication is that if we promote a deep sense of place as a critical component of belonging, we must be promoting an odd kind of intellectual conservatism that is quite out of step with the times.

Whether rootedness in place is a fashionable idea or not, whether it fits with the 'Modern condition' or not, there's little doubt that both our environmental and our existential crises derive in good part from a dissociation between people and the places they live. We have grown to see the physical world around us as empty of significance, as inanimate. We call the places where we live 'property'. And we inhabit our dualistic worldview so completely that we aren't even aware that there is another way to be. What is that other way? What could it mean, to truly belong to a place?

It isn't simply about whether or not you were born there. It is about whether your identity has been and is being in some way shaped by that place; having a sense that its stories, its topography, its weather, have formed you – formed your character and your values. It is feeling yourself to be profoundly rooted in the sand or soil of a place, having both a deep knowledge of and a sense of affinity with the non-human others which inhabit it along with you – both plant and animal. It's about experiencing your place as living, as animate. It's about living in physical, hands-in-the-dirt, feet-in-the-water relationship with it – in some way, about seeing

281

yourself as inextricable from it. This way of being in the world is possible wherever you live. For some of us, it is easier in wild places, or at least in the countryside. Others – like Viv Palmer, the Bug Woman; like Jacqueline Woodward-Smith, who we'll meet later in this chapter – find it just as easy in a city.

More than half of the world's population live in cities and towns, and that percentage is forecast to continue to rise. Environmental social scientist Julian Agyeman believes that a reinvention and revival of sharing in our cities could enhance equity, rebuild community and dramatically cut resource use. He suggests that the intersection of urban space and cyberspace provides an unsurpassed platform for more just, inclusive and environmentally efficient economies and societies rooted in a sharing culture.[15] The environmental organisation Friends of the Earth also argues for towns and cities which are controlled by the people living there: 'It's not the people who are the problem,' their website states:

> It's the way we build, organise and run our cities . . . Imagine a city that asks you what it should spend money on. A city that funds affordable housing and prevents rip-off landlords. One that can raise money without going to central government with a begging bowl. Where education empowers you to participate in decisions on big issues like economic policy, air pollution, transport, energy and food. Instead of treating kids as future cogs in a consumer machine. Imagine a city where sharing is the norm – from cars to pets. From skills to community-owned energy. Where libraries aren't just council-owned places we go to borrow books. They're 3D printing labs where residents lend and repair household tools. Places where nature thrives – fruit and vegetables growing on our streets, walls and the roofs of high-rise flats.[16]

The idea of living in place in a deeply connected way isn't new. It's something that all people would once have had, and which indigenous peoples around the world still do – but which most of us in the West now lack. It's radically different from the way that most of us live, those of us who, though of course born somewhere, are in no meaningful sense *of* anywhere. Unable to belong to any particular place, we so often find ourselves unable to belong to the world, from which as a consequence we hold ourselves separate.

Aggravating this problem of belonging is our tendency (the result of 2,000 years of human-centred Western philosophy) to retreat inside our own heads and look there for solutions to all of our problems. We spend our lives searching for meaning in ourselves, engaged in deep conversations with our 'inner child', meditating on a mat indoors, trained to be ever-mindful of what's going on inside us – our breath and our thoughts and emotions – when so much of the meaning we need is beneath our feet, in the plants and animals around us, in the air we breathe. We swaddle ourselves so tightly in the centrality of our own self-referential humanness that we forget that we are creatures of the Earth, and need also to connect with the land. We need to get out of the confines of our own heads. We need – we badly need – grounding; we need to find our anchor in place, wherever it is that we live. Once we find that anchor, so many of our problems fade away. And once we find that anchor, so often we uncover the nature of our true work, the nature of the gift we can offer up to the world.

In May 2010, we took up residence in our new house at the end of the world, and we called it Taigh nam Fitheach: House of the Ravens. It was one of three dwellings along a tiny side road which branched off from the main village street and stretched all the way down to a wild, rocky headland studded with hidden beaches. This one-and-a-half-storey house, the main part of which had been built on the croft from local stone sometime around the very end of the nineteenth century, had fallen into disrepair. The heating didn't work; the roof was a haphazard patchwork quilt of tile, asbestos and slate; there was no damp-proof course and so all the concrete floors in the downstairs rooms were sodden. The croft was in no better shape. A bizarrely ramshackle, mostly derelict 'shed' constructed from a miscellany of old windows and doors was the only infrastructure on the land, and although the external border was solidly deer-fenced against the resident marauding gangs of thirty or more stags, every internal strainer and fencepost was rotten. We immediately launched ourselves into a renovation project, and then set about expanding both our crofting and our business activities, working hard to find a place and a function in that widely dispersed and sometimes challenging community at the end of the world.

Eventually, we were both going to reap the consequences of the excesses of energy and activity that we were sowing during those years. But in the meantime, precisely because of the way we were now living, close to the many animals we kept on the croft, close to the land which I walked as well as worked, a different kind of learning was taking place. After all my vagabonding ways, my fleeting glimpses of heaven in this place and that, I was finally learning to truly belong to the land. And out of that most precious of all journeys, I was slowly developing the unique gift that I was going to bring back to the world. I was learning to become what I had always wanted to become, to reclaim that dream I had had, so many years before: the woman on the night hill, listening to the birds and the foxes, hands in the rich soil, feet cold and bare in a fast-flowing river. Embodying her sense of her own deep belonging to this world, utterly rooted in the land in which she lived. I didn't have a name for her then, but I did now: the *bean feasa*, the Wise Woman of my native tradition.

It wasn't an active strategy; it simply happened. It happened because of the hours I spent outside each day in all weathers, tending to the vegetables, doing my chores around the croft. It happened because, whatever else might be going on in the house or out on the land, twice a day I went out walking. I spent so much time walking simply because this beautiful, hard, radically wild land called to me. It had shouted out my name into the fierce Hebridean wind the first time I had seen it, as if it had been waiting for me for years. Longing for someone who would see it for what it really was. Like a lover, I crashed headlong into its arms. I wanted to be out there, walking the shoreline, clambering over rocks, peering into rock-pools, face turned always to the sea like Miranda gazing out into the tempest. The gales and the rain and the storms weren't a hindrance; in so many ways they were an essential part of it.

The pull of that land was like a drug, and I couldn't seem to do without it. Every morning, before the rest of the world was awake, I would take the dogs out onto the *aird*. Down to the small, tidal sandy beach which no one else ever came to, or along to the bay where the tiny Breanish River runs into the sea. I would walk the same familiar paths and sometimes I would stake out new ones. I knew that land as I had never come close to knowing anywhere else, and I knew it intensely in every season. Not just the plants, but the birds and the animals too. I watched in February for the oystercatchers to return, then the lapwings in May; I tracked the migrations of large flocks of whooper swans who descended twice-yearly on the loch at the bottom of the croft. I walked in storms so fierce that I could hardly stand up, and I stretched out and dozed on hot sunny summer rocks. In the tiny, inward-looking community we lived in, there was no one else out there to fall in love with that place as I had fallen in love; there was only ever me, and the dogs, and the land.

More than just knowing the place, I came to know its stories. In the mountains to the east of Taigh nam Fitheach, filling the view from every front window, the reclining figure of a woman could be seen – hair rippling out in long waves, with one arm thrown back behind her head. There are other places throughout the islands and mainland Scotland where the shapes of specific mountains or ranges represent the silhouette of the old goddess of the land. The best-known of them is Lewis' 'Sleeping Beauty' mountain, which in Gaelic is called Cailleach na Mointeach – the old woman of the moors; she can be seen on the far south-eastern horizon from the Callanish stone circle. I looked out onto our own reclining goddess every morning when I opened the bedroom curtains; she was visible from my desk as I worked, and she dominated the landscape when I walked or worked outside. I whispered my hopes and fears to her each day as I walked the headland. She was always there, a constant, vivid reminder of the divine feminine in the landscape whose stories exist still both in Scottish and Irish mythology.

Woman in the mountains, Breanish, Isle of Lewis

In the Western Isles, the stories tell of her two aspects: Brigid, known there as Bride, and the hard, stony blue-faced Cailleach – the Gaelic word for old woman, crone or hag – who we will meet more fully in the next chapter. One version of the story says that the old woman of winter, the Cailleach, dies and is reborn as Bride the spring maiden on the old festival day of Imbolc (1 February). Bride is fragile at first, but grows stronger each day as the sun rekindles its fire, and turns scarcity into abundance. But as autumn approaches and the light begins to fade she weakens again, and her sister the Cailleach begins to awaken. And by the old festival of Samhain (1 November) it is the Cailleach who rules the season, and Bride who sleeps quietly in the hills. There are many stories about this battle for the seasons which takes place between Bride and the Cailleach, but they can clearly be seen as two aspects of life in balance, of the need for both darkness and light, for both summer and winter, the ever-renewing cyclical nature of the world.

Wherever I walked, this and other stories of the land were made visible in its permanent features. That reclining figure in the landscape became my confidant, living as I did at the far edge of the world with nobody much to talk to or relate to other than David. The land became my best friend. It was perfectly animate to me, utterly alive. I was deep in relationship with it. And as I walked, day after day, year after year, I began to feel as if I were merging with the land, becoming it, not only knowing but living within its stories. This is the deepest connection of all, a facility that can only come from years of grounding in a place, and from paying more attention to it than to anything else. When you live as I lived, when you are with the land as I was with it during those years, loving it, tending it, talking to it − in some strange but very real sense you fall into its story. You become part of the land's story of itself, part of the land's dreaming. And when you reach out to the land in the way that I reached out, there are consequences. It engages with you, in turn. It reflects you back to yourself. It teaches you, and if the land you inhabit is hard and bleak, then its lessons may be as hard and as bleak as it is. Because above all, the land tests you.

I had a dream, a few months after we first moved to Lewis, after I had stumbled across an especially remarkable and hidden part of the coastline, all rock beds and carved-out cliffs. It was what I have always thought of as a Big Dream: the kind you might have just a few times in your life. The kind of dream you know is telling you something, though often enough you have no idea what. A mythic dream. I dreamed that this rocky place I had discovered was peopled with animals, and those animals were formed from carved-out rocks in the cliffs and the ground. A cliff face above a rock pool became an eagle with outstretched wings, and a little further along was a stalking wolf with holes for eyes where the sky shone through. In a shallow channel of sea water which I would somehow have to cross if I wanted to carry on walking, an enormous whale offered its body for a stepping stone. I could sense something stirring in the air around me, and it was redolent of power and danger. *If you tread on that sleeping whale*, the place seemed to be saying to me, *the keeper of the stories; if you waken the animals; if you talk to the sleeping heart of the rock; if you risk the wakening of the sleeping power of this abandoned land – you never quite know just what it is you are going to awaken in yourself. Will you wake them anyway? Will you do it? Will you risk it, without fear of the consequences?*

I put the dream to one side; I didn't know what it meant. Three years later the image of that wolf with holes for eyes where the sky shone through would come back to me in a powerful wave of understanding of my own needs and nature . . . but that is a story for the following chapter. I risked it, anyway; I was too far gone to hold back now.

My intense identification with that place began to have a strong effect on me, to follow through into other parts of my life. How could it not be utterly transformative, this process of shape-shifting into the land? I began to think about the things in my life which really mattered to me, and which nourished, rather than depleted, and I began to long to downsize and simplify. I wanted only to indulge in activities that derived their meaning from the land. I grew fascinated by traditional herbalism, and as well as the practice of wildcrafting, I began to cultivate medicinal herbs in the tiny area of our garden which we'd been able to make windproof. I learned to spin, so that I could turn the fleeces from our own beautiful sheep into yarn – spinning, spinning myself into being – and then I learned how to use the wild plants on the headland for dyeing that yarn. I learned how to weave baskets from willow, and planted osier on sheltered areas of the croft.

As Alice Starmore would tell me some time later, if you don't know a place then you don't feel responsible for it. I knew this place and loved it deeply, and as a consequence I was beginning to fully take on my feelings of responsibility not just for this very specific patch of land, but for the wider Earth of which it was a part. I began to think about what I might offer to a world in crisis, and to examine the skills I had, the opportunities to make a difference. What was the gift that could I bring back from my long, swithering journeys? It soon became clear that the most obvious vehicle which we had for change-making was the fact that we still ran a small publishing company. And so I set about founding a quarterly magazine which we called *EarthLines*,[17] to publish articles and showcase art which explored our complex relationship with the natural world. It had a strong land ethic and a focus on the culture and lore of place. We wanted to find people who were living authentically in the face of environmental crisis, who were prepared to unflinchingly explore the challenges that we all now face. We wanted to provide inspiration for change.

Although it had been years since I'd actually practised any of these skills, in theory I was still a writer, a psychologist, and an 'expert' in the use of myth and story as vehicles for transformation. For a long time, I'd been mourning the loss of my own writing practice. After *The Long Delirious Burning Blue* was published back in 2008, when it had been well received and generously reviewed, I'd found it impossible to find the time to work on a new book. I'd received a Writer's Bursary from the Scottish Arts Council to complete a new novel, but sadly, the pressure of running Two Ravens Press, of always having to focus on the writing of others, meant that there was never enough energy for my own. And in my growing despair about the state of the world around me, I'd lost more than energy: I'd lost heart. I'd lost faith in words. Words had ruled me for far too much of my life, and I'd simply run out of them. I'd begun to feel again as if I had nothing to say. But now, inspired and nurtured by the land, quickened by the warm, fertile silence inside me, my own work was pushing to be reborn.

I sat one bright, calm morning on a rocky outcrop down at the headland, watching a seal watching me. It made me remember the Selkie stories that I'd always loved so much, and which so obviously emerged directly out of the deep relationship that people in these islands have always had with the sea and its creatures.

The stories that were resonating with me right now were stories that offer insights not just into our own lives and problems, but insights into our relationship with the land and its non-human inhabitants. But almost all the ideas and practices I'd ever encountered while working therapeutically with myth and story originated in the work of Jungians – fine, popular writers like Marie-Louise von Franz and Clarissa Pinkola Estés – and focused entirely on the plotlines and archetypes which illuminate the dark, hidden corners of our own individual psyches. And by this stage in my life, I was convinced that one of the major problems with Western civilisation was the fact that too many of us spend far too much time in our own heads, analysing and over-analysing, and then going back around and analysing some more.

I was so very tired of our endless, exhausting, human-centred psychology, and in therapeutic work which used narrative it so often seemed as if the stories had been dumbed down, scaled down to fit us: the big bad wolf reduced to a mere bit-player on the vast stage of our individual egos, wandering in ever-decreasing circles around the neatly fenced forests of our inner landscapes. What if we let the wolf out, put him back in the real world where he belongs? What about the stories which re-animate not just our own souls, but the soul of the outer landscape, and which bring us into relationship with it? The stories which are embedded in place, and which, by listening to them, embed us in place in turn? The myths that Canadian writer Sean Kane calls 'the power of the place speaking'?[18]

These were the kind of myths that come from my own Celtic traditions, our own Dreamtime stories which tell us how the land came into being, our own mythlines, peopled with characters and gods and goddesses who arose directly out of the land I was walking on now. Peopled with women who were literally the power of the place speaking, for they spoke with the Voices of the Wells. I realised that – perhaps precisely because of their strong rootedness in place, their refusal to reduce key characters to easily assimilated archetypes, and the lack of an obvious simple take-home message in most of them – these Celtic myths (and especially the complex, ambiguous myths from the Gaelic tradition) so rarely appeared in books and articles by Jungians. Almost everyone focused on Greek myths and the archetypal characters which could be derived from them, with all the Greek gods and goddesses neatly categorised and their some-times complex histories simplified and, more often than not, reduced to clusters of straightforward personality traits which people were encouraged to identify with and somehow assimilate into their own lives. But regardless of whether this kind of thing made sense as a strategy for 'personal growth', those archetypes, and in particular those divine women, had no resonance in my land – they were so deeply enmeshed in the Mediterranean lands in which they arose. Hera never made it as far as the Outer Hebrides, and nor did Athena: they'd have run back shrieking to the olive groves if they'd so much as set foot on these icy, rain-soaked, windswept shores. They didn't belong here; they made no sense here.

So back I went again to those old Celtic stories, thinking about the ways they informed our connections to place. I started to write about them, to work with them, in the context of my own increasingly rich experience of place and belonging. And I found myself, more by instinct than by specific design, focusing exclu-sively on stories and mythology about women. Over time, ever since I had begun while in America to explore the nature of my own womanhood, I had become more and more interested in women's unique ways of experiencing the natural world, and their relationships with the land. Since that time of reawakening, as well as finding myself making women friends much more easily, I had begun to read almost exclusively books by women. I had discovered the great female 'nature writers' – writers like Annie Dillard, Terry Tempest Williams, Jay Griffiths – whose relationships with the natural world seemed so very physical, so sensual, so deeply embodied, and so very different from the ways in which male writers often wrote about their relationships with nature.

Perhaps it was inevitable, then, that very soon I would turn to writing about and working exclusively with women. I began to run creative retreats for women, bringing them to the place where we lived, holding the space for them while the hard, beautiful landscape worked its transformational magic. It was a nourishing combination of writing, story and therapy. I was finally in my element. I had finally found that unique gift I'd been searching for all my life: the gift of the *bean feasa*. I was finally getting ready to Return.

If the power of the Celtic woman is the power of place speaking, then this is the gift that we can offer to our world, the contribution that we can make to the healing of our Wasteland. We are the carriers of the wisdom of our native places, the knowledge of the plants and the animals, the rich intelligence of the cycles of life and the seasons. We are the mediators of the wisdom of the Otherworld, the Voices of the Wells. We are the Wise Women.

The Journey of the Heroine we've been following in this book is a journey back to the ground of our own belonging in the world, a retrieval of our life-giving feminine wisdom and the regrowth of the roots that nourish it. Our own roots, which reach down into the soil, push down into the cracks in the rocks, drink from the groundwater that flows down the mountains. This is not a journey which takes place in our heads. It is a journey which takes us out of our heads and weaves us back into the shimmering web of life – life, with all its beauty and its chaos, its caresses and its stings, its dangers and its blessings. In this journey we learn to get our hands dirty – to thrust them into the fecund earth and plant the seeds of the world's new becomings. We learn to listen again to the stories told to us by the land in which we walk. These stories are a gift and a terrible burden; there is joy and abundance, and then, in the passing of a cloud over the sun, there is sudden loss and a grief which is almost too heavy to carry.

Carry it anyway; we were built for it, we women. It was always our role to carry these stories and it must be so again, now that the world calls out in its agonies for us to rise up and speak the truth. Now that the Earth calls out for us to speak again with its voice. The stories are everywhere still: listen, and you will find them.

They are the tentative flowering of a dog-violet in spring. They are the thunder of rock fall in winter ice. They are told by the heron, as she shrieks her grief for the death of the salmon into an early morning sky. They are told by the hare, remembering the days when the fields were filled with poppy and corncockle, and the grass was long and gave shelter. They are told by our sisters around the planet.

We do not do this alone. We do not do this without the world, which listens in its turn as we tell the stories back to it. The world does not see that we are 'other', that we have made ourselves separate. It sees only a dog-violet, hears the clattering fall of winter rock, feels a woman's hands on the bark of a tree. The world is listening to you; you are in this world and of it and it is in and of you and wherever you go you carry this gift with you. Be the power of the land speaking. Pass the gift on. Pass it on, and in this way we, like our female ancestors from long ago, like the goddesses of Sovereignty in our native mythology, become guardians and protectors of the land. By taking up these ancient roles, we begin to restore life to the Wasteland. Refuse the continuing destruction, because what hurts the Earth hurts us. Because we are the whole Earth. We are the Voices of the Wells; we are the power of the land, speaking. Use your voice. Speak.

This path, this revolution of belonging, necessarily entails accepting our responsibility towards our own places and communities. It might be impossible to save the world all in one go, but it is possible to protect, guard – and yes, even save, when necessary – our home places and our communities. If we have to do it little by little, one place at a time, then now is a good time to begin. Each of us sewing just one of the squares which contributes to the vast, growing patchwork quilt of the world's renewal. So many of the women I spoke to while I was writing this book showed me that it can be done, and in so many different ways: we each bring our own unique gifts to the process, and we each have our own unique place to protect.

Jacqueline Woodward-Smith practises her gift of place not in the wild, green Celtic heartlands, but in the seething centre of population that is the city of London. That's where I first met her, under the arrival and departure boards of Liverpool Street station in the evening rush-hour, shuffling from side to side to avoid being run over by endless swarming masses of tired, aggressive men and women intent only on finding their way to a train and getting the hell out of Dodge as soon as possible. There she was, the perfect antidote to it all: very much larger than what passes for life in all this insanity, with a big wide smile, bright red hair, wearing large glasses and a full, long black cotton skirt patterned around the edge with large white skulls.

Like so many of the women I've spoken to, Jacqueline began by working within what she calls 'the system', spending twenty-four years in the British government's Home Office – the epitome of uncaring, institutionalised bureaucracy. One day, heart-sick, she watched a sunbeam reach through a window and light up a corner of the paper-filled desk she occupied in the bowels of a building filled with others just like her. Sometimes it's the simple things which break us, and something had been building up inside her for a long while. She handed in her notice, and off she went to train as a counsellor. Now she works in schools, helping young children whose family lives are difficult, whose ways of being in the world are different, and who find it hard to fit into a school system which is, as Jacqueline says, 'designed for conformity', in which there are 'no wild edges where you can be yourself'.

It's not necessary, she tells me firmly as we forge a path out of the teeming station (I'm just closing my eyes and hoping for the best), to live in a wild place or in the countryside to have a strong connection with the natural world. It happens in the city too, and Jacqueline's own connection to London is deep. 'In some funny sense, my attachment is about the physical layers of history here, about continuity,' she says, as we sip tea in a busy coffee bar behind the station. 'A strong sense of relationship with the gener-ations of people who lived out their lives in this place. Of course they would have had deep connections with it, and those of us who make it our home still do. Yes, it's a city; yes, there's concrete

– but it's not a dead place. There's still nature, it just expresses itself differently. I've counted twenty-seven different wildflowers along the verge by the side of a road in Blackheath which I walk along every day. Wherever you are, even in the heart of the city, at the very least you can find a plant growing out of a wall! That's the gift of a city. The city teaches you to focus on the small things. I look at London and I don't think "Wow, this is a big city, all concreted over." I think, "Look – there's some common vetch growing over there, and it's beautiful."'

Jacqueline's gift is to teach as many people as she can to see what she calls these 'small beauties': from the disturbed and disadvantaged children she counsels for her day-job, to the many fans of her popular Facebook page, where most days she posts a list of those small beauties she's encountered herself. Today's list of ten things includes the following: 'Hearing a high-pitched peeping as I left the Crossbones Garden and seeing that it was a fledgling blackbird calling for food from its mother, who was digging about in some fallen leaves to find morsels to share. I watched them for ages. A beautiful moment of intimacy with the wild.'

In a city perhaps more than anywhere else, Jacqueline suggests, community is critical if you plan on changing the world. 'London is really just a load of little villages joined together,' she says. 'Most places have their own centre. I live in Blackheath. I know its shape, I know where the middle of it is. I shop in local shops and I talk to local people. There's a community orchard, and a park at the bottom of the road where lots of people go. Caring about places, caring for the environment, isn't just for people who live in the country. There are people in cities who are just as concerned about the state of the planet. We might sometimes need to approach it in different ways, but there is a surprising, sometimes hidden resilience in London's communities. I see it in practice every day.'

Jacqueline is as inspired as any country-dweller by the myths and stories which come out of this land. 'They're incredibly important to me, and I can feel them just as deeply in London, where so much of the history of this land has been centred.

I feel as if I would die without those stories. They illuminate my life, my concerns, my place. Take the story of Blodeuwedd, the Flower Maiden. It's a story I've always felt strongly about, and whenever I look at those wildflowers along the verge, it floods back into my heart.'

The old *Mabinogion* myth Jacqueline is talking about begins with the Welsh hero Lleu Llaw Gyffes, who has been placed under a *tynged*[19] by his mother Arianrhod which prevents him from ever taking a human wife. And so instead, Lleu's magicians Math and Gwydion '[take] the flowers of the oak, and the flowers of the broom, and the flowers of the meadowsweet, and from those they conjured up the fairest and most beautiful maiden anyone had ever seen.' Blodeuwedd may have been created to satisfy one man's needs, but she falls in love with another, and together they conspire to kill Lleu – the only way that she might have her freedom. But Lleu escapes, and Gwydion takes revenge by turning Blodeuwedd into an owl. It's an interesting story about woman as property – full, like so many Celtic myths, of ambiguity and complexity. As ambiguous and complex as these vast cities that we have created, so easy to dismiss as 'urban jungles', so easy for those of us who thirst for more wild places in the world to abhor.

'It's easy to dismiss the cities and its wastelands,' Jacqueline says as I stand up to leave, 'but wildflowers grow there as well.'

Love the place you are in, is the message; it doesn't matter what the place is. Even the broken places need to be cherished. And as I make my way back through steaming summer streets to my friend's flat in the Barbican, my eyes find a way to tune out the crowds and to focus instead on the green things pushing their way out through the cracks in the pavement, taking every opportunity to bloom.

Back in the Celtic heartlands, Loveday Jenkin works in quite a different way to change the system that so many of us seek to escape: she turns her gifts to politics. She is the spokesperson on environmental issues for Mebyon Kernow, the Cornish nationalist party, and is a passionate advocate for Cornwall's Celtic identity. For Loveday, trained in ecological biochemistry, that identity is strongly associated both with attachment to and a sense of responsibility for place. 'My sense of being Cornish – and therefore Celtic – relates very strongly to my environmental activity,' she tells me over coffee and chocolate brownies amid the mid-morning clamour at the Godrevy Beach Café, on Cornwall's north-west Atlantic coast. 'Part of the bones of my identity is that feeling of being an intrinsic part of this place, and so understanding how it works. I believe strongly that we can learn from the place itself how best to manage its ecosystems, and to deal with any environmental issues that arise in them.'

Loveday's parents were both founder members of Mebyon Kernow, and key shapers of the Cornish cultural revival. 'I've been politically aware for as long as I can remember,' she laughs. 'It was impossible not to be, in our house. I remember hand-addressing envelopes containing party information when I was ten, and at sixteen I was knocking on doors to try to persuade people to vote for Mebyon Kernow. Today, even though the percentage of people who actually vote for us is quite low, our policies are very popular because our focus is on doing things locally, trying to make sure that decisions are made which are right for Cornwall. Because a lot of the English government's policies don't work for us. Our environment is similar to that of Wales, Ireland and the Highlands and Islands of Scotland – it consists of a lot of dispersed small settlements, rather than a big city playing a central role. And so Mebyon Kernow's policies are much more environmentally focused and community-based; it's a left-wing, social, green party. That focus on the environment and the community comes from a strong feeling that this is our place. We belong to it, we care for it.'

In the early part of the last century, she tells me as we walk in a chill, gusty Atlantic wind to the place where the Red River meets the sea, Cornish culture had been so strongly overlaid by the dominant English culture that the customs, stories and language which sprang from the land had almost vanished. Now, after decades of hard work from cultural activists, there is a strong and spirited cultural resurgence. 'Cornish culture has grown phenomenally during my lifetime, and in particular the old Celtic aspects of it. The majority of people here now recognise that Cornwall is a Celtic nation. We've seen that unique Celtic culture flourish again with the revival of Cornish dancing and music, and the rebirth of traditional Cornish festivals. Part of the vestiges of old Cornish culture which have been reclaimed are the folk tales and stories, a sense of Cornwall as a mythic place. That sense had always been there, though awareness of the stories had begun to slip away. But those tales come directly out of place, and so they still have relevance and meaning to people who live here when they recover them. They can just plug right back in.'

At the heart of this cultural revival is a revival of the Cornish language; Loveday is also a major contributor to that process, having brought up her two children to speak Cornish as their first language. 'There's a sense here now that it's okay to be Cornish. It's different, yes – but it's okay to be different, because there's something here in this land that's unique, and rich, and it is ours. Now, there are a lot of cultural exchanges with other Celtic nations – especially the speakers of other Brythonic languages in Brittany and Wales.'

Loveday is very clear that her passionate advocacy for the natural world, place and community all spring directly from her strong sense of identity as a Celt. 'There is something different about us. It's hard to find the words to describe it. If I'm away, as soon as I come back across the border to Cornwall, I recognise it. But I also recognise it in other Celtic countries. If I had to try to define it, I'd say it's that we are rooted in the land. We're a part of it. There's an element of survivorship which is part of the innate character of the Celtic people, I think; there's an extremity in these countries, both in the landscape and in the weather. Being Celtic is about standing up in the face of those elements. Whatever happens, we'll still be there. Because we're rooted here, we're grounded.'

9

Mountains and Rocky Heights

Becoming Elder

An Chailleach Bhéarra, Co. Cork, Ireland

Hag

Once I dreamt I was the earth,
the parish of Ventry its length and breadth,
east and west, as far as it runs,
that the brow of the Maoileann
was my forehead, Mount Eagle
the swell of my flank,
the side of the mountain
my shanks and backbone,
that the sea was lapping
the twin rocks of my feet,
the twin rocks of Parkmore
from the old Fenian tales.

That dream was so real
that when I woke the next morning
I glanced down to see if, perchance,
my feet were still wet.
Then off I went, and promptly forgot
all about my vision until,
O, when was it exactly, nearly
two years later, the fright
of my daughter stirred again
the dregs of that dream.

We were strolling the strand
but she was so dead-beat
she turned towards home, while
I trudged onwards alone.
Before I got far, I heard
her come running back, snivelling
and sobbing at every step's breath.
'What's wrong?' 'O, Mam, I'm scared stiff,
I thought I saw the mountains heaving
like a giantess, with her breasts swaying,
about to loom over, and gobble me up.'

Nuala Ní Dhomhnaill
Translated from the Irish by John Montague[1]

The early morning sky is fractious, mottled with the ragged remnants of an earlier storm. Bright blue over bare grey mountains to the north, midnight across the dark glowing bay to the south. A hint of early-morning red in the east colours the tarmac ahead of me a peculiar shade of midnight-purple. Rain lances over a slate-grey sea out west, and a sudden squall whips up the rushes on the road's verge. This is hag weather, for sure. Fitting weather, because I am on the Beara Peninsula in the far south-west of Ireland, exploring the country of An Chailleach Bhéarra, the Hag of Beara. 'She is older than time,' a local guide-book says of her, and indeed it is told that she is the oldest of the old, the creator and guardian of the wild land of Ireland.

On the small peninsula of Kilcatherine, to the north and west of the village of Eyeries with its brightly painted, many-coloured houses, sits a large boulder in a small, fenced-off patch of land. Seen from the side, it looks like an ancient hag in profile: scabrous skin, hooked nose and firm, jutting chin; and indeed, so a local legend tells us, these are the fossilised remains of An Chailleach Bhéarra herself. Here she sits, looking out to sea and (according to that local guidebook again) 'waiting for the cosmic tides to turn'. An official plaque near the boulder offers up the following story to explain her presence:

An Chailleach Bhéarra (the Hag of Beara) is one of the oldest mythological beings associated with Ireland and she is particularly associated with Kilcatherine in the Beara Peninsula, where she mostly lived. She was considered a goddess of Sovereignty, giving the kings the right to rule their lands. According to legend, she had seven periods of youth one after another, so that every man who had lived with her came to die of old age. Her grandsons and great-grandsons were so many that they made up entire tribes and races and as a result she was known in many parts of Ireland and up along the west coast of Scotland. She considered the arrival of Naomh (Saint) Caitiarin, who preached Christianity in Kilcatherine and the surrounding districts, as a threat to her powers. One day, after gathering seaweed along the shore of Whiddy Island in Bantry Bay, the hag returned to Kilcatherine to find the saint asleep on a bare hillock. She approached him quietly, grabbed his prayer book, and ran off. A cripple who lived nearby saw what happened and shouted at Naomh Caitiarin, who then woke up and saw the hag running off. The saint ran after her, caught up with her in Ard na Caillí, and recovered his prayer book. He then turned her into a grey pillar-stone with her back to the hill and her face to the sea. There she remains to the present day.

So they say, those who tried to overthrow the old ways and diminish the women who held the moral and spiritual authority which they then usurped. So they say – but there are other stories, and better. The older stories tell that she sits there, patient as time itself, looking out to sea, waiting for the return of her husband, the sea-god Manannán Mac Lir. There she sits, waiting for one last kiss before the world ends. How could you not sit with her for a while, and tell her some of your own story to help her pass the time?

The boulder and the surrounding ground are strewn with gifts left by others who have come to visit her. A colourful scarf, a bangle, shells and many copper coins. And so I leave a gift of my own: rummaging deep in the many pockets of my old walking jacket for something to offer, I find a small polished piece of lapis lazuli. I have no idea when it came to be there, or why. But I know what it is for. On the left side of her face I find a hollow that might well be an eye-socket. It is there that I place the lapis lazuli stone, so that the sea and the sky might be reflected in her eye and she might see her husband more clearly, when finally he comes. And so a hag with one blue eye sits now on the rocky shores of Beara. I share her long vigil for a while, sit with her as I often sat with the Cailleach on the rocky western shore of another wild island far to the north. I tell her stories of that northern sister, whispering into the lichen-encrusted bulge that passes for an ear. I kiss her rough old mouth, for you must always kiss the hag, and then I leave.

They might try to tell you that she is dead, the Wise Old Woman of Beara, but I can tell you that she lives on. That afternoon I lose myself in a hag-ridden hidden valley over which towers a sun-drenched mountain called The Tooth. I find her there, and as I approach the mountain she opens her mouth and breathes on me, and a mist rolls out over the hills and a sudden fierce wind whips up and blows it down into the valley. Her sighs are still carried in the wind which sweeps down her mountains, that old hag of Beara, her strong breath moistening the ancient bones of this land which she herself made. She will not be so easily dismissed.

Propped up against a giant boulder, I wait out the brief storm, and watch until the mist fades and the sun begins to creep out once again. Then, hill-blind, I leave.

In Irish and Scottish mythology, the Cailleach[2] is the divine hag, the Old Woman of the World, the creator-goddess of the land. Gaelic mythology has no story which specifically explains the creation of the universe, but the old stories of the Cailleach explain the formation of the land. She is the geotectonic power of the land itself, who gives shape to the Earth throughout all its ages. Stories tell of how she constructed enormous mounds, megaliths and towers in a single night. Like the natural world over which she presides, she renews herself constantly: each year in spring, or every hundred years, by bathing in a certain body of water, depending on the story.

In Ireland, her landscapes are craggy, prominent mountains and outcroppings, from the Cailleach stone on Beara to the Hag's Head (Ceann Caillí) at the southernmost tip of the Cliffs of Moher in County Clare. On top of Slieve na Calliagh (Sliabh na Caillí, 'the hag's mountain') at Loughcrew in County Meath are megalithic tombs which include a kerbstone known as 'the hag's chair'. In Scotland, she is also known as Beira, Queen of Winter, an altogether more fearsome character with white hair, a dark blue face, rust-coloured teeth, and a single eye in the middle of her forehead. She created the mountains; they formed when, striding in giant steps across the land, she accidentally dropped rocks from her creel. In some stories she is said to have built the mountains intention-ally, pouring them from her apron to serve as her stepping stones as she walked; in others she created rivers and lochs, and carried a hammer which she used to shape the hills and valleys. She leapt from hilltop to hilltop followed by herds of deer and families of wild pigs; sometimes she rode a wolf.[3] She is a wilderness spirit who protects wild animals; she is a seasonal deity too, the elemental power of storms and of winter.

In Ireland she lacks this sometimes negative and limiting connec-tion with winter, and is strongly linked with cows, with fertility, and with the sowing and harvesting of grain. The stories tell that she taught the people how to thresh using a holly-stick flail and a hazel-wood striker, threshing the sheaves on a clean floor, one at a time. They followed her custom of sowing seed in late winter and harvesting green corn before the autumn storms came. In many Irish-speaking areas the last sheaf of the harvest was called the Cailleach, and it was treated with great ceremony and respect. As folklorist Gearoid Ó Crualaoich declares in his extensive study of Cailleach traditions,[4] she personifies the 'proactive, female creativity and power . . . seen, in Irish ancestral culture, to be the major source from which emerges both the general form of the physical universe and the security and wellbeing of the social order in times of stress.'

Although she appears nowhere else in so critical a cosmological role as she does in Irish and Scottish mythology, we find the Cailleach's equivalent in other Celtic lands too. In the Isle of Man, just as in Ireland and Scotland, the Caillagh appears sometimes as the *bean nighe*: the Washer at the Ford who washes the blood-stained shirts of slain warriors. In Manx legend she haunts the banks of inland streams, is often dressed in red, carries a candle and wields a wooden stick to beat the washing. The legend of the 'Caillagh ny Groamagh' ('Old Woman of the Gloom') is a related Manx tradition which associates the Cailleach with the shoreline. She was important enough to have a day named after her: Caillagh ny Groamagh's Day, which happens to be the same date as Brigid's day, Imbolc, on 1 February. She is also called the Caillagh ny Gueshag: Old Woman of the Spells. In Brittany she is called the Groac'h, an old woman or witch, a shape-shifter who possesses the elemental powers of nature; many landscape features are attributed to her. Sometimes, she is portrayed as a solitary old fairy who offers gifts to the humans who visit her. The hag also appears in a number of Celtic myths in which she presents herself as another face of the goddess of Sovereignty. As in the story 'What Do Women Want?', in these tales the Hero must kiss the hag in spite of his distaste for her ugliness or immense age; if he passes the test he is rewarded by her transformation into a beautiful young woman, who then recognises his worthiness to rule.

The Cailleach, then, has numerous roles: she is a goddess of Sovereignty, she is creator of the land, she is the guardian and protector of wild nature. She is able to restore her youth periodically, so living forever . . . but inevitably, as the centuries pass and patriarchal beliefs take ever-greater hold, she comes into conflict with Christianity and is finally overthrown by it. In later stories she is dismissed as little more than a wicked old witch.

'The Lament of the Old Woman of Beare', a well-known ninth-century poem, bemoans the power which the Cailleach lost with the coming of Christianity during the Middle Ages, and the associated degradation of the concept of Sovereignty. In this particularly striking example of patriarchal revisionism, the powerful, untamed Cailleach – who created the landscape and leaped across hilltops – converted to Christianity, and is now pictured as a miserable old nun who waits only for death. In this brave new world, age is no longer revered; it is seen as a weakness, something to be dreaded and abhorred.

And yet in Ireland, as Gearoid Ó Crualaoich has shown, despite all attempts by the over-culture to declare her dead (turned to stone by a priest, slipping off a cliff, drowning in a deep Sligo loch, crumbling to dust on hearing the early-morning bark of a dog . . .) the Cailleach lives on in folk culture, and continued to strongly influence cultural development in the early modern era. Ireland's tradition of female power was so ancient and so embedded that neither Christianity nor other male-dominated state institutions could ever fully eradicate it. She lives on still, that old hag of Beara, in the form of the Wise Woman. In most folk stories about her, the knowledge of the *bean feasa* is always shown to be greater than that of the priest, and she often teaches him a lesson. So it is that the Cailleach in all her forms has always opposed the patriarchy, even when she's been driven underground.

As the Heroine moves on through her life and through whatever new Journeys may come, the time will come to work on becoming Elder. The word 'elder', of course, can mean many things. The Elder may be fierce, eccentric, wild; she may be the Trickster energy that sets about disrupting the status quo. She may also (or later) represent the deep, restful dark: the slow sinking back into the quietness within that is arguably one of the greatest gifts of extreme old age. To a woman of the Celtic nations, to become Elder is above all to become Cailleach: to represent the integrity and health of the wild places and creatures of this world. To become Elder is to become strong – strong as the white old bones of the earth, strong enough to endure the long, lonely vigil to the end of the world. To become Elder is to hold the power, stay the course. Above all, to become Elder is to become the *bean feasa*, the Wise Woman: the one who knows the secrets and speaks the languages of the land, who speaks with the moral authority of the Otherworld, who weaves the dreaming of the world.

In many stories of the Cailleach she is represented as a solitary creature, but in both the Irish and the Scottish traditions it is also told that she had a husband – sometimes called simply 'the Bodach' (*bodach* means 'old man' in Gaelic), sometimes identified as the sea-god Manannán Mac Lir. This old and beautiful tale from the Isle of Skye shows a Cailleach figure weaving her magic not alone, but in perfect harmony with her husband: two elders working together, masculine and feminine principles in perfect harmony.[5]

~

The Dream-makers

One beautiful morning in later summer, a group of young women from the village on the edge of the world, all the way down there by the sea, set off into the mountains to gather blaeberries. One of them, daydreaming and enjoying the sun on her shoulders, strayed away from the rest, climbing up higher and higher in search of larger and finer berries. But then suddenly the air grew chilly, and she looked up, shivering, only to see a wall of mist rolling down the slopes of the mountain towards her.

Startled out of her reverie, she realised that she was alone, and at once turned to retrace her steps and to find her friends – but the mist whirled around her, and in no time at all she became lost. Slowly and cautiously she moved on through the mist, only understanding that she was going in the wrong direction when the heather through which she had originally climbed suddenly gave way to rock. She stood still, frightened now, afraid to move for fear of stepping over a cliff edge, or falling into the deep cut of a mountain burn.

And then she heard footsteps behind her. She whirled around, peering into the mist, and saw a band of huge ghostly forms moving towards her. Fearful, she would have stepped back – but a sudden small breeze shifted the fog for a moment, and she saw that the visitors were deer. Most of them were hinds, with calves at foot. They didn't seem to be afraid of her and so she decided to join them, thinking that they at least would know where they were going, and might even lead her to safety. The deer moved slowly through the mist, grazing here and there, and so it was easy for the girl to keep up with them. A few steps at a time, they led her high up into the dark Cuillins, where eventually she found herself standing beside them at the opening of a cave.

Thinking to wait there in safety until the mist dissolved, the girl entered the cave. But the cave was inhabited; inside she found an old man and an old woman, each seated upon a wooden stool, gazing into a dark rock pool in the cave's floor. The old woman turned to the girl and courteously asked her how she had come to be there; the girl told her tale and begged shelter for the night or until the mist would clear. 'Shelter for one night we cannot give,' the old woman said, 'but shelter for a year and a night you may have if you will help me in the dairy, for I grow old. The deer will take you back down the mountain when the time is done.'

As she looked into the depths of the old woman's dark eyes, the girl found herself agreeing. And so she spent busy days caring for and milking the hinds, and gathering sweet-scented herbs from the mountains which the old woman showed her how to find. There was thyme, meadowsweet and wild mint; there was golden asphodel and bog myrtle. The old woman dried them and sprinkled them on the fire which she lit each day out of dried heather. Then she would heat the deer's milk, and make crowdie cheese. While the old woman worked at the fire with herbs and milk, the old man sat gazing into the rock pool, in which all the world was mirrored. And then, when the crowdie was made, he fashioned from it shapes and figures of the things that he had seen on the pool's surface. For he and his wife were the makers of the world's dreams.

Every evening as the sun set below the sea, the old man carried their white dreams to the cave mouth, and held them up to take on colour from the sunset. The dreams that he held in his right hand were true dreams, and out of the blue sky came eagles and falcons, larks and wrens, to carry them throughout the world. But the dreams in his left hand were false phantoms, designed to mislead. Out of the dark cracks of the mountain came the crows and ravens, to spread the shadows around the world.

When the year and the night of the girl's service were ended, the old woman came out of the cave and spoke in a strange tongue to the leader of the herd of deer, a gentle hind with glowing eyes who now was grey with age. She said farewell to the girl, telling her that her service had been honest and true, and that she would find a reward waiting for her when she returned home to the seashore.

The deer led her by a hidden, easy route down the mountain, and they came sooner than she had thought to the sea – but this was not the shore that the girl knew. She started to walk along the beach to see if she could discover where she might be, but the deer wouldn't allow it, and they gathered around her, enclosing her in a circle, and stood looking out to sea.

The girl looked too, and soon she saw, coming out of the sunset, a boat made all of skins; and as it came closer she saw that in the boat was a fair young man with a golden torc at his throat. He landed his coracle and came to her, hands outstretched, and at once she knew that she loved him. He called her 'the fair one of dreams', and told her that he had dreamed of her many times over the past year, back home in his father the king's halls. Last night, he said, he had been shown in another dream the way to find her, and so he had followed the dreampaths, and had come to ask her to marry him.

The girl of course agreed, and they sailed away together across the sea. And when she became queen of her husband's country, she taught the people the meaning of many dreams which the old woman had shown her during the time of her service in the mountains, and they grew wondrously wise.

But now much is forgotten.

~

311

I remember, years ago, laughing at the title of a book on the psychology of mindfulness by American therapist Jon Kabat-Zinn: *Wherever You Go, There You Are*. Since then, I've often thought that it might make a suitable epitaph, because for sure, it's easier to change places than it is to change yourself. How many times must we make what seems to be the same journey, spin round and around what seems to be the same circle? Three years into our time on Lewis, the answer was beginning to become clear to me: *until you learn*. Life is a series of journeys, and every lesson that it offers to us comes around again, in the same form or a different form, until we learn it. Each time around, there is more to be lost – but each time around, there is also more to be gained.

Lewis. I loved that island with all my heart, but that didn't mean it was the right place to stay. You may love someone more than anything else in the whole world – but that doesn't mean you can live with them. Not all love affairs are forever.

We had arrived in this place in the spring of 2010 burned out, exhausted and in a state of deep disrepair. What we needed more than anything was time. Time to slow down, to surrender to our despair, to embrace the darkness without fighting it. Time to let that despair and darkness connect us back to ourselves, and then to the world again, and to the land. We needed not only to lick our wounds but to fully explore them, and then to let them heal. We had argued to ourselves and everyone around us that we weren't running *away* from the world; we were running *towards* a new way of living, a new way of being in it. Instead, we lived in exactly the same way we had always done, and we did exactly what we had always done. Only the scenery had changed.

We arrived, and we instantly threw ourselves into a major project to renovate the house and croft. We put most of our furniture, clothes and the Two Ravens Press book stock into storage, camped out in the house until the builders came, and then we lived with them for four months while they dug up floors and reinstalled pipes and reslated the roof and put in a shower room and constructed a utility room . . . While all this was going on, we ran the publishing business from a single small closed-off room, sometimes climbing through the window to get into it when access from inside the house wasn't possible.

Meanwhile, the poultry needed housing, the croft needed internal fencing and paddocks to make it safe and practical for the sheep, and we needed a proper shed to store food and bedding for the animals. David spent months re-fencing, hanging gates, constructing paddocks, erecting hen houses and duck houses and goose houses. I wanted to grow vegetables and so a polytunnel arrived and was duly erected; David spent more weeks constructing wooden slatted wind-breaks for a fruit and vegetable garden, and to fortify the polytunnel against the regular salt-laden storms. Everything that we built had to be tied down; poultry houses, sheds and even polytunnels were known to regularly blow away in winter, and there was nothing but a flat headland between us and the prevailing gales from the south and west.

We worked hard and built strong because we planned to stay there forever; after all, where else was there to go? We were already on the far edge of the world, and we couldn't imagine how it might ever be possible to come back from such a place – or where we might ever want to come back to.

One day, a couple of years later, we had a moment to breathe. The house was warm and cosy; we had an enormous steel barn with electricity on the croft – more space than we imagined we'd ever need. The beautiful black, horned Hebridean sheep were safe and happy; now they had been hefted to the land and spent most of the year out on the vast Breanish common grazings, which ran from the sea all the way across the mountains to the east, and included the beautiful deserted village of Mealista with its spectacular sandy beach, as well as the uninhabited Mealista Island, half a mile offshore. They had been joined by a small flock of black-and-white Jacob ewes that I'd been hankering after for years, and we loved them all dearly. The geese and ducks took more looking after than they'd ever seemed to need on the mainland, but we loved them too. The polytunnel was flourishing, and we were mostly self-sufficient in vegetables. The hens were thriving and I sold the extra eggs around the village and to local hotels and bed-and-breakfasts.

We had cut back a little on the number of books we were publishing . . . and if we had had any sense at all, we would have thought about resting for a while. But rather than stopping, we saw the breathing space as time to conceive a few new projects, because wasn't that who we were, and wasn't that what we did?

Wouldn't it be great if we kept pigs? I helpfully suggested. Maybe a breeding sow? – I had always wanted to live with a sow. But then we discovered that you should never keep just a single sow, because they're intensely social animals – and so along came Doris, a beautiful pedigree Saddleback, and Edna, a Gloucester Old Spot/Berkshire cross. We had to construct two more sets of pig-proof housing, safe and warm for farrowing – but my long-suffering husband was used to all of that by now, and within a fairly short period of time the pigs had summer and winter quarters, complete with their own nice little patio areas so that they had somewhere hard to stand when the ground got too boggy. Karen Taylor's boar Rufus came to service them each year, and they produced litters of beautiful piglets which we sold on easily once they had been weaned.

And then, I suggested a few months on, once the pigs were all settled in, if we were going to try to do this self-sufficiency lark properly, how about a milk cow? I'd always wanted a milk cow. Wouldn't it be great, to milk a cow? And so off David went again, to build a milking pen in another corner of the barn, ordering in a cattle crush, creating a place from which we could safely load a cow into a trailer . . . Off he went, to bring home a beautiful black wild, horned Kerry calf from the mainland. She arrived on the old seasonal festival of Imbolc, and so I called her Brigid. We adored her, and David spent months training her to a cattle crush and a halter so that one day we might be able to milk her and make cheese.

There was, of course, a continuing madness in all of this, an ongoing lifelong imbalance which I had yet to learn to recognise, let alone correct, and which was augmented by David's own particular brand of excess. He had been elected as chairman of the local Grazings Committee and, in a crofting township which had long been divided by feuding and bickering, he was determined to bring everyone together. And so he had conceived of and was driving and managing the first community activity in the village for many years: an ambitious project involving three kilometres of fencing, to enclose a beautiful area of lush parkland by the wide sandy beach at Mealista. Saving the world, one fencepost at a time. He was out working at it all day, every Saturday, and often for the odd day during the week as well, because of course the mission must be accomplished. I too was working hard in the community, helping a local group put together a business plan to construct a St Kilda heritage centre a few miles away, near the lovely coastal village of Mangurstadh.

Two Ravens Press, the new *EarthLines* magazine, the croft, the community work ... we were each running the equivalent of two or three full-time jobs at once. It was impossible, and it was getting more impossible by the day. Again, that sense of being on a runaway train, watching horrified as history repeated itself. The sense of complete powerlessness, the impossibility of bringing it to a halt. I had come full circle: there I was, at fifty-two years old, all burned out once more. I had given up safe corporate jobs in England and then in America, and embraced the financial and personal risks of moving to wild, remote places – not once, but twice – because I saw the Wasteland for what it was, and because my life felt shallow and disconnected. I left those jobs because I longed for a deeper relationship with the land and a more meaningful, grounded way of being in the world.

Later, I had moved from Ullapool to Lewis because I was all burned out again and had grown too busy to nurture the connection with the land that I'd started to develop. I'd been in a different kind of Wasteland then – a Wasteland of my own making – but

I was occupying the same dysfunctional psychological space nevertheless. Three times before, I had seen this problem arise and
taken major, life-changing steps to solve it. And yet, here I was
for a fourth time.

There was something in me which still hadn't properly learned,
which still hadn't fully recognised a pattern which badly needed
to be broken. My way of being in the world wasn't working, and,
in spite of the fact that I thought I was a pretty good psychologist, I hadn't really grasped that *I* was the problem. I was so
focused on the need to keep the wheels turning, any wheels at
all, and along whatever road they might be travelling. If a space
opened up in my life, I'd rush to fill it. I knew intellectually that
something wasn't right, but I couldn't seem to learn it instinctively,
applying the wisdom of my body, which was exhausted again.
Exhausted, because I was once more living with that sensation
of giant hands clutching at my throat, squeezing and letting go,
over and over. Because I was experiencing again that feeling that
I couldn't breathe, that I couldn't get enough air into my lungs.

The only thing that was different this time around, and that
was keeping me sane and still standing, was my increasing focus
on and attachment to the land: the remarkable and intensely
moving sense of deep relationship to this place which was rooting
me, grounding me, almost in spite of myself. Whatever else might
be going on, whatever madness awaited me in the house or the
croft or the wider world, still I fell into the deep, powerful spell
of the land twice a day. On Lewis, I felt as if the land was all
there was, the only thing – for all its harsh, stormy lessons – that
nourished and supported me. It was loud, extreme, vivid; it refused
to be ignored.

Sometimes, when you're not paying attention, life steps in and
deals you a major blow to the head, to make sure that you do.
'The universe', by this stage in my life, had had quite enough of
me – and so along came the lesson that finally ended all lessons.
It began in early 2013, with exhaustion and a recurrence of those

old symptoms of anxiety. It began with a series of deaths and losses. It began with a hard spring: icy temperatures, drought followed by serious rain. The grass wasn't growing and the pregnant ewes were struggling; the wildflowers which should have bloomed by then were non-existent and the bees were struggling too. David cut and brought home huge branches of flowering gorse every time he ventured into more sheltered parts of the island, and for a little while longer they managed to hang on.

Then lambing came, and we lost a pair of twin lambs, from a beautiful Jacob ewe we loved dearly. Drowned in a ditch while we weren't paying attention, or maybe while we were paying too much. We buried them at the bottom of the croft, by the loch. Red-eyed, David paced the kitchen floor for hours, unable to live with what he insisted was a dereliction of duty. We almost lost a wether who fell into another deep ditch and was swept away in torrential rain, but thankfully a watchful neighbour was keeping an eye out. We carried him into the utility room and I lay on the floor with my arms wrapped around his shivering body to keep him warm while David tried to dry him out with a hairdryer. He survived.

But we lost a goose – a delicate white Roman goose, the daughter of the old goose who I had hatched from an incubator and hand-reared along with her sibling back in the spring of 2006, in the rich, vivid days after I'd first met David. The dead goose's name was Blue, because of the colour of her leg ring. We buried her on the croft, in the field where the remaining geese lived. A raven carried off another goose's hatchling, the only gosling from that year; we heard the goose's long drawn-out cries of distress in the early morning while we were still in bed. The raven left a tail-feather behind as compensation; it seemed like a poor exchange.

I struggled on, because that's what I did best, and we had *responsibilities*; there was no time to grieve, no time to stop. Chin up; soldier on. We borrowed a fine and experienced Shetland bull to mate with Brigid, who was now two years old. The bull, while mating, went right through the wall of Brigid's vagina and into her abdomen. A totally freak thing, according to the vet: she was abnormally small. But she now had a large tear inside her which couldn't be mended and which meant that even if she survived she would never be able to mate again or carry a calf and give us milk, and she would always be prone to infection. A croft with very limited grazing has no room for a pet cow, especially an invalid, and keeping a cow is enormously expensive. Which meant that Brigid, my beautiful love with her sweet-smelling breath, silky black coat, long sweeping horns and Kerry temper, would probably need to be killed and eaten.

On the lessons came, thick and fast throughout that spring and summer, dealing one blow after another. They didn't all come from animals. I began to get anonymous hate mail – emails and comments on my blog – from someone in America who had discovered that I'd once worked for a tobacco company and imagined that it was some big secret and that they were going to 'out' me. It had never been a big secret – why would it be? – and I'd talked about it publicly on a number of occasions. But that didn't prevent the intensity of the unpleasantness, the curious sense of violation added to the isolation I was feeling and the death and dying all around me, from almost toppling me.

A part-time elderly neighbour took exception to the way David and I had voted (along with a majority of the community, but that didn't seem to matter) in an election at a local Grazings Committee meeting which she had not attended, and flew at me with a surprisingly unpleasant verbal attack one afternoon as I walked past her house with the dogs and waved a cheerful greeting. It was crazy, out of all proportion. I'd never experienced anything like it before; I was shaken. I began to walk another way. I began to hate the world.

On it went. I broke a wrist, falling flat on my face while struggling to help David carry a too-heavy metal farm gate down the hard stony track to the headland. I limped back to the house alone, cradling the wrist in my other hand, while he made sure that the gate arrived safely at its destination: the mission must be accomplished.

Finally, David buckled under the strain of a mission or two that could not, for the first time in his life, be accomplished. The community obstinately refused to be brought together, and although, with a great deal of local pride and delight, the fencing project had been completed on schedule, enthusiasm for another round had been short-lived. Other plans dreamed up by the fencing cartel rapidly faded once the project had ended and everyone drifted back to their own lives and reclaimed their weekends. The local warmongers started a new campaign. His vision of a busy, thriving crofting community which depended on and helped each other – the way it was in the old days – was never going to be. He was, he declared, the last man standing, and he grew bitter and angry. The harder he grew, the more I withdrew. Back to the land, back to my own work. Eventually, barely holding myself together and worn out with his dissatisfactions, I persuaded him to take some time away from the village and the croft in July 2013 to attend a week-long Gaelic language intensive on the other side of the island.

He came back home completely transformed. Smiling, softer, excited again by life.

He came back home and announced that he didn't want to be a crofter any more, but wanted instead to do a degree at the University of the Highlands and Islands, an hour's drive away in the island's only town of Stornoway, and devote himself to learning Gaelic. He'd be gone three or four days a week.

And so they went, one by one, the animals that we'd tended so lovingly and for so long; the animals which I would find it impossible to manage alone. Doris and Edna, the big friendly sows, went to a new home on the neighbouring island of North Uist. My small, funny, gentle flock of Jacob sheep went to a young couple on the east side of the island. Off they went, all packed together into a trailer: Norma, Just Jacob, Pirate, Little Sister, Big Sister. Their ewe-lambs Princess, Wobble and Catwoman. Yes, each of them had a name; we had thought hard and long about their names, choosing them carefully for a particular personality trait or other defining characteristic. Freya the Shetland cow, who we had very recently acquired along with her calf, Corra, and who David had begun to milk, went to a new home in Carloway. Brigid – too big to kill carefully and lovingly on the croft and butcher ourselves, as we had done with all our other animals – went to the abattoir.

Cailleach silhouette, Breanish, Isle of Lewis

Our relationship buckled under the strain of the past several years, and under the weight of my desolation as well as my fury at the ease with which David seemed to have shrugged off bonds and responsibilities which only a week earlier had been sacred. It buckled in the face of the changes in each of us which seemed to be taking us in different directions. Finally, my much-loved old golden retriever dog Frodo, who was getting on for ten years old and had been suffering from a mystery illness for a couple of weeks, died on a small patch of grass outside the back door.

It was enough. Finally, I let myself break; after I had broken, I finally came to understand.

Lewis, in the final days, standing on a cliff-edge, looking out across a stormy sea to the Flannan Isles. Standing in the one place which I believed I could never leave. My place. I recognised it the first moment I saw it. In some curious way it has defined this four-year period of my life, here on this bleakly beautiful, unrelenting island. In some even more curious way, it has defined me. This place, with its vast expanse of slabbed rock extending underfoot like a multicoloured, layered carpet which slopes gradually down to a smattering of boulders, coated with emerald green algae, onto which the sea continually crashes. This undulating rock floor is founded on Lewisian gneiss, one of the oldest rocks in the world. Metamorphic rock – yes, metamorphic: a word shot through with all the possibilities of transformation that I could ever want. How could such a place not define me? It changes in form, it adapts to whatever storms and stresses may come along. It is phoenix rock, emerging renewed from temperatures greater than 1,500 degrees Celsius and pressure that is greater than 1,500 bars. Such things of necessity cause profound change if you mean to survive them. More than simply transformed, this rock has endured, and there are times in everyone's life when endurance matters. The past year has been such a time in mine.

There is a corner of this place which is a shrine. Cliff walls provide a home to succulent plants and to miniature Scots lovage; a clear, sparkling pool in one corner is inhabited by a species of fairy shrimp, or maybe *Gammarus*. I have sat here often by that pool, cross-legged, back cradled by the smooth ancient stone behind me. In the rock wall at the back of the pool, if the light is right and your mind is open, you can make out several faces in the shadows and hollows. A young woman with a snub nose; a craggier face which belongs to a crone. Pan your eyes left, and at the edge of the cliff nearest to the sea you may see the silhouette of a hag, and indeed it is known that in such places the

Cailleach may stand and stare out to sea, perhaps waiting for the return of her husband, the sea-god.

Here, I have sat and immersed myself in stories of the Cailleach, the creator-goddess of this land. Here, I have become Cailleach for a time. Here, I have become Storm. I have stood for long periods of time by the side of that old hag and stared out to sea with her, imagining the long ages and the unyielding rock and the unending power of the sea. Here, I have learned about endurance. I have learned about standing – and more than I ever wanted to know about making a stand. I have learned about digging in, and for sure I have learned about digging too deep. I have remembered that the Cailleach, for all her seemingly harsh ways, danced her wild way across the mountains even as she brought the onset of winter, and I have remembered that I too have always loved to dance.

This place has seen me grieve, but it has also seen me dance barefooted across its warm rock. I slept here once, at the end of a long, slowly darkening August, after four months of those endless and exhausting too-light Hebridean summer nights during which I hadn't once seen a black sky. I slept fitfully on a flat slab of rock, a person-sized niche carved out of the cliff-face which I called the Cailleach's bed, waking at intervals during the night to see the stars bright above me, and the moon, and the regular flashing of the Flannan light like the pulsing heart of the sea.

Leaving? Yes, we are leaving – leaving again, and what breaks my heart more than any of the other things that have been and remain still to be endured is the leaving of this old Cailleach. She's been alone before, standing sentinel to the swell of the sea, waiting for her husband to return. She's been there alone through all the recent ages of man. So why do I feel I'm abandoning her? Perhaps it's because of my own old fear of abandonment, my terror of being left. Perhaps it's because there have been so many who abandoned this land, so many who deserted her for an ungenerous and unforgiving god. Still, there she stands, back proudly turned to the poor, straggling remnants of a people who once sang to her beauty. Look at her there, with her heavy brow, chiselled cheeks and sharply jutting jaw. She may be old, but there is a fierceness in her still.

There is a fierceness in me still.

On 1 August 2013, on the old harvest festival-day of Lughnasa, the time for reaping what you sow, I sat by the rock-pool shrine next to that silhouetted old Cailleach, looking with her out to sea, and I finally let myself fall into the dark Otherworldly cave I'd avoided all my life. A time came that I can hardly bear to remember now; it was as if all the stresses and the strains of the past seven years had crashed in on me, all at once. I'd always seen myself as unassailable, but for the first time in my life, I broke. Weeping for hours at a time on the sofa, with only the presence of a little border collie dog climbing onto my lap and licking the tears from my cheeks keeping me going. All the anger I'd never been allowed to express as a child ('Don't you dare shout at me; you're just like your father') spewing out in huge great globs of white-hot rage. Crazy nights in the kitchen with 'Raggle-Taggle Gypsy' playing at full volume, whirling around the table like a dervish while the dogs barked along for the fun of it. I was mad as Mis, for sure. If it hadn't been for my *responsibilities* I'd likely have taken off into the hills and woven rushes through my hair and feasted on shoots and grubs.

The truth of it is, I needed this. We both needed it. We needed something radical to break through the dogged lunacy of our lives, something powerful enough to burn it all away. I burned and I burned. Burned myself alive in some great conflagration of long-suppressed emotion, but instead of being consumed I was transformed. 'Do you want to know how I feel?' I shouted at David one night over dinner in the thick of it all, flushed, wild-eyed, and probably slightly drunk. 'I feel utterly *incandescent.*'

Sometimes, like peace, wisdom comes dropping slow. Sometimes, when you are stuck and have been stuck for years without even realising it, it falls from the sky, lands bang-smack on the top of your head, and knocks you out for the count. The wisdom that descended on me was the wisdom which belonged to the place I was living. It wasn't a gentle wisdom, or an easy one. It was the wisdom of the oldest rock on the planet; the hard, unyielding stony Hebridean earth; the sharp, treacherous shore – and above all, the wisdom of that old Cailleach at the end of the world who had seen it all before and who had ceased to take prisoners long ages ago.

In order to come into my wisdom, in order to finally see the patterns which needed to be broken before I could move on through my journey, I'd had to be cracked open. And now everything I'd suppressed or tidied neatly away over the years came oozing out of that fractured shell, sticky and gelid and puddling messily on the floor. There it was, all laid out in front of me; and day by day, week by week, pounding the headland, staring blindly into the sea, I examined every choice I'd ever made, took my life and myself to pieces. Things I'd never understood suddenly made sense, dysfunctional behaviour patterns suddenly became clear. That cracked and blackened mirror I was holding up to myself told one hell of a story.

Recognising the source of many of our problems as simple overwork, we came slowly to the difficult but necessary decision to sell Two Ravens Press; it was taken over by a crofter in Ness who had previously bought lambs from us. Only *EarthLines* remained. All of a sudden, I had time on my hands: not only time to think, but time to start again learning how to simply be.

David, meanwhile, immersed himself in the study of Gaelic. At first I'd rather ungenerously imagined it was just another displacement activity, but it turned out otherwise. It was a genuine passion, and for something very much more than the fact of wanting simply to speak another language. It was a passion for the sound of the words, for the way they rolled off the tongue – but above all, a passion for a different way of looking at the world, for a language which expressed things which could not be well expressed in English, or which couldn't be expressed at all.

Ultimately, a passion for a culture, and a way of life: a way of life deeply rooted in place.

I'd begun, when everything went so horribly wrong, to seriously contemplate leaving him ... but then curiously, just as radically as it had broken, and in ways I would never have begun to imagine, our relationship began to reweave itself. Once upon a time I had married a man who had the heart of a poet – but who had no time for stories. A man who was (though he hated the very notion of it, and found the idea that there might be any significance in myth deeply iniquitous) on a classic Hero's Journey. A former student of Western philosophy, a lover of Nietzsche, a frowner upon anything mythic or fey. Gentle in so many ways, and yet the perfect product of the patriarchy in others. Thoroughly dis-enchanted, utterly in love with the rational, the intellectual, the conservative, the secular, the institutional.

I had (foolishly) spent the seven years we'd been together suppressing everything in my own presentation of myself that he might find offensive, that he might be able to mock, or otherwise 'deconstruct'. My tarot cards were hidden deep in a drawer; I never used the word 'soul' in conversation. Now, in an astonishing act of dissolution, in the space of that one week's exposure to the music and poetry and laughter of his fellow students on that course, and the sudden blossoming of love for an old language and a deeply place-based culture, he had begun to unravel that old hardness and rigidity, and then to reassemble himself into something altogether more interesting. Each night over dinner, like a red-haired Celtic Scheherazade, I fed him a new story from Irish or Scottish mythology. He listened, and sometimes he asked for more.

All the while, throughout all of this, it was the land which held me together. The wildflowers which appeared exactly when they always came, even though my world had ceased to bloom; the whooper swans who still stopped off for a while on their long migration south, even though my heart had broken and crashed to earth. The land held me, and I told my stories to the stones. I howled my anger at the sea and took the salty spray it threw back in my face, and somehow I managed to laugh. I took my strength from it – and yet, some new and fatal softening in me was for the first time rubbing up uncomfortably against the harshness of this place. And quite simply, without the animals on the croft, with David away in Stornoway for much of each week, I was lonely.

The community around us was mostly made up of incomers and was small, disputatious and inward-looking; all of my friends were either back on the mainland or lived on the far side of the world. I had no one to talk to, and no one other than David with whom I could exchange ideas. I began to long for music and laughter of my own; I began to long for a tribe that I could properly belong to. Nursing another dead tree, cradling another dead herb bed, killed by the constant salt spray and never-ending vicious winds, I began to long for a place where things actually wanted to grow. This land had challenged me and pushed me to the brink; now, I just wanted to be held. There are times when you need the extremity of rock, the hardness of an old, cold place against which you can measure yourself. There are times when you need to retreat to the wilderness. But there are times when you need the subtle flow of a river, the song of a waterfall and the deep, slow presence of trees. Times when you need to Return. There are times for holding on, and times for letting go.

The final insight came during a small, week-long creative retreat for women that I was leading during an improbably hot and sunny spell at the beginning of October 2013. The wildness of the land and the stories we explored worked their magic on the seven participants, who found themselves spontaneously skinny-dipping in rock-pools, rolling in muddy bogs, dancing on rocky outcrops at the edge of the sea. We spoke of the Cailleach, of becoming hag; we wrote and we wept and we shared each other's stories.

One bright sunny morning, about to begin the day's workshop, I sat down on a hard chair with my back to an enormous window in the main room of the property I had rented to host the course. All of a sudden, one of the older women said to me, 'You know, I've been thinking about you, sitting there morning after morning, with your back to the sea and the sky. And somehow you look right there. Light. As if you're part of the distance. Yes, that's how I see you: light, like the sweep of that distant horizon' – and what little there was left in me to break by then shattered, because I had come to think of myself as so heavy and hard. Heavy and hard, like this beautiful but unforgiving old land.

I remembered that there had indeed been a lightness in me once, in that time of learning to fly and of breaking free: a lightness which I had lost somewhere along the way. I remembered that wolf in my dream, the wolf with holes for eyes where the sky shone through, and I thought that I had left no room in the rocky edifice, the impenetrable stone-skin I'd constructed around myself, for the sky to shine through. And I remembered that the sea and the sky – water and air – had always been my elements, but I had weighted myself down with work and *responsibilities*, and buried myself far too deeply in the cold, harsh, solitary earth of this magnificent but unrelenting place. I had learned to live without trees and fertile ground and green grass. I had learned to live without people.

Now, I was learning new things. I was learning that the pendulum of our lives had swung too far. I was learning that for all its failures and horrors, for all the things that I find abhorrent in this civilisation, I was nevertheless a human being and human culture is something I couldn't seem entirely to eschew.

Sometimes, if you dig yourself too deeply into an element that is not your natural element, then if you are very, very lucky it will spit you out rather than swallow you up. And she spat me out, that stony old Cailleach. She chewed me up a little before she sent me on my way, but she spat me out. These are the lessons of the land; this is the power of place speaking. It speaks, if you choose to listen. I listened, and so it was that I came to leave that place that I couldn't ever have imagined leaving, and I returned to Ireland after all.

Len had died a few years earlier, leaving our old cottage (which I had signed over to him in order to achieve my divorce) to his daughter, who soon sold it on. The way was open . . . but much as I had loved the place, something in me resisted going back to Connemara. I felt as if I needed to move firmly forwards rather than circling back to a place where I'd been a couple of decades earlier. And so instead we came to Donegal, to this wild north-western outpost where still, on my doorstep, I can find the bleak mountains and the high, windy bog and the vast sweep of a white, stormy strand – but also, a tiny house in a gentle green valley, in a small wood, by a fast-flowing, light-hearted river. A house that is set apart in the hills, but just a few minutes away from a thriving village with a friendly community, and year-round festivals filled with fiddle music, poetry and song.

Here, we are in the Gaeltacht, an Irish-speaking territory where there is a new language for David to learn, not so very different from Scottish Gaelic. Here, too, in an Ireland that still hugs its stories close to its heart. Here, where that old Cailleach hugs me still to hers, for there is a strong thread between Donegal and the Hebrides, a thread which binds us tightly together: two old Gaelic provinces, cultures and languages, with just a thin, bright strip of ocean between. From An Chailleach Bhéarra in Ireland to the south, to An Chailleach Bheur in the Hebrides to the north. The line is unbroken; the line is true. This centre holds.

To this place I bring the lessons I learned in Lewis: not just the personal and emotional insights, but the greatest learning of all: the remarkable, transformative lessons of the land. I believe I would take those lessons with me wherever I should go, but this land fits me like a glove, and my writing and story work thrive in this Ireland I've always loved, this country where the Otherworld is a fact of life, absolutely as real as our own. ('If you are wise,' says our neighbour the poet, matter-of-factly, in passing, pointing to a cluster of ancient hawthorns known locally

as the 'fairy wood', 'you will never steal a stick from that place.')
My work springs directly out of this land, too: I earn my living
from online courses in place-based story and personal myth-
making, teaching people how to build belonging, and from the
'Singing Over the Bones' creative retreats for women which I
continue to offer on this new, wild Atlantic fringe. And through
this work I am nurtured by a different kind of community: a
large and vibrant international network of women with whom
to exchange stories, ideas and laughter.

There had always been a part of me that pined still for Ireland,
however much I might have loved the other places I'd lived in.
Something about it that I couldn't seem to let go. Why is it that
some of us come to so deeply identify with one place and not
another? I have no easy answers, only the knowledge that for all
my wanderings and switherings, this is the place I have always
wanted to run back to when things grew difficult, the only place
which makes me feel healthy and whole and full of joyful heart.
There is an idea in this country, a belief in the 'place of resur-
rection': the place where a soul is happiest on earth and, at the
same time, most in touch with all that is eternal. Perhaps Ireland
is simply that place, for me.

Becoming elder begins at menopause, an entire journey all of its
own: a biological, spiritual and emotional rite of passage whose
impact is often underrated. Menopause is not a medical condition,
it is an earthquake, shaking us to our deepest foundations, wiping
out the edifices we've so carefully constructed on what we once
imagined to be the solid ground of our life. Menopause hacks us
open; it is the cleaving to end all cleavings.

It was no surprise that during that cataclysmic last year on
Lewis I was also experiencing the beginnings of menopause. It
may creep up on you gently, with the occasional hot flush and
disruptions of the menstrual cycle – but then, one by one, it
systematically strips away all the trappings of womanhood and
sexuality which we've clung to – or had foisted upon us – for

the whole of our lives. It can be hard to surrender, to relinquish our identification with fertility, youth and motherhood. Often that relinquishment entails a time of deep grieving. Sometimes we clutch at all that is vanishing, unable or unwilling to learn to love our beautiful silver or white hair, to live comfortably with our new wrinkles and our sagging skin. Sometimes we refuse it, postponing the inevitable with hormone therapy and hair dye. It seems like the harshest and loneliest of all lessons, in this society where elderhood is so little valued.

Yes, menopause is an ending, and it is natural to mourn an ending – but it is not a disability. It is also a new beginning. In some indigenous cultures, medicine women are not allowed to practise till they've reached menopause. There are new wisdoms now to be learned. Life is not over, it has simply changed irrevocably. We might fear disappearing – and yet there is a freedom in invisibility. We are no longer tied to the endless ups and downs of hormonal fluctuations, the endless seething cycles of emotion that accompany them. The life-passage of menopause is above all else a response to the many changes our body is undergoing. Menopausal wisdom is the deep wisdom of the body, which calls us to shrug off the glitter, to divest ourselves of the trimmings which no longer matter. We are no longer defined by old roles and expectations. We are freed from those old shackles, and with that freedom comes a new focus, a clarity, and almost always a desire to simplify. This is a time to reflect on what is still to be done in our lives; a time to turn our attention to things we've put aside. It is also a time for seeing the truth about our lives, and finally understanding our patterns. For many there is also a freedom from perpetual strivings to become, from the need to constantly accomplish; instead, there is the slow dawning of a passion for creating necessary change. Because menopause doesn't strip us of our passions: it simply shifts their focus. That heart still thunders; that fire still burns. It burns us from the inside out, hot flush after hot flush, year after long year, burning away all that we no longer need.

As menopause progresses, we begin to look outside ourselves; our attention moves from the individual to the collective. We begin to think more about passing on what we have learned; about offering up our wisdom for the benefit of the community, of the Earth. Healthy elders, no longer needing to assert themselves, to be competitive with each other, are especially skilled at forging alliances, building communities and creating networks. In indigenous cultures, they are deeply respected for it. Carol Schaefer tells us in her inspiring book *Grandmothers Counsel the World*[6] that in Native American societies:

> the women elders, the grandmothers, were the ones who were looked up to as guardians to watch over the physical and spiritual survival of the family, and thus the tribe. They became the keepers of the teachings and rituals that allowed the tribe to flourish, and they upheld the social order. In many of the tribes around the world . . . the Council of Grandmothers was always consulted before any major decision was made, including the decision of whether or not to go to war.

But in our Western societies, we are so rarely presented with positive images of older women. We have lost respect for the grandmothers.

A vision of understated elegance walks into The Jam Factory, a bright, sunny café just across the road from Oxford railway station. Her white hair is perfectly bobbed and she is dressed all in white too, because, she tells me as we find a table and order coffee, later today she is off on a three-day meditation retreat with some friends. I'm not especially tall and I'm pretty slim, but I feel like a great hulking giant next to her.

Don't be fooled: Scilla Elworthy[7] may be petite, but she has enormous presence – the steely, but warm and entirely unthreatening presence which enabled her to initiate and then lead a series of ground-breaking dialogues between nuclear weapons policy-makers worldwide and their critics during the 1990s. Those meetings formed the basis for later global disarmament treaties, and caused her to be nominated three times for the Nobel Peace Prize. As if that wasn't enough achievement for one lifetime, she followed it up in 2002 with the founding of Peace Direct,[8] an international charity which works at the grassroots level to support local peacebuilding activities around the world. And then, in 2005, she became a key adviser to Peter Gabriel, Archbishop Desmond Tutu and Sir Richard Branson in setting up The Elders,[9] an independent group of global leaders who work together for peace and human rights. I'm exhausted just thinking about it, but she hasn't stopped there; now an elder herself, Scilla has turned her attention to what she describes as 'the ways women have lost their power and the ways we are re-finding it', and a couple of years ago she co-founded another organisation, Rising Women, Rising World,[10] to work with just these issues.

'I was seventy-two two days ago,' she tells me when I express my surprise at her determination to keep on fighting for positive change in the world, 'and I'm feeling an ever-stronger calling to serve the Earth in some way. For me, the postmenopausal years have been filled with zest. My elderhood isn't about contemplation, that image of going deep into the cave, consulting the dark and coming out with great wisdom. My path is more active. I'm an initiator. Though I'm beginning to think I've had enough of starting new things now!'

Although for much of her life her focus has been on peacemaking, Scilla's interest in women's issues began back in 1978, when she was living in Paris and was asked by the Minority Rights Group to co-author the first-ever report on female genital mutilation. But it was during her time working with nuclear policy-makers and their critics that she first began to have a sense of the specific, valuable qualities that women could bring to the table.

'I found myself in the presence of very powerful men, and their underlying assumption was that to progress in this world, you have to dominate. Such a masculine way of operating! And then we, a mixed group with a significant proportion of women, were the ones who were creating this safe space in which they began to feel, remarkably, that they could all remove their masks and for the first time ever talk openly to each other. That experience made me realise that what women brought to politics was an entirely different realm of experience. It was to do with connection, and with relationship. A completely different way of influencing others which had nothing to do with domination.'

Scilla began to think more about what this uniquely feminine expression of power might consist of and where it might originate, and in her 1996 book *Power and Sex*[11] she targeted her research on other ways in which it seemed to be manifesting itself in the world.

'I started to notice that women were doing something more than just standing up for themselves and making their voices heard. I saw that there was something tangible in what might be called the "deep feminine": a profound power that comes from the belly, a creative power, deeply calming – it can calm an atmosphere even at a distance. It's safe and nurturing of course, but it's also to do with birth-giving. To me, that ability women have to birth things is very much bound up with our connection to the seasons and the Earth, with a devotion to the regeneration of the Earth, helping and supporting her to recover from what we've done to her.'

In *Power and Sex*, Scilla describes the impact of a woman who has this form of inner power: 'People feel safe with her,' she writes, 'because she has her feet planted within the earth.' She is very clear that her own nourishment, and her own sense of inner power, derives from precisely such a sense of rootedness. Although she was born in Scotland and professes to an 'attachment' to it, and later studied in Ireland, her real attachment is to the Earth as a whole.

'I have a passionate devotion to the physical Earth,' she tells me, leaning forward with her hands on the table and, characteristically, making me the focus of her full attention. 'I have a garden, and I assist plants to grow in it. It's not just a wonderful antidote to all the hurly-burly, it's about the privilege of being able to have one's feet and hands in and on the Earth.' I find myself wondering whether she has always felt like this, and she tells me about her mother, who was also a passionate gardener. 'We lived on a farm, and she grew most of the things we ate. Yes, she talked to plants too! I remember sitting next to her while she planted a flowerbed when I was very small, somehow understanding without being able to express it, this very strong connection to the Earth that she had. It really was as if she was a part of it. That image has been with me all my life. And so it's like coming home, in a way, this work I'm doing now to serve the Earth. The desire for it goes back a long way.'

This new work that she is speaking about is focused around Rising Women, Rising World, the organisation which Scilla and her friends Jean Houston from the USA and Rama Mani from India set up to harness that unique feminine power she's been talking about, and to put it to good use. 'We decided that now was the time to use the strength and imagination of the deep feminine to build a world that works for all of us – both human and non-human – on this planet. We realised that between us we knew at least twenty wise and talented women from so many different cultures around the world, some indigenous, some not. A number of those women were specialists in fields like economics, education, arts, governance, food and water management, peace-building, and so we asked each of them to be a "pioneer" in this new organisation, to lay out their vision of how the future could be if feminine values were brought to the fore.'

The way that Rising Women, Rising World works, Scilla explains, is that each woman 'pioneer' gathers around herself a constellation of twelve others who are also passionate about her subject, and she mentors them, works with them to formulate a project, ensures they're clear about exactly what it is they want to achieve. And then eventually each of them in turn works with twelve more . . . and so the network, she hopes, will spread exponentially throughout the world. 'Investigate what breaks your heart,' she says. 'Then ask yourself whether that is where your passion lies, think about what your key skills are, marry the two – then you have your initiative.'

Interestingly, although the focus is very much on women's unique skills and power, the organisation actively welcomes the participation of men, and Scilla is very clear that the feminine qualities being sought and cultivated are available to men too. 'It isn't about gender, it's about ways of being in the world. It's absolutely about working together. That's how we're going to create real change. You can't do it without men. And to do it with them is a joy.'

Over the years, Scilla's focus has changed from working within the system – her years in the United Nations, working with top decision-makers, endeavouring to shift their mind-sets and approaches – to working predominantly at the other end of the spectrum, with grassroots movements. I ask her whether she feels that age has changed her perspective on where real change in the world is most likely to come from. 'Yes,' she nods. 'Now I think I've come to the point where I feel that the important change is really coming up from below. In the same way as green shoots find their way through concrete, yes – but also as earthquakes, as really big sudden shifts. So I'm really interested now in the ReGeneration generation, and especially in millennials – those born between 1980 and 2000 – because their priorities are so different from their predecessors. Surveys done by KPMG and Goldman Sachs show that millennials prioritise climate change, resource scarcity, inequality and the regeneration of the planet over personal gain and achievement. There's a huge new energy building up in the world, especially among young people – but I also see it being led by the elders.'

I'm curious about how that might work. What does she think are the contributions that elders can make to Western societies which seem to have lost respect for them? 'My vision of elderhood comes from two places: first, my experience of really getting to know some older women who made a big impact on me, especially one specific wise and wonderful Maori woman, and a Native American woman,' she tells me. 'And then of course growing myself into elderhood and realising what a lot of unused wisdom, power and conviction so many of us have. I believe it's a huge unused untapped source. The postmenopausal woman everywhere is totally under-used. In the West, the norm seems to be that, after meno-pause, women are made to feel useless. But when women come through menopause with the idea that it's a new beginning rather than the end of everything, there can be an incredible influx of energy and clarity. I believe we haven't even begun to harvest the energy and wisdom that's available to us in women over fifty-five.'

As Scilla speaks, always looking directly into my eyes, always asking questions in her turn, always making me feel that this a conversation, a genuine exchange of ideas rather than a one-sided interview, it's easy to see how she embodies the honest, openly communicating feminine power she talks about. And I am reminded of Jungian Marion Woodman's definition of that most iconic of all images of elder women, the Crone. 'She is not withdrawn,' declares Woodman. 'She is alarmingly present. Like a tuning fork her truth shatters hypocrisy. Others in her presence are released into what is true in themselves. Or flee.'[12]

Scilla tells me that her own initiation into elderhood began quite early. 'The post-menopausal energy I'm talking about begins to emerge when women are released from the need to be sex objects, which our culture imposes on us. When we suddenly become invisible. This happened to me at quite a young age. My hair had been white since I was thirty-five, and like so many do, I spent years dying it. And then, when I was fifty, I decided I'd had enough. I stopped treating the roots, cut it off to a centimetre long all over, and then I was all white. I became invisible over-night. It was an utterly fascinating experience. All of a sudden, I found I had to use my energy differently. But really,' she laughs, 'it was incredibly liberating. Your energy becomes your own, instead of thinking all the time about who is looking at you, who might desire you.'

I find myself wondering whether her fierce energy and determination to create change will ever run out. Has she felt even just the tiniest glimmer of that possibility yet, I ask her? 'Yes,' she nods. 'I've reached a point in my life where I'm changing my patterns a bit. A while ago I became ill, and that made me think about conserving some of my energy, so that I finally stopped saying yes to every demand. I'm focusing in. I think that's very much a part of elderhood: getting very clear about how to use the rest of your life. The possibilities of course are fewer, the time shorter. You can't any longer imagine that you can change everything! I focus now on just one or two things that I'm most passionate about. And focused passion is important, as you grow older: a refusal to tolerate the intolerable.'

I wonder whether that passion springs from anger, from rage, but she is very clear that rage is not what she is talking about. 'I think the nature of what needs to be conveyed by women now is *wrath* rather than rage,' she says firmly. 'Wrath is different. To me, it means an incontrovertible statement, put across fiercely, and also carrying an urgent instruction about what needs to happen. Wrath carries no hate, but for sure – just like the utterances of the women Oracles of old – it comes with dire warning.'

Dire warnings abound in Celtic mythology too, and our old women are not to be messed with. If, as a Celtic woman, to be Elder is to be Cailleach, then to be Elder is above all to be the fierce protector of the Earth, guardian of its balance. In the Scottish Highlands she was known as the Cailleach Beinne Bric, protector of the deer, the 'fairy cattle'. Hunters had a great respect for her and, if they followed her instructions on which deer to cull and when, she ensured that they were always provided with enough food and pelts. So she is seen to be carefully guarding the balance of the natural world – but if her instructions were not followed, there were serious consequences.

In some of these old stories the Cailleach might appear as a Glastaig (a Maighdean Uaine, or Green Maiden);[13] one such story tells of a Glastaig who prevented Donald Cameron, a hunter in Lochaber, from killing a herd of hinds which she was driving. Seeing him raise his gun, she called to him: 'You are too hard on my hinds, Donald! You must not be so hard on them!' Donald, quick-witted, answered her with this swift reply: 'I have never killed a hind where I could find a stag.' He allowed the hinds to pass, concentrated ever afterwards on taking the occasional stag, and the Glastaig never bothered him again.

In another story, a man returned from hunting on Beinn Bhric one day when he heard a sound like the cracking of two rocks against each other. At the base of a large stone by the road he found a woman with a green shawl around her shoulders. The woman, clearly a Glastaig, held a deer shank in each hand, and constantly struck them together. He asked her what she was doing, but she cried only, over and over again, 'Since the forest was burnt! Since the forest was burnt!' And she kept repeating this refrain for as long as he could hear her.[14] Here, the Cailleach mourns the cutting of the forest; here, she mourns the loss of her deer. Here perhaps she mourns the coming of the road, the coming of man, and of progress. Here, like the Old Woman of Beare, she seems to have been dethroned, deprived of her power to protect.

The Elder, fully embedded in and belonging to her place, is fierce in her protection of it. Love and respect your place, she will tell you, for there is a strong argument that you begin to love the whole – not just a pretty idea of Earth, but the complex, thorny reality of it – by learning to fully love your own part. We engage in a meaningful way with our current environmental crisis by starting with the place that we call home, so that, in whatever ways are open to us, we can take responsibility for, and help to protect, the land that we occupy. The land which we personify.

To become Elder, then, is to protect the living – but it is also to be able to face death. The Cailleach in Scotland, whipping up the winter storms, striking the ground hard with her staff so that frost forms where it falls, represents the dying half of the year. And yet, she is able to constantly renew herself – a reminder that the creative process which is so fundamental an aspect of womanhood is a cycle of birth and rebirth, founded on the principle that death constantly gives birth to life. In order to embrace the creation of life, you must be able to live with the knowledge of death. This is the heart of what it is to fully be a human being. It is also at the heart of our old native ways of knowing: the Celts viewed time, and so life, as cyclical rather than linear.

This cyclicity isn't just an interesting historical curiosity lacking in practical consequence: it is evidence of an entirely different worldview. If you see the world as linear, then the dynamic forces which underlie existence are progress and growth. And over the past couple of thousand years, these concepts have become more than just the bedrock of Western economics; they have become the foundational ideas of our civilisation. If you see life as linear, so that progress and growth are what give it meaning, then it is hard to endure impermanence of any kind. It is especially hard to live with death, because death is the ultimate impermanence. In modern Western society, we want to preserve everything, and we want to live forever. We wage war on old age and write songs about being forever young. And because death is seen as no more nor less than the end of the line, and so something to be held off and resisted, we live in constant fear of it.

But to the Celts, death was inextricably intertwined with life. Every month, the moon died and was reborn. Every winter, the sun died and was reborn. The tide came in, and the tide receded. To imagine that you could avoid these natural cycles was not only unthinkable, but undesirable. Out of all the dying, something precious and new is always born. Unending transformation, the greatest of all the gifts the Earth offers us. Life in death and death in life. It's the secret that's contained in the Grail, in the ancient cauldron of rebirth.

Perhaps more than anything, to become Elder is to be comfortable with your place in the world, finally to have understood where all of your various journeys have been leading you, to understand your gifts as well as your limitations, and to tightly focus those gifts on service to the Earth and community. To become the Elder who can express her wrath rather than her rage, and warn of the dire consequences of ignoring it, is to have stepped fully into your own power as a woman. To become Elder is to have found the courage to reclaim the moral authority which we once lost. That reclaiming takes courage, because women have been so very well trained to be afraid – and it isn't always our impotence which makes us most afraid: it's our power. We are not accustomed to it, and so we fear its consequences. To step into your power means to trust yourself, your instincts and your intuition. To let the fear go, and the shame, and tell the stories which need to be told.

Arthur, Dartmoor, England (*Diane Banks*)

I think that I'm about to choose Arthur, but it turns out that Arthur is choosing me. Just as I open my mouth to say his name, he turns away from his two companions and strolls purposefully across the field towards me. I stand still, awe-struck, as he gently lays his beautiful brown head on my right shoulder. It feels like an anointing. I can hear Sue laughing at my side as I lift my hand to stroke the side of his warm brown neck. 'See?' she says. 'He's chosen you.'

Earlier this morning, a perfect, crisp and sunny late-February morning, I drove east across the Tamar and headed north to Sue Blagburn's home just outside the small village of Holne in the green, rolling hills of the south-eastern Dartmoor National Park, deep in the heart of the old Celtic kingdom of Dumnonia. I am here to talk to her about her work, but most of all I am here to meet her horses. She might be the owner of the company through which she offers a variety of different workshops and individual sessions in equine-facilitated learning, but she considers the horses to be the true educators. Adventures with Horses[15] is located at the converted stone barn in which Sue lives; her three horses – Arthur, William and Harry – live there too and have the run of a couple of lush paddocks bordered with native hedges and trees.

Although I've ridden horses at various times in the past, I do not really know 'horse'. Dogs are my animal, and I've lived with them for many years – working Border collie sheepdogs, for the most part – so I know what it is to be part of a pack, to walk with animals who are hunters at heart. But horses are prey animals, and women are often prey. I wanted to learn from them, and to understand them. What I needed more than anything now was to find a way of assimilating all that I had learned on my journey. If women are the Voices of the Wells, if women are the power of the land speaking, how do I step into that power? Could a horse show me the way?

'Horses,' Sue states, as she leads me into a small frosty paddock where the three horses are engrossed in a morning meal of hay, 'teach us to be braver, more aware, more alive in the present moment, more balanced, more coordinated. They teach us to surrender to something bigger and stronger than ourselves. This can happen just by being around them, by merging with their way of being. By understanding the culture of the herd.'

The herd is at the heart of it. Although they form very inclusive communities, Sue tells me, they do nevertheless have a 'pecking order', and one of the three horses in front of me is the clear leader of this tiny group. I can't see any obvious clues at this point, but then I don't really know what signs I should be looking for. And it has to be said that they are rather more interested in breakfast than anything else just at the moment. Arthur, a brown thoroughbred with a white mark rather like a lopsided heart on his forehead, stands slightly to one side; William and Harry, smaller native New Forest ponies, are a little closer together. In spite of the chill which is creeping up through my boots from the icy ground and making me shiver, there is something very restful about just standing there with the horses as Sue tells me their individual stories. It feels . . . natural.

'So it should,' Sue says as we walk back to the house. 'People and horses have worked together in partnership for thousands of years – the art of horsemanship has been traced back to 8000 BC, and less than a hundred years ago horses were still our main form of transport, as well as our agricultural support workers. Now that machines have taken over their jobs as workhorses and war horses, they've become our recreation, or our pets. But there's much more to horses than that, and now, as we think about reinventing what it is to be human among all the challenges of the twenty-first century, a growing number of us feel certain that horses have a new role to play in teaching us.'

I am especially interested in horses because, in Celtic mythology, they are strongly identified with women. The story of Rhiannon is one such example: she first appears to Pwyll riding a magical white horse; later she is forced herself to act as a horse, carrying travellers into the castle on her back. She is often described as a horse-goddess, though the most prominent of Celtic horse-goddesses was undoubtedly Epona, who in the first three centuries AD was worshipped across Western Europe.

I ask Sue why she thinks there was such a strong relationship between horses and the feminine, distracting her sufficiently that she burns the toast and sets off the kitchen fire alarm, and so I hold off until everything is ready and we are seated at the table in a cosy, light-filled sitting room.

'In wild or natural herds, there's always a lead stallion,' she explains over tea, toast and a boiled egg, 'but somewhere in the herd there's also usually a lead mare. She's an older mare, chosen not on the grounds of dominance, but on her ability to pay attention, to know the land, to know where the best grass is, what the weather will be doing. On Dartmoor I've sat and watched lots of wild herds. They'll suddenly move, on some subtle signal from a lead mare. She sets the direction and pace of the herd. The lead stallion is at the edges, keeping the herd together and protecting it from predators.'

A few days before I came to see Sue, on her recommendation I read Linda Kohanov's ground-breaking book, *The Tao of Equus*.[16] Kohanov suggests that horses relate to the world in ways which traditionally and archetypally are associated with the feminine, choosing 'cooperation over competition, responsiveness over strategy, emotion and intuition over logic, process over goal, and the creative approach to life that those qualities engender.' She writes about a persistent connection in mythology between horses and aspects of female knowledge that are routinely suppressed in patriarchal cultures. As we have treated horses, so we have treated women, Kohanov says. We break their spirit, believe we must dominate and control them through fear and intimidation. The wisdom which women bring – the wisdom of the body and the senses, the wisdom of intuition and of relationship – has been sidelined, ridiculed, suppressed. But maybe horses can help to show us the way back. Now, I ask Sue how she thinks this might work.

'Over all the years I've been working with horses,' she says, 'as a riding instructor, a competitor, a breeder, I began to see that horses can teach us a better way of being in the world. It's about learning to find, or reconnect to, what has heart and meaning in our lives. Horses can help us with this. The horse asks us to become honest, authentic in our behaviour and emotions, because horses are prey animals and want to feel safe in our presence. When you approach horses, they're not listening to your agenda, status or outer persona; instead, they're watching your body language, assessing your emotions . . . they're listening to your inner story, not your outer story.

'Horses see through to our internal states. They reflect them back at us, make the invisible visible. They respond to who and how you really are, in your body, in the present moment. A horse can give accurate and instant feedback about what is real and truthful in us. And so they can become our allies and our guides as we explore our inner stories, and as we start to understand how they are tied up with our external challenges, ambitions or stuck places. All of this helps us to see our lives with new eyes, to shift and to become more authentic. Horses teach us how to re-align mind, body and spirit so that we can walk on into our future with courage, grace and integrity.'

With breakfast over, it is time to head back out into the sunshine so that I can experience a session with the horses. 'The horses do most of the work,' Sue tells me as we walk back out to the paddock, where the horses have finished their hay and are standing together quietly in a group. 'I simply hold the space. How much you challenge yourself is your choice, but if you step out of your comfort zone and trust your instincts, the process of working with the horses can be enlightening.'

We open the gate to a larger, sunnier field and the horses follow us in and on into the centre. Clearly taking delight in the more open space and the increasing warmth of the sunny morning, the three horses run around us, bucking and leaping. To my surprise, I stand my ground, finding only pleasure rather than threat in the spontaneous display of exhilaration and power. But then I trust Sue, who clearly knows her horses. And I am here to give up control, and to learn. I have to trust the horses, too.

The horses settle down and move to the edge of the field near a tall hedge, where they stand still and clearly are contemplating a nap in the sun. Sue invites me to approach them, and, when I feel comfortable, to touch them. At first I feel reticent. Who am I, that they should take notice of me? Who am I to impose myself on them, to invade their herd? Sue has told me that as soon as we start to connect with a horse she or he will be evaluating us, asking, who is leading? 'One of the big learnings is the fine line between not being assertive enough and being too dominant or demanding. Horses help us find the middle path, where we step into our power.'

I approach William first, who I have sized up as the calmest of the horses. Although they are all more or less the same age, there is something about William which seems older, more serene. I creep closer, and he shows no signs of objecting. Hesitantly, I reach out a hand and stroke the side of his head. I still feel diffident. I know that a dog loves to be stroked; does a horse? Or is he just tolerating me? I feel uncomfortable, not knowing. I don't like it when someone I don't know invades my personal space; does a horse feel the same?

Arthur is close by; he is a tall, leggy horse who from the beginning has struck me as rather more restless than the two solid, earthy native ponies. He tosses his head a little more, moves around a little more. And so I am more cautious, but he stands still and allows me to come close. And then Harry, though for some reason I'm not especially drawn to Harry. Something in his energy seemed a bit . . . laddish. Boisterous.

I spend a few moments with each of them and then retreat a little to what I hope is a respectful distance. I don't want to press too hard; I just want to stand with them. I really want to just stand with them. Since I have come among them my breathing has slowed and my body is so relaxed that if someone pushes me ever so gently, I'll likely fall over.

I de-focus my eyes and stand still, entering into a pleasant trancelike state; eventually, slowly, the horses drift away, nibbling at the ground. When they reach the other side of the field, Sue's soft voice breaks into my reverie.

'So, which horse do you think you would like to work with?'

And that was the moment the real learning begins. It starts with my choice – and his.

I am a little distracted, hardly listening as Sue tells me about the lives of her horses, utterly astonished at myself for choosing Arthur. Arthur is absolutely not the kind of horse I would have thought to choose. I would expect to have chosen William: quiet, meditative William, the Wise Old Man archetype in horse form, and who, Sue tells me after I fail completely to work it out for myself, is the real leader of the herd. That surprises me at first, until I think about it some more. The leader of a herd of prey animals isn't going to be the most boisterous, or the horse with the biggest personality, or the largest physically. The leader of the herd is going to be the horse they can trust to keep them away from danger.

But I haven't chosen the herd leader, the sensible native pony who is most likely to keep me away from danger. I've chosen the horse I am least sure of, the horse I feel both most drawn to and most challenged by. I've chosen the thoroughbred, and he has chosen me. The horse who seems to me (whether it is true or not – I am for sure no expert in reading horse behaviour) to be flightier, and very much less predictable. William would have been the safer choice; he exudes a more familiar energy. And so often in my life I have made the safe choices, the sensible choices . . .

There isn't time to reflect on this now: Arthur and I have work to do.

First, I get to know him a little better. I massage his flanks, scratch his back, put my head against his neck, breathe in the subtle smell of warm horse. I am loving this, and Arthur seems happy enough; but then Sue suggests that I lead him around the field for a while, first of all using a rope, and then without. Arthur seems quite agreeable to walking with me while I have the rope, but as soon as we take it away and he has freedom of choice, he instantly loses interest and starts to wander off to the edge of the fence, bellowing out to his friends across the way.

Another native pony in a neighbouring field, who I am told is called Tristan, comes to see what all the fuss is about. Arthur is delighted, and at this point is clearly finding Tristan very much more interesting than me. Arthur is finding a quarter-inch blade of grass several feet beyond the fence more interesting than me. And I have no idea what to do about it. I turn to look to Sue for advice, and then decide that I should be working it out for myself.

I follow him over to the fence and talk to him, stroke him. He moves away. I wonder if I should be more assertive; I follow him again and place myself directly in front of him, insisting; he bats me out of the way with his nose as if I'm an irritating, improperly socialised young foal. I cajole, run backwards for a few steps to persuade him I'm really a playful and fascinating person and there's nothing on the planet he'd rather be doing than following me round a rectangular yard as I mutter loving inanities and tell him what a lot of fun we're having. Arthur doesn't seem to be buying it. He follows me for a few steps, head thrust forwards and low, as if to say, 'Oh, all right' . . . but just as quickly, he loses interest again; his ears prick up, and off he goes. I stand still, sighing, and put my hands on my hips. How am I going to get his attention? How do you make yourself interesting to a horse?

Finally, Sue takes pity on me. 'You're a storyteller. Why don't you tell him a story?'

I look at her as if she's mad. She wants me to tell a story to a horse? Stories are human magic; I believe that for sure. But to a horse? That would be ridiculous, wouldn't it? – thinks the woman who has on several occasions told stories to stones . . . but no one was watching me at the time, no one was judging me. My mind goes blank. I don't know what to do. I look at Arthur not looking at me. Why did I choose him? Why didn't I choose William, who might at least have been kinder? But here is Arthur, and he happens also to be the horse who chose me. Why? Did he think I might be more interesting than I am? Did he imagine I'd have something important to say? I look at Sue in desperation. I look at Arthur in desperation. Arthur is still intensely focused on the field where William and Harry are, somewhere beyond the trees. What if I tell him a story and he doesn't listen? What if I can't persuade him to listen? What if he thinks I have nothing worth listening to? What if the story doesn't work? What if the magic fails? What if I fail?

The ghost of a small child hovers somewhere over there in the trees, floating a foot or two above the ground. Quiet as a mouse, she slinks back into the shadows. She is trying to make herself as small as she can, so no one will notice her. Her head is filled with fairy tales, but she isn't going to tell them. Her teachers complain that they can't get a word out of her. She locks her stories up in a big bag which she carries slung around her shoulders. Heavy, so heavy. She ties the bag up so very tightly that they can't get out . . . Sue clears her throat, and the memory of her voice slips into my head: *Step out of your comfort zone and trust your instincts* . . . and all at once she fades a little, that child, self-conscious to the point of paralysis, who feared nothing more than failure. I close my eyes on her, and whatever it is that I am now steps forward, feet firmly planted on this lush, green ground, and takes a deep breath.

'Okay, Arthur,' I say. 'I'm going to tell you a story.' And all at once, I know which story it is that Arthur needs to be told – Arthur, the one-time great competitor, the well-bred racehorse who had to be retired early after an unexpected injury. Something in me shifts and clarifies, because this is what I am: a storyteller who is also a psychologist; someone who chooses the story that is right for the person, for the narrative of their life, and for the times. Someone who knows the stories that are the power of place speaking. Someone who knows that, in the telling of the right story, enchantment, inspiration and healing are to be found.

I walk up to Arthur, and I begin.

'Would you like to hear the story of Macha[17] and the men of Ulster, Arthur?' He flicks his head towards me for little more than a second, and then looks away. I carry on. No one can resist a good story; why should a horse be any different? 'It's a story about a woman who was really a goddess, and a goddess who was really a horse.' I stand next to him for a while, murmuring the story into his pricked-up ear. 'Crunnchu mac Agnoman was a farmer in the rich hills of the great and fertile province of Ulster. A few months after his first wife died, a beautiful young woman came one day to his door. She told him that her name was Macha and, saying no more to him, she came into the house, turned herself around sunwise in a circle, and then began to act as if she were his wife.'

I carefully start to walk backwards, away from him, one slow step at a time. 'She sat herself down on a chair near the hearth, and stirred up the fire. She spent the whole day there, without exchanging a word with anyone. Then she fetched a kneading-trough and a sieve, and began to prepare a meal. And as the day drew to an end she took a bucket and milked the cow, still without speaking.'

My voice is confident. Story is magic, and now I am casting a spell. I call to Arthur, and he turns towards me and begins to follow as I continue to walk slowly backwards. 'When Macha returned to the house, she turned herself around sunwise in a circle, then went into Crunnchu's kitchen and gave orders to his servants. She took a seat next to Crunnchu and waited until the other members of the household had gone to bed. And then she put out the fire, left the house, came back inside, turned herself around sunwise in a circle, and went to Crunnchu's bed.'

Arthur is still following, so I pick up my pace. 'They lived together for a long time, and because of his marriage to her his wealth increased. She brought fertility to his fields and health to his crops and herds. She seemed always to shine and be healthy and she could run like the wind. Truly, Arthur. Like the wind!

And then, to add to Crunnchu's joy, Macha became pregnant.' I stop; Arthur stops too. 'And here is where it begins to go wrong.' I start to walk again; Arthur follows.

'Shortly before Macha was due to give birth, Crunnchu was invited to a festival organised by Conchobar, the king of Ulster. Macha looked at him gravely, and warned him that he must not mention her to anyone there, otherwise she would not be able to stay with him. He promised to say nothing, and went on his way.

'The festival was a fine one, full of tournaments, games and processions. Finest of all were the horse races, and finest of all the horses were the horses of Conchobar, king of Ulster. But none of those horses was as fine as you, Arthur! Wine flowed freely in Conchobar's company, and as his horses won each of the races in turn, the king grew proud. The final race was a chariot race, and once again, the king's two horses won. And then the bards came out and praised the king and the queen, the poets and the druids, his household, the people and the entire assembly. The people cried: "Never before has a horse been seen that is the equal to these two horses of the king. In all Ireland there is no swifter horse!"

'But then – "My wife runs quicker than these two horses," said Crunnchu. And, taking offence, Conchobar demanded that Crunnchu should be seized and held until his wife could be brought before him and the truth of his words could be tested.'

Arthur isn't just following me now; he has caught up to me and is walking by my side. And so I begin to trot; Arthur trots too. 'So messengers went out to Crunnchu's house, and they told Macha what Crunnchu had said, and that she must go to the festival if she wanted to save her husband's life. "My husband has spoken unwisely," said Macha; "it was not fitting that he should say such things. As for me, I may not come. I am about to be delivered of a child." "That is unfortunate," said the messengers, "because your husband will be put to death if you don't come with us." And so Macha said, "Then I must go."

'She followed the messengers down to the field, where everyone crowded round to see her. "It is not becoming," she said, "that I should be looked at in this way while I am pregnant. Why have I been brought here?" "To race against the two horses of the king," shouted the crowd. "I cannot!" she cried. "I am about to give birth." And so Conchobar, in all his kingly pride, commanded that Crunnchu should be put to death. "Help me," Macha called out to the bystanders, "for a mother has borne each one of you. Allow me, Conchobar, a short delay, until I am delivered of my children." But Conchobar refused.'

Arthur is pulling ahead of me, so I move faster, almost shouting now, skipping a little, caught up in the pleasure of telling the story, caught up in the joy of running with a horse. '"Then shame upon you who have shown so little respect for me," she cried. "And because you take no pity upon me, a curse will fall upon you." "What is your name?" asked the king. "My name," she said, drawing herself up, tall and proud, "and the name of the children I will bear, will forever live on in the place of this assembly. I am Macha, daughter of Sainreth mac Imbaith. Bring up the horses beside me!"

'And so it was that Macha raced against the horses of the king of Ulster and outran them both, and she arrived first at the finishing line. Then she fell to the ground and, clutching her great belly, she cried out so loudly that her cry pierced the ears of all those in the assembly. She gave birth to twins, a son and a daughter, before Conchobar's horses even reached the end of the track. And so the place of that assembly now is called Emain Macha, the Twins of Macha.'

Now I am slowing down again, and Arthur adjusts to match my pace. 'But everyone who heard Macha's cry was suddenly overcome with weakness, so that they had no more strength than had a woman in labour. And with her dying breath, Macha said, "From this day onwards, the dishonour that you have inflicted upon me will rebound on all of you. When a time of oppression falls upon you, each one of you who lives in this province of

Ulster will be overcome with weakness, the weakness of a woman in childbirth, and this weakness will remain with you for five days and four nights. For nine generations it shall be so." And then Macha died, Arthur—' and slowly, I bring us both to a halt. 'Macha died.'

Something in me has shifted, something else has settled. Something has been revealed. I put my arms around the big horse's neck and hug him tightly; a shiny brown head comes to rest gently on my right shoulder. When I look back to the trees, the ghost of the little girl has vanished.

10
If Women Rose Rooted

Doorway through an ancient yew tree,
Paimpont, Brittany

When we say the Okanagan word for ourselves, we are actually saying 'the ones who are dream and land together'. That is our original identity. Before anything else, we are the living, dreaming Earth pieces. The Okanagan perception of the self and that of the dominant culture has to do with the 'us' that is place: the capacity to know we are everything that surrounds us; to experience our humanness in relation to all else and, in consequence, to know how we affect the world around us . . . We also refer to the land and our bodies with the same root syllable. This means that the flesh that is our body is pieces of the land come to us through the things that the land is. The soil, the water, the air, and all the other life forms contributed parts to be our flesh. We are our land/place. Not to know and to celebrate this is to be without language and without land. It is to be 'dis-placed'. The Okanagan teach that anything displaced from all that it requires to survive in health will eventually perish. Unless place can be relearned, all other life forms will face displacement and then ruin. As Okanagan, our most essential responsibility is to bond our whole individual and communal selves to the land. Many of our ceremonies have been constructed for this. We join with the larger self and with the land, and rejoice in all that we are. We are this one part of the Earth. Without this self and this bond, we are not human.

Jeanette Armstrong[1]

Once upon a time, the people of our Celtic nations knew what the indigenous people of other lands knew: that our fate is inseparable from the fate of the land we live on, and the fate of wider Earth. Once upon a time, Celtic women knew that we are the land, and the land is us. Once upon a time, we spoke with the moral and spiritual authority of the ancestors and the Otherworld. Once upon a time, before the coming of the Wasteland. Before the forces of the patriarchy systematically stripped us of that knowledge and of our power. Before the great patriarchal religions and the men who spoke for their misogynistic gods systematically rewrote our stories.

Once, we were native to our own places; once, we belonged. There is a Gaelic word for it, and like so many Gaelic words, coming from a language which rises out of a deeply connected, animistic worldview, it is not easily translatable into English. These are the languages of root and leaf, of field and stone, of seaweed and salt. These are words whispered in our ears by the land as if by a lover; the languages which tell us that we and the land are one. In Irish, the word is *dúchas;* in Scottish Gaelic, *dùthchas.*[2] It expresses a sense of belonging to place, to a certain area of land; it expresses a sense of rootedness, by ancient lineage and ancestry, in the community which has responsibility for that place. In Welsh, the word *cynefin* has a similar meaning. This is the way our ancestors lived.

Early Gaelic and Welsh literature paints word-pictures of a

culture in which there was little separation between plant, animal and human. A culture whose coexistence with and co-dependence on the rest of the natural world was a given, founded on the principle of taking no more than the local land could support. In Ireland the *dinnseanchas*, the stories and lore of place, were the foundation stones both of personal and communal identity, and of moral obligations to the land and the tribe. There was no dualism in this culture; the everyday world and the Otherworld were woven together in a shimmering web of complex, inter-dependent entanglements.

This way of being in the world is the key to our native tradi-tions – but now, that sense of belonging to the world that those of us in these Western lands once had, that sense of deep rooting in the Earth, is all but dead. The patriarchy crippled it; Modernity dealt it the final blow.

As a woman, I want to make it live again. My own womanhood is expressed in the stories and traditions of my native lands, for this little fragment of the Earth not only nourishes me, it made me. My body is created and recreated from these Celtic home-lands, from the ever-transforming particles of life which once formed the bodies of my ancestors, or the bark of a tree, or the outer skin of a stone. I will give what is left of me back to it when I am dead. This land hasn't just formed my physical self, it has shaped my character, my identity. It knows me. The mountains have heard and echoed back the sound of my voice; the wind has carried and recognises my scent. This land is who I am. We belong to each other, this land and I, and the Heroine's Journey, the Eco-Heroine's Journey, I've written about in this book is above all a journey to that way of belonging. A journey back to a solid rooting in the land where we live, and the traditions of our native places.

But if the power of Celtic women springs directly out of these Celtic lands and our native traditions, what happens when we move away from those places? Is there something we can carry away with us? Is there some sense of belonging, some way of being in the world that we can derive from our ancestry, even if we are physically rooted in another country entirely? It's a problem which many women in the Celtic 'diaspora' wrestle with – and there are many such women. Estimates suggest that there might be as many as 70 million people of Irish descent around the world, another 20 million people who claim Scottish ancestry, and several million more whose ancestors were Welsh, Breton and Cornish. Many of the women I have spoken to, often several generations after their ancestors first emigrated from these lands, still identify strongly with their Celtic ancestry, and hunger to find ways of meaningfully incorporating Celtic traditions into their lives.

Sylvia Linsteadt is a slim, blonde, twenty-five-year-old writer who lives with her partner in part of an old Victorian house in Oakland, California. She may inhabit the dense urban centre of this sprawling city, but her large backyard is teeming with chickens and bees, flowers, vegetables and herbs. There, she lovingly tends an angora rabbit called Hawthorn, whose coat she clips and spins into yarn. Culturally, she describes herself as 'a bit of a mongrel', but she tells me that her Irish roots call to her more than any others, and have done ever since she was a small child. 'When I was younger,' she says, turning a mug of tea round and around in her hands, 'I read a lot of books about Celtic beliefs and customs. My deep sense of the land as sacred came first to me through Celtic literature and spirituality. My sense of the Earth as wholly animate came out of the native traditions not of America, where I live, but the Celtic lands of my ancestors.'

That way of seeing the world – and being in it – pervades Sylvia's work and life. A few years ago she made an enormous leap of faith and gave up her first ever full-time job – working in an office as an assistant to a small publisher – to follow her dream of becoming a writer. 'It's the only thing I ever wanted to do,' she says. 'It was a choice between compromising, struggling on for the sake of a safe job, closing myself inside, away from the land and the world I loved – or I could take a chance early on in my life, now, when there's less to lose.'

Today, Sylvia earns a small living from selling heartfelt and beautifully packaged stories and fairy tales which come in hand-addressed envelopes in the mail, crammed with dried leaves and petals and tied up with hand-woven yarn. She spends as much time as she can outdoors, walking and practising the art of animal tracking; her beautiful blog, The Indigo Vat,[3] is filled with tales of her meanderings around her beloved Point Reyes peninsula and the Coast Range foothills of central-northern California. Sylvia's stories are unique: straddling the continents, they have one foot in the Celtic lands of her ancestry and the other firmly planted in the Californian landscape to which she is deeply attached.

'I do feel deeply rooted in this land, yes,' she says. 'But I wish that the heritage of my immediate ancestors in this place wasn't predicated directly upon violence, slaughter and the oppression of a people and a way of life that had been grounded here for at least 9,000 years. The old stories of this land, the old native traditions of its people, are not mine to touch. My own people have done enough meddling, enough ruining, enough destroying, and I have no right now, a white girl made up of almost every imaginable European culture, regardless of my longing for rootedness, my longing to belong to the land into which I was born, to go adapting and adopting the sacred stories of a people who my direct ancestors probably discriminated against, probably even killed.'

For Sylvia, as for so many of the women I spoke to, this is a vein of shame, anger and humiliation that runs very deep, and she holds strongly to the view that Native American stories are not to be appropriated. 'Certainly those are stories to be learned, revered, respected; but not retold, not in my voice. And that would be too easy, anyway, taking stories from other people about the land you live on, instead of listening and learning its stories yourself. Those were stories gathered and earned over millennia. Those of us who came later need to work for our own wild myths, break ourselves open to let them in.'

Sylvia's yearning to find a way to merge her ancestral traditions with the physical reality of the land she now lives on, led her to look at the old European stories she once devoured as a child in a different way: she began to wonder whether they could adapt themselves, whether somehow they could shape-shift to fit a very different ecosystem.

Although she speaks passionately about the ways in which this wild and rocky coastal landscape of Northern California reminds her of the Celtic countries where her ancestors came from, the native creatures and the plants here are quite different. This is a land of redwood, coyote brush, red alder and thimble-berry; of mountain lions and tule elk, coyotes and gray foxes, orange-bellied newts and red-legged frogs. But, she tells me, there are Snow White tales from West Africa to Chile, from Albania to Iraq and from France to Louisiana. So while it's true that those tales were born originally out of specific landscapes, languages and cultural contexts, they too, like the people who carried them, are migrants.

'I began to wonder,' she says, purposefully twisting a stray lock of long hair with long fingers as she speaks, as if somehow she could use it to weave one of her tales, 'if I could walk with old stories over these landscapes, plant them here, see how they take to the bobcats, the Douglas firs, the manzanitas and kestrels. My heritage and the traditions of my "people" are based in lands far away. But can we break open the old stories like you break open a fruit, find the seeds, and regrow them here? See if they can find their gray fox whiskers, their elk hooves, their red-legged frog songs? To see how they can shape-shift with the redwood-coastal fog on their necks, the resin of chaparral on their tongues?

'I don't know what it's like to live in Scotland, so I have to find and to write stories that are based here, where I live. And so the story of the sealwoman who lost her skin becomes the story of a sea lion. My story "The Children of the Land Under This Land" came from the old Irish myth, "The Children of Lir", in which four children are turned into swans by their jealous stepmother. This retelling, set along the wild California coast, begins when the famed pirate Sir Francis Drake drops the anchor of his *Golden Hind* along the shore of a Point Reyes estuary in the year 1579, altering the lives of the Coast Miwok who have lived there for millennia.'

The characters and landscapes which inhabit the stories may shift, but the heart of the stories does not change. You cannot transport the Cailleach Bhéarra to the deserts of New Mexico; her place is here, in the wild, wet, stony land she created and personifies. But you can carry the ancestral memory with you; a memory that will help you to find the Old Woman of the World in whatever shape and form she manifests in the place where you live. You can carry with you our native ways of looking at the world, a knowledge that the Earth is animate, a sense of life as sacred, a need to live in harmony with the cycles and seasons of the year. These are the native traditions of your people; they belong to you. The old stories will teach you, wherever you take them. They will show you how to become the *bean feasa*, the Wise Woman.

There she goes now, the young one, walking the old stories into a new land. Standing tall, with long flowing skirts and long wavy hair piled high on top of her head. There she goes, the perfect reminder that it is not just the mothers and the grand-mothers that we need, but the daughters too – the ones who might yet find the courage to live as we did not. 'I take them out with me, the stories,' Sylvia says. 'I take them out walking alongside the courting coyote prints and the place where brush rabbits come to graze the long grass in the early morning next to the salmonberry canes.'

The themes and threads of the story remain, and women like Sylvia are taking up those threads, using them to weave connected, grounded ways of being in the world – ways of being that are not based on impossible yearnings for an overseas land which they will not live in and can never physically belong to, but which are deeply rooted in the place where they live now. 'I am here,' Sylvia says. 'This land is my home, whatever colonial baggage that statement carries with it. I have a duty and a longing to know it and to belong to it. The stories of my people, my ancestors, can help me do that.'

Women are spinners and weavers; we are the ones who spin the threads and weave them into meaning and pattern. Like silkworms, we create those threads out of our own substance, pulling the strong, fine fibres out of our own hearts and wombs. It's time to make some new threads; time to strengthen the frayed wild edges of our own being and then weave ourselves back into the fabric of our culture. Once we knew the patterns for weaving the world; we can piece them together again. Women can heal the Wasteland. We can remake the world. This is what women do. This is our work.

In these times it's not enough to awaken ourselves, to find our community: the world is in need of restoration, and each one of us is challenged to do the work of collective change. The day of the Heroic quest is over, with its all-conquering, dragon-slaying Hero saving the world, one sword-stroke at a time. The Journey we need now is not a journey of active, world-beating individualism, it is a journey of collective re-enchantment – a re-animation of the Earth. It's time to become native to our places again. It's time for women to shrug off the yoke of the patriarchy, and reclaim our native power. The power that is the Earth itself speaking; the authority of the Voices which came out of the Wells. If there is to be change, it will come from us. Right here, where we stand. Women were always the story-givers, the memory-keepers, the dreamers. Listen now to the land's long dreaming. Do you see what it's dreaming? It's dreaming you.

On the Ordnance Survey map, the waterfall which lies just upriver from our cottage is named Asnanomedan: an anglicised corruption of Eas an Amadáin, Waterfall of the Fool. I sit here for a while every day among the trees which cluster thickly around and obscure it, listening to the water's flow. I close my eyes and concentrate; one day I'll understand what this Riverwitch is saying to me. I sing to her sometimes, so that she will know my voice in turn. Sometimes, I bring a poem; I say it aloud to the trees so that they too can know me.

After years of being uprooted myself, I'm finally learning about trees. Here is what I have learned about trees: they are tenacious. A rowan tree is beginning to grow out of a tiny crack in the old bedrock exposed by the river. The stone protects the seedling from the worst of the winds and gives it shelter. It clings tight; it will not let go. Here is what I have learned about trees: their roots are deep. They establish their roots first, and then they reach for the sky.

I have sat here by this waterfall for over a year now, and I am learning to stay still. Sit long enough in the same place, dreaming and singing, and you may learn to hear its voice. But through four swirling seasons I sat, the fool by the waterfall, and still I failed to hear. I was surrounded by ash and alder and willow, dense and interwoven along the sheltered river banks. I appreciated their beauty, learnt of their waxing and waning as the year's wheel turned. Still, I mourned the lost oaks of Min Doire, plain of the oaks. This place cries out for oaks. We had been told that the ancient oak woodlands were cleared here to the last tree, and amid the press of rich foliage I feared that it must be true. And then I saw it, one morning in April, before the ashes had burst their buds.

Hidden in a gorge, protected by the waterfall – an oak tree. A sessile oak: the last old native oak in Min Doire. Its bony hand clutches as fiercely to the bare rock in the middle of the divided river as does an eagle to a rabbit. There is no guessing how old the tree may be. Older perhaps than I dare imagine. It stands there still, all moss and knots. Every morning I see it, that old tree, clinging on with such a determination to live this very day.

It will never give up. But it is not trying to live forever. That would be something different entirely. The tree has many beautiful, strong words for 'today'. It has none for 'forever'.

The last of the ancient trees. See, they hide there still; they have not left us. We can find them, if we only learn how to look.

This old oak remembers a time when there were so many others of its kind, a time that is encoded deep in the earth-memory of this land. And so, a few days later, a spade cuts deeply into the scrap of land which runs down from our cottage to the river. I stand and watch while David digs. When he's done and the hole is big enough, I take the seedling. This tree-to-be, this tiny thing, has grown from an acorn gathered in County Tyrone from one of the oldest oak trees in Ireland. The man who grew it is passionate about keeping the ancient, native tree stock alive. He grows the trees and hands them on, freely, to anyone who will take them. Carefully, I lower it in. I am careful with its roots; they're fragile still. A little light compost, a little fish-and-bone meal. Together, we put our hands to work, each of us patting and firming the soil around it.

Gently, little tree; it'll be a good many years before you grow, a good many years before you reach the stature of the last native oak of this old land of Min Doire. We will not live to see it. But if we tend you, sit by you each day and whisper our stories as we listen in turn to yours, you may yet root. You may yet rise.

Postscript

The Eco-Heroine's Journey

A Guide

'Riverwitch', Donegal, Ireland

The Eco-Heroine's Journey which we've followed in this book is a path to understanding how deeply enmeshed we are in the web of life on this planet. In many ways, it is an antidote to the swashbuckling action-adventure that is the Hero's Journey: it is a woman's journey, based on a woman's way of being in the world. This path forces us first to examine ourselves and the world we live in, to face up to all that is broken and dysfunctional in it and in our own lives. Then it calls us to change – first ourselves, and then the world around us. It leads us back to our own sense of grounded belonging to this Earth, and asks us what we have to offer to the places and communities in which we live. Finally, it requires us to step into our own power and take back our ancient, native role as its guardians and protectors. To rise up rooted, like trees.

The Journey is necessary for each one of us. Not just for our own personal growth and greater wellbeing, but because our places and people need us. The beautiful, ailing Earth needs us, and the non-human others who inhabit this planet along with us. Our children, our descendants, need us to fight for their future. Each of us has something unique to offer to the world; each of us occupies a node in the web of life on this planet. And so we all need to make the Journey, and no matter how challenging the path may be, there is richness and beauty along the way.

Every pilgrim needs help on her path; all of us need guidance at some point on the Journey. In writing this book, and in sharing the twists and turns, the failures and the lessons learned from my own long, convoluted Journey, I'm offering myself as an ally on yours. And in these final few pages, I offer you – out of my own personal experience as well as my professional work with narrative psychology – some specific tips, and some questions to ask yourself which I hope will help you get started in thinking about how you might tell your own story.

1. The Wasteland

This first stage of the Eco-Heroine's Journey asks us to sweep aside the veil which prevents us from seeing the world as it is: to understand what is broken, and what needs to change. This isn't just about understanding climate change and failing ecosystems: it is about acknowledging social, economic and political injustices too. This stage requires us to examine the ways in which women are treated in the world, and minorities, and animals – any groups and clusterings that are considered to be 'other' – any groups who do not fit the preferred archetypes in our dominant culture.

Flinch, but don't look away. It is easy not to think about these things, and to put uncomfortable emotions to one side out of a sense of powerlessness. It is easy to get disheartened. So many of us go through stages of feeling helpless, or believing there's nothing that can be done. But there's always something that can be done, no matter how small. The Journey is not about saving the world with one dramatic action: that is beyond our reach, and besides, it's not the Eco-Heroine's way. The Journey is about accepting that we each have a responsibility for the way we live our lives, for our footprint on the planet. It's about accepting that we each have a responsibility for the local places we live in, and for the communities around us. It's necessary first of all to see and under-stand the big picture – but then we need to zoom in, and focus on our own particular part of it.

- What are the ecological, social and political injustices in the world you live in?

- How is the Wasteland manifested in your own life? What kills or confines all that is vibrant and alive in you? In what ways have you been cut off from the wellspring, from the source of life?
- Have you assumed any archetypes of the patriarchy which do not fit you? Have you launched yourself on a Hero's Journey, adopted a Heroic way of being in the world?

2. The Call

Now we must decide whether we will listen to the Call which lures us down a path that we know will lead to change. We have seen the Wasteland for what it is: what will we do now? Do we dare listen to the Call? Will we follow it, will we step off the edge?

It is possible to refuse the Call, just as I did for many years, paralysed by my own fear. But life is not about being safe and secure; life is about growing, learning, transforming. The Journey is life, and if you refuse it, it will come calling again. Each time, the Call will be louder; each time, the stakes will be higher and there will be more to lose. Think of the Selkie: to stay is ultimately to die.

- In what ways have you lost your skin, and what does that skin represent? How did you lose it? Is there a lost part of yourself which you yearn for now? Have you ever constructed a new skin which is false, or which does not belong to the person you believe yourself to be?
- Is there a phase in your life which seems to be ending?
- What is the Call which you hear? Where does it come from?
- Will you go? What does it mean, to go? How will you begin?
- What are you going to seek? What is the nature of your quest?

369

3. The Cauldron of Transformation

Step off the edge . . . and then, if it happens, let yourself fall. Feel the grief and the loss; feel the environmental despair. Feel the rage.

Do you fear it? Stay with the dark anyway. Don't fight it; don't try to manage your way out. You will simply postpone the inevitable, and it will come around again. Don't fear the dark: it's a natural part of the Journey. The most beautiful butterflies emerge from the darkness of the cocoon; the finest plants push their way out of the deep, rich, fertile soil. Out of the darkness comes strength, and focus. There is always another rebirth. But it always begins in the dark.

Be still. Listen. Let yourself disintegrate.

- What are your dysfunctional ways of being, your patterns? What are the parts of you which must be left behind?
- What is it which sustains you, when everything else around you dissolves? What holds you up, when all support structures fail?
- How will you learn to be still, and listen?

4. The Pilgrim's Way

Stay for a while in the dark, lick your bleeding wounds – but then pick yourself up, and find your way to the path. Put one foot in front of the other, and walk: a pilgrimage begins with one small step.

Don't be proud; even if your path is a solitary one right now, the Eco-Heroine's Journey is co-creational at heart, focused on building relationships – with other humans, with plants and animals, with the land itself. Accept the help which is offered; make friends and allies wherever you can.

- What is it that shows you the way? Who or what offers hints about the path you might follow? Do you find clues in your dreams? Do synchronicities occur, or has someone appeared in your life who sets you off on your way?

- Who are your allies, human, plant and animal?
- What tests and temptations might you face? What cultural myths must you uncover and overcome in your own life?
- Like Rhiannon, what truth about yourself must you insist on and uphold throughout the long passage of your Journey?

5. Retrieving the Buried Feminine

Creativity is at the heart of the feminine mystery. We are the ones who give birth, who bring life to the world. Creativity isn't just about knitting scarves or going on painting courses; it isn't about creating great works of art or writing bestselling books. Creativity is an authentic approach to life: an openness, a spontaneity; a determination to nurture rather than destroy. Stop telling yourself you're not a creative person; think about the ways you can manifest that deep, life-giving feminine wisdom in your own life.

- What is your relationship to the feminine, and who are your role models, if any?
- Do you feel as if you are comfortable with your body, and fully inhabit it? Do you have a sense of being grounded, rooted in the Earth?
- What aspects of being a woman have you buried deeply?
- What does creativity mean to you, and in what ways do you offer the gift of life?

6. Restoring the Balance

The fight against the patriarchy isn't always a fight between men and women. There are masculine and feminine qualities in each of us, and each of us has those qualities in differing amounts – and sometimes at levels which naturally fluctuate at different times in our lives. This part of the Journey is about understanding, appreciating and embodying the qualities which fall into both categories, and bringing ourselves – and the world – back into harmony.

But in our own culture we still need urgently to fight against the dominant masculine, to ensure that women are listened to as well as men, to demand that we are respected and kept safe, and to insist that our ways of knowing and being are valued. It can be exhausting, but always insist on these things, and always fight for them where you can. We can only change the world if we have authority, and the power to act.

- How do masculine and feminine qualities express themselves in you and in your own life and relationships? Does one way of being dominate?
- In what other ways are you out of balance?
- In what ways do imbalances manifest themselves in your place and your community?
- How might you begin to restore those imbalances and fight for women's voices to be heard, for feminine qualities to be recognised and respected?

7. The Heroine's Return

As Alice Starmore so clearly and evocatively stated, it's hard to care for what you don't know. So many of us have lost the deep knowledge of our places and communities which our ancestors once had, and as a result we no longer feel that we belong to them, no longer feel that it is our place to guard and protect them. If we want to bring our unique gifts to the world, to speak for the Earth, to recover the Voices of the Wells, we have to do so from a place and a community to which we belong.

It is perfectly possible to create a deep sense of belonging, either to a new place or to a place you have lived in for a long while. Wherever you are, for however long or short a period of time you stay there, it is important to learn to belong. Learn the history and the stories of the place and its people. Learn the ecology and geology, and come to know the landscape. If you live in a bog, what does bog mean to you? What is the black, buttery peat at the heart of you? If you live in a city, what do its tower blocks and skyscrapers represent to you? An urban forest, concrete trees reaching for the sky? What webs are woven with its roads? Stand under the skies of your place, understand and anticipate the changing of its seasons, and know the phase of today's moon. Embrace the weather with all its vagaries, for a place cannot be separated from its weather. Walk your streets, explore your woods, and always, always take account of the small beauties.

- What do you already know about the place you live, and what do you think you need to learn in order to feel a sense of belonging?
- Do you know its plants and animals, understand its ecology and geology?
- What do you know about the community around you – the origins and history of the people who live in your place?
- What myths and stories arise from your place?
- In the context of your own Return, what do you think is the unique gift that you are bringing back to the world, or your community?

8. Becoming Elder

Becoming elder is a Journey all of its own. It is a Journey to accepting and valuing the richness of ageing. It is joy in freedom from old constraints.

If you haven't already experienced it, think of menopause as a new Journey. This is not simply a physical change, it is a spiritual and psychological transition too.

Pass your wisdom on. Think about telling your own story. No one experiences life as you do: you have a unique story, a unique set of experiences, a unique way of seeing the world. Tell that story; use it to inspire and encourage others.

Remember that old age is not always sleepy or withdrawn. Remember the archetypal fierce crone. Remember Marion Woodman's description: 'She is not withdrawn. She is alarmingly present. Like a tuning fork her truth shatters hypocrisy. Others in her presence are released into what is true in themselves. Or flee.' When it is necessary, become fierce. Be wrathful.

- What does this Journey through menopause or to elder-hood mean for you?
- How might it better equip you to continue to offer your gifts to the Earth and the community around you?
- What will you welcome letting go of?
- Embracing the simplified clarity of elderhood, what will you focus on now?

When the journey you are presently on seems to be over, remember that there is no real end. There may be new journeys ahead; there may be journeys-within-journeys. There is always something new to learn, always another gift to be brought out into the world. Embrace each new cycle; welcome every twist and turn. It is how we know we are alive.

References

1. From 'The Women Speaking' by Linda Hogan, in *Dark. Sweet.: New & Selected Poems* (Coffee House Press, 2014). Reprinted with permission of the author.

Reclaiming Our Stories

1. From *A Propos of Lady Chatterley's Lover and Other Essays* (Penguin, 1961).
2. Samhain was later called All Hallows, or Hallowe'en.
3. *Aos Sí* (sometimes *daoine sí*) means 'people of the *sí*', the Irish word for the hollow hills to which they were banished. (The older form of *sí* is spelled *sidhe*, and writers such as W.B. Yeats omitted *aos* or *daoine* and referred to the fairy folk simply by the word for the hollow hills themselves, calling them 'the sidhe'.) They are believed to be the remnants of the Tuatha Dé Danann (the people of the goddess Danú), an ancient people who invaded Ireland long ago, and whose presence in Ireland was recorded in ancient historical texts such as the *Book of Invasions*. The Tuatha Dé Danann lost control of Ireland to the Milesians (humans, the Gaels, ancestors of modern Irish), and were forced to flee the land and take up residence in the hollow hills and mounds which are the entrances to the Otherworld where the *Aos Sí* now live.
4. An addition to this story is sometimes told: Just as the ceremony ended and the feast began, there came a hammering on the walls and doors of the hall. The fairy folk looked out, and saw the hill covered with latecomers who had arrived after the doors were closed.

They had been unable to enter, and were now too late to receive the gift of wisdom. There is still a saying in Gaelic about a foolish woman: 'She was out on the hill when the wisdom was distributed.'

5.   Also known in some countries/regions as Anu; and as Dôn in Wales.

6.   WHO, Department of Reproductive Health and Research, London School of Hygiene and Tropical Medicine, South African Medical Research Council, *Global and regional estimates of violence against women: prevalence and health effects of intimate partner violence and non-partner sexual violence* (World Health Organization, 2013).

7.   Mary Kaldor, *New and Old Wars: Organized Violence in a Global Era*, 3rd edition (Stanford University Press, 2013).

8.   See, for example, www.theguardian.com/commentisfree/2015/aug/20/sexual-harassment-women-curfew.

9.   Beatrix Campbell, *End of Equality* (Seagull Books, 2014).

10.   www.un.org/disarmament/WMD/Nuclear.

11.   Gedge's book is still available (Chicago Review Press, 2007); however, I highly recommend Manda Scott's 'Boudica' series of novels for a unique in-depth exploration of the character of Boudica and the world she lived in: *Dreaming the Eagle*, *Dreaming the Bull*, *Dreaming the Hound* and *Dreaming the Serpent Spear* (Bantam).

12.   Kenneth Jackson concludes, based on later development of Welsh and Irish, that the name derives from the Proto-Celtic feminine adjective *boudika*, 'victorious', that in turn is derived from the word *bouda*, 'victory'.

13.   The label 'Celtic' is usually bestowed on people who speak Celtic languages: either of the Brythonic branch (Wales, Cornwall, Brittany) or the Goidelic/Gaelic branch (Ireland, Scotland, Isle of Man). Once all of Britain was 'Celtic' and spoke some form of Common Brittonic, an old Brythonic language which preceded modern Welsh. After the Romans departed from Britain, Germanic-speaking Saxons began a migration to the eastern coast of Britain, where they established their own kingdoms. Eventually, the Brythonic language in these areas was replaced by that of the Anglo-Saxons. By the end of the 1st millennium, the Anglo-Saxons and the Gaels between them had conquered most of the Brittonic

territory in Britain, and the language and culture of the native Britons had largely been extinguished, remaining only in Wales, Cornwall, parts of Cumbria and Eastern Galloway.

14. Cassius Dio, *Roman History* (Harvard University Press, 1987).

15. In Greek mythology, Pandora, the first human woman created by the gods, opened a jar and let loose all the evils of the world.

16. Joseph Campbell, *The Hero With a Thousand Faces* (Princeton University Press, 1949).

17. Maureen Murdock, *The Heroine's Journey* (Shambhala, 1990).

18. www.greenbeltmovement.org.

19. www.eradicatingecocide.com.

20. www.vandanashiva.com.

21. www.idlenomore.ca.

22. The statement was made at the Vancouver Peace Summit, in September 2009. A session, 'Nobel Laureates in Dialogue: Connecting for Peace', was moderated by former Irish president and peace activist Mary Robinson, and featured four Nobel Peace Prize Laureates: the Dalai Lama; Mairead Maguire and Betty Williams, founders of the Northern Ireland Peace Movement; and American anti-landmine crusader Jody Williams.

Wells and Waters: The Wasteland

1. Reprinted with the permission of the author.

2. Modron ('mother') is a figure in Welsh mythology, known as the mother of the hero Mabon ap Modron. Cornwall shares a Brythonic language and story tradition with Wales, and so it is likely that Modron would have been known there too.

3. William Hals, *The Compleat History of Cornwal, part being the parochial history* (*c.* 1750).

4. For the original text in translation, see http://d.lib.rochester.edu/camelot/text/elucidation.

5. For a full treatment of these issues and an overview of ecofeminist philosophy, see Val Plumwood, *Feminism and the Mastery of Nature* (Routledge, 1993).

6. bugwomanlondon.com.

7. http://www.theguardian.com/commentisfree/2015/aug/20/sexual-harassment-women-curfew.

8. T.S. Eliot, *Complete Poems and Plays* (Faber and Faber, 2004).

9. Black Friday is an import from the US, where retailers have offered steep discounts in the past decade on the day after the Thanksgiving holiday. This traditionally marks the day when stores start to make a profit for the year.

10. http://www.ft.com/intl/cms/s/0/7c92013a-76d1-11e4-8273-001 44feabdc0.html#slide0.

11. Aldous Huxley, *Brave New World* (Chatto & Windus, 1932).

12. See for example Michelle Mech, 'A Comprehensive Guide to the Alberta Tar Sands' (Green Party of Canada, 2011). http://www. greenparty.ca/sites/default/files/a_comprehensive_guide_to_the_ alberta_oil_sands_-_may_2011_-_last_revised_march_2012.pdf.

13. http://www.fao.org/food-loss-and-food-waste/en/.

14. http://wwf.panda.org/about_our_earth/all_publications/living_ planet_report.

15. See Elizabeth Kolbert, *The Sixth Extinction: An Unnatural History* (Bloomsbury, 2014).

16. S.L. Pimm, G.J. Russell, J.L. Gittleman and T.M. Brooks, 'The Future of Biodiversity', *Science* 269: 5222 (1995), 347–50.

17. http://www.un.org/climatechange/blog/2014/03/ipcc-report-severe-and-pervasive-impacts-of-climate-change-will-be-felt-everywhere.

18. http://www.iea.org/publications/scenariosandprojections.

19. Michael Specter, 'The Climate Fixers', *The New Yorker* (May 2012).

20. J. Hansen, et al., 'Ice melt, sea level rise and superstorms: evidence from paleoclimate data, climate modeling, and modern observations that 2 °C global warming is highly dangerous', *Atmospheric Chemistry and Physics Discussions* 15 (2015), 20059–20179.

21. http://www.populationmatters.org/issues-solutions/population.

22. www.pollyhiggins.com.

23. Although in the earliest centuries of the Christian church women took minor leadership roles and contributed significantly to its intel-lectual culture (for example: St Brigid of Kildare's leadership in the founding of the monastery at Kildare in Ireland; St Hilda's establishment

of Whitby Abbey; the rich writings of St Hildegard of Bingen), women were denied many of the spiritual powers allowed to men. As Rebecca Moore in *Women in Christian Traditions* says, they faced 'increasingly repressive efforts by ecclesiastical authorities to control, and then to exclude, women from religious life', as 'the institutional church and its male hierarchy reasserted its power over women in a series of reforms in the ninth, tenth and eleventh centuries' (NYU Press, 2015).

24. For more information, see Peter Berresford Ellis, *Celtic Women* (Constable, 1996).

25. See Miranda J. Green, *Celtic Goddesses* (British Museum Press, 1995).

26. Although in those days she could no longer be worshipped as a goddess because of the dominance of Christianity, the 'lady of Sovereignty' was present still in a symbolic role.

Islands of the Heart: Embracing the Call

1. I later discovered that these are the first two lines from a poem by Adeleine Anne Proctor.

Deep Caves and Bottomless Lakes: The Cauldron of Transformation

1. 'It's possible I am pushing through solid rock' [10.1] from *Selected Poems of Rainer Maria Rilke, a Translation from the German and Commentary* by Robert Bly. Copyright 1981 by Robert Bly. Reprinted by permission of HarperCollins Publishers.

2. The Eleusinian mysteries in ancient Greece partly took place in caves which represented the entrance to the Underworld; these mysteries re-enacted the myth of the abduction of the Kore (also called Persephone) by Hades, ruler of the world below, her subsequent descent to the Underworld, and her eventual return to the world above. The Eleusinian cycle parallels the three primary phases of the Hero or Heroine's Journey: the first stage ends with the descent of the Kore to the Underworld; the second represents the search for her; and the third ends with her ascent and return to the upper world where she is reunited with her mother, Demeter.

3. John Waddell, *Archaeology and Celtic Myth* (Four Courts Press, 2014).

4. The Welsh name for the Otherworld.

5. This story appears in the late medieval *Tale of Taliesin*, and is included in some editions of *The Mabinogion*, a collection of stories compiled by Welsh authors in the twelfth and thirteenth centuries from earlier oral traditions.

6. The Gaelic equivalent of the Brythonic *awen* is *iomas*.

7. www.listentoatale.com.

8. Mis is pronounced 'Mish'. For the original text see Brian Ó Cúiv, 'The Romance of Mis and Dubh Ruis', *Celtica* 2:2 (1954).

9. In early Irish, 'dark knowledge'.

10. See Alexandra Bergholm, in *Approaches to Religion and Mythology in Celtic Studies* edited by Katja Ritari & Alexandra Bergholm (Cambridge Scholars Publishing, 2008).

11. www.sophiemckeand.com.

12. Kat Duff, *The Alchemy of Illness* (Random House USA, 2003).

Finding the Path: The Pilgrim's Way

1. Copyright © 2004 by Ursula K. Le Guin. First appeared in *The Wave in the Mind: Talks and Essays on the Writer, The Reader, and the Imagination*, published by Shambhala in 2004. Reprinted by permission of Curtis Brown, Ltd.

2. Graham Robb, *The Ancient Paths: Discovering the Lost Map of Celtic Europe* (Picador, 2013).

3. www.tranquilpaths.com.

4. As depicted in the form of ancient statues, plaques and other archaeological artefacts – see Miranda J. Green, *Celtic Goddesses* (British Museum Press, 1995).

5. The story of Rhiannon is told in *The Mabinogion*.

6. Wendell Berry, 'The Problem of Tobacco' in *Sex, Economy, Freedom & Community* (Pantheon Books, 1992). For the text, see http://forum.ra.utk.edu/1999fall/problem-tobacco.htm.

Moor and Bog: Retrieving the Buried Feminine

1. From 'Creation of the Himalayas' in *The Treekeeper's Tale* by Pascale Petit (Seren, 2008). Reprinted by permission of Seren Books.

2. http://www.monbiot.com/2013/07/16/the-naturalists-who-are-terrified-of-nature.

3. Edward Broadbridge (ed.), *Seamus Heaney* (Skolerradioen Danmarks Radio, 1997).

4. Seamus Heaney, *Preoccupations: Selected Prose, 1968–1978* (Faber and Faber, 1980).

5. 'Bogland' is from *Door Into the Dark* (Faber and Faber, 1969).

6. M.C. Balfour, 'Legends of the Cars', *Folk-Lore* (Folklore Enterprises, Ltd.) 2: 2 (1891).

7. Naomi Wolf, *The Beauty Myth: How Images of Beauty Are Used Against Women* (William Morrow, 1991).

8. http://www.people.com/people/archive/article/0,,20115393,00.html.

9. For more statistics and information, see http://www.stopstreet harassment.org/about/what-is-street-harassment.

10. See, for example, http://news.sky.com/story/1502776/harassment-of-women-endemic-at-universities.

11. http://www.huffingtonpost.co.uk/anneliese-midgley/we-need-to-stop-street-harassment_b_8044470.html.

12. www.dreamingaloud.net.

13. See, for example, http://redtenttemplemovement.com.

14. Eleanor Agnew and Sharon Robideaux *My Mama's Waltz: a Book for Daughters of Alcoholic Mothers* (Simon & Schuster, 1998).

15. A fictionalised account of my journey through learning to fly is in my novel, *The Long Delirious Burning Blue* (Two Ravens Press, 2008).

16. From 'The Blanket Around Her' in Joy Harjo, *What Moon Drove Me to This?* (Reed Cannon & Johnson, 1979).

17. See, for example, Jeffrey Gantz, *The Mabinogion* (Penguin Classics, 1976); *Lady Gregory's Complete Irish Mythology* (Bounty Books, 2004); W.B. Yeats, *Irish Fairy and Folk Tales* (Modern Library Classics, 2003).

18. www.virtualyarns.com.

19. http://www.theguardian.com/books/2006/jul/29/featuresreviews.guardianreview14.

20. www.mamba.org.uk.

The Enchanted Forest: Restoring the Balance

1.   'The Creel' from *The Tree House* by Kathleen Jamie (Picador, 2004). Reprinted with the permission of Macmillan Publishers.

2.   Most scholars believe that the Arthurian legends originated in Wales, and spread by virtue of a related Brythonic language first to Cornwall, and then with the British settlers, across to Brittany.

3.   From Wolfram von Eschenbach, *Parzifal* (Penguin Classics, 1980).

4.   Jessie L. Weston, *From Ritual to Romance* (Cambridge University Press, 1920).

5.   Robert A. Johnson, *The Fisher King and the Handless Maiden: Understanding the Wounded Feeling Function in Masculine and Feminine Psychology* (HarperSanFrancisco, 1993).

6.   In the *Echtrae Airt meic Cuinn* (The Otherworldly Adventure of Art mac Cuinn). In this story, Conn, High King of Ireland, marries the wicked Bé Chuma, who becomes infatuated with his son, Art. Conn's druids announce that because of his unacceptable marriage, his land will become a Wasteland. He searches for a way to restore his country by sailing towards the mystical western isles, and when he returns his wife has been banished, lifting the curse.

7.   John Carey, *Ireland and the Grail* (Celtic Studies Publications, 2007).

8.   In the old Welsh story of Dorn, a precious cup is taken from Otherworldly women at the bottom of a spring well, and in the medieval Welsh poem 'Preiddeu Annwn' ('The Spoils of Annwn') Arthur raids Annwn, the Welsh Otherworld, to seize a magical cauldron which is guarded by nine maidens. Another old Irish tale has Conn Cétchathach, Conn of the Hundred Battles, visiting the Otherworldly home of Lug, one of the great lords of the Tuatha Dé Danann. They entered, and were welcomed by a woman in a gold crown. Next to her they saw a silver vat, bound with gold hoops, full of red ale, and a golden cup and serving spoon. Then they saw a tall beautiful man on a throne, who introduced himself as Lug. The woman with the gold crown was introduced as the 'Sovereignty of Ireland', and after serving a meal she poured drinks, and said to the people who were assembled, 'To whom shall this

cup be given?' Lug then recited a poem which told Conn how many years he would reign, and the names of the kings who would follow him. The house and its inhabitants disappeared, but the cup and serving spoon remained, and Conn found himself back in Ireland where he soon became king.

9. See, for example, J.P. Mallory, *In Search of the Indo-Europeans: Language, Archaeology and Myth* (Thames & Hudson, 1991).
10. Robert Bly, *Iron John: A Book about Men* (Addison-Wesley, 1990).
11. http://www.theguardian.com/society/2014/feb/18/male-suicides-three-times-women-samaritans-bristol.
12. Scilla Elworthy, *Pioneering the Possible* (North Atlantic Books, 2014).
13. Cori Howard, 'How Avatar got it right: "Mother trees" use fungal systems to feed the forest', *Canadian Geographic* (Jan–Feb 2011).
14. www.treesforlife.org.
15. mandyhaggith.worldforests.org.
16. A network of nearly 200 NGOs from North America, Europe, Scandinavia and Russia working for the protection of boreal forests.
17. www.thousandhuts.org.
18. Gerry Loose, 'The Hutting Instinct', *EarthLines*, 12 (July 2015).
19. In Theodore Roszak et al. (eds), *Ecopsychology: Restoring the Earth, Healing the Mind* (University of California Press, 2002).
20. G. Albrecht et al., 'Solastalgia: The Distress Caused by Environmental Change', *Australasian Psychiatry*, 15: Suppl 1 (2007), S95–8.
21. Cormac McCarthy, *The Border Trilogy* (Picador, 2007).

The Fertile Fields: The Heroine's Return

1. 'Curandera' is reprinted with permission from the publisher of *Chants* by Pat Mora (© 1985 Arte Público Press, University of Houston).
2. http://www.theguardian.com/books/2015/jan/13/oxford-junior-dictionary-replacement-natural-words.
3. ibid.
4. Michael McCarthy, *The Moth Snowstorm: Nature and Joy* (John Murray, 2015).

5. http://intothehermitage.blogspot.ie/2013/07/weed-wife.html.

6. For example, the archive of oral narrative collected by the Irish Folklore Commission in the 1930s still showed evidence of this.

7. Gearóid Ó Crualaoich, *The Book of the Cailleach: Stories of the Wise-Woman Healer* (Cork University Press, 2003).

8. ibid.

9. Jeanne Achterberg, *Woman as Healer* (Shambhala, 1991).

10. The story first appears in the fourteenth-century *Red Book of Hergest*. Legend says that her children grew up to be the famous twelfth-century herbalists, the Physicians of Myddfai. Using natural products gathered from the surrounding area, the Physicians created cures and remedies for headaches, sunburn, swellings, coughs and sneezes. Some of these ancient remedies are recorded in the *Red Book*.

11. www.veriditashibernica.org.

12. Joseph Campbell, *The Hero with a Thousand Faces* (Princeton University Press, 1949).

13. Marion Woodman, *Leaving My Father's House: A Journey to Conscious Femininity* (Shambhala, 1993).

14. Robert A. Johnson, *The Fisher King and the Handless Maiden: Understanding the Wounded Feeling Function in Masculine and Feminine Psychology* (HarperSanFrancisco, 1993).

15. Duncan McLaren and Julian Agyeman, *Sharing Cities: A Case for Truly Smart and Sustainable Cities* (MIT Press, 2015).

16. http://www.foe.co.uk/page/big-ideas-cities.

17. www.earthlines.org.uk.

18. Sean Kane, *The Wisdom of the Mythtellers* (Broadview Press, 1998), p78.

19. The Welsh equivalent of the Irish *geis*: a doom, a fate, a forbidding.

Mountains and Rocky Heights: Becoming Elder

1. 'Hag', a translation by John Montague of Nuala Ní Dhomhnaill's poem 'Cailleach', from *Pharaoh's Daughter* (1990), by kind permission of the author and The Gallery Press.

2. The word *cailleach* in modern Irish and Scottish Gaelic is used to

mean 'old woman', but it derives originally from the Old Irish word *Caillech*: 'veiled one' (from *caille*, veil). In Ireland she is usually referred to as the Cailleach Bhéarra, but in Scotland she is more often known as Cailleach Bheur. It's been suggested that these names are unrelated to the Cailleach's strong associations with the Beara peninsula, but might rather derive from the old Irish word *biorach*, meaning 'sharp, shrill, inimical' and so referring to her association with winter and wilderness.

3. Donald MacKenzie, *Scottish Folk Lore and Folk Life* (Blackie, 1935).
4. Gearóid Ó Crualaoich, *The Book of the Cailleach* (Cork University Press, 2003).
5. Based on a story in Otta F. Swire, *The Inner Hebrides and Their Legends* (Collins, 1964).
6. Carol Schaefer, *Grandmothers Counsel the World: Women Elders Offer Their Vision for Our Planet* (Trumpeter Books, 2006).
7. www.scillaelworthy.com.
8. www.peacedirect.org.
9. www.theelders.org.
10. www.risingwomenrisingworld.org.
11. Scilla Elworthy, *Power and Sex* (Element Books, 1996).
12. Marion Woodman, *Leaving My Father's House: A Journey to Conscious Femininity* (Shambhala, 1993).
13. A Glaistaig, in Scottish mythology, can be either malign or benign; she most often appears as a protector spirit of cattle and cattle herders. In this example, as in others, she is more closely associated with the Cailleach in her role as protector of wild creatures, and of deer.
14. Both of these stories are from the translation by Michael Newton, printed in *Warriors of the Word* (Birlinn, 2009), of the original Gaelic in James Macdougall's 1910 book, *Folk Tales and Fairy Lore in Gaelic and English* (J. Grant). Translations quoted with the author's permission.
15. www.adventureswithhorses.co.uk.
16. Linda Kohanov, *The Tao of Equus: A Woman's Journey of Healing and Transformation Through the Way of the Horse* (New World Library, 2001).

17.   There are several women named Macha in Irish mythology, which often causes confusion. Macha Mong Ruad ('red mane') was the daughter of Áed Rúad, and according to medieval legend and historical tradition was the only Queen in the List of High Kings of Ireland. Her father rotated the kingship every seven years with his cousins Díthorba and Cimbáeth. Áed died after his third stint as king, and when his turn came round again, Macha claimed the kingship. But Díthorba and Cimbáeth refused to allow a woman to take the throne, and a battle followed. Macha won, and Díthorba was killed. She married Cimbáeth, with whom she shared the kingship for seven years, until he died of plague at Emain Macha, and then she ruled for fourteen more years on her own, until she was killed by Rechtaid Rígderg. Various sources record another Macha, the wife of Nemed, leader of the second settlement of Ireland after the flood. She was the first of Nemed's people to die in Ireland. Macha, daughter of Ernmas of the Tuatha Dé Danann, appears in many early sources. She is often mentioned together with her sisters, Badb and Ana (or Morrigu; names vary according to the source). The three are said to represent the Morrigan, a triple goddess associated with war. Macha, wife of Crunnchu, who appears in this story, was a different character altogether.

If Women Rose Rooted

1.   Jeanette Armstrong, 'Sharing One Skin', *Cultural Survival Quarterly*, 30: 4 (Winter 2006) Land & Resources in the Americas. Included with the permission of the publishers.
2.   The word is derived from the Irish / Gaelic word *dú* / *dùth* which can mean 'earth' or 'land'.
3.   http://theindigovat.blogspot.com.

Acknowledgements

There are two people without whom this book would never have come into being. Kirsty McLachlan, my agent, who was kind enough to email me out of the blue one day and ask if I'd ever thought about writing a book on place and belonging. I hadn't, but then of course I did. And my publisher, Hannah Macdonald, who, during the course of a telephone discussion about a quite different piece of work, allowed me to persuade her that a book on Celtic women and their landscapes and stories might be just the thing for her new publishing house. And who then trusted that I'd go away and actually write it. I've very much appreciated her editorial insights, clarity and focus. I'm also profoundly indebted to Charlotte Cole for her skilful and sensitive copy-editing, and to Sue Amaradivakara and the extended team who've worked on this book for their commitment and support.

I'm immensely grateful to all the women from around the world who so generously and openly shared their stories with me while I was researching and writing this book. Some of those stories made it into print, some can be found on the book's website (ifwomenroserooted.com), and a few more were told in confidence and are written only in my heart.

So many others provided support in so many different ways. Claire Cummings, for thoughtful and eye-opening discussions around the issues of indigeneity. Jane Galer Barnes, for many exchanges of ideas on place, belonging and Celticity. Claire Aumenier and Judith Hoad for their contributions to some of the journeys I undertook to research this book. All the women who are part of the Facebook group for my Sisterhood of the Bones course, for their enthusiasm and love of myth and story. Angela Piears, for forty-three years of love and friendship and a spare bed in London whenever it was needed. Moya McGinley, for a constant supply of laughter, scones and a good strong 'hot drop'. Tasmanian treasure Désirée Fitzgibbon for sharing so many things, and for coming with me on my second visit to kiss the Hag. Sara Firman, always, for being there – even an ocean away – when it all came tumbling down. Ceaití Ní Bheildiúin for poems, mountains, and the most surprising friendship of all. Pascal Lamour, electro-shaman extraordinaire, provided invaluable and entertaining insight into Breton culture and mythology. Very welcome encouragement and engagement in the earliest of stages came from Tim and Mairead Robinson, John Waddell, Leslie van Gelder and all at the 2014 Roundstone Conversation.

I might never have had the stamina to finish this book without the love and support of my husband, David. I'm deeply thankful for his insights, built-in bullshit detector, and for finding words when they failed me; for feathers and fur and mermaid's purses brought to my desk to brighten long writing days – but more than anything, for a strong hand to hold along the Journey.

Many writers and texts have provided me with crucial insights along my own Journey – far too many to list here. But I'd like to highlight a few whose influence was particularly formative along the path to conceiving this book. Clarissa Pinkola Estés, for her seminal work *Women Who Run with the Wolves*. Sue Monk Kidd, for *The Dance of the Dissident Daughter*. Martin Shaw, for *A Branch from the Lightning Tree*, and many lively exchanges of ideas about myth-telling and the storying of place. Michael Newton, for *Warriors of the Word* and his rich, extensive and thought-provoking body of work on Gaelic culture. Various works cited in this book by Peter Berresford Ellis, Miranda Green, J.P. Mallory, Barry Cunliffe, Gearóid Ó Crualaoich, John Carey, Rosalind Clark and Anne Ross were also critical to the development of my thought on Celtic origins, beliefs, culture and women.

Finally, I'd like to honour and offer my thanks to the Native American and Hispanic writers – Leslie Hogan, Joy Harjo, Louise Erdrich, Pat Mora and others – who, when I was lost in America many years ago, helped me to see what it might mean for a woman not only to be native to place, but to be one with the land. And to the heart-filled poets from my native traditions – Nuala Ní Dhomhnaill, Eiléan Ní Chuilleanáin, Eavan Boland and many more – who showed me so many ways in which myth, land and woman are one.